PSYCHOANALYSIS AND PHILOSOPHY OF MIND

PSYCHOANALYSIS AND PHILOSOPHY OF MIND

Unconscious Mentality in the Twenty-first Century

Edited by

Simon Boag, Linda A. W. Brakel, and Vesa Talvitie

Routledge
Taylor & Francis Group
LONDON AND NEW YORK

First published 2015 by Karnac Books Ltd.

Published 2018 by Routledge
2 Park Square, Milton Park, Abingdon, Oxon OX14 4RN
711 Third Avenue, New York, NY 10017, USA

Routledge is an imprint of the Taylor & Francis Group, an informa business

British Library Cataloguing in Publication Data

A C.I.P. for this book is available from the British Library

ISBN-13: 9781782201793 (pbk)

Typeset by V Publishing Solutions Pvt Ltd., Chennai, India

CONTENTS

ABOUT THE EDITORS AND CONTRIBUTORS

Simon Boag is a senior lecturer in psychology at Macquarie University where he teaches personality theory, research methods and the history and philosophy of psychology. He has published extensively in the area of Freudian repression and unconscious mental processes, philosophy of mind, conceptual research and is the author of *Freudian Repression, the Unconscious, and the Dynamics of Inhibition* (Karnac). He can be contacted at: simon.boag@mq.edu.au (see also his website: www.simon.boag.com)

Linda A. W. Brakel is associate professor (adjunct) of psychiatry and research associate in philosophy at the University of Michigan. She is also on the faculty of Michigan Psychoanalytic Institute and practises psychoanalysis in Ann Arbor, Michigan. She has authored and co-authored articles on topics ranging from empirical studies testing psychoanalytic concepts to those on the philosophy of mind and action. Her most recent works are three interdisciplinary books: *Philosophy, Psychoanalysis, and the A-Rational* Mind (Oxford), *Unconscious Knowing and Other Essays in Psycho-Philosophical Analysis* (Oxford), and *The Ontology of Psychology: Questioning Foundations in the Philosophy of Mind* (Routledge). She can be contacted at: brakel@umich.edu

Jim Hopkins is visiting professor in the psychoanalysis unit of the Research Department of Clinical and Health Psychology at University College London, and was Kohut visiting professor of social thought in the School of Social Thought, The University of Chicago, for 2008. He is also emeritus reader in the philosophy department, King's College London. He has co-edited books including *Psychoanalysis, Mind, and Art: Perspectives on Richard Wollheim* (Blackwell) and *Philosophical Essays on Freud* (Cambridge University Press) and has published numerous articles on the philosophy of psychoanalysis, as well as other topics, such as consciousness and interpretation. He can be contacted at: jim.hopkins@kcl.ac.uk (see also his website: www.jimhopkins.org).

Michael P. Levine is professor of philosophy at the University of Western Australia. He is editor of *The Analytic Freud* (Routledge) and has recently co-authored *Prospects for an Ethics of Architecture* (Routledge), *Thinking Through Film* (Wiley-Blackwell), *Politics Most Unusual* (Palgrave Macmillan), *Integrity and the Fragile Self* (Ashgate), *Racism in Mind* (Cornell University Press). He is currently writing a book with Bill Taylor on catastrophe, urban disaster, ethics and the built environment. He can be contacted at: michael.levine@uwa.edu.au

Tamas Pataki is an honorary senior fellow in the School of Historical and Philosophical Studies, University of Melbourne. He has published extensively on the philosophy of mind and co-edited with Michael Levine *Racism in Mind* (Cornell University Press) and is the author of *Against Religion* (Scribe) and *Wishfulfilment in Philosophy and Psychoanalysis: The Tyranny of Desire* (Routledge). He can be contacted at: tpataki@unimelb.edu.au

Vesa Talvitie is a doctor of psychology, licensed psychotherapist, organisational consultant (FINOD), and currently works as an occupational psychologist for the City of Helsinki. In addition to numerous articles on psychoanalysis in Finnish and English, he is the author of *Freudian Unconscious and Cognitive Neuroscience: From Unconscious Fantasies to Neural Algorithms* (Karnac) and *The Foundations of psychoanalytic theories—Project for a scientific enough psychoanalysis* (Karnac). He can be contacted at: vesa.talvitie@alumni.helsinki.fi (see also his website www.vesatalvitie.fi)

INTRODUCTION

Psychoanalysis and philosophy of mind

Simon Boag, Vesa Talvitie, and Linda A. W. Brakel

Freud's philosophy of mind is at once one of his most contentious and enduring contributions to our understanding of human functioning. Psychoanalytic theory makes bold claims about the significance of unconscious mental processes and the wish-fulfilling activity of the mind, citing their importance for understanding the nature of dreams and explaining both normal and pathological behaviour alike. If true, then psychoanalytic explanation makes a substantial impact to our understanding of human behaviour; it informs us that what people do often belies their true motives—and that these motives themselves may not even be known to the person who holds them. However, since Freud's initial work, both modern psychology and philosophy have had much to say about the merits of psychoanalysis, especially with respect to the possibility of unconscious mentality. Freudian thinking has been heavily criticised by both those outside of psychoanalysis and those within. Of the latter, the tension between clinicians and theoretician/scientists has been pronounced: Freud's metapsychology has fallen out of favour with many for not reflecting the clinical situation, and the development of object-relations accounts has called into question the fundamental motives that Freud proposed. Whether psychoanalysis is a scientific or hermeneutic exercise has also been debated.

The state of affairs is reflected in the current discussions of plurality in psychoanalysis—or psychoanalys*es*, as some would say (e.g., Wallerstein, 1995). Changes in mainstream psychology have also led to adaptations within psychoanalytic theory. For instance, psychoanalysis has been re-conceptualised in terms of cognitive theory and information-processing (Erdelyi, 1974, 1985), and the developments in affective neuroscience have underscored the development of neuropsychoanalysis (Panksepp, 1998, 1999). The increasing interest in neuropsychoanalysis is itself a new direction that is not welcomed by all (Blass & Carmeli, 2007) and its conceptual underpinnings are critically questioned (Talvitie, 2009, this volume). One also wonders what Freud would make of some of the developments in psychoanalysis, including the mentalisation movement as advanced by Fonagy and colleagues (e.g., Fonagy, 1999; Fonagy & Target, 2000); therein defence and unconscious processes recede into the background and instead a failure to develop a theory of mind finds prominence.

Given the current state of psychoanalysis, one may then wonder whether there is any merit in revisiting the fundamentals of Freudian theory again. After all, some may think, surely advances in science generally and psychology specifically have overtaken Freud's anachronistic, early twentieth-century thinking. There are, however, several reasons for re-examining the fundamentals of the psychoanalytic conception of mind. For a start, while some of the specifics of Freudian theory have found little currency in contemporary discussions, it is the fundamental factors in Freudian thinking—unconscious mentality, wish-fulfilment, and defence—that nevertheless generally enjoy prominence across the various psychoanalytic perspectives. Furthermore, any new psychoanalytic perspective tends to define itself by specific differences with classical Freudian theory. However, even more fundamentally, Freud in many respects left more questions than answers. His theory was never completed and his aversion to philosophy possibly prevented him paying critical attention to fundamental issues that can only be addressed philosophically, such as the relation between mind and body, or mind and consciousness. What is required then is a critical re-examination of Freudian concepts via a joint scientific and philosophical appraisal of psychoanalytic theory.

The new developments in psychology, philosophy and psychoanalysis raise new challenges and questions concerning Freud's theory of mind. This book centres upon the major concepts in psychoanalysis, including the notion of unconscious mental processes and wish-fulfilment and their relationship to dreams, fantasy, repression, religion, art, and morality. These are central concepts because they provide the theoretical building blocks that allow a move beyond describing psychological and behavioural phenomena in order to explain them in terms of complex psychodynamic processes. However, these concepts are not all considered equally coherent. Taken as such, this volume can be considered a companion volume to our other edited work (*Philosophy, Science and Psychoanalysis*—Boag, Brakel, & Talvitie, 2015). In both volumes we provide a fresh, critical appraisal and reflection on Freudian concepts, and address how the current evidence and scientific thinking bears upon Freud's original ideas.

There are two major themes contained within this volume. The first theme addresses the topic of explanation in psychoanalysis. Freud's theory is seen by many as situated within, and extending, the ordinary folk-psychological "desire plus belief model" (Boag, 2012; Brakel, 2009; Cavell, 1993; Gardner, 1993; Hopkins, 1988, this volume; Mackay, 1996, 1999; Pataki, 2000; this volume; Petocz, 1999; Wollheim, 1991, 1993). On this view, *intentional* action arises from a motivational state or "desire" component, guided by an instrumental cognitive or "belief" component. Here, when explaining person *P*'s doing *A*, it is understood that: (i) *P* desires *B*; and (ii) *P* believes that doing *A* leads to *B*. The "belief" component includes knowledge, memory and phantasy and specifies the known possible means of satisfaction (or of avoiding frustration). One could say here that explanation could thereby never be reduced to neural events alone, even if neural events are nevertheless implicated in believing and desiring. Accordingly, the relation of neuropsychoanalysis to psychoanalytic explanation requires very careful consideration—and Talvitie (this volume) proposes that this has yet to occur. However, there are also opportunities for enhancing psychoanalytic explanations in terms of current research, neuroscientific or otherwise, even if philosophical issues still require much further consideration.

Tamas Pataki opens this section by addressing the fundamental psychoanalytic thesis of wish-fulfilment and its relevance to unconscious intentionality. He argues for the fundamental role of Freudian wish-fulfilment for both interpretation and explanation of symptoms, the analysis of dreams, and the understanding of art, religion, and even prejudice. Jim Hopkins then examines psychoanalysis in the context of modern neuroscience and evolutionary theory, as well as refreshing psychoanalysis in terms of insights from attachment research. He examines the explanatory context of Freudian theory, demonstrating similarities between the types of explanations both Freud and Darwin employ, and how Freud's explanation then deepens our understanding of human existence. Hopkins' contemporary stance, moreover, draws upon current research from a variety of fields, including neuroscience and sleep research. Next, Michael Levine develops a psychoanalytic discussion about understanding art and the mind of the artist. He addresses views about art and the artist in terms of key long-standing questions concerning the ethics of art and their relation to art's aesthetic.

The second major theme addresses the current debate concerning the nature of unconscious processes. Vesa Talvitie critically assesses whether the cornerstone of psychoanalysis—the unconscious and the possibility of repressed ideas located in the unconscious part of the mind—can be coherently sustained, drawing attention to the sociological factors impinging on scientific discourse generally and psychoanalysis specifically. Linda A. W. Brakel then examines the psychoanalytic topic of primary process mentation, providing both theoretical and empirical evidence for unconscious processes. Finally, Simon Boag raises philosophical arguments in defence of unconscious mental processes, through a fresh examination of Brentano's argument against unconscious mentality.

This debate presented here is an extension of Freud's view on the unconscious, under critical discussion during Freud's lifetime (for example, see Münsterberg, 1909, pp. 125–157). This topic still draws attention to the conflict between empirical findings that suggest the possibility of unconscious mentation, and philosophical perspectives claiming that the very notion of an unconscious *mental* process is untenable. As the philosopher Ernest Nagel states: "And as for the notions of unconscious psychic processes processing causal efficacies—of unconscious, causally operative motives and wishes that are not somatic dispositions and activities—I will not venture to say that such locutions are inherently nonsense, since a great many people claim to make good sense of them. But in all candour I must admit that such locutions are just nonsense to me" (Nagel, 1959, p. 47). Indeed, in the same volume in which Nagel's comments appear, the psychoanalyst Heinz Hartmann admits that Freud himself gave reason for such criticism: "As to the psychology of unconscious processes, I think it can be said that Freud in developing that part of analysis was much less interested in the ultimate 'nature' or 'essence' of such processes—whatever that means—than in finding a suitable conceptual framework for the phenomena he had discovered" (Hartmann, 1959, p. 7).

In the pre-analytic philosophy era, Freud's restricted exploration regarding the ontology of mental processes and unconscious mentation was perhaps both understandable and prevalent. However, ever since Freud's time there has been considerable pressure from two directions to rigorously account for the mental unconscious and to minimally describe what it actually refers. One direction is the fast developing field of neuroscience, which has challenged the division of labour between psychology and brain science. Multicolour brain-scan images and high-tech methods, in general, attract people, and there is a danger that the weight of neuroscience-driven viewpoints will become far overemphasised. Thus there is a growing need to determine the nature and essence of mind and its relation to neuroscience (see, for example, Bem & Looren de Jong, 2006; Bennett & Hacker, 2003; Boag, 2012; Talvitie, & Ihanus, (2011a, 2011b), especially with respect to the mind-body problem (see Brakel, 2013 for extended discussion of this issue)).

The other (related) direction pressing for explanation of unconscious mentation involves the philosophy of mind. Here, too, technological innovations have played a considerable role. The development of computers, for instance, has given rise to the computer-metaphor for understanding brain-mind processes (i.e., the analogy between the brain and computer's hardware, and mind and computer's software). The computer analogy provided a fresh viewpoint to the age-old Cartesian mind-body problem, and inspired philosophers to engage in lively discussions concerning epistemology. Thought-experiments like the "Chinese Room Argument" (Searle, 2002), "Twin earth" (Putnam, 1975), and "Mary the super color scientist" (Jackson, 1982) have figured in these debates. Clearly, especially as the questions concerning the essence of mind and mental phenomena have become extremely topical in other domains, psychoanalysis cannot be a credible academic discipline if it (still) ignores the challenge of providing a coherent account of unconscious mentality. Our volume is an attempt to do just that.

CHAPTER ONE

Wish-fulfilment revisited*

Tamas Pataki

Freudian wish-fulfilment

In the first edition of *The Interpretation of Dreams* (1900a) Freud introduced a theory according to which dreams, some neurotic symptoms and delusions are wish-fulfilments.[1] The scope of his investigations quickly expanded and he eventually concluded that not only dreams and symptoms but also phantasy (or fantasy) such as daydream, some unconscious phantasy, other neurotic and some psychotic symptoms—delusions, hallucinations—jokes and art, slips of the tongue, bungled actions, magical or omnipotent thinking, illusions such as religion and aspects of morality and social organisation were also wish-fulfilling or, recognising that action can fall short of its objective, attempts at wish-fulfilment.[2]

It is evident that Freud's conception of wish-fulfilment (henceforth: FWT), exemplified in the phenomena listed above, cannot be the same as our ordinary conception of what it is for a wish to be fulfilled, and I will outline its distinctive features presently. Although FWT was clearly

---

*I would like to thank Michael Levine and the editors of this volume for many helpful suggestions.

a fundamental concept for Freud, its novelty, scope and implications have been underappreciated, and it has received little explicit critical attention in the psychoanalytic literature. Nevertheless, it remains fundamental to the psychoanalytic understanding of many of the phenomena Freud had identified, though often appearing under different guises: for example, as omnipotent phantasy; as underlying defences such as projective identification; in "actualization" in the transference, acting out and symptom (Sandler 1976, 1989). We shall see that even if Freud was only approximately right about the nature and scope of FWT, then it must also form an important compartment of any philosophy of mind that seeks to understand irrational action and belief formation in Intentional[3] or common-sense psychological terms, and, indeed, it now seems increasingly likely in neuroscientific terms as well. This chapter revisits Freud's conception, locates its significance in clinical and theoretical contexts, and examines some recent philosophical and scientific work bearing on it. Several disputative and polemical remarks are included in the endnotes.

Outline of the conception

Our ordinary understanding of wish-fulfilment can be articulated like this:[4]

A. In the *ordinary sense*, any wish that *p* is fulfilled only if:

i. the wish is terminated: the agent ceases to wish that *p*;
ii. the agent comes to believe that *p*;
iii. it is a fact that *p*: the wished-for state of affairs or action occurs;
iv. the wish is extinguished *because* of the occurrence or institution of *p*.

FWT is importantly different from this core conception. Freud maintained consistently that one of the mind's principal tasks is the relief of tensions created by needs (or drives), mentally expressed as desires or wishes.[5] Ordinarily, when we wish to perform some action or establish a state of affairs and no countervailing conditions prevail, we will act to satisfy the wish. Acting in such instances is a case of fulfilling wishes on model (A). But if prevented from acting because of sleep, inhibition, or other constraints, then sometimes we can produce transformations in ourselves—self-deceptive or consoling beliefs and phantasies, hallucinatory experiences, delusions, or other symptoms—which manage to substitute for the real objects of those wishes and, in a manner, satisfy or temporarily terminate them. Here the mind has recourse to FWT or, as Freud often says, "substitutive satisfaction". Evidently this conception differs from the ordinary understanding of wish-fulfilment summarised in (A).

It is distinctive of those phenomena identified by Freud as wish-fulfilling—dreams, hallucinations and so on—that whilst conditions (i) and (ii) are necessary, conditions (iii) and (iv) are not. Characteristically in FWT either the wished-for states of affairs do not exist or come to pass, or if they do they have no causal role in the extinction of the wish. The causal role must therefore rest entirely with (ii) "coming to believe that p" (or with mental states functioning terminatively in the manner of belief, if such there are). Moreover, in nearly all cases of wish-fulfilment described by Freud the agent *initiates* the wish-fulfilling process.[6] Wish-fulfilment cannot entirely *befall* an agent. Thus, Freud's patient Dora periodically succumbed to hysterical coughing and aphonia that were causally overdetermined; one such cause, according to Freud, was Dora's intention to separate her father from his mistress. Even if the symptoms were not manufactured intentionally, even if, say, they were produced sub-intentionally (by desire alone) or as the expression of affective processes, they could still have succeeded fortuitously in separating the lovers, and thus be wish-fulfilling in the Freudian sense. What would *not* count as wish-fulfilment in this sense is if, for example, a brick fell on the mistress's head. That would have served to satisfy Dora's wish to separate her father from his mistress but it would not count as an instance of FWT. So further conditions incorporating degrees of agency must be added to (i) and (ii). Since intentional involvement can come in degrees, in different phases of action, it will be useful to mark the limits, from the (let's say) *maximally* intentional cases where FWT is itself intended to the simplest cases where no intention (though perhaps desire acting sub-intentionally or as a sub-personal mechanism) is at work. This can be done by distinguishing two forms of a condition, which replaces conditions (iii) and (iv). The weaker form (v(a)) is that the agent initiates the wish-fulfilling process, in a sense that does not entail but does not exclude intention. The stronger form (v(b)) identifies the maximal cases of wish-fulfilment: where a wish that *p* of an agent A is fulfilled, the process that fulfils the wish can be truly described as intentional under some such descriptions as "A fulfilling A's wish that *p*" or "A gratifying (consoling, appeasing ...) A".

So we may imagine a spectrum of cases. In the simplest type of wish-fulfilment, such as the hallucinatory gratification in infant mental life posited by Freud, a wish directly instigates the process but intention plays no role in the satisfaction of the instigating wish: these are sub-intentional phenomena. In a second possible type, in which intention is not yet in play, a wish may be conceived to activate mental activity or automatism of the sort proposed by Wollheim (see below), the operation of which leads to the satisfaction of the wish. Perhaps defence mechanisms such as repression and projection are examples. In a third type, representations or pictures of wished-for states of affairs—wishful phantasy or fond memory—may be generated intentionally, though not yet for the purpose of achieving wish-fulfilment. One may summon up remembrance of things past or review the nicer aspects of the holidays, but FWT can overtake this process if regressive conditions of engrossment or reverie impose and wishful phantasy is ephemerally mistaken for reality. Children easily become engrossed in play and wishful phantasies, but engrossment also occurs later, in dozing, daydreaming, or states of withdrawal or dissociation. A fourth possible type—the maximal cases—presupposes a mind capable of intentionally providing for itself substitutive satisfactions. Some so-called "lucid dreams" in which there appears to be intentional direction of the course of the dream, some phantasy, neurotic and psychotic symptoms and enactments are of this kind. In the preceding types, the relation between the wish and its expression or representation in wishful phantasy (i.e., not wish-fulfilling phantasy), on the one hand, and the fulfilment of the wish, on the other, was adventitious. There was a role for intention in the third type, but not for intended wish-fulfilment. In all these cases wish-fulfilment befell the wish. The expressions of the wish or wishful phantasy were mistaken for what would satisfy the wish in the first and third types, and mental mechanism subvened to satisfy the wish in the second. In the present class of cases the relations between wish, the vehicle of wish-fulfilment—phantasy, symptom, or action—and the satisfaction of wish are not adventitious. Wish-fulfilment is itself either intended or is instrumental to another form of self-solicitude that is intended—and, for reasons to be explored, it must be intended unconsciously.

Now we can summarise the conditions for FWT:

B. For any wish that p, it will be fulfilled in the manner of FWT only if:

i. the wish is temporarily terminated: the agent ceases to wish that *p*;
ii. the agent comes (transiently) to believe that *p*;
v(a). the agent initiates the wish-fulfilling process, in a sense that does not entail but does not exclude intention; or
v(b). in maximal cases, the process that fulfils the wish can be truly described as intentional under some such descriptions as "A fulfilling A's wish that *p*" or "A gratifying (consoling, appeasing …) A."

This conception, entirely original to Freud (though not of course articulated this way), was muddied by him in three different ways. First, he regularly conflated the ordinary kind of wish-fulfilment with his novel discovery, FWT. Second, he conflated FWT with the conceptions of precursors, especially the ancient oneiromancers, who had hit on wishful interpretations of dreams: dreams that were wishfully prognostic or instructive but patently not wish-fulfilments in the way Freud proposed. But most importantly, he failed consistently to distinguish between (i) the representation of a wish being fulfilled, and (ii) the fulfilment of the wish, either as the process or, what is different, the end state. Consider some typical statements:

1. Of the famous Irma dream Freud says that its content was "the fulfilment of a wish and its motive was a wish" (1900a, p. 119).
2. Hysterical acts are "mimetic or hallucinatory representations of phantasies" (Freud, 1913, p. 173).
3. Freud writes of a "delusion having as content the fulfilment of the wish" (Freud, 1922b, p. 226).
4. *A dream is a (disguised) fulfilment of a (suppressed or repressed) wish.* (Freud, 1900a, p. 160, his italics)
5. *Dreams are not disturbers of sleep … but guardians of sleep which get rid of disturbances of sleep …* a dream does not simply give expression to a thought, but represents the wish fulfilled as a hallucinatory experience … the dream does not simply reproduce the stimulus [the wish], but removes it, gets rid of it, deals with it, by means of a kind of experience. (Freud, 1916–1917, p. 129, his italics)
6. Every dream may be a wish-fulfilment, but apart from dreams there must be other forms of abnormal wish-fulfilments. And it is a fact

that the theory governing all psychoneurotic symptoms culminates in a single proposition, which asserts that they too are to be regarded as fulfilments of unconscious wishes. (Freud, 1900a, pp. 568–569)

7. The motive force of phantasies are unsatisfied wishes, and every single phantasy is the fulfilment of a wish, a correction of unsatisfying reality. (Freud, 1908e, p. 146)
8. Symptoms serve for the patient's sexual satisfaction; they are a substitute for satisfaction of this kind, which the patients are without in their lives … This symptom was fundamentally a wish-fulfilment, just like a dream—and moreover what is not always true of a dream, an erotic wish-fulfilment. (Freud, 1916–1917, p. 299)

Many similar passages could be adduced, treating of hallucinations, art, and so on. Inspection shows that Freud says at least two quite different things about wish-fulfilling processes. In (1)–(3) the processes are said to be *representations* of wish-fulfilment, or to have as their *content* representations of wish-fulfilment. But in (4)–(8) the processes are said to *be* wish-fulfilments. This difference has important implications. I suggest that Freud's considered view is that dreams, symptoms and their kin do not just represent the objects of wishes (e.g., a cake I crave) or, what is different, scenarios of wishes being fulfilled (my eating the cake); they actually fulfil them, though they do this in a qualified way (it is *as if* I had eaten the cake). This understanding is supported by the fact noted above that Freud frequently refers to wish-fulfilments as "substitutive satisfactions", by which he appears to mean that they are real, albeit attenuated satisfactions of wishes, achieved by roundabout means. But we must see why this is a theoretical necessity in Freud's work and not just loose language.

The idea that representation suffices for FWT fails to capture the specific roles that Freud assigns to the function of dreams and symptoms: for example, to preserve sleep or to circumvent realistic action. FWT involves less than full satisfaction in the ordinary sense (A) but more than the mere representation of satisfaction: it involves, as well, a *temporary cessation of wishing*; or, in Jim Hopkins' term, a "pacification" of the wish (Hopkins, 1995, 2012, this volume).[7] Just as there is a difference between entertaining a thought and believing it, so there is between experiencing an imaginal representation of wish-fulfilment and taking it "for real". The person who has a wishful phantasy or thought of killing his father, consciously or unconsciously, who represents to himself this wish fulfilled, may feel guilt at having evil thoughts. But this is evidently different from the fully fledged wish-fulfilling phantasy or delusion that he has killed his father. The significance of termination (or pacification) in wish-fulfilment emerges clearly from an adaptational (Hartmann, 1939) perspective. There is no advantage to an incapacitated organism in merely expressing or representing wishes as fulfilled: the organism that cannot change the world to accord with its desires still demands an end to the painful stimulus of an ineluctable wish or desire and tries to terminate it, in default of realistic action. Dreams and the rest of the wish-fulfilling series aim to fulfil wishes in order to prevent or delay action, not *just* to represent them. Dreams are guardians of sleep. Symptoms are not merely representations but satisfactions achieved in the manner of FWT (e.g., Freud, 1916–1917, pp. 350, 361).

Now, we have traced a rough outline of the concept of FWT but have no assurance that the concept is coherent or that there are mental processes or actions actually falling under it: the features of the concept were extracted from Freud's understanding of dreams, symptoms, and so on; but of course he may have gone astray. It may be that *nothing* satisfies the concept whose features are set out in (B). For (1) there may be no psychic or circumstantial conditions under which any form of FWT can be realised. And, (2), the problematic *maximal* forms of FWT—in which FWT is itself intended—seem particularly fraught. I will address these issues below, after providing some historical context for our discussion.

A very short history of wish-fulfilment

That frustrated desire can sicken and kill was recognised in ancient cultures. When the seventeenth century missionary Father Ragueneau visited North America he found that the Huron people recognised a class of illness caused by unfulfilled wishes, some of them unconscious, diagnosed by their medical specialists, and treated with a "festival of dreams" in which desirable objects would be collected from the community and given to the patient during a banquet and public rejoicing (Ellenberger, 1970, p. 26). Plato and later Hellenic philosophers were insightful about pathologies of desire and disrupted selves (Sorabji, 2006), and Augustine wrote brilliantly on the conflicted will. But in the long period of Christian totalitarianism that followed, philosophical interest in the appetitive or orectic roots of action, internal conflict and self-partition waned. Eros and will were deprecated, and the immortality of the soul, implying indivisibility, obviated questions about partition. It was not till the late Enlightenment that philosophical interest turned once again to the ineluctability of desire and will, and their capacity to divide the self against itself. Arthur Schopenhauer identified the will with the Kantian thing-in-itself, and so as noumenally constitutive of everything in the cosmos. He made acute observations about various expressions of will, including relations between sexual striving and insanity. In its personal expression the will was conceived largely as unconscious striving, without knowledge, aided by an intellect that is generally "a mere tool in the service of the will" (Schopenhauer, 1844, p. 205).

> In fact, the intellect remains so much excluded from the real resolutions and secret decisions of its own will that sometimes it can only get to know them, like those of a stranger, by spying out and taking it unawares; and it must surprise the will in the act of expressing itself, in order merely to discover its real intentions. (Schopenhauer, 1844, p. 209)

Under Schopenhauer's influence and the *Naturphilosophie* founded by F. W. von Schelling, the will came to be identified with a kind of universal unconscious, and thinkers such as Carl Gustav Carus and Eduard von Hartmann developed elaborate and extravagant accounts of unconscious processes animating nature as well as humankind. In the prevailing psychological schools of "voluntarism" *striving* or *willing* were regarded as the dominant principles of human psychology (Alexander & Selesnick, 1966, pp. 218ff; Ellenberger, 1970, Chapter Five). William James and F. H. Bradley (the great proponent of absolute idealism) wrote extensively on the will, both of them in ways that still command great interest. Towards the end of the nineteenth century, Nietzsche insisted, with unparalleled intensity (though not plausibility), that the *will to power* is the fundamental motivation in human psychology and cosmos.

A little earlier, Romantic psychiatrists—such as Johann Heinroth (1773–1843), Johann Christian Reil (1759–1813), and Karl Wilhelm Ideler (1795–1860)—recognised the paramount importance of the passions and of inner conflict in the genesis of mental illness. Ideler emphasised the aetiological significance of sexual love and traced delusions back to childhood experiences. Heinroth expressed an acute awareness of the pathogenic role of guilt (sin, he termed it). Like their precursors, the magnetists, these alienists intuitively grasped the significance of *the rapport*, transference and suggestion, of unconscious motivation and the therapeutic import of "unmasking" or revealing "the pathogenic secret", all of which, as Ellenberger remarks (Ellenberger, 1970, p. 277), became characteristic of the later dynamic psychiatry of the 1880s and 1890s, though their source had by then been forgotten.

So the causal connection between desire and emotion, on the one hand, and mental pathology, on the other, was recognised by the middle of the nineteenth century; but then rapidly eclipsed by the *Somatiker* or neurological movement in psychiatry in the last half of the century. Freud is usually appreciated as a scientist steeped in the spirit of the Enlightenment, educated in the reductionist biophysics movement of that period associated with Herman von Helmholtz, and his teachers Ernst Brücke and Theodor Meynert. We have Freud's testimony to the influence of these men on his early work (Freud, 1925d; Makari, 2008, parts I and II). And, of course, it is so. Yet in his authoritative work, Ellenberger (1970, p. 199) describes Freud and Jung as the late great epigones of Romanticism; and this, thematically, as I have adumbrated, is also true. Despite accepting the reductionist materialism of his teachers, which he never abandoned in principle, some of Freud's earliest defining doctrines and preoccupations were more in harmony with his Romantic predecessors than his scientific milieu. It is unlikely that there was direct influence from the philosophers or Romantic psychiatrists: there is no evidence in his writings that Freud possessed anything like a *scholarly* knowledge of Schopenhauer, Carus, Nietzsche, Brentano, or the others, but, of course, their popularised ideas were in the air, and so large a mind as Freud's could scarcely have failed to assimilate them.[8] And it was with Bernheim in 1889 (in one of the last pockets of Romantic medicine) Freud tells, that he "received the profoundest impression of the possibility that there could be powerful mental processes which nevertheless remained hidden from the consciousness of men" (Freud, 1925d, p. 17).

His earliest psychoanalytic work ran counter to the dominant scientific positivism and neurological psychiatry in several respects. In contrast to the spirit of the biophysics movement, Freud insisted on the causality of *subjective* motives, on the orectic (desiring, appetitive, wishful), conative (willing, striving, decisive), and affective aspects of mind, particularly sexuality, in the aetiology of psychopathology—a salient theme in Schopenhauer and some contemporary sexologists, but not in the milieu in which he worked. He frequently cast mental conflict in terms of will or intention and counter-will; hysteria, specifically, was posited to be an unforeseen consequence of intentional or willed splitting of consciousness (Freud, 1892–1893, pp. 122–128; 1894a).[9] And with Freud something entirely new appears: mental pathology is not just *caused* by orectic or affective states, most specifically desire or wish; symptoms and their kin are the *fulfilments* of these states. Eventually, Freud's apparently incompatible commitments to a reductive scientific materialism, on the one hand, and to subjective causality and the Intentional psychology indispensable for the expression of subjective states, on the other, created a schism in his theorising between a quasi-neurological framework—the "metapsychology" that was the lingering ghost of his earliest neurobiological tenets—and an augmented Intentional psychology. In struggling with these dual commitments Freud is quite our philosophical contemporary. At the foundation of psychoanalysis Freud realised that all that needed to be said about the neuroses could not be said without the Intentional idiom:

> I have not always been a psychotherapist. Like other neuropathologists, I was trained to employ local diagnoses and electro-prognosis, and it still strikes me myself as strange that the case histories I write should read like stories and that, as one might say, they lack the serious stamp of science. I must console myself with the reflection that the nature of the subject is evidently responsible for this, rather than any preference of my own. The fact is that local diagnosis and electrical reactions lead nowhere in the study of hysteria, whereas a detailed description of mental processes such as we are accustomed to find in the works of imaginative writers enables me, with the use of a few psychological formulas, to at least obtain some kind of insight into the course of that affection. (Freud in Breuer & Freud, 1895d, pp. 160–161)

By the 1970s it was obvious that fundamental parts of the Freudian metapsychology intricately developed by his ego-psychologist heirs (e.g., Hartmann, Kris, & Loewenstein, 1964; Hartmann, 1964) were inadequate to the explanatory demands made on it. In particular, the drive-discharge model of motivation, in which Hartmann had with deliberation placed his hopes (Hartmann, 1948), failed to provide a plausible account of action. Hartmann complained that despite theoretical progress in other areas there was "still no systematic presentation of an *analytic theory of action*" (Hartmann, 1947, p. 37). Melanie Klein and her followers, while accepting Freud's dual drive model, shifted their emphasis to phantasy; and other object-relational thinkers retreated from drive psychology altogether. Although wish-fulfilment as articulated by Freud is implicit in the Kleinian concept(s) of phantasy, especially in the notion of omnipotent phantasy, it was not recognised as such. Such psychoanalytic interest as there was in systematic accounts of motivation and action, in the conceptual exploration of FWT, largely evaporated.

Freud's failure to recognise FWT's singularity and to distinguish it as a fundamental tenet[10] no doubt contributed to the concept's neglect. Because wish-fulfilment tends to be associated with drive theory, the false dichotomy still present in much psychoanalytic thought between drive and object relations or interpersonal theory—as if object-relating somehow precluded mutual desiderative relations between subject and object—has led to further neglect. Moreover, the classical preoccupation with neuroses, considered largely as pathologies of desire and conflict, has given way in contemporary theory to a dominant concern with pathologies of developmental, predominantly cognitive deficits resulting from environmental or interactional failure: failure in attachment leading to incapacity for "mentalisation" (Fonagy et al., 2004; Holmes, 2010); disrupted (preverbal) internalisation leading to defective "internal working models" (IWMs) (Bowlby, 1971) or "representations of interactions generalized" (RIGs) (Stern, 1985); and the acquisition of unconscious pathogenic beliefs (Weiss & Sampson, 1986). This attention to impaired (broadly) cognitive structures and associated failures in affect regulation appears to have diminished interest in the active, desiderative, wish-fulfilling aspects of mind. Psychoanalysis appears now less concerned with the pathology of desire than of belief—or the various proposed belief-like structures anteceding beliefs (IWMs, RIGs, procedural memories, etc.). It is less concerned with the consequences of frustrated wishes than with deficits in cognitive functions.

Notwithstanding these developments, interest in Freud's pre-drive account of motivation based on the wish and wish-fulfilment was revived.[11] Classical drive psychology is problematic, but the notion of unmotivated object-relations is, after all, incoherent. The revival can be observed in the volume edited by Gill and Holzmann (1976), Holt

(1976), Hopkins (1982), Sandler (1976), Sandler and Sandler (1978), Schafer (1976), Wollheim (1991[1971]; 1979) and many other articles of this period. At the same time significant developments in the analytic philosophy of mind were taking place, with renewed interest in motivation and action initiated by Wittgenstein, Elizabeth Anscombe, Hampshire, and, especially, a brilliant series of papers in the 1960s and 1970s by Donald Davidson, amongst others (Anscombe, 1957; Davidson, 1980; Goldman, 1970). Eventually there appeared a promising survey of a stretch of conceptual terrain, which could account in reasonably systematic ways for the causal and conceptual relations between the terms of common-sense psychology (desire, belief, choice, decision, intention, etc.) and for some understanding of how these terms may be physically realised.

Analytic philosophers initially gave scant consideration to psychoanalysis—except for dismissive assessments of its scientific status. As late as 1974 Richard Wollheim complained in the preface to his important anthology (Wollheim (Ed.), 1974) that Freud's ideas "have barely impinged upon philosophers." Then, about the time classical metapsychology collapsed, a number of psychoanalytically informed philosophers, principally Wollheim and Jim Hopkins, began to view psychoanalysis through the lens of analytic action theory, and showed persuasively how an augmented common-sense psychology vindicated the concepts and provided the causal structure of much of the psychoanalytic domain (Hopkins, 1982, 1988, 1995; Wollheim, 1979, 1984, 1991, 1993). Their approach invigorated work in the philosophy of psychoanalysis (Boag, Brakel and Talvitie (Eds.) 2015; Brakel, 2009; Cavell, 1993, 2006; Gardner, 1993; Lacewing, 2012, 2013; Lear, 1998; Levine, 2000; Pataki, 1996b, 2000, 2014a; Petocz, 1999) but has not been as influential within psychoanalysis or philosophy as it should be. Today it seems that the rapid development of a predominantly reductive neuroscience may once again overshadow the Intentional project. I will reflect on this development briefly in the concluding section, but my immediate task is to locate FWT in the context of an extended common-sense psychology.

Psychoanalysis and common-sense psychology

Although there are important variations, the general view of the psychoanalytic extension of common-sense or Intentional psychology undertaken by Wollheim, Hopkins and those who have followed can be summarised as follows:

i. a significant part of psychoanalytic theory is an extension and deepening of common-sense psychology; this can be viewed in two parts:
i(a). some key concepts of psychoanalysis are extensions of common-sense-psychological concepts; for example, *introjection* and *unconscious phantasy* are extensions—are based on our understanding of—*imagination*, and;
i(b). the forms of causal explanation used in psychoanalysis are in some cases the same as, and in others extensions of, those of common-sense psychology, and;
ii. the distinctive forms of causal explanation in psychoanalysis are those of Freudian wish-fulfilment (FWT) and phantasy (where phantasy is regarded as distinct from FWT);
iii. FWT involves modes of causal explanation that are non-intentional.

It is a feature—it is the point—of this extension of Intentional or common-sense psychology that it remains Intentional. In common-sense psychology we explain actions and mental activity, as well as dispositions and the occurrence of sensations, emotions, and moods, using an immense variety of mental concepts—desire, belief, rage, joy, envy, disappointment, fear, cowardice, generosity, malice, etc. It is necessary to recall how rich and heterogeneous this cluster of concepts is—evolved over millennia of human social life—and to resist the temptation to suppose that these "thick" concepts can be neatly reduced to, and behaviour explained in terms of, a few basic concepts such as belief and desire; let alone be reduced to, or correlated with, neural or computational states. (Nevertheless, belief and desire are basic to the causal explanation of *much* action and mental activity, and for this reason, as well as for reasons of economy, the focus will generally be on them.)

Not all explanation of action is causal. Sometimes action is explained by re-description. Money is seen to be changing hands and we explain that our friend is repaying a debt, bribing an official, buying a car. These re-descriptions are explanations, and useful ones. The brain sciences cannot displace such explanations because they presuppose concepts foreign to them. The concepts of *debt, bribe* and *buying* supervene on conventions, practices and institutions that cannot conceivably figure as concepts of any possible brain science. However, we may become interested in *how* actions (the activation of the musculature, etc.) are performed, in what *manner* they are performed (resentfully, with trepidation), and *why* (because she wanted to clear a debt, to win) they are performed. And to satisfy such interests the sciences as well as Intentional psychology may be invoked. The most straightforward explanation in Intentional psychology is the providing of reasons for intentional action. This usually involves specifying desires and instrumental beliefs about how to satisfy those desires, which, together, both cause and rationalise the action; it may also involve specifying executive states such as intending, deciding, and choosing.

Various non-intentional modes of causal explanation are available to common-sense psychology (see condition (iii)). Some of these may be mentioned briefly. Brian O'Shaughnessy (1980) highlighted the notion of sub-intentional action. The concept compasses all those acts, including mental acts, which are caused by wish or desire without facilitation by instrumental beliefs or anything else. Such action has teleology but is caused non-rationally (i.e., is not performed for a reason, understood as a belief-desire pair, or initiated by an executive state). Some wishful imagination, unconscious phantasy[12] and daydreaming may quite naturally be thought to be caused in this way. Our Intentional framework also recognises other motives—I use "motive" loosely to signify anything that instigates action. There are forms of *expression* that have archaeology but no teleology, as when I clench my fists in (out of) anguish, or laugh, or shudder with fear. Explanation along these lines would, in the framework adopted here, be Intentional, but neither intentional nor sub-intentional. We also recognise reactive motives, as when I spring up from fright; and a range of other motives animating thought.

These modes of explanation have a secure home in common-sense psychology but now we must consider the more fraught extensions proposed for psychoanalytic explanation. Richard Wollheim (1991, pp. xixff, 1993a) has usefully (and I think more or less correctly) summarised these and I will summarise his summary. First, *non-conscious* desires and beliefs operating as non-conscious reasons (Wollheim leaves it open whether the reasons are preconscious or dynamically unconscious) explain some intentional actions, such as some parapraxes: the "accidental" dropping of vases and the like (Freud, 1901b). Second, unconscious desire and belief, and a chain of association that leads to what Wollheim calls a *displaced action*. Freud's patient, the Rat Man, wanted to kill his competitor, Dick (in German = fat), and embarked on a strenuous course of exercise to "lose fat". Through that chain of association, losing fat takes on the symbolic meaning of killing Dick. A third motive, the conjunction of desire and what Wollheim calls (infelicitously) "instinct", results in processes designated *"mental activity"*. Wollheim includes (some) of the defence mechanisms in this category, such activities as disavowal, projection, and repression. In such cases it *looks as if* an agent believed that initiating a defence mechanism would further her desire, but it is not plausible, Wollheim contends, to posit instrumental beliefs (1991, p. xxxiii). (Wollheim next mentions the conjunction of desire and phantasy, but it is unclear how or in what instances he conceived of this motive's application, so I leave it aside.) Fourth, the operation of desire (in the absence of an instrumental belief and "instinct") plus some precipitating factor leading to a special sense of expression: "Expression includes dreams, those neurotic symptoms which are not to be thought of as displaced actions and those parapraxes which are not to be thought of either as displaced actions or as actions with unconscious motivation" (Wollheim, 1991, p. xxxv). Expression, Wollheim says, is clearly not action; it is also not activity (1991, p. xxxv). Yet it is more in keeping with Freud's approach, he continues, to hold "that the person would not have done what he did were it not for the gratification that ensued" (1991, p. xxxiv). Wollheim's thought seems unclear here: he seems to be identifying a motive different from the ("archaic") expression of emotion noted above, as in smiling or shuddering, as well as from the sub-intentional causation of action.

The programme of using only the common-sense concepts and extended patterns of causal explanation in the Intentional accounting of psychoanalytic phenomena is not an easy one, and some authors have seen a need to introduce (to "discover") new Intentional concepts with special explanatory qualities for that purpose. For example: *the wish* and *phantasy* understood as "pre-propositional" by Gardner (1993) and Lear (1995, 1998a); and as "technical terms" by Brakel (2009); *propositional reflection* in Gardner (1993); and *neurotic-belief* again in Brakel (2009). In my view, these innovations are superfluous, the extension of the common-sense idiom as set out by Wollheim suffices. Moreover, I will contend that intentional explanation (belief-desire explanation) runs deeper and more widely than Wollheim—or indeed most commentators—has allowed.

Intention in wish-fulfilment

In seminal formulations Hopkins (1982, 1988) placed FWT at the centre of the Intentional explanation of the psychoanalytic domain but explicitly contrasted FWT with intentional action. FWT was conceived sub-intentionally, the result of a kind of imaginative activity animated by desire. "In rational action", Hopkins wrote, "motives produce willed intentions and real actions aimed at satisfaction. Here [in dreams] they produce wishes and mere representations of satisfaction, on the pattern of wishful imagining" (1988, p. 41). This sub-intentional mode of wishful imagining was enlisted in the explanation of complex enactments such as obsessional symptoms (1982, pp. xxi–xxvii; 1988, p. 55) as well as dreams. Similarly, Gardner (1993) maintained that "[t]he fundamental idea on which a psychoanalytic extension of ordinary psychology hinges is that of a connection of content, driven by the operation of desire freed from rational constraints" (1993, pp. 229, 88–89). He concedes that in a case history there are "many [intentional], strategy-suggestive phenomena, some of which are genuinely strategic." But "[t]he crucial point is that these do not stand at the core of psychoanalytic irrational phenomena …" (p. 191).[13]

Hopkins adopted a non-intentional analysis of FWT partly because he recognised a major difficulty with the view that I dub "intentionalism" (i.e., the notion that intention plays a role in FWT)—that of identifying suitable practical syllogisms—schemas whose main premise is a desire, minor premise an instrumental belief, and conclusion an action—for most of the material psychoanalysis attends (1982, p. xixff). That difficulty is discussed below in the section on practical reasoning. Gardner (1993) added to intentionalism's problems by advancing concerns about the partition of mind ("second-mind personology") that intentionalism appears to entail. To see the problem, consider a situation discussed by David Pears (1984, p. 79). A girl "persuaded herself that her lover was not unfaithful … (but avoided) … a particular cafe because she believed that she might find him there with her rival …" Let's suppose, in a psychoanalytic frame, that consciously she was persuaded of her lover's fidelity, and the troubling belief that he was unfaithful was unconscious or otherwise dissociated. Then she harbours contradictory and segregated beliefs about her lover's fidelity. The more important point to notice, however, is that by intentionally avoiding the cafe she seems to be *actively protecting* herself against acknowledging a belief that she (unconsciously) already has; and *that* unconscious belief plays a part in motivating her protective activity. For the manoeuvre to succeed she must be unaware of her *intentionally* avoiding the cafe; for her intention is predicated on a reason that contains the disavowed belief, and knowledge of it would unravel her purpose. The right hand cannot know what the left hand is doing. But then the supposition of *unconscious intentional agency* seems to entail two controversial conclusions: that there is unconscious practical reasoning or deliberation leading to (a) (unconscious) intentional action (i.e., there may be conscious knowledge that an action is performed but its grounds or causes are unconscious) and (b) a dissociation of self into at least two quasi-independent, self-like centres of agency. In addition to these two difficulties for intentionalism, two others, of hoarier complexion, are immediately sparked: (c) scepticism about the concept of unconscious intention, and (d) Sartre's formidable "censor argument", according to which any attempt to introduce duality (or multiplicity) in mind by the interposition of a censor opens up an untenable duality in the censor, and institutes a vicious regress.

Because of these difficulties, most philosophers have rejected partitive conceptions of mind and pursued non-intentional analyses of wish-fulfilment, phantasy, and symptom formation; and largely ignored the role of FWT in art, religion, and prejudice (Cox, Levine and Neuman, 2009; Levine, this volume; Pataki, 2007, 2014b are recent exceptions).[14] I have criticised several sub-intentional analyses and other forms of non-intentional analyses in detail elsewhere (Pataki, 1996b, 2000, 2014a) and here I will repeat only one telling criticism (in the next section). However it is incumbent on me to state that recent work on the implications of the so-called Bayesian theory of mind/brain, according to which the brain is essentially a prediction-processing machine producing updated models of the world by reducing prediction error over its sensory and interoceptive presentations, has produced sub-intentional accounts of FWT, which appear to be immune to some of those criticisms. The ground-breaking applications of this theory to wish-fulfilment may be found in Hopkins (2012) and Andy Sims (2015). One main line of criticism I pursued was that sub-intentional accounts provided no persuasive explanation, in any but the most primitive cases, of how desire alone could cause beliefs that pacified it. The mechanism presupposed by the sub-intentional accounts was obscure. The Bayesian theory illuminates it. I am not competent to assess the success or otherwise of this suggestive but complex neuroscientific theory which is, of course, subject to empirical evaluation. But I will venture two points about its application to the phenomena of FWT, indicating directions along which further consideration could be pursued. The mechanism it describes, basically construing desires as a kind of "doxastic representation" (compassing belief and experiential content) with which beliefs are then brought into line in the process of reducing prediction error (surprise or free energy), may still be inadequate, as Sims concedes, to explain complex wish-fulfilling enactments of the sort I have described as involving maximal intentionality. The theory may require modification or augmentation to account for these types; alternatively, it may entail that these types are not in fact wish-fulfilling. Second, the theory's radical reconstrual of common-sense psychological terms such as belief and desire, and the fact that it generally supervenes on a number of controversial philosophical doctrines—a representational theory of mind, a biosemantic theory of content, reductive physicalism—leave it vulnerable to future refutation on non-empirical grounds; how the theory would look without those (more or less) fraught philosophical foundations is difficult to envisage.

I will now proceed by trying to make the intentionalist position I enjoin plausible, and so shed some light on the alternatives by contrast. The position can be expressed briefly. FWT involves a variety of techniques and processes, with varying degrees of agential involvement, from zero to maximal intentionality. The simplest forms, hallucinatory wish-fulfilment and most dreaming (so-called "lucid" or "directed" dreams being the exception), involve only non-intentional mechanisms operating in primitive mental conditions. But at the other, maximal, end of the spectrum there are complex, reflexive processes in which phantastic (imaginal or plastic) representations, enactments, manipulation of other people or tendentious selections from available evidence are used intentionally and unconsciously for such purposes as fulfilling wishes, or consoling, protecting or appeasing one's self. Some compensatory daydreams and masturbatory phantasies are obvious examples of this kind, as are, less obviously, some forms of wish-fulfilling symptom and enactment. These reflexive forms of FWT may be viewed as falling into a compartment of self-caring or self-solicitous activities that, sometimes perversely, enter into auxiliary or superordinate relations. For example, self-abasement can be an instrument of self-appeasement, and self-deception is often in the strategic service of superordinate modes of self-solicitude, such as self-consolation or self-justification. (Clearly, self-solicitude is the larger class of which FWT is a member; but since most self-solicitude involves FWT, this may be ignored for present purposes.) In failing to recognise unconscious intentionality or strategy in FWT, non-intentionalists have neglected important aspects of the self's activity—those adaptive, self-solicitous activities in which the self takes itself as an object to be cared for.

Some grounds for intentionalism

Freud seems to have been an intentionalist. Certainly, the notion of unconscious intentionality—that the reasons for intentional action may be unconscious—seemed to him unproblematic. He enjoined the homogeneity of conscious and descriptively unconscious mental types and there is nothing in his views to suggest that he thought unconscious intentions operated in ways radically different to conscious ones.[15] He invoked unconscious intentions to explain the wish-fulfilling phenomena of symptoms (e.g., 1916–1917: chapters xix–xiii, esp. pp. 298–299; 1909a, p. 231); parapraxes (1901b, passim); phantasies (1908a, pp. 159, 164, 1909a); play (1908e, p. 146; 1911b, p. 39); and art (1908e, passim). He presents daydreams and masturbation phantasies (1912f; Stoller, 1979) as crafted products intentionally manufactured for the purpose of gaining satisfaction, in phantasy as well as in physical discharge. In his structural model Freud assimilates hallucination to phantasy and emphasises the ego's intentional role in its construction (1924b, 1924e). The dream too is described "as a piece of phantasy working on behalf of the maintenance of sleep" (1923b, p. 151): the ego responds to disturbing demands by "what appears to be an act of compliance: it meets the demand with what is in the circumstances a harmless fulfilment of a wish and so gets rid of it" (1940a, p. 170). In later editions of *The Interpretation of Dreams* Freud included striking examples of intentional control over the shape of the dream (lucid dreams):

> ... there are some people who are quite clearly aware during the night that they are asleep and dreaming and who thus seem to possess the faculty of consciously directing their dreams. If, for instance, a dreamer of this kind is dissatisfied with the turn taken by the dream, he can break it off without waking up and start it

> again in another direction—just as a popular dramatist may under pressure give his play a happier ending. (Freud, 1900a, pp. 571–572)

Finally, consider Freud's remarks on the evocation of hysterical symptoms. He first recognises precipitation by economic and associative factors, but then adds that they may also be evoked:

> (3) in the service of the primary purpose—as an expression of the 'flight into illness', when reality becomes distressing or frightening—that is, as a consolation; (4) in the service of the secondary purposes, with which the illness allies itself, as soon as, by producing an attack, the patient can achieve an aim that is useful to him. In the last case the attack is directed at particular individuals, and can be put off till they are present, and it gives an impression of being consciously simulated. (Freud, 1909a, pp. 231–232)

The description of neurosis as consoling flight into illness is certainly suggestive of intentional strategy, and Freud could hardly have made it plainer that this was his view of the secondary purpose in neurosis. It is true, as Gardner (1993, p. 192) observes, that the secondary purpose is preconscious and does not shape the symptom, but this does not alter its unconscious strategic character. The secondary purpose is descriptively unconscious, subject to the potent censorship between the *Pcs.* and the *Cs.* systems (Freud, 1915, p. 196), perhaps permanently inaccessible to the patient, probably running counter to the patient's conscious intentions, and an intentional cause of the precipitation of the symptom.

Freud's description of this broad range of phenomena as manifesting intention is suggestive but not conclusive: his considerations may be subject to systematic error. But consider now a specific case and ponder the alternatives:

> A patient, a successful scientist in his own field, came to analysis because (amongst other things) he had a severe work problem. He could, in fact, produce the work required of him, and had made several notable contributions in his field. He had previously had analysis for some years, and at the beginning of his current analysis it seemed that all the well-known factors causing a work difficulty of the sort he had were present. His need to delay getting down to work till the very last minute was quite clearly an oedipal problem,

> in which he could not allow himself to feel that he had satisfied oedipal sexual and aggressive wishes by working well. It was also seen to be part of an anal-retentive tendency, which had persisted for most of his life, and so on. Analysis of his fear of success, of his need to hold on until the last moment, and of many other elements that were clearly related to his work problems did not do more than give him greater insight ... Eventually ... the significant function of his symptom became clear. By allowing himself to get into a state of anxiety, and by creating a feeling of great internal pressure as the time passed and his work was not done, he could recreate, to a degree which was almost hallucinatory in intensity, the feeling of being nagged at and even screamed at by his mother. It became clear that he used his symptom to re-experience an object-relationship, one in which a wished-for sado-masochistic relationship with his mother was actualised. However, what was present was more than the simple sexualisation of anxiety, but a real need to feel secure by re-experiencing the earlier relationship to the mother, even though he had to pay a rather painful price for this. (Sandler & Sandler, 1978, pp. 290–291)

It is suggested that the symptom was created by the scientist to satisfy "a wished-for sado-masochistic relationship with his mother." On the Sandlers' interpretation the anxiety state that the scientist induces in himself can be re-described as representing (*being experienced as*) mother's presence in near hallucinatory form. There is, we may assume, good reason why he wants to experience mother's presence, painful to be sure, but satisfying the patient's overriding need for security or attachment. Can this wish-fulfilling end—that it be for the scientist *as if mother were present*—be achieved non-intentionally?

Notice that the panic that the scientist manufactures is not the product of a single stroke. What we would find is endless procrastination, strolling, eating; a veritable programme of postponement. In other words, the strategy invades more or less every corner of his life and intentional projects: *a thousand intentional acts pointing in the same direction*. It seems evident that the process of creating the near hallucinatory experience of mother, which is the vehicle for the wish-fulfilling belief that she is present, is an intentional strategy. For it seems inconceivable how, on alternative non-intentionalist accounts (whether sub-intentionalist, expressive, and so on), a vast array of non-intentional mechanisms could be strung together in the service of the one unified purpose. How could such mechanisms have come to infect the thousand acts that contrive themselves into the achievement of that purpose? If such cases cannot be explained non-intentionally then intentionalism does seem a promising possibility; but another possibility is the failure of the psychoanalytic project to understand such cases in Intentional or common-sense psychological terms. I will come to that presently, but first let us turn to the prospects of intentionalism.

Unconscious intention and practical reasoning

A necessary condition of the operation of intentional FWT is the existence of unconscious intentions operating in much the same way as conscious intentions do. But there is a widespread intuition that intentions are the kind of thing that can only be conscious. As Stuart Hampshire wrote: "Intention is the one concept that ought to be preserved free from any taint of the less-than-conscious. Its function, across the whole range of its applications, is to mark the kind of knowledge of what one is doing, and of what one is inclined to do, that is fully conscious and explicit" (Hampshire, 1974, p. 125). The psychologist Daniel Wegner shares a similar intuition: "*Intention* is normally understood as an idea of what one is going to do that appears in consciousness just before one does it" (2002, p. 18). Curiously—partly through the work of Wegner (2002), Benjamin Libet (2004), and others—the view that there exist unconscious or non-conscious intentions seems now to prevail. Indeed, the shoe is on the other foot and the contemporary challenge is to demonstrate that there are causally efficacious, proximate *conscious* intentions (Mele, 2009). A large body of experimental evidence seems to support the existence of unconscious intentions, and therefore unconscious efficacious reasons and other executive states.

One well-confirmed experimental finding is that certain non-conscious neural events, causally sufficient for some prescribed action *A*, occur a significant period of time before the agent becomes aware of a conscious experience of intending, deciding, or willing *A*. (It is unclear what the supposedly conscious experiences of intending and willing *are*; but the argument here is ad hominem, and this particular obscurity does not affect it.) Wegner, who thinks that willing and intention *are* conscious ideas or experiences, concludes that because the non-conscious neural states are sufficient for action, conscious will, the allegedly subsequent conscious experience, is not part of the causal process in acting, and is therefore an illusion.

But if we take a different tack and abandon Wegner's supposition that willing or the other executive states are *conscious ideas or experiences*, and consider them instead as functional states initiating, sustaining, and guiding intentional actions, then another possibility opens up: that the causal antecedents of action detected in the experiments are a species of these functional states—that is, non-conscious intentions, urges, or decisions, or the neural substrates of them (Mele, 2009, p. 38). We have, after all, long recognised non-conscious *standing*, as opposed to occurrent, intentions guiding action (my long-standing intention to visit Paris), as well as enthymematic intentions in the causal process of skilled action, such as playing tennis. In fact, there seems to be no reasoned objection to non-conscious intentions, even to dynamically unconscious intentions; and experiments such as those just noted provide evidence for precisely such states.

Also significant is a convergence of various lines of thought on Freud's view that the "executive agency of mind" is unconscious—or more precisely that it need not be conscious, that in pathology, at least, elements of it recede into the unconscious. On the basis of controlled clinical investigations the Mt. Zion group concluded that "a person is able unconsciously to exert some control over his behaviour, that he regulates it unconsciously in accordance with thoughts, beliefs, and assessments of current reality, and that he attempts, by his regulation of behaviour, to avoid putting himself in dangerous situations" (Weiss and Sampson 1986: 5). The clinical material they record leading to this conclusion is most compelling. In their neuropsychoanalytic tour de force Kaplan-Solms and Solms (2000, pp. 90–115) discuss a patient with a serious language disorder experienced subjectively as "an inability to think", but more accurately described as an "inability to *attach words to her thoughts,* resulting in an inability to *bring her thoughts to consciousness* (and to *keep* them there)" (2000, p. 108, their italics). The patient suffered a functional dissociation between her consciousness and executive control, yet "continued to behave in an essentially reasonable way … to function as an essentially rational and reality oriented agent" (2000, pp. 110–111). The authors conclude that the patient "retained executive control over her *behaviour;* all that she lost was control over her *consciousness* … This confirms Freud's revised (1923b) topographical proposals, to the effect that consciousness is not the executive agency of the mind, and that even the ego itself is fundamentally unconscious" (2000, p. 111). It is integral to the conception of an *executive agency of mind* that it forms and acts on intentions.

These are not conclusive but they are compelling considerations supporting the notion that actions can be caused by unconscious efficacious reasons and executive states such as proximal intentions. If so, then objection (c) to intentionalism noted earlier can be put aside. I will assume that the considerations do show that scepticism about unconscious intention is unwarranted. But now the most serious objection looms. Can coherent, plausible unconscious intentional structures—practical syllogisms—be constructed for the maximal cases of FWT, the type for which we made provision at the start of the chapter? Attempts to do so run into formidable obstacles. Non-intentionalism appears an attractive option because intentionalism appears impossible.

In Lecture 17 of the *Introductory Lectures* (1916–1917) Freud discusses a compulsive symptom in a nineteen-year-old girl:

> [T]he most important stipulation related to the bed itself. The pillow at the top end of the bed must not touch the wooden back of the bedstead. The small top pillow must lie on this large pillow in one specific way only—namely, so as to form a diamond shape. Her head had then to lie exactly along the long diameter of the diamond. The eiderdown had to be shaken before being laid on the bed so that its bottom end became very thick; afterwards, however she never failed to even out this accumulation of feathers by pressing them apart ... She found out the central meaning of the bed ceremonial one day when she suddenly understood the meaning of the rule that the pillow must not touch the back of the bedstead. The pillow, she said, had always been a woman to her and the upright wooden back a man ... If the pillow was a woman, then the shaking of the eiderdown till all the feathers were at the bottom and caused a swelling there had a sense as well. It meant making a woman pregnant; but she never failed to smooth away the pregnancy again, for she had for years been afraid that her parents' intercourse would result in another child and so present her with a competitor. (pp. 265–268)

Freud interpreted this ritual as the girl's "magical" attempt to keep her parents separated, to prevent their sexual intercourse and to ward off anxieties connected with the birth of a competitor. The ritual seems to be a sequence of intentional actions but the girl could provide no reasons for performing it and initially found her own actions unintelligible. Presumably she would have rehearsed some such syllogism as: "I want to sleep; if I want to sleep then I must first perform these acts (I can't resist anyway) of separating bedstead from pillow; therefore I perform these acts." But these thoughts do nothing to illuminate the symptom. How has she come to think such things, how has she come to such a pass?

If we follow Freud's principal interpretation we can construct another practical syllogism for her behaviour:

> Girl wants to separate mother and father.
>
> Girl believes that by separating bedstead and pillow she will separate mother and father.
>
> --
>
> Girl separates bedstead and pillow.

If the girl's action accords with this unconscious syllogism then it is intentional. The major premise, the girl's desire, is not in doubt but the minor premise expresses what appears to be a "mad belief". Several commentators have questioned whether it is possible to hold such bizarre beliefs or to have them engage as motives to action (Hopkins, 1982, pp. xxiff). Michael Moore writes:

> [O]ne should question whether the association of one thing with another [her father with the bedstead] is evidence that the girl believes the two things to be the same … In addition, there is evidence to the contrary; unless she is more than neurotic, she would surely declare that she knows the difference between her father and her bedstead. Given the usual assumptions about the consistency of a person's beliefs, there is strong evidence that she does not believe that her father and her bedstead are one. (1984, pp. 335–336)

Moore assumes that the girl could have held the belief expressed in the minor premise only if she believed that the bedstead was identical with her father (ditto: mother) and this he believes is unlikely on the basis of an expected denial, had she been asked, and the fact that the belief would be inconsistent with her other, rational conscious beliefs.

He concedes, though, that the girl *might* have had the mad belief if she were "more than neurotic". Moore accepts that the "ritual is plainly an action of hers", by which he means that the action of separating the bedstead and the pillow is intentional. He follows Jeremy Bentham's inclusive definition of "intentional" as qualifying all actions performed by an actor who knows she is performing them. Since the girl knows "what she is doing", separating bedstead and pillow, it follows on this criterion that she is acting intentionally. Bentham's definition cannot be right but let's go along with it. So, then, what *is* the practical syllogism that explains her action? If she is acting intentionally then there is a reason for her action. To deny that the action is intentional is a position that is defensible—the symptom is, after all, compulsive. But if intentionality is imputed then either a reason for acting—conscious or unconscious—had better be produced, or, failing that, a sound argument demonstrating that acting intentionally does not entail having efficacious reasons for acting. Bentham's definition is clearly flawed and Moore's use of it here, combined with his rejection of the unconscious syllogism, leads to the untenable position of affirming that the ritual is intentional, without an explanation of how it can be.

It is a mark of *conscious* intention that it is sensitive to circumstance; that it can be withheld or modified in light of relevant rational considerations. These features are lacking in the girl's ritual. So it seems that the act, under the description "separating bedstead and pillow", is not intentional: there are no conscious efficacious reasons for it and it is not (immediately) vulnerable to rational revision. But the same act-event could be intentional under other descriptions. Several different practical syllogisms concluding with the required action can be constructed. Recall Moore's claim that in order to arrive at the sort of practical syllogism instanced above, the girl must have *believed* that the bedstead was her father. In fact, that is not implied in the material and it is not necessary for the girl to have believed it. What she appears to believe, unconsciously, is that if she separates the bedstead and the pillow she will have separated her parents. Believing this proposition is not the same as, nor does it presuppose, believing that her parents were identical with the furniture. The sorcerer who sticks pins into an effigy doesn't believe that the effigy *is* his enemy. The distinction underlying the difference here is between one thing *operationally symbolising* another and that thing being *believed to be identical with* the other. And both of these circumstances can be distinguished from a third, where one thing is functionally *equated* with another: where there is a Segalian symbolic equation, as I shall say.

Unconscious symbolism hugely extends the scope of FWT, as our cases illustrate. It is clear that such symbolism doesn't necessarily entail belief in identity of symbol and thing symbolised, though there may be such a belief, and it may be operative. If the bedstead girl believes unconsciously that the bedstead is her father (ditto: mother) then from the fact that she separates bedstead from pillow she will be able to *infer* (unconsciously) that she has separated her parents. In the case I referred to as operational symbolism, what the girl does *seems* to separate her parents when she separates the bedstead and pillow—as she apprehends it unconsciously. It is *as if* she separated them, at least transiently.

It is easy to find unconscious intention conferring reasons on each scenario. The practical syllogism set out above is an example using the sorcery-like belief ("if she separates the furnishings she will separate her parents"). And the following is an example for the operational symbolic equation:

> Girl wants to prevent the conception of a baby-competitor.
>
> Girl believes that by keeping her father/bedstead and her mother/pillow apart she could prevent that conception.
>
> ---
>
> Girl separates bedstead and pillow.

The "/" sign here is meant to indicate that it is not a case of *believing* that father and bedstead (ditto: mother) are numerically identical, but of failing to distinguish between them *qualitatively in certain important respects*. The bedroom furniture, in the girl's case, may symbolise parents, and action upon the furniture may be perceived as affecting the parents. But there is neither numerical nor full qualitative identity here. This is therefore different from the relation I referred to as Segalian symbolic equation (Bott Spillius et al., 2011, pp. 514–515; Segal, 1957, 1991) where there appears to be almost complete indiscernibility between symbol and thing symbolised, and different processes underlying the equation. In this kind of symbolic equation "the symbol is so equated with the object symbolized that the two are felt to be identical." On the other hand, in "true symbolism or symbolic representation, the symbol represents the object but is not entirely equated with it" (Segal, 1991, p. 35). Incorporating Segalian symbolism, a third practical syllogism can be generated:

> Girl wants to prevent the conception of a baby-competitor.
> Girl believes that by keeping her father = bedstead and her mother = pillow apart she could prevent that conception.
> --
> Girl separates bedstead and pillow.

I don't wish to suggest that any one of these syllogisms is *the* correct one. It seems to me that such mad beliefs as considered here may indeed enter into unconscious practical reasoning. But in light of what has been said about maximal FWT and self-solicitude another possibility arises.

Dissociation

Accept for the moment the coherence of the notion of divided minds and the possibility of maximal forms of FWT. Allow one part of the mind (B) to be in solicitous, caring relation to another, "client", part (A). Then we can generate valid practical syllogisms that do not contain outlandish desires or mad beliefs. For example:

> B wants to console (protect, pacify, etc.) A.
> B believes that by separating bedstead and pillow A will be consoled (protected, pacified, etc.).
> --
> B separates bedstead and pillow.

Notice here that B's belief is not mad; it is solicitous, the kind of belief a concerned mother may develop for a child. Such intrapsychic solicitous roles are noted frequently in Freud's work and in many of the pioneer object-relations theorists. Freud writes, for example, of the ego's protection of the id (1940a, pp. 197–199) and of the superego's solicitude for the ego: "To the ego … living means the same as being loved—being loved by the superego … The superego fulfils the same function of protecting and saving that was fulfilled in earlier days by the father …" (1923b, p. 58); and "if the super-ego does try to comfort the ego by humour and to protect it from suffering, this does not conflict with its derivation from the parental function" (1927d, p. 166). He eventually emphasised that some of these self-solicitous relations are "decisively influenced by the identification with the nursing mother" (Hartmann, Kris, & Loewenstein, 1946, p. 39). Spitz (1965, p. 179) noted that internalisation of maternal functions was necessary for the infant's acquiring independence and the capacity for self-regulation. Winnicott wrote: "The infant develops means for doing without actual care. This is accomplished through the accumulation of memories of care, the projection of personal needs and the introjection of care details, with the development of confidence in the environment" (Winnicott, 1965, p. 48). The investigation of such healthy internalisation of caring functions has been pursued (e.g., Kumin, 1996; Schore, 2003) though, to my knowledge, its implications for mental structure, for dissociation of mind leading to the kind of mental opacity implied in the last practical syllogism, has not.

Considerably more is known about pathological dissociations in which the infant faced with an intolerable environment internalises and identifies with its frustrating or hated objects, or complies with them, splits itself, and takes itself as an object. Winnicott's (1965) views on the false self's protection and solicitude for the true self are well known. A number of Kleinian analysts (Bion, 1967; Rosenfeld, 1987) as well as some strongly influenced by Klein (Kernberg, 1966, 1975; Ogden, 1986) and others (Bollas, 1987) have written about these pathological reflexive attitudes in which the management or solicitude for the object self has become perversely hostile. It is possibly because the self-solicitous relations, including the intentional forms of wish-fulfilment, are so frequently dominated by pathological developments that they often take the form of self-deceit, symptom, delusion, and pernicious illusion.

At this point we can discern some closure. We can begin to see the capacity for maximal FWT as a consequence primarily of the internalisation of caretakers and their functions—though, of course, such functions may be augmented from elsewhere. There is a relationship that the self has to itself that is one of solicitude, caring, consolation, and, at its best, cherishing; though, perhaps more often, it degenerates into pandering, appeasement, and deceit. Much care-taking is conscious, but much, as considerations concerning unconscious executive agency suggest, may be unconscious. Maximal FWT, it is proposed, involves strategies in which the self, dissociated by its internalisations, sets out unconsciously but intentionally to provide for itself gratification or consolation or protection. It does this by telling itself stories (as in dreams and daydreams), manufacturing phantasies and symptoms or delusional scenes that, so to speak, alter the evidential field for the client self. It creates a congenial imaginary world in which mere wishing *seems* to have made it so. And now it appears how the practical syllogisms for FWT set out earlier articulate the practical expression of this dissociated condition of mind. Of course, many difficulties with the notion of a dissociated mind remain, but the very possibility of maximal FWT constitutes a new argument for just such dissociation. We have now travelled some way to allaying objections (a) and (b) above.

Moreover, we can now see in outline how the Sartrean censor argument, (d), can be expeditiously dispatched. David Pears (1984) had already proposed a means of dealing with it. He suggested in effect that the duality in the protective sub-system—the censor—of knowing what is not supposed to be known didn't matter because the protective system has as its environment and concern the well-being of the defended system and can therefore tolerate duality without embarrassment. This, I think, is essentially correct. Gardner (1993) advanced what he thought were two conclusive objections to the manoeuvre: no adequate explanation has been provided of either (i) the causal origin of the protective sub-system (pp. 76–77) or (ii) the irrational contents of the sub-system (p. 114). But we can now see how psychoanalytic theory can answer these objections. As regards (i) the self-like structures of the unconscious protective ego may be seen as products of the internalisation of maternal and other caring functions, and their dissociation. And (ii): psychoanalysis gives us insight into the many ways in which irrational, bizarre and pathogenic beliefs are retained in unconscious and, indeed, conscious mental life.

The circumstantial conditions for successful FWT

We have charted the scope of agency in FWT but have not yet described the psychic or circumstantial conditions that enable its various forms to succeed. Freud provided a metapsychological account of wish-fulfilment that is intended to provide those conditions (1900a, pp. 533ff). It could be glossed as follows: when a wishful impulse's immediate access to satisfaction is frustrated, as it is in the helpless, hungry infant and the sleeper, a topographical regression of psychic energy ("quantity") to the perceptual system of the mental apparatus ensues, and a reactivation of a memory of satisfaction as a hallucinatory experience provides a "perceptual identity" with the original satisfaction. A memory of a previously satisfying experience is thus mistaken for a perception of the wished-for object, and wish-fulfilment (or discharge) is achieved. The "mistake" is an expression of the regression to primary-process functioning, whose key characteristics include mobility of cathexis and "*the replacement of external by psychical reality*" (Freud, 1915e, p. 187, his italics). However, in his most careful consideration Freud realised that the revival of a memory-percept in a primitive mode of functioning won't quite deliver the required result:

> If the secret of hallucination is nothing else than that of regression, every regression of sufficient intensity would produce hallucination with belief in its reality. But we are quite familiar with situations in which a process of regressive reflection brings to consciousness very clear mnemic images, though we do not on that account for a single moment take them for real perceptions. Again, we could well imagine the dream-work penetrating to mnemic images of this kind, making conscious to us what was previously unconscious, and holding up to us a wishful phantasy which rouses our longing, but which we should not regard as a real fulfilment of the wish. (1917d: 231)

Dreams, he had earlier observed, are not just thoughts or sensory images: "their ideational content being transformed from thoughts into sensory images *to which belief is attached* and which appear to be experienced" (1900a, p. 535; italics added). In the later metapsychology paper he emphasises that hallucination "brings belief in reality with it" (1917d, p. 230). And how does belief do that? Freud harks back to an old view: when an idea isn't contradicted, it's believed (1900a, pp. 50–52, 535; 1917d, pp. 230, 234). When nothing in the mind "contradicts" or is incompatible with a particular idea or perception, because all incompatible ideas or perceptions have been excluded or "decathected"—have *Cs.* and *Pcs.* attention withdrawn from them—then "reality testing" is inoperative, and the particular idea or perception is "believed". We may say that in such circumstances when wishful representations brook no contradiction and succeed in presenting themselves as wish-fulfilling representations, as the irrecusable evidence on which critical occurrent beliefs are based, the agent is *engrossed* (Wollheim, 1979, p. 53).

On this analysis, the aspect of primary process functioning that enables psychic reality to replace external reality turns in part on the liability of the regressed mind to become engrossed in its psychic experience, which then generates terminating beliefs. This view seems to be consistent with the Bayesian account of Freudian wish-fulfilment developed in Hopkins (2012). The general idea is that the brain's main (or perhaps only) function is reliable prediction of sensory experience and so avoidance of conflict between its sensory and interoceptive inputs with the current dominant model that the brain is using to make sense of experience. To do this the brain suppresses/represses representations inconsistent with that model, but where it cannot explain them away it keeps them alive as potential correction to its current state. (We might say that the representations remain unconsciously cathected or objects of preoccupation.) Confronted with an internal stimulus when action is impossible (as in sleep), or because the desire conflicts with the dominant model, the brain, governed by the imperatives of homeostasis and conflict avoidance, may rapidly repress the desire and produce in its place "an *internal representation of the experience of satisfaction the desire predicts*" (2012, p. 258, original italics). In the case of dreaming: "this neurologically intelligible way of managing conflict related to internal sensory input appears as a kind of *perfect and all-encompassing miniature hallucination,* in which the deluded dreaming subject utterly obliterates both what is happening in his mind and how things are in the world … his dreaming brain (as ego) is producing a *double denial of reality …*" (2012, p. 258). This, as Freud supposed, would seem tailored by the ego to enable sleep undisturbed. In the case of some symptoms, such as the Rat Man's torturing and tormenting phantasies, we may see the brain as:

> pacifying [the repressed, animating] desires as soon as they arose by the most direct means possible, that is … by falsely but immediately representing the predictions to which the repressed desires gave rise as having been fulfilled. In this way the brain succeeded in suspending the working of such desires, in the absence of any real attempt at satisfaction. This dreamlike process of pacification, however, was also the symptom which rendered the patient anxious, depressed, and obsessional. (Hopkins, 2012, pp. 262–263)

Thus the Bayesian account of wish-fulfilment in terms of repression and conflict avoidance would also seem to supervene on something like imaginative engrossment as we have conceived it. The efficacy of both the dream and the kind of wish-fulfilling phantasy that partly constitutes the Rat Man's obsessional symptoms are predicated on absorption in a kind of "miniature hallucination": in dream "all-encompassing", in the symptom less so. But this difference between dream and symptom suggests that the Bayesian account must be supplemented by some index of the efficacy of phantasy, whether it be the degree of belief generated by engrossment that underlies Freud's account (and ours), or another factor, such as *experiential vivacity,* informally proposed by Hopkins (see Pataki, 2014b, pp. 79–80). This issue of an index of efficacy seems to me uncertain, but in my view treating the phantasy involved in dream and symptom as a kind of non-canonical but irrecusable "agent's-evidence" that generates wish-fulfilling beliefs is the most cogent solution to the problem.

In any case, both the account of engrossment I have outlined and the neuroscientific model appear to have serious limitations in accounting for the full range of FWT. Although they may be adequate for explaining primitive instances of FWT—hallucinatory wish-fulfilment, dreams, and some features of symptoms—it is difficult to see how they can accommodate enactments such as the anxious scientist's, the wish-fulfilling character of personality disorders, religion, and art. Precisely what are the objects of engrossment in obsessional *acts*, for example, and who or what elements of self are engrossed? To answer these questions requires, I think, a radical extension of the notion of engrossment, applying not only to features of internal psychic experience (dreams, phantasies) but to engrossment in the enactment of *roles* by dissociated aspects of the self. I have explored this proposal elsewhere (Pataki, 2014b, Chapter Five). But other, and perhaps more attractive, alternatives may present themselves: (i) to abandon altogether the attempt to provide Intentional explanations for the more complex symptoms and their kin; or, less radically, (ii) to abandon Freudian wish-fulfilment as the fitting mode of explanation for these phenomena.

Freudian wish-fulfilment abandoned

In the classical *economic* account, neurotic symptoms (and their kin) were conceived as products of conflict, as compromise formations between, at first, libidinal drives and egodrives, and later between id drives and ego structures. Instinctual drives incompatible with the ego are repressed but, given their natural tendency to seek discharge, continue to strive for expression. When the ego's counter-cathectic or defensive forces weaken, a "return of the repressed" ensues and the repressed material, modified by the defences, achieves expression or discharge in disguised or attenuated form. These expressions are the neurotic symptoms and may be regarded as secondary attempts to bind the anxiety associated with repressed material. They provide partial release of drive tension or excitations. This economic conception of drive discharge is not in principle dependent on the representational content of the symptom. It is generally agreed that this account is faced with insurmountable problems.[16]

The view explored in this chapter enlarges on another strand in Freud's thought. Symptoms (and their kin) are states or acts with sense or meaning. They have representational content that is a compromise between the fulfilments of wishes originating from opposing elements of the personality. They are wish-fulfilling not just in that the drive of which the wish is the representative achieves "discharge", but in depicting a "scene", in facilitating circumstances, in which contending wishes are fulfilled (in the manner of FWT), or from which it can be unconsciously inferred (after unravelling the primary process and defensive distortions) that they have been fulfilled (Freud, 1916–1917, chapters xix–xxiii). This construal of symptoms requires specification of Intentional content and therefore turns on characterisation in the Intentional idiom.

Embracing common-sense psychology we must now face the consequences. In contemporary mainstream psychiatry the dominant view of the major mental disorders—schizophrenia, bipolar disorder, major depression, a range of anxiety disorders—is that they are essentially neurobiological conditions. Their symptoms are alleged to be manifestations of a "broken brain", though (on most accounts) they may be triggered by environmental factors, so-called "significant life events". A description of neurobiological conditions (anatomical, chemical, physiological) is believed to suffice; Intentional explanation doesn't enter the story. The less profound neurotic and borderline conditions, and the various phenomena that Freud assimilated to neurosis, are also viewed by many investigators in this reductive light. The contrary idea that most mental disorders, even most psychotic disorders, can be understood entirely in Intentional terms does not have a large following.

Across the various relevant disciplines there is in fact a spectrum of perspectives, ranging from neurobiological exclusivism or "neuralism", as George Graham (2010) dubs it, to those that employ the ambiguous mental mechanics of cognitive neuroscience, to approaches that figure mental disorder largely in Intentional terms but invoke, to different degrees, the intervention of neurobiological mechanisms or mental but a-rational forces. As an example of the latter, Graham argues for the necessity of Intentional characterisation of all mental disorders and rejects exclusive "neuralism". But he also insists that understanding the major disorders requires reference to a-rational neural causes that "gum up" the mind and explain why the patient is "unreason-responsive" and the disorders are involuntary and unintended (Graham, 2010, p. 47).[17] The gum consists (in part) "of non-rational/a-rational/mechanical/ brute neural forces irrupting into the space of a person's reasons or Intentionality and being partly responsible for the truncation or impairment in reason and rational control that helps constitute a disorder" (2010, p. 126). The brain in mental illness, on this account, is just a little bit broken.

In a hybrid account of mental illness, such as the one proposed by Graham, in which Intentionality is an essential feature, there certainly seems space for FWT. It will remain an open question whether or not particular disorders are instances of, or to some degree manifest, FWT. This would not appear to be the case if exclusive neuralism is true and mental disorders are entirely disorders of the brain. Where the Intentional idiom has no purchase, neither has FWT as we have characterised it. It must be observed, however, that if exclusive neuralism is true then it should be possible to fully describe the mental disorders in the languages of neurobiology; and no one has a clue how to do that. There are powerful philosophical reasons behind this insufficiency that can only be touched on here. It may prove possible to identify various neurobiological configurations—or, perhaps, mechanisms defined in cognitive science—that are active across a diagnostic class. But the identification of such an entity, or a group of such pathogenic entities, in a particular case of mental disorder would fall far short of a complete characterisation of the disorder. For each disorder has mental content, distinctive thoughts, fears and phantasies responsive to the present environment and to the past (and future) that are not irrelevant to the nature of the disorder. These the physical characterisations cannot capture. So it would seem on the face of it that neither exclusive neuralism nor a non-Intentional cognitive neuroscience poses an imminent threat to the scope of FWT.

But now there may be another objection to the scope of FWT. Not that FWT is misapplied altogether or superfluous, but that it does not apply beyond the narrow range of intrapsychic phenomena such as the dream or delusion. Noted above was the possibility of disburdening an account of complex symptoms such as enactments of the obligation to explain the refractory feature of pacification, indeed of representation, by jettisoning the supposition of wish-fulfilment. Gardner in his incisive work argued that when psychoanalysis needs to pass beyond intrapsychic processes to explain what appear, at least prima facie, to be intentional actions then wish-fulfilment is superseded (1993, pp. 140–141, 172) and we must employ phantasy, "a new theoretical concept", which "differs from wish-fulfilment in having the power to manifest itself in intentional action" (1993, p. 141). Given the manifest difficulties of construing intentional action as wish-fulfilling, the temptation to pursue this, or a related course, is considerable. Of course, this tack would detach FWT from essential Freudian conceptions with which it is imbricated, but that is scarcely a decisive objection to it. An adequate response to this challenge must demonstrate how the phenomena in question—enactments such as the anxious scientist's—can possibly be wish-fulfilling, and indeed that they are. I think that the adequate response requires working out the implications of the kind of self-solicitous dissociation of the self touched on above. I have attempted that in Pataki (2014b); but uncertainties abound.

Notes

1. The theory was famously adumbrated in explicitly mechanistic form in 1895 (Freud, 1950a), a form Freud subsequently considered unsatisfactory.
2. Freud writes: "the principal function of the mental mechanism is to relieve the individual from the tensions created in him by his needs ... But the satisfaction of ... part of these needs ... is regularly frustrated by reality. This leads to the further task of finding some other means of dealing with the unsatisfied impulses. The whole course of the history of civilization is no more than an account of the various methods adopted by mankind for 'binding' their unsatisfied wishes. Myths, religion and morality find their place in this scheme as attempts to seek a compensation for the lack of satisfaction of human

wishes ... [T]he neuroses themselves have turned out to be attempts to find individual solutions for the problems of compensating for unsatisfied wishes, while the institutions seek to provide social solutions for these same problems ... [T]he exercising of an art [is] once again an activity intended to allay ungratified wishes—in the first place in the creative artist himself and subsequently in his audience or spectators" (Freud, 1913j, pp. 186–187).

3. As well as the common usage in which "intentional" qualifies action as "purposeful", "meant" or "aimed at", the term is used in a technical sense in philosophy, which, following common practice, I capitalise: "Intentional". (It is important in what follows not to confuse intentionality with Intentionality.) The Latin root is *intentio*, in scholastic idiom meaning "representation". In a famous passage (cited by Boag, this volume, "Brentano and the intentionality of mental acts") Brentano refers to a mental phenomenon as including "something as an object within itself" and defines mental phenomena as "those which contain an object intentionally within themselves". Elsewhere he refers to the "intentional existence" (or again, "inexistence") of the objects of mentality. His thought (at times) seems to be that such objects exist representationally. Be that as it may, in contemporary philosophy and psychology, Intentionality is most commonly explicated as the property of "aboutness", supposedly possessed only by mental states—"states" understood in the broadest sense, without commitment to a specific ontology. Thus belief, fear and desire are said to have Intentional objects that they are about, and since we can think about, fear and desire things that don't exist, Intentional objects need not exist or even be possible. Intentional objects are what we think (that grass is green) or what we think about (grass, greenness). Intentionality has been said to be the mark of the mental, but this is incorrect. Mental states such as bare awareness (Damasio et al., 2000), moods, pain and other sensations fail to have Intentional objects: a headache, for example, is not about pain, it is pain. This claim challenging Intentionality as a criterion of the mental may be disputed, as it is by Simon Boag (this volume, p. 264*n*). He observes that "to say that a person feels pain is to simply say that the pain is the *object* of the mental act of feeling" (cf. Brentano, 1874, pp. 90–91; Boag's italics). Maybe so, but not to the point. The point is not that pain and some other sensations cannot be *the objects* of Intentional states—*anything* can—but that pain and some other sensations do not *have* Intentional objects, as the Intentionality criterion requires, in the manner that beliefs, desires and so on do. Boag suggests that pain may be the object of "paining", and so presumably moods may be the objects of "mooding". It is then not pain and moods

that have Intentional objects, as the criterion requires, but "paining" and "mooding"; but this is lapsing into unintelligibility. The insistence on finding Intentional objects may be part of a broader Realist-tinctured project in which Intentionality is the relation that binds brains to their (unconditioned) objects. For example, Boag (this volume, p. 248) writes:

> Cognition here refers to acts of *knowing*, such as believing, thinking, remembering, wishing, and desiring, which may either be veridical or non-veridical: "psychological processes are … typified by a kind of relation not to be found in merely physical interactions, and that is the relation of *knowing about* or *referring to*" (Maze, 1983, p. 83, his italics; cf. Maze & Henry, 1996, p. 1089) … The cognitive relation itself "is not a kind of *stuff* that binds the terms. It is just how the terms are with respect to each other" (Michell, 1988, p. 234). Accordingly, as a relation, to be conscious of something is not to ascribe properties (qualities) to either the knower or the state of affairs cognised, and thus care is required when conceptualising mentality to avoid the possibility of reifying relations into qualities.

Since the *Theatetus* much epistemological endeavour has been directed at articulating the *differences* between the various Intentional states that are all subsumed here under "acts of *knowing*". The subsumption is unhelpful. Believing, for example, is not an act (an action, though there are mental acts, like deliberating or projecting) as Boag suggests—and neither is knowing for that matter—but even if it were, it cannot be a species of knowing. You can believe what is false but not know what is false; if belief were a species of knowing you could know what was false. This is a terminological issue, though of consequence. A less easily repaired problem with this expression of Realism, however, is its poverty, clearly revealed in the blunt quotations from Maze and Michell above: how *are* "the terms with respect to each other"? We are told a priori that all mental states are relational, having the logical form SRp, where the relation is external, in the early Bradley-Russellian sense. This may be of interest to a logician. (Actually, it is almost certainly wrong because the logical form of mental action sentences likely involves quantification over events not relations.) But what we want to know is what knowing, believing, fearing and wishing *are*, and their differences. Treating them as Intentional relations, or relational states of affairs, obscures this requirement. And if one *looks*, one finds great variety. The mental is not all of a piece.

4. I have discussed Freudian wish-fulfilment and its relation to the ordinary conception at length elsewhere (Pataki, 1996, 2000, 2014b) and provide only a summary account here.
5. Although there are important conceptual differences between them, I will generally use "wish" and "desire" interchangeably. In its *conceptually central* instances, wishing presupposes an acknowledgement that action is impossible, or close to being so. "How I wish I could have been there" or, even, "I do wish I could go", do not place me in causal relation to action in a time frame but tell, instead, of my preferences. That is why although one cannot desire what one knows to be impossible, one can certainly wish for it. I cannot knowingly desire to undo the past, but wishing that I had been born into wealth or had gone to a better school is something I still do.

   The German *wunsch*, however, has a stronger affiliation with action than our "wish" does, and neither Freud nor his translators distinguished systematically between wishing and desiring. Although it is clear from Freud's texts that he was using "wish" (*wunsch*) in an ordinary way, some of Freud's recent philosophical commentators have claimed to identify in Freud's account of wish-fulfilment a systematically quasi-technical notion of the "wish" to be distinguished from desire. Sebastian Gardner (1993, pp. 124, 140) claims that the "psychoanalytic wish" uncovered by Freud is a novel kind of mental creature, "a sort of hybrid", different from both desire and ordinary wishes, though related to the ordinary kind of wish, and is "necessarily engaged in the process of wish-fulfilment" (1993, p. 126). The difference he alleges is underlined in his claim that "Freud did not envisage wish-fulfilment as a mode of satisfaction available to propositional desires" (1993, p. 123), though desires (according to Gardner) can exploit wish-fulfilment by regressing to a state of instinctual demand and give rise to a wish susceptible to wish-fulfilment (1993, p. 123). Richard Wollheim (1984, pp. 85, 90ff) also discerns a quasi-technical notion of the "wish" that acquires its significance in the context of the archaic operation of mind. Jonathan Lear (1990, pp. 75–76) says that "a wish is a motivating force, but, unlike desire, its products are not actions. Freud implicitly recognizes that a wish differs from a desire. For he characterizes a wish by its role within the archaic functioning of the infantile mind." Similarly, Brakel (2009, p. 139) thinks that "wish" is a term of art for Freud, and wishing, unlike desire, is exclusively satisfied by phantasy. Jim Hopkins, who does not usually put much weight on this distinction (1982, pp. xixff, 1995) did wonder though (1988, pp. 44–45) whether in consequence of the irrationality and detachment from reality of the wishes fulfilled in dreams Freud should not have "introduced a special theoretical term—perhaps something like 'night-time motive derivative'—instead of the common-sense term 'wish'".

The attributions of these categorical distinctions to Freud are mistaken and lead their authors to distorted accounts of wish-fulfilment. Freud does not distinguish between orectic kinds *wish* and *desire*, between pre-propositional wishes (or some hybrid of wish and desire) and propositional desires (Gardner, 1993, pp. 153–156), nor between ordinary and "psychoanalytic wishes". He distinguishes among kinds of wishes in terms of their content and topographical location: whether they are conscious, preconscious, or unconscious (roughly, in the later structural account, whether they are in ego or id). Depending on their location, both wishes and desires can be taken as materials for the primary and secondary processes. That Freud did not entertain a technical notion of "the wish" is easily demonstrable. First, he frequently uses "wish" in an inclusive way to cover for all the conative and orectic states that set our minds turning, as when he writes, Hume-like, that "nothing but a wish can set our mental apparatus working" (Freud, 1900a, p. 567). Second, in relation to the formation of the dream, Freud contends that there has to be at least one wish "dating from earliest childhood" (1900a, p. 269) that is strong enough to instigate the dream (1900a, p. 553); these unconscious wishes, invariably associated with wish-fulfilment, have some of the properties attributed to them by the commentators. But Freud then goes on to explain that in dreams there is a *layering* of wish-fulfilments in which all manner of wishes and quite ordinary desires left over from the "day residues" are also fulfilled—in the peculiar manner of FWT (1900a, pp. 550–572). Third, Freud conceived of daydream, art, religion and other things as fulfilling wishes and desires equally: "Only in art does it still happen that a man who is consumed by desires performs something resembling the accomplishment of those desires and that what he does in play produces emotional effects—thanks to artistic illusion—just as though it were something real" (Freud, 1912–1913, p. 90). What are those desires? Principally, they are commonplace (propositional) "desires to win honour, power, wealth and the love of women" (1916–17, p. 376). Here "wish" could be substituted without loss for "desire", as could the reverse substitution in Freud's characterisation of religious ideas as "illusions, fulfilments of the oldest, strongest and most urgent wishes of mankind" (Freud, 1927c, p. 30).

6. The unconscious wish-fulfilment achieved through art or religious worship may be exceptions to this condition, though even here it seems likely that wish-fulfilment occurs only as a consequence of projective

and introjective engagement with art or religious conception, in which unconscious wishes find or generate representations of their fulfilment and achieve FWT.

7. As I observed in Pataki 1996, Hopkins was wrong in earlier work to impute to Freud (1988, p. 40) the reasoning that: "Since the dream represents the wish as fulfilled, the dream can be regarded as wish-fulfilment"; see also (1982, passim; 1991, p. 97) and Cavell (1993, p. 44). In later papers (1995, 2012, this volume) Hopkins recognises that FWT requires pacification also. Freudian wish-fulfilment is "a form of wishful thinking or imagining, in which a wish or desire causes an imaginative representation of its fulfilment, which is experience—or belief-like" and yields "pacification without satisfaction" (1995, pp. 461, 471). Thus the formula for action in case of thirst:

   A des P [I drink] → P [I drink] → A exps, bels P [I drink] → A des P [I drink] pacified

   I think there are difficulties with this commodious construction of "experience or belief-like representation" (Pataki, 2000, 2014b), and whilst the formula may articulate the causal structure of some symptom formation, such as the Rat Man's obsessive thoughts, it does not serve for complex symptoms, such as the Rat Man's obsessive *actions*, or phenomena like wish-fulfilling religiosity or aesthetic experience.

8. A large body of recent work depicts Freud as one who sold out on science, developing psychoanalysis a priori fashion from philosophical and dated nineteenth century scientific conceptions (Sulloway, 1992; Kitcher, 1992; Smith, 2003; Brook, 2003; Tauber, 2010). This work, diverse in many ways, is remarkable for its indifference to the impact and import of Freud's clinical experience. Kitcher (1992, pp. 102–111), for example, argues that the superego concept was derived essentially from Freud's covert commitments in biology and anthropology; but Freud tried to conceal that, according to Kitcher, and presented the superego concept as a clinical discovery. Yet entirely absent in her book is any clinically informed discussion of guilt, melancholia, negative therapeutic reaction, masochism, or persecutory delusions; that is, all those conditions which would deeply impress a sensitive clinician, and whose manifestations cry out for a conceptualisation of intrapsychic relations of kinds like those of which the superego concept is an instance. Freud certainly knew the biology, neuroscience and anthropology of his day. But it is the most bookish of turns to suppose that the clinical phenomena he confronted daily played no part, or only a

negligible part, in the construction of theories designed to explain such self-reflexive phenomena.

Remarkable also is Tauber (2010), who portrays Freud as an engaged philosopher responding to the doctrines of Brentano, Kant, Schopenhauer, Lange, and others. In Tauber's vision, Freud is concerned explicitly to counter Brentano's denial of unconscious mentation while adopting the philosopher's thesis of Intentionality. Freud's conceptions of reason and freedom are said to be "ideas lifted directly from Kant" (pp. 9, 22, 125), and "the entire psychoanalytic edifice rested upon a version of Kant's philosophy of mind" (p. 123). Freud is also "profoundly indebted" to Schopenhauer and Nietzsche, a claim made by many others who have mined this field. On the biological conception of human nature Freud "closely aligned himself with the Nietzschean-Schopenhaurian line" (p. 19). "The Schopenhaurian Will is the direct precursor of Freud's id" (p. 156) and "Freud would later formulate this drive [Schopenhaurian Will to life] into the various instincts" (p. 159). And so on. These claims are speculations based on superficial thematic affinity, and completely ignore the far-reaching impact of clinical encounter. The more cogent picture is that the philosophical themes detectable in Freud's work were common coin of educated folk in the last quarter of the nineteenth century. Freud was largely indifferent to traditional philosophical problems. Thus, he was committed to strong determinism, though it is possible, as Tauber argues, to extract a view of rational autonomy in his later work when he turned his attention to ego autonomy. Tauber thinks that this view of rational autonomy or free will was adopted from Kant. But rather than demonstrating direct philosophical engagement, as Tauber supposes, Freud's attitude shows the opposite: the striking fact in relation to the incompatibility between psychic determinism and rational autonomy is that Freud made no attempt whatsoever to resolve it. There is little evidence that Freud even felt the philosophical tension. Such insensitivity may be a vice, but it is beside the point to complain, as Tauber does (p. 138), that Freud failed to "explicitly develop psychoanalysis as a moral enterprise." Few things could have been further from his mind.

9. "*[T]he splitting of the content of consciousness is the result of an act of will on the part of the patient.* By this I do not, of course, mean that the patient intends to bring about a splitting of consciousness. His intention is a different one; but, instead of attaining its aim, it produces a splitting of consciousness" (Freud, 1894a, pp. 46–47, italics in original).
10. "The theories of resistance and repression, of the unconscious, of the etiological significance of sexual life and of the importance of infantile

experiences—these form the principal constituents of the theoretical structure of psychoanalysis" (Freud, 1925d, p. 40).

11. The account of motivation based on wish and wish-fulfilment is found principally in Freud's *Project* (1950a [1895]) and *The Interpretation of Dreams* (1900a) but continues alongside the drive account introduced in the "Three Essays on Sexuality" (1905d). The integration of evolutionary theory, neuroscience, attachment theory and psychoanalysis exemplified in the work of Hopkins (2012, this volume), Panksepp (1998), Panksepp and Biven (2012), Schore (1994, 2003), Solms and Turnbull (2002), and others, will refocus attention, as Hopkins (2012) indicates, on Freudian wish-fulfilment. It now seems fairly clear that Freudian drive theory is bound to make way for the type of affective theory of motivation charted by Panksepp, in which primary subcortical emotional command systems—SEEKING, RAGE, CARE, etc.—are the basic motivational forces that stimulate or energise tertiary neocortical systems to produce purposeful action. This rather Humean account of motivation can be seen as having picked up the leads of the older orectic and conative faculties. The neuroscientific theory cannot undermine our ordinary understanding of action using Intentional concepts, however, any more than the atomic theory undermines the existence of furniture.
12. Despite Freud's official view of phantasying as proceeding from play (1908e, p. 144; 1911, p. 222), and so purposive, as play is, there are passages where he recognises unconscious phantasy that obviously antedates play (1908a, p. 161), and others where he is at pains to distinguish "freely wandering fantastic thinking" from intentionally directed reflection (Freud, 1921b; Kris, 1952, p. 311).
13. Gardner recognises that *preconscious* intentional (strategic) activity—that is to say descriptively unconscious mental activity originating with the ego—has a place in psychoanalytic explanation. This concession is fatal, I believe, to his larger project of constructing a metapsychology using largely "pre-propositional" materials. See Pataki (1998, 2000), Petocz (1999, pp. 158ff, 187ff).
14. Rejecting partitive conceptions: Thalberg (1974); De Sousa (1976); Davidson (1982); Moore (1984); Johnston (1988); Gardner (1993); Graham (2010). Davidson, it is true, argued for segregating constellations of propositional attitudes; but he did not hold that these constellations constitute independent centres of agency: "such constellations", as Hopkins (1995, p. 473) says, "do not *have* motives; rather they *are* (groups of) motives" (his italics). To my knowledge, only David Pears (1984), Rorty (1988); Pataki (1996, 2000, 2003, 2014a) and Boag (2005) have, though along different lines, argued for a conception of mind

whose parts satisfy sufficient conditions for independent agency; albeit in Pears' case only a transient independence. Petocz (1999, p. 164) is also receptive to mental plurality. Within psychoanalysis, on the other hand, it is commonplace to hold that the mind is constituted by independent agencies. Freud, Fairbairn, (arguably) M. Klein, Winnicott, Bion, Ogden, Symington and S. Mitchell have explicitly embraced partitive conceptions of mind or self. Of course, a roll call doesn't settle anything about the adequacy of partitive conceptualisation, but it can suggest that the observed clinical phenomena do press strongly in its direction.

For non-intentional readings of FWT (or wishful thinking) within a broadly common-sense psychological framework: Wollheim (1979, 1984, 1991, 1993); Hopkins (1982, 1988, 1991, 1995, 2012); Moore (1984; Eagle 1984, 2011); Johnston (1988); Lear (1998); Gardner (1991, 1993); Cavell (1993, 2006); Marshall (2000). McLaughlin (1988) and Brakel (2009) possibly also belong here. R.K. Shope (1967, 1970) had earlier argued that psychoanalytic explanation was non-intentional. Wollheim's account of the motivational structures found in symptoms and their kin allows for some instances of intentional activity, as in his notion of "displaced action", but he essentially comes down on the side of the sub-intentional and the expressive at the expense of the intentional. See the "Supplementary Preface" to his (1991 [1971]). For some early attempts to explicate enactments (obsessive acts in the main) as intentional see the papers by Alexander and Mischell in Wollheim (Ed.) (1974), and Hopkins (1982, p. xxiff).

15. "All the categories which we employ to describe conscious mental acts, such as ideas, purposes, resolutions, and so on, can be applied to them [unconscious mental acts]. Indeed, we are obliged to say of some of these latent states that the only respect in which they differ from conscious ones is precisely in the absence of consciousness." (Freud, 1915e, p. 168)

There is a long history of scepticism about unconscious mentality so conceived. Vesa Talvitie (this volume) rehearses several objections that he thinks are part of some bad news for psychoanalysis. I don't think we should worry.

Talvitie says that Freud's statements in the quoted passage are like those of an oracle or Zen master, suggestive, presumably, but unpersuasive. The first objection he presents concerns the nature and location of unconscious mental contents: "it is very unclear what a repressed mental content is, and where and how it exists". Another objection concerns the causality of unconscious mental events or states: how can they cause disorders? A third objection is epistemological: "it is very unclear where the non-perceived (and also perceived) mental contents lie, and what sense-organ is used to perceive them; we see with the help of our eyes, hear with ears, but *what is the organ that perceives mental contents*?"

In light of these objections, Talvitie, possibly following John Searle, suggests that if unconscious mentality is anything then it is neurological. On the other hand, conscious mentality is given the palm. A conception of "ordinary mentalism" is a sine qua non of clinical work: "that conception presupposes that mental matters like contents of consciousness, feelings and mental images have causal power over other mental states and behaviour". Now, Talvitie is familiar with some recent philosophy of mind, and he knows that substance dualisms and property dualisms appear to face insuperable obstacles; presumably he would find those positions unacceptable. So what does he think is the ontology of his "ordinary mentalism"? How does ordinary mentalism evade the objections brought against unconscious mentality? How and where do conscious mental states exist? How are *they* causally efficacious? And what organ perceives them? The most cogent solution to the ontological problem seems to be a token identity reductive materialism: every mental event (or at least the core group of items that we describe as mental) is identical with a physical event. Not everyone is convinced, but there does seem to be an "honest difference", as Kim (2005, p. 160) says, between such reduction and eliminativism. Mental causality is preserved, since every mental event is a physical event and the causal closedness of the physical is maintained. The (core) mental events, being neurological, are located in the brain. The problem of inner sense can be sorted out one way or another.

But notice that from an ontological perspective unconscious mentality is exactly on the same level as conscious mentality. Both are neurological. So, on the most plausible account of the mental that we have, Talvitie's strictures against unconscious mentality come to nothing. Of course, there remains an epistemological issue about our unawareness of unconscious states. But Freud's notion of repression being a withdrawal of Pcs. cathexis, about consciousness depending on the vicissitudes of attention surely points in the right direction. If I am not mistaken, Boag's response to Talvitie (this volume) is a cogent elaboration along these lines.

16. More sophisticated models of drives have been developed that may rescue key features of the drive-discharge account. Notable is the model found in the work of Maze, Petocz, Boag, Newberry and others (see papers in Mackay & Petocz (Eds.), 2011; cf. Boag, 2005). On their views, drives incorporate complex cognitive and consummatory machinery. Irrespective of their success within the framework of

psychoanalytic theory, it seems to me that such complexity is foreign to most traditional conceptions of drives, and the models should be seen as an innovation in search of another name.

17. The fact that symptoms appear to be unintended, involuntary and unpleasant is problematic for psychoanalytic explanation, which seeks to preserve wish-fulfilment as a feature of symptoms. Morris Eagle says that "neurotic symptoms are certainly not understood in the ordinary sense as intended acts" (2011, p. 70). But his dilemma is that his own clinical experience gainsays him. He discusses the case of a patient ST who whenever he came close to intimacy and marriage ruminated on his potential homosexuality and dithered until the liaison was broken. And he did this repeatedly. Eagle reaffirms that neurotic symptoms are "experienced as unintended, ego-alien happenings over which one has no control" (2011, p. 70) but is forced to conclude that "the symptom served to protect my patient from the danger that engagement and marriage represented to him … I do not begin to adequately understand the mechanism or process that can generate a symptom that is experienced as unbidden, unintended, and involuntary and yet can be purposive" (2011, p. 71). The considerations in this chapter should begin to indicate how that might happen.

CHAPTER TWO

The significance of consilience: psychoanalysis, attachment, neuroscience, and evolution

Jim Hopkins

From shortly before the start of this century students of the mind began increasingly to relate psychoanalysis to both developmental psychology and neuroscience. A recent example is a neuroimaging study by ten collaborating authors on the effectiveness and mode of action of psychoanalytic therapy in treating depression (Buchheim et al., 2012). This attempts to co-ordinate converging research from a number of fields—including psychoanalytic theory, attachment research, and neuroscience—to relate the way depressed patients have improved during psychoanalytic therapy to hypothesised alterations in their internal models of their emotional bonds with their parents.

Although such convergences have been accumulating over many years, they have as yet been given little attention in overall assessments of psychoanalytic theory, particularly in the philosophy of science. So in what follows I want to consider the consiliences upon which this study draws in more detail, and discuss what they mean for the understanding of psychoanalysis more generally. Research of this kind began in disciplines that were regarded as separate from one another, and is conducted in theoretical vocabularies that—like most human concepts—remain distinct and irreducible. But we are now well aware that radically different concepts or vocabularies can constitute compatible ways of understanding the one world—including our bodies, brains, and the minds these realise—that we describe in terms of them. So let us begin by sketching a framework for thinking about explanation, confirmation and disconfirmation that may facilitate comparisons among irreducibly different theories in different but connected fields.

Causal explanations as working hypotheses tested by data they explain

In these theories—in almost all theories—we can regard ourselves as framing causal explanations by proposing causal hypotheses to explain data we want to explain. Characteristically, we do this because although we accept the data (they are, after all, data), we cannot see, and want to understand, *why the data are as they are*. Our hypotheses explain and unify data by integrating them into larger but hypothetical causal patterns—those produced (caused) by the causal mechanisms or processes that the explanations hypothesise. So, such hypotheses explain why the data are as they are, in the sense that they enable us to see that the data are as we should expect them to be, given the causal mechanisms and processes by which they are explained. And it is because an hypothesis enables us to see the data as expectable in this way that we accept that hypothesis as providing a good explanation of the data with which we are concerned.

Such explanatory hypotheses perforce predict the data they explain. A degree of prediction is inherent in showing that the data are as we should *expect* them to be, given the hypothesis that explains them. For in this, data are represented as *expectable* in a way they were not before we brought the hypothesis to bear on them, and as they would not be, given the negation of the hypothesis. Explanatory hypotheses that are predictive in this minimal sense are therefore liable to confirmation or disconfirmation in the basic sense that we regard the probability of the data given such an hypothesis as greater than the probability of the data given the negation of the hypothesis.

Using "P" for "the probability of" we can write this as P(D given H) > P(D given not-H). Probability is standardly measured by numbers between 0 representing certain falsity and 1 representing certain truth, so that the probability we would assign to the H that a fair coin flipped randomly will land heads would be .5. The probabilities we can assign to H and D can vary in this range. We may regard the probability of what we are taking as data as approaching 1, but when we seek to explain data so as to see why we might expect them to be as they are, we are considering what their probability *would be*, had they been generated in accord with the explanatory hypothesis we are considering. This will differ from hypothesis to hypothesis.

To appreciate this let us simplify some of our intellectual history and imagine ourselves in the position of people who have not yet become clear that the earth moves, and are beginning scientific observation by charting the movements of the clearly visible celestial objects (the stars and planets) in the night sky. Having done this over a long period we are struck by the regularities in the data we have accumulated; for example, by the nightly movements of the constellations around the North Star, which seems nearly immobile in relation to them. Taking these naked-eye observations as our data, we want to know why they are as they are. Since we have made them by fallible eyesight, and using records from observers that may not perfectly agree, etc., we cannot take all our data as certain. Still we can be clear that, overall, the data accord with generalisations such as that above.

We can also imagine that we have framed one of the first great explanatory hypotheses, namely that the celestial objects are on a sphere that moves around the earth, as described in Kuhn (1957). We could test this by building small models of the earth as surrounded by such a sphere, or a map of the sky as it would appear in looking up at such a sphere, or even better by constructing a sphere—a partial model of the universe as we are conceiving it—to which we can attach lights representing the celestial objects in their relative positions in the sky. In this case we can imagine that an observer can sit inside the sphere (as in a planetarium) to see how well rotating it generates hypothetical data—appearances to the observer inside the sphere—that match those we record for the celestial objects themselves.

This would be a way of estimating the P(D given H) for the H we have framed, via a model of the generation of the data that we could use to reproduce them. Probably we would find that between the difficulties in observing and recording the data and those of building a sphere to try to reproduce the data everything would be more or less approximate. Still even in these circumstances we might find that the movements of the main constellations were modelled fairly well by their representations on our sphere, so that P(D given H) would seem high for them. For others, such as the morning star and the evening star, we would find that their movements were not well modelled in this way, so that P(D given H) apparently went towards nil.

In light of this we might tentatively accept our hypothesis and model as a good explanation and the best we can frame for the movements of the "fixed stars", but as not yet providing a satisfactory account of the "wanderers" or planets. Focusing on them, we might attempt to explain their motion, say, by modelling their movement with wheels attached to the sphere, which are then free to move in further ways that we could attempt to specify.

As this illustrates, when we explain data by hypotheses, those data become evidence by which the hypothesis can be tested. For by Bayes' theorem (see Hawthorne, 2012; Joyce, 2008; Talbot, 2011) the credibility (probability) we assign to an hypothesis given data it succeeds in predicting [P(H given D)] should be greater than the credibility or probability [P(H)] we assign to the hypothesis prior to the prediction. But for data to increase the credibility (probability) of an hypothesis that predicts them is for those data to confirm that hypothesis; and likewise for decrease in probability and disconfirmation; and this will be so just if P(D given H) > P(D given not-H), as above.[1] So inference to the best explanation, taken as a form of Bayesian abduction (Douven, 2011), naturally renders causal hypotheses that explain data testable by reference to them. In such an account, which I have briefly applied to clinical psychoanalysis elsewhere (Hopkins, 2013b; see also the recent discussions in Lacewing, 2012, 2013), causal explanation and unification go hand in hand with testability, and in whatever domain they are found.

Causal explanation in Darwin

To understand the role of these concepts in psychoanalysis it may be useful to compare their role in Darwin's account of natural selection. Few would deny that Darwin's hypotheses have been highly confirmed. But they also have striking methodological similarities to those of Freud—similarities, for example, that led the celebrated philosopher of science Sir Karl Popper to declare both theories unscientific, and on nearly identical grounds.

Popper's claim that Freud's theories are not scientific but "metaphysical", because they are not (what Popper called) *falsifiable*, is well known. In calling a theory falsifiable Popper meant that it was comparable to a generalisation like "all swans are white", which could be falsified by a single instance or datum (a single black swan). This is evidently a great simplification, since observing white swans and hypothesising that all swans are white seems a much simpler thing than trying to get to grips with the kind of observational data considered in our already simplified scientific example above. Still, we can say that Popper was taking an hypothesis as falsifiable, and so scientific, just if it predicted the data D that it was meant to explain with near certainty, so the P(D given H) approached 1. (Given that all swans are white, the probability that any swan observed will be white is 1.) In this case P(not-H given not-D) would also approach 1, so H would be refuted. This simple and straightforward account won many converts, although it (apparently arbitrarily) restricted the probabilities that could be considered in thinking about confirmation and disconfirmation to those approaching 1 or 0, and so left most actual scientific data out of account.

Popper seems to have applied such an account in assessing Darwin and Freud, and since their hypotheses rarely predicted the data they explained with a probability approaching 1 he found them wanting. In the case of Darwin, acknowledged by almost everyone as among the greatest of scientists, Popper (1978) argued that it was "important to show that Darwinism [by which he meant the more recent versions of Darwin's theory held by evolutionary biologists] is not scientific but metaphysical." So he argued, using "testable" as if it meant "strictly falsifiable":

> Darwinism ... is metaphysical because it is not testable ... Darwinism does not really *predict* the evolution of variety. It therefore cannot really *explain* it ... there is hardly any possibility of testing a theory as feeble as this. (Popper, 1978, p. 136)

Here the feebleness that Popper ascribes to Darwin's theory is apparently the inability to "really *predict*" that data it covers—that is, to predict it with a sufficiently high probability. This he apparently took to show that the theory also cannot "really *explain*"—as if we could not really determine why something had happened unless we could have predicted it.

But while dismissing Darwin's theory in this way, Popper, who rightly admired Darwin, also tried to do justice to it. So he stressed that the theory had been "invaluable" in adding to the growth of knowledge.

He illustrated this by saying "it is clear that we are helped by the theory of natural selection" in "trying to explain experiments in which bacteria become adapted to, say, penicillin". This was because the theory "suggests the existence of a mechanism of adaptation, and it even allows us to study in detail the mechanism at work. And it is the only theory at all which does all that" (Popper, 1978, pp. 136–137).

It has now been widely recognised that Popper's description of Darwin's theory as non-scientific, non-explanatory and "feeble" is incoherent, given his acknowledgement of the unique role of the theory in guiding biological research and experiment. This is clear in the very terms of his account. To say that in experiments certain bacteria have "become adapted to penicillin" is not just to "suggest the existence of a mechanism of adaptation". Rather it is to assert that there is a particular kind of mechanism in particular organisms, and that this mechanism has operated in a specific and predicted way in experimental conditions. The claim, roughly, is that the bacteria in question: (i) have particular mechanisms of reproduction; (ii) that these enable them to reproduce themselves with heritable variation, including variants that can survive in various concentrations of penicillin (as determined by experiment), and; (iii) that, as predicted by Darwin's theory, the superior reproductive success of these variants in these circumstances produces populations that are penicillin-resistant.

This is clearly a scientific hypothesis predicting experimental results that accord with Darwin's theory. Popper could say that it did not *really* predict only if by "*really* predict" he meant "predict with near certainty", which, as noted above, would be arbitrarily to restrict the probabilities that might be considered in assessing prediction and confirmation or disconfirmation. Moreover, since Popper was reporting on experiments that had already been done, this was a scientific hypothesis that had already been confirmed by experiment, and one whose confirmation was already taken to support Darwin, although not in the way Popper required.

The kinds of experiments Popper was describing, moreover, were direct applications of Darwin's original hypotheses. Darwin had begun his account by describing the long-standing agricultural practice of selective breeding, and these were experiments in the selective breeding of bacteria. So here the science was an extension of common knowledge as well. In particular, people had known for centuries that:

i. Living things have physical mechanisms of reproduction (differentiating male from female organisms, for example), whose working
ii. yields the kinds of similarities between parents and offspring that impel us to regard them as members of the same species, and also
iii. yields differences between parents and offspring—variations that can be bred from, and so are heritable, as can be readily observed in families, fields, and farms.

Such general but common-sense understanding of heritable variation and selective breeding lay behind the selective breeding of bacilli in controlled experimental conditions by which, as Popper records, the common-sense generalisations have been extended and refined and the mechanisms underlying them specified. Such extension of common-sense causal understanding is an important part of both causal explanation and scientific progress.

Causal explanation and scientific progress

In causal explanation, as said above, we hypothesise causal mechanisms in order to explain particular data as effects of these mechanisms. This means that we almost inevitably start with hypotheses that explain many fewer data, and much less rigorously, than we will do as explanation progresses. The path to the precise and all-encompassing theories of Newton and Einstein started with hypothesis about the movements of the visible celestial objects like those discussed above: that these objects moved as they did because they were (in some way) attached to (some kind of) spheres that (for some reason) circled the earth.

The vagueness of this initial form of hypothesis did not deprive it of explanatory power and practical utility, and the progress that began with it constitutes an important part of the history of science. So let us note, first, that in such progress we characteristically start with hypotheses that initially improve our ability to unify the data more than our ability to predict them. This is because the data have already attracted our attention as having common features that we feel cannot have arisen by mere chance, and so already seem to require unification as effects of a causal mechanism. The regularities in the way celestial objects moved, such as the predictable progress of the constellations in the night sky, had been noted from before historical record.

In such a situation the framing of a particular hypothesis—even a relatively vague one—about how the data are generated is an important step forward. Even if the hypothesis does not enable us to predict the data that have drawn our attention better than before, it will enable us to draw further conclusions about them (e.g., if they are on a sphere they should move in a uniform way). This will enable us to gather further data with an eye to confirmation or disconfirmation (do they actually move in a uniform way?) and so to focus on data that require further explanation (the planets move differently from the fixed stars). The hypotheses we frame to explain these data may elaborate the initial one, and so remain as consistent as the original with common sense (there are mechanisms on the sphere that produce the planetary movements). But also they may differ from the original one, and from common sense, in deep ways (the earth itself is a planet and a satellite of the sun).

If these more radical hypotheses prove better (no epicycles, a single form for all motions, consistent with data from telescopes, etc.) we can adopt them as our main working hypotheses, despite their departure from common sense (the earth moves, we are not at the centre of the universe, etc.). Then the process or refinement and replacement of hypotheses starts again (Kepler, Newton, Einstein ...). But this also means that the most important scientific hypotheses are liable to take us further and further from common-sense ideas that are also important in our lives. So, inevitably, those less concerned with understanding the data will have greater reason to reject the hypotheses as destructive of the common views they cherish, and to resent those who have encouraged this destruction by framing them (Copernicus, Darwin, Freud). This too is a characteristic part of progress in causal explanation.

Common sense and causal explanation in Darwin

We can see this a bit more clearly by considering a diagram from *L'Histoire de la Nature des Oyseaux*, published in 1555 by the French naturalist and diplomat Pierre Belon.[2]

Here Belon charts a sample of the kinds of data about plants and animals that, in his view (as that of very many others prior to Darwin), required to be explained. Although such similarities and differences had been observed many times, no one had been able to understand why they were as they were—why they should be *expected to be* as they had

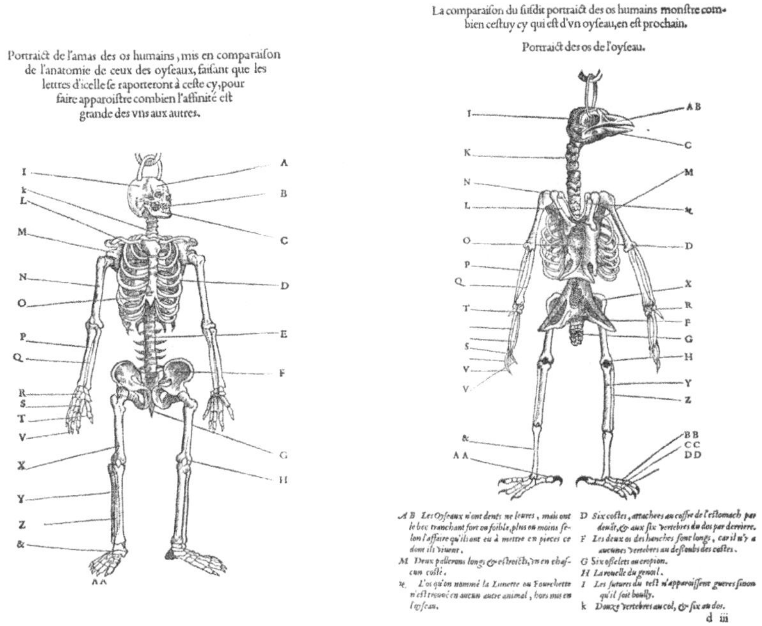

Figure 1. From *L'Histoire de la Nature des Oyseaux.*

been observed to be. The similarities in these skeletons are particularly puzzling because they appear at the joints and bones of nature itself. We know that similarities and differences like these would be replicated in skeletons and structures of countless living things. So they indicate many natural kinds of similarities among living things that seemingly could not arise by chance.

As in the case of the movements of celestial objects, such similarities require explanation as effects of a causal mechanism; but it is not easy to see what sort of mechanism this could be. Even if we were to take them as fashioned by a Creator, why should He or She make humans to be so much like chickens? (or again, as Darwin remarked, the creator would seem to have been inordinately fond of beetles …). And if humans are so like chickens, why are they also so different? This too points to a vast range of things that could not be a matter of chance, and hence require a causal mechanism to explain them.

Darwin explained such data about similarity and difference by *extending* the long-familiar common-sense ideas about living things that we set out just above. These were: (i) that they reproduced or replicated themselves via physical mechanisms of inheritance that yield the kind of similarities in virtue of which we regard them as members of a single species, and; (ii) that these mechanisms also yielded the breedable (heritable) differences among plant and animal parents and offspring that were familiar to all who took the trouble to observe them.

Darwin's extension of common sense

Darwin's extension of these similarity- and difference-producing roles yielded his account of evolution as proceeding by a process of *descent* (producing similarity) with *modification* (producing difference). Roughly:

i. Darwin extended the role of the mechanisms in producing inherited similarities, so as to explain data consisting in similarities between organisms that were members of distinct species. These could readily be observed, both superficially (in examples such as lions and leopards, horses and zebras, apes and humans) and also (as naturalists like Belon had noted) between species otherwise as different as humans and chickens. (And likewise for the fossil remains of past species.) Such similarities, Darwin held, were as might be expected—such as might be thought probable—given his hypothesis that the organisms in question shared common and perhaps simpler ancestors, from a time in the long history of life on earth before their species had become differentiated.
ii. Darwin likewise extended the role of the mechanisms as producing heritable differences (variations), so as to explain data consisting in differences between varieties within species, and again differences between members of different species. Again these included the small but crucial differences that prevented members of very similar species from breeding with one another to produce fertile offspring, as well as the larger differences between species like Belon's human and chicken (and likewise for fossil species). These differences, Darwin held, were such as might be expected, given his hypothesis that living organisms were continually modified over repeated generations. This, as he explained, occurred via their participation in an inescapable reproductive competition that preserved, and so accumulated, heritable differences that

> augmented reproductive success. Indeed, such modifying accumulation, operating on a single original kind of reproducing organism, might be expected—over the countless generations and situations of the very long history of life on earth—to produce "from so simple a beginning" the "endless forms most beautiful and most wonderful" that "have been, and are being, evolved" (Darwin, 1859, p. 490).

This again illustrates how scientific hypotheses can be developed by extending ideas that are already accepted as matters of common sense and common observation, as well as how upsetting such hypotheses can be as they progress further and further from common sense. (We are descended from apes, and worse, from forms like amoebas and bacilli, and like them we are adaptations that facilitate the replication of genes.)

They also illustrate the particular point that such hypotheses can combine great explanatory scope with relatively weak prediction, by enabling us to see how a large range of data are as we should expect them to be, given the causes hypothesised to explain them; and how such hypotheses can be confirmed by the breadth of their explanatory role. On this point Darwin gave a far better account than Popper as to why his hypotheses should be accepted. He urged that we should credit them because they explained a great range of phenomena that no others did, and also because these explanations were predictive in the weak but essential sense we set out at the beginning.[3]

This seems right, although the probabilities involved are intuitive, unquantifiable, and (as Darwin himself stressed) insufficient to support precise predictions. It seems also to be why, although arousing vehement opposition, Darwin's theories were from the outset recognised *by those who studied them together with the data* (although not, of course, by many others) as confirmed by their explanatory role.

From weak but broad prediction to strongly confirmed science

Taking the history of science subsequent to Darwin into account, we can also see that his hypotheses illustrate an important scientific possibility, and one that may also be realised by Freud's. This is that causal hypotheses that predict only weakly but explain very broadly (as do both Darwin's and Freud's) *may have these features because they strike deeply into the nature of things*. They do this by recruiting causal mechanisms that operate over the broad range of phenomena that they serve to unify, and so are common to many things and processes. Given that this is so, these mechanisms—however vaguely they are initially specified—may prove important for understanding in many fields.

In this, however, their role can be fully appreciated only *after* the mechanisms have been understood more deeply, and in the fields that specify their working more precisely. This will be especially so if, as in both Darwin and Freud, the initial hypotheses are cast in a vocabulary that differs from those of the scientific disciplines that are destined to draw out their consequences. In this case the deeper understanding of the mechanisms that these disciplines permit will be framed in concepts, or modes of explanation, that differ, perhaps radically, from those of the original hypotheses—as Freud's original psychological hypotheses cast in terms of memory, emotion, desire and belief differ from those of the explanatory vocabularies (including, in Freud's case, the vocabulary of neuroscience) in which the causal mechanisms recruited in these hypotheses require to be elaborated.

In such a case the deeper understanding of the mechanisms may yield better predictions, but these will be evident mainly in the conceptually disparate disciplines in which their working is specified. If we describe the mechanisms generally but vaguely, as in the initial hypotheses that specify them, then we can use them to predict only weakly. But when we describe them in more detail in other disciplines, although this generates better predictions, it does so only in terms articulated within these disciplines, and in the range of cases then under investigation. So we may gain a better understanding of the mechanisms, and a deeper sense of the explanatory power of the original hypotheses, while leaving the predictive weaknesses of the hypotheses that indicate the full scope of the mechanisms intact.

This is arguably what we find in the unification of Darwinian natural selection and the molecular biology of reproduction. Our increasing knowledge of the mechanisms of heredity has gone with attaining many stronger generalisations down to sub-cellular and molecular levels. These, however, still do not enable us to predict how even single-celled organisms like bacilli will evolve outside controlled conditions. At the same time, and despite this continuing predictive weakness, the generality of Darwin's hypotheses has entailed that this deeper understanding has brought far stronger confirmation of those hypotheses than anyone might originally have thought possible.

Darwin's original hypotheses entailed that "the endless forms" would bear similarities inherited by descent from their "simple beginnings". In learning about the mechanisms of reproductive inheritance we have learned that all living things reproduce themselves via a relatively small family of molecules and processes (DNA, RNA, the production of peptides, and so forth). On the account we have given, the fact that these same molecules play a central role in producing the "endless forms" of all living things strongly supports Darwin's claims as to how these forms "have been, and are being, evolved". For such a vast similarity, holding down to every cell of every living thing, would be expected given Darwin's hypothesis that all these forms are descended from the same "simple beginnings"; but it would seem to have a probability approaching 0—a universal sheer coincidence, with trillions upon growing trillions of instances—on the negation of that hypothesis. So although we remain unable, say, to be clear as to how much of evolution is due to natural selection as opposed to the underlying dispositions of the materials on which selection works, we have evidently put some of Darwin's "simple beginnings" beyond reasonable doubt.

Taking Freud in these terms

We will start to consider Freud by comparing him with Darwin. Whereas Darwin's discoveries relate to almost all features of living things, Freud's are restricted to the thoughts and feelings of human beings, and the motives upon which we act. Still, our own thoughts, feelings, and motives, and those of others, are of central importance in our lives, so that Freud's discoveries also have great potential significance.

Disciplinary consequences of broad but weak prediction

As an initial point it is worth noting that we can better understand the disagreements and differences in formulation that we find in Freudian and post-Freudian depth psychology by considering Darwin and the predictive weakness of his theory. It is relatively easy to frame hypotheses in both Darwinian biology and post-Freudian psychology, and the explanatory predictions these hypotheses generate are often, as Popper complained, too weak to provide clear grounds for choice between competitors. Despite the clearly scientific nature of evolutionary biology, this has the consequence that adherents of different hypotheses often engage in seemingly irresoluable disputes—about whether particular features of living things are to be understood as adaptations or "spandrels"; about lumping organisms together in the same species or splitting them into different species; about whether evolution is rapid, gradual, or sometimes one, sometimes the other; about whether genes should be described as "selfish" and what this might mean; about the role of groups in natural selection; and so on and so on. Hence the field has seemed constantly liable to fragment into opposing groups generated by such disputes, and one can find different competing groups of theorists, like varieties of the same species of bird, on almost every branch of the tree of life (see http://tolweb.org/tree/).[4]

Post-Freudian depth psychology is, explicably, similar—but worse. The reason is the same in both cases. Extant forms of explanation are too predictively weak to compel decision between competing hypotheses. Still, this is plainly consistent with describing the hypotheses of schools of depth psychology, like those of post-Darwinian evolutionary biology, as issuing from competing varieties of a single viable and vigorous species of explanation, generated by the work of the founder in question. Darwin's successors show how even in biological science weakness in prediction can foster explanatory competition that obscures underlying theoretical similarity (Freud's (1930a) "narcissism of small differences"—p. 305). In psychoanalysis this is amplified by insurmountable difficulties in communicating clinical data among investigators and groups.

The clinical data of depth psychology, like human thought and feeling generally, vary unpredictably from individual to individual, moment to moment, context to context, and therapy to therapy. This are no skeletons, fossils, or colour-coded representation of gene expression for everyone to examine publicly and come to agree about; videos and physiological monitoring catch only a fraction of what participants actually think and feel; and even for a single dream, as Freud's writings illustrate, the associations and hypotheses required to understand the motives expressed in it are so lengthy, disconnected and hard to scan that they can only rarely serve as instruments of communication.

As a result, psychoanalytic clinical data—even those that are well understood—remain impossible to compress or survey. Discussion often centres on clinical vignettes, which inevitably display only a minute fraction of the data on which the hypotheses they illustrate are actually based, and are naturally cast in the theoretical vocabularies that serve as marks of distinction for differing schools. In these circumstances cross-school discussion requires both translation of vocabulary and suspension of group loyalty—difficult matters even in more favourable evidential circumstances, as disputes among Darwinians indicate. In both cases deeper inspection makes clear that similarities in empirical content outweigh the differences that demarcate competing schools; but disputation remains liable to obscure theoretical claims tacitly shared by all.[5]

The ease and rapidity with which different investigators can share data is an important factor in the collaboration and progress characteristic of science (see Hopkins, 1992, for further discussion). In light of this we should not be surprised that Freud's successors are less able to secure agreement among one another, and are slower to do so, than Darwin's. This is just what we should expect, given the nature of the data; and it would be expected even if, as I think, hypotheses cast in psychoanalytic terms are very often good explanations, as well as the best we have, of the vast range of data they cover.

The case is similar for the hostility and scepticism that psychoanalysis arouses. These are clearly comparable to now familiar forms of outrage at Darwinian claims that violate what was once regarded as common sense. Darwinian scientists, together with allied disciplines and scientific institutions generally, work continually to mitigate these reactions. They provide public rehearsals of data and explanation, such as we see in schools and museums, on websites like *The Tree of Life* mentioned above, and in many other places; and they combine these with prestige- and solidarity-building group celebrations like *Darwin 200*. In the case of Freud's hypotheses, and despite their widespread diffusion, the relative incommunicability of data—even for hypotheses of great explanatory scope—undermines such attempts at education and mitigation of outrage.

Progress in Darwin and Freud

We saw in Darwin how a theory that predicted weakly but very broadly could engender scientific progress, and in the process come to enjoy stronger confirmation than seemed possible at the outset. We find an analogous combination of weak but broad prediction in Freud. Even allowing for differences that have grown up among his successors, the mechanisms hypothesised by Freud have a strong overall claim, supported by very many instances of good explanation, to play a significant role in the understanding of the working of motive in individual psychology, dreaming, and mental disorder; and also in group psychology, and particularly in understanding the dispositions to group-on-group conflict that have punctuated our history, and now may put a stop to it. So if there is a Freudian analogue to the kind of progress that resulted from the work of Darwin, we should surely seek to understand and explore it.

This kind of progress requires that the broad, weak predictions of the initial basic hypotheses be borne out later, but in further and perhaps very distinct disciplines that investigate the working of the causal mechanisms originally hypothesised. As the scanning experiment with which we began illustrates, such investigation is now under way for the neural mechanisms of human motivation. Many findings seem to be such as we might expect, given that the mechanisms operate in ways previously indicated by Freud and his successors.

Common sense and causal explanation in Freud

In the work of Freud, like that of Darwin, we find both beginnings in common sense and a kind of progress that rapidly comes to contradict common-sense ideas. We can trace Freud's step-by-step progress from common sense to radically different conclusions in works such as *The Interpretation of Dreams* (Freud, 1900a), and indeed even in the single specimen dream—the dream of Irma's injection—with which he begins that book. Even Popper, when he finally studied Freud's explanations there closely, wrote that:

> [Freud's theory of dreams] contains, beyond any reasonable doubt, a great discovery. I at least feel convinced that there is a world of the unconscious, and that Freud's account of dreams given in his book are fundamentally correct, though no doubt incomplete. (Popper, 1983, p. 164; cf. Grünbaum, 1989)[6]

We saw above that Popper's methodology does not readily explain his favourable judgement on Darwin, and the same, as Grünbaum has stressed, applies to this judgement on Freud's account of dreams. So it may be worth applying the sketch with which we began, as this relates to accounts of Freud on dreams that have been given elsewhere.[7]

Desire, belief, and intentional action

The common-sense concepts that Freud extends are the basic ones of desire and belief. These are related by one of the deepest generalisations of common-sense psychology, that which concerns the relation of desire and belief in successful intentional action. An example of such an action would be one in which a person desires to drink from a glass in front of her, and does so. For purposes of generalisation we can represent this as:

A (the agent) desires that A drinks → A drinks

The arrow represents the causal working of the agent's desire to drink in governing the motor activations via which she drinks, and thereby succeeds in satisfying her desire. This illustrates the way we describe desires to perform actions of particular kinds in terms of the kinds of actions that would satisfy those desires, and hence in terms of effects those desires would have if acted on.

This evolved conceptual and linguistic practice[8] enables us to understand the causal working of desires, beliefs and other states of mind without explicit use of the concept of causality, and via our understanding of the sentences we use to describe them. So our practice yields a general causal and linguistic pattern that holds in all cases of successful intentional action, which, keeping our original in brackets, we can abbreviate using the schematic letter "P".

A des P [e.g., I drink] → P [I drink]

In the example, drinking the agent's desire would have operated via her belief that if she moved in certain ways she would drink, and this would have combined with her desire that she drink to produce a desire to move in the way she did to do so. Let us describe A's belief as the belief that if she moves in the D ways she will drink, and abbreviate the sentence describing the belief by "Q". Then we can represent the causal combining of her desire and belief by the so-called "practical syllogism":

A des P and A bel if Q then P → A des Q

If we write this in another way we can see why people have spoken of a syllogism in this kind of case:

A des P
A bel if Q then P
A des Q

When an agent forms a means-end desire in this way, the linguistic form of the sentences in terms of which we describe the process (taken from the bottom up) is that of modus ponens. This indicates the rationality of this kind of alteration of desire in light of belief. It shows that if we satisfy the desire for the means (des Q) and if our belief about the means-end connection (if Q then P) is true, then the satisfaction of the desire that is our end (des P) is logically guaranteed.

This action-guiding role of belief in the satisfaction of desire is familiar. Equally important, however, is another role, which we encounter when we consider what happens after an agent has acted to satisfy a desire. In this case the agent receives perceptual feedback from her own action, so that she has what Freud called "the experience of satisfaction". This perceptual experience pacifies the desire—inhibits it, or causes it to cease to operate. So the overall pattern, including in brackets the particular desire—action—perception- and belief-describing sentence with which we are concerned, is:

A des P [I drink] → P [I drink] → A exps, bels P [I drink] → A des P [I drink] pacified

This is one of the most basic patterns of common-sense psychological understanding. It registers the fact that experience and belief not only guide desire but also cause it to cease to operate. This is particularly important for understanding Freud.

Wish-fulfilment, projection, and simple dreams from sensory impingement

This emerges if we consider simple dreams. An example would be the dream of *drinking delicious cool water* that Freud often had after eating salty foods (Freud, 1900a). He would have this dream several times, before waking up thirsty and getting a drink. Many people have had such a dream: and even more, probably, its counterpart of dreaming the experience of a satisfying micturition, after repetitions of which one wakes with a full bladder.

Someone who has a dream of this kind characteristically understands it in terms of a causal pattern like that above. Thus someone who wakes up thirsty after a dream of drinking takes it that the thirst caused the dream, as someone who wakes up after a dream—or series of dreams—of micturition takes it that the cause of these dreams is the full bladder that they go on to relieve in reality. Such dreams seem clear examples of the causal pattern of Freudian wish-fulfilment—that is, of an *imaginary* experience of satisfaction of some desire or wish, but *in the absence of real satisfaction*, and caused by the desire or wish itself.

This pattern is very similar to that of the working of desire in intentional action above, except that the causal role of the real satisfaction of the desire—as abbreviated by "→ P [I drink] →"—is left out. So we have:

> A des P [I drink] → A dream exps, bels P [I drink] → A des P [I drink] pacified
>
> or again:
>
> A des P [I micturate] → A dream exps, bels P [I micturate] → A des P [I micturate] pacified

These dreams thus consist in imaginary experiences of satisfaction. The imaginary experiences, in turn, seem to have two connected causal roles:

i. They (temporarily) pacify the nascent desires to drink or micturate that the dreamers experience and act on when they finally wake up; and at the same time
ii. they mask (inhibit, suppress, repress) both the desire and the *veridical* internally caused sensory experience (of thirst or a full bladder) that causes the desires in question.

In this they apparently exemplify Freud's (1900a) conception of dreams as "guardians of sleep", and also, as Freud held, to serve in managing conflict among sources of motivation.

As accords with these general ideas we now have a range of connected grounds for holding that sleep and dreaming are important physiological and psychological processes, and such as would naturally be protected from interruption. Long-term sleep deprivation causes laboratory rats to become extremely aggressive and finally kills them (Cartwright 2010; Rechtschaffen & Bergmann, 1995) and is liable to cause paranoid hallucinations and delusions in human beings (Coren, 1998);[9] and even mild short-term deprivation renders individuals more liable to false memory (Diekelmann, Landolt, Born, & Wagner, 2008). Conversely, sleep and dreaming apparently serve in the processing of both memory and emotion, consolidating new memories and reactivating and reconsolidating old ones at the same time as they "knit up the raveled sleeve of care" to mitigate the role of adverse emotions in the mind as a whole (Cartwright, 2010; Rasch & Born, 2013: "The Active Systems Consolidation Hypothesis"). In this, slow wave sleep (SWS) and rapid eye movement (REM) sleep appear to play complementary roles (Cairney et al., 2014; Cartwright 2010; Rasch & Born, 2013).[10] Concurrently, turning to the physiological level of description, they are hypothesised to reduce the metabolic load on the synapses that connect neural cells, thereby effecting synaptic homeostasis (Tononi & Cirelli, 2014), and to cleanse the brain of metabolic waste (Xie et al., 2013).

These processes, moreover, seem to be systematically related. Hobson and Friston (2012) and Hobson, Hong and Friston (2014) have recently hypothesised that REM dreams, and vivid hallucinatory conscious experiences and the powerful activations of emotion that they involve, have the particular function of optimising the models of the world via which the brains of dreaming creatures effect waking perception and action. This process of optimisation reduces the *complexity* of the neural models, rendering them simpler and better in their functions of representing sensory input as conscious experience of its causes. Since the brain's models function like hypotheses that predict future experience, this process is comparable to that by which scientists revise theories to make them simpler and better at predicting the data they explain (see Sober & Forster, 1997, for a related notion of simplicity). We should expect the nocturnal consolidation of memory and recalibration of emotion to be part of such an optimising process, and argue that the reduction of complexity in the model involves the reduction of synapses required for synaptic homeostasis (Hobson & Friston, 2012; Hobson Hong & Friston, 2014). So the hypothesised processes of consolidation and optimisation might themselves yield metabolic waste that sleep eliminates.

These hypotheses, and particularly those concerning the REM processing of emotionally aversive memories (Cartwright, 2010; Cairney et al., 2014; Rasch & Born, 2013), cohere with psychoanalytic accounts of the role of dreaming. In explaining the role of conflict in dreams, Freud sometimes hypothesised that dreaming was prompted by a wish to sleep, which conflicted, say, with the wish to drink or to micturate. In light of the importance of sleep and dreaming, however, it seems unnecessary to assimilate sleep to intentional action in this way. The conflict may be between the nascent desires to act and physiological mechanisms that operate to preserve sleep and dreaming without the intervention of desire, as with the mechanisms that maintain breathing. In either case we can assume that such simple wish-fulfilling dreams work, as they seem to do, by masking sensory input and pacifying desires that might interrupt these vital processes.

A similar sleep- and dream-preserving function can also be seen in dreams caused by ongoing pain, such as the projective dream reported by the neuroscience blogger Neurocritic in discussing this topic:

> Yesterday morning, I had a terrible nightmare in which my real life leg pain was projected onto someone else in an exceptionally gruesome way. I was driving along an unknown neighborhood street when suddenly a man … had fallen under my car and had both his legs amputated from being run over … The gravely injured man was still alive … I was absolutely horrified. All I could do is say "oh my god oh my god oh my god" over and over … It was an awful nightmare, and in the dream I was quite traumatized by the entire experience.

As Neurocritic observes, neuroscientists investigating the mechanisms by which the pain-sensing systems are altered in REM sleep take them to explain "why nociceptive stimuli can be either neglected or incorporated into dreams without awakening the subject." This again would accord with the Freudian sleep- and dream-guarding function, as well as the emotional processing, memory consolidation and model optimisation mentioned above.[11] His own dream, however, illustrates the capacity of projection to cause nightmares that may interrupt these functions, as do the apparently unassimilable and consolidation-resistant memories of those who suffer from post-traumatic stress disorder (PTSD). The Freudian notion of projection he uses in describing this dream is also a way of managing motivational conflict, and can be understood by contrast with the more familiar notion of identification.

Freud understood identification as "the assimilation of one ego to another" (Freud, 1933a, p. 63), and took this as an important mechanism of learning and development. Projection, by contrast, effects the *differentiation* of one ego from another, and Freud conceived it as involving the imaginary relocation of some (often unwanted or self-condemned) aspect of the self as in the other, thereby creating an image of the self as lacking, and the other as having, whatever was projected. We see this very clearly in the dream above, in which pain of the kind the dreamer perceives in himself is represented as in another person. Such nightmare-like hallucinations are also seen in sleep-deprived individuals, and again in paranoid schizophrenia, suggesting that they have a common underlying physiological basis, and one related to the kind of conflict that projection works to mitigate.

The virtual reality that projection creates for a dreamer seems very far from wished-for, although it is certainly created by their own motivational systems and from within their own brains. Hence in post-Freudian psychoanalysis it is commonly described in terms of the notion of *phantasy*—a more general form of experience- or belief-like mental activity that encompasses daydream and other forms of make-believe or fictitious experience as well as wish-fulfilment. (Moreover, since the dreamer is so deeply identified with the person into whom his pain has been projected, the phantasy would be one of *projective identification*, as described by Melanie Klein (1946). This illustrates how later psychoanalytic concepts have grown out of Freud's early notion of wish-fulfilment, while retaining parts of the same basic logical and causal structure.

To see the working of Freudian and post-Freudian hypotheses in these instances it may help to represent things visually. So let us set out data and hypotheses in the simple format below. The data with which we are concerned come, on the one hand, from the dreamer's free associations, and on the other from the manifest content of the dream. So we can tabulate them as follows:

Data from associations	Data from dream

Then we can put in the hypotheses that we take to explain, unify and (weakly) predict the data between the columns in which the data are specified, to make clearer how the hypotheses relate to them. This will give:

Data from associations	Hypothesis that explains, unifies and predicts data	Data from dream

Taking the simple examples so far, we have:

Data from associations	*Data from dream*
Freud has eaten salty food, wakes up thirsty and with a desire to drink	Freud dreams he is drinking, quenching his thirst, satisfying his desire to drink
Agent has full bladder, wakes up desiring to micturate	Agent dreams he is micturating, emptying his bladder, and satisfying his desire to micturate
Neurocritic has pain in his leg	Neurocritic has nightmare about pain in another man's legs

As this makes clear, the data have the kind of common-sense causal pattern we saw above (they are correlated in content as **P** to **P**, and also as desire to experience of satisfaction, or again as beginning to end of a process of projection, as illustrated below). These patterns in content seem inexplicable by mere chance. So as accords with Bayesian methodology,[12] the correlation seems to require a causal explanation:

Data from associations	*Data from dream*
Agent desires that **P** [I drink]	Agent experiences satisfaction of desire that **P** [I drink]
Agent desires that **P** [I micturate]	Agent experiences satisfaction of desire that **P** [I micturate]
Agent suffers **P** [I have pain in my leg]	Agent experiences another suffering **P** [Another has pain in his legs]

Using the notions of wish-fulfilment and projection, we can explain these data as follows:

Data from associations	*Hypothesis that explains, unifies and predicts data*	*Data from dream*
Agent desires that **P** [I drink]	Agent's mind/brain manages conflict between nocturnal arousal of motive and continuing sleeping and dreaming by dreamt wish-fulfilling representation of satisfaction that pacifies (inhibits) activation of motives that might interrupt sleep and dreaming	Agent experiences satisfaction of desire that **P** [I drink]
Agent desires that **P** [I micturate]	As above	Agent experiences satisfaction of desire that **P** [I micturate]
Agent suffers **P** [I have pain in my leg]	Agent's mind/brain manages conflict between nascent perception of pain and continuing sleeping/dreaming by dreamt projection of pain into another	Agent experiences projection of **P** into another [Agent causes another to have pain in his legs]

Here the explanations unify the data by representing them as the result of the management of nocturnal motivational conflict, and in a way that is clearly also predictive. For given the hypothesis that wish-fulfilment and projection in dreams are means of resolving conflict of this kind, we can see how entries from the first two columns tend to predict the third, and entries from second and third tend to retrodict the first. We can also apply the same mode of explication to Freud's analysis of his dream of Irma's injection. Taking even a few parts from this may help give some sense of the intuitive grounds Popper, as well as many others, have had for accepting Freud's explanations as likewise confirmed by data from his associations and dream.

Part of Freud's dream of Irma's injection

This dream originated from a visit paid to Freud by his close friend and family doctor Otto (Freud, 1900a). He had recently visited the family of Freud's patient Irma and been called away to give someone an injection. When Freud asked about Irma, Otto replied that she was "better, but not yet well". As Freud describes in the preamble to his analysis, he was annoyed by Otto's remark and sat down later that evening to write up Irma's case history to show it to another friend, M, who was a leading figure in their circle, in order to justify himself. That night Freud had a dream, some parts of which are quoted below, in which Irma, having apparently sent him a message ahead of time, came to a gathering at his house and complained to him about her pains:

> … I at once took [Irma] on one side, as though to answer her letter and to reproach her for not having accepted my 'solution' yet. I said to her: 'If you still get pains, it is really only your fault.' She replied: 'If you only knew what pains I've got now in my throat and stomach and abdomen—it's choking me'—I was alarmed … I thought to myself that after all I must be missing some organic trouble. I took her to the window and looked down her throat … I at once called in Dr. M., and he repeated the examination and confirmed it … M. said 'There's no doubt it is an infection … the toxin will be eliminated'. We were directly aware, too, of the origin of her infection. Not long before, when she was feeling unwell, my friend Otto had given her an injection of a preparation of propyl, propyls … propionic acid … trimethylamin (and I saw before me the formula for this printed in heavy type) … One does not make injections of that sort so thoughtlessly … And probably the syringe had not been clean. (Freud, 1900a, p. 107)

In light of his analysis Freud took this dream—and particularly the final part about Otto having given Irma an injection of trimethylamin with a dirty syringe—as a wish-fulfilment. As he says:

> The dream fulfilled certain wishes which were started in me by the events of the previous evening (the news given me by Otto and my writing out of the case history). The conclusion of the dream, that is to say, was that I was not responsible for the persistence of Irma's pains, but that Otto was. Otto had in fact annoyed me by his remarks about Irma's incomplete cure, and the dream gave me my revenge by throwing the reproach back on to him … I was not

> to blame for Irma's pains, since she herself was to blame for them by refusing to accept my solution. I was not concerned with Irma's pains, since they were of an organic nature and quite incurable by psychological treatment. Irma's pains could be satisfactorily explained by her widowhood (cf. the trimethylamin) which I had no means of altering. Irma's pains had been caused by Otto giving her an incautious injection of an unsuitable drug—a thing I should never have done. (p. 143)

The associations and thoughts on which Freud bases this interpretation run to some fifteen pages in the *Standard Edition* (Freud, 1900a, pp. 96–121), and many more pages would be required here to explain which aspects of his account should be regarded as cogent. Still we can flag some points as before:

Data from associations	*Data from dream*
Freud wants not to be responsible for Irma's suffering	Freud says to Irma "If you still get pains, it is really only your fault"
Freud wants not to be responsible for Irma's suffering	Irma is suffering from an organic complaint, so Freud is not responsible for Irma's suffering
Freud is annoyed with Otto, for his remark implying that Freud was in some way at fault in his practice with Irma	Otto is at fault in his practice with Irma
Otto had given someone an injection while at Irma's, and Freud has been contemplating that his injections never cause infection	Otto gave Irma an injection that caused an infection
Freud desires to clear himself of responsibility for Irma's suffering	Otto bears sole responsibility for Irma's suffering
Freud was hoping that M's opinion of his treatment of Irma would clear him of responsibility	M observes Otto's bad practice and recognises that Otto bears full responsibility for Irma's suffering
Freud thought Otto's remark thoughtless	Otto's injection of Irma was thoughtless

Here again, although less precisely specifiable, we find a series of correlations in content among the data that seem to require explanation by a causal connection, and that also suggest the kind of explanatory hypothesis that would do so. So, combining the Freudian hypotheses we used for the simple cases above, we have:

Data from associations	*Hypothesis that explains, unifies and predicts data. As in the simple cases above, Freud's mind/brain manages conflict between the nocturnal arousal of motive and the processes of sleep and dreaming by wish-fulfilment and/or projection*	*Data from dream*
Freud wants not to be responsible for Irma's suffering	Freud wishfully and / or projectively locates responsibility for Irma's suffering	Freud says to Irma "If you still get pains, it is really only your fault"
Freud wants not to be responsible for Irma's suffering	Freud wishfully / projectively represents Irma as suffering from something for which he is not responsible	Irma is suffering from an organic complaint, for the treatment of which Freud is not responsible
Freud is annoyed with Otto, for his remark implying that Freud was in some way at fault in his practice with Irma	Freud wishfully / projectively represents the situation as the reverse of that he took to be implied by Otto, so that it is Otto, not Freud himself, who can be accused of fault connected with Irma's suffering	Otto is at fault in his practice with Irma

(*Continued*)

Continued.

Data from associations	*Hypothesis that explains, unifies and predicts data. As in the simple cases above, Freud's mind/brain manages conflict between the nocturnal arousal of motive and the processes of sleep and dreaming by wish-fulfilment and/or projection*	*Data from dream*
Otto had given someone an injection while at Irma's, and Freud has been contemplating that his injections never cause infection	Freud uses elements from reality to wishfully/projectively represent the situation as one in which Otto, not Freud himself, should be accused of fault connected with Irma's suffering	Otto gave Irma an injection that caused an infection
Freud desires to clear himself of responsibility for Irma's suffering	Freud wishfully/projectively represents the situation as one in which he has no responsibility for Irma's suffering	Otto bears sole responsibility for Irma's suffering
Freud was hoping that M's opinion of his treatment of Irma would clear him of responsibility	Freud wishfully/projectively represents M as finding that Irma's suffering was Otto's fault	M observes Otto's bad practice and recognises that Otto bears full responsibility for Irma's suffering
Freud thought Otto's remark thoughtless	Freud wishfully/projectively represents Otto as thoughtless	Otto's injection of Irma was thoughtless

As this illustrates, Freud's associations enable us to see this more complex dream as a mosaic of elements, each of which is comparable to the simple examples we took previously. As the use of "and/or" indicates, although Freud's data can be understood in terms of the concept of wish-fulfilment that he originally used to explain them, they are in fact better understood in terms of an hypothesis (projection, or projective identification) that he did not originally use. This concept was to be used for understanding dreams later, and mainly by other analysts. This clearly improves explanation, since the hypothesis of projection predicts—as wish-fulfilment alone does not—the displacement of traits from Freud to Otto.

This also illustrates something about Freud's data, and those recorded by other analysts. It is characteristically the case that clinical data explained by the hypotheses of a particular analyst at a particular time are better explained by hypotheses framed by other analysts later for the explanation of different data. This tends to disconfirm the most popular non-psychoanalytic explanation of the kind of apparently confirmatory relation between data and hypotheses illustrated above, namely that analysts' data seem explained by their hypotheses only because the data are, in one way or another, produced in response to, or "contaminated by", those hypotheses. Insofar as Freud's data are better explained by hypotheses he did not have in mind, this criticism is disconfirmed.

We can see more of this if we consider a further and deeper layer of data, concerning Freud's memories not from the day of the dream, but from events some way in the past. (On the understanding of dreams as consolidating memories, these would be not memories under first consolidation, but rather emotionally important memories from the past, aroused for reconsolidation with those of the day.) Freud's associations took him to a series of his own medical failures and derelictions. Thus he recalled that he had heard a few days earlier that a patient to whom he had recommended the use of cocaine "had developed an extensive necrosis of the nasal mucous membrane" (Freud, 1900a, p. 111) and in connection with this that he "had been the first to recommend the use of cocaine, in 1885, and this recommendation had brought serious reproaches down on me. The misuse of that drug had hastened the death of a dear friend of mine" (p. 111).

The "serious reproaches" were the result, among other things, of Freud's claiming that cocaine was not addictive, and this had also been his reason for recommending that his friend use it to withdraw from the morphine that he was using (and becoming addicted to) for the control of incurable nerve pain. But his friend "had at once given himself cocaine injections", and had ultimately died as a result. Likewise, Freud recalled "a tragic event in my practice. I had on one occasion produced a severe toxic state in a woman patient by prescribing what was at that time regarded as a harmless remedy ... My patient, who succumbed to the poison, had the same name as my eldest daughter" (p. 111). This prompted him to reflect: "It seemed as if I had been collecting all the occasions I could bring up against myself as evidence of lack of medical conscientiousness." This had apparently been an unconscious response to Otto's remark, or to his own activity in writing up Irma's case history afterwards.

This enables us to see more clearly that a main theme of Freud's dream (and tacitly of his analysis) was guilt and potential shame about these evidences of lack of medical conscientiousness. The medical circle that materialises in this dream and assesses Freud's and Otto's treatment of Irma was one of Jewish physicians in Vienna, all of whom were aware that "doctrinal considerations" might impede their professional lives, and hence also aware of the importance of their reputation for medical competence and conscientiousness. Freud also makes the importance of his own self-reproaches clear in his associations to his final reproach to Otto, saying:

> *One does not make injections of that kind so thoughtlessly* ... this sentence in the dream reminded me once more of my dead friend who had so hastily resorted to cocaine injections ... I had never contemplated the drug being given by injection. I noticed too that in accusing Otto of thoughtlessness in handling chemical substances I was once more touching upon the story of the unfortunate Mathilde, which gave grounds for the same accusation against myself .... (Freud, 1900a, p. 106, his italics)
>
> *And probably the syringe had not been clean.* This was yet another accusation against Otto ... I was proud of the fact that in two years I had not caused a single infiltration; I took constant pains to be sure that the syringe was clean. In short, I was conscientious. The phlebitis brought me back once more to my wife ... and now three similar situations came to my recollection involving my wife, Irma and the dead Mathilde .... (p. 107, his italics)

From these associations we can again see the importance Freud attached to these two deaths, for both of which he felt personally responsible, and both of which were the result of the misuse of toxic substances in injection. Taking these associations into account, we have:

Data from associations	*Data from dream*
Freud's advocacy of the medical use of cocaine brought "serious reproaches down on me"	Otto thoughtlessly misuses trimethylamin
Freud feels guilt because he accidentally killed a patient by giving her toxic injections	Otto gives Irma a toxic injection of trimethylamin
Freud feels guilt because he advised a friend to take cocaine, and his friend later died from cocaine injections	Freud reproaches Otto before M and their other medical colleagues, saying that one does not make injections of that kind so thoughtlessly
Freud was proud that he is careful to give injections that do not cause infection	Freud reproaches Otto before M and their other medical colleagues, saying that Otto's syringe had probably not been clean

And again:

Data from associations	*Hypothesis that explains, unifies and predicts data: Freud manages conflicts arising from his own guilt about thoughtless use of toxic substances and injections by wishfully/projectively representing Otto, as opposed to himself, as deserving such blame, and himself as censuring Otto accordingly*	*Data from dream*
Freud's advocacy of the medical use of cocaine brought "serious reproaches down on me"	Freud wishfully/projectively represents Otto as misusing potentially toxic substances	Otto misuses trimethylamin

(*Continued*)

Continued.

Data from associations	*Hypothesis that explains, unifies and predicts data: Freud manages conflicts arising from his own guilt about thoughtless use of toxic substances and injections by wishfully/projectively representing Otto, as opposed to himself, as deserving such blame, and himself as censuring Otto accordingly*	*Data from dream*
Freud feels guilt because he accidentally killed a patient by giving her toxic injections	Freud wishfully/projectively represents Otto as opposed to himself as giving a thoughtless toxic injection	Otto gives Irma a toxic injection of trimethylamin
Freud feels guilt because he advised a friend to take cocaine, and his friend later died from cocaine injections.	Freud wishfully/projectively represents Otto rather than himself as liable to reproach for damaging injections	Freud reproaches Otto before M and their other medical colleagues, saying that one does not make injections of that kind so thoughtlessly
Freud was proud that he is careful to give injections that do not cause infection	Freud wishfully/projectively represents Otto as opposed to himself as giving injections of the kind that cause infection	Freud reproaches Otto before M and their other medical colleagues, saying that Otto's syringe had probably not been clean

In this we can see the role of guilt and shame more clearly, and with this the additional significance of the projection into Otto that enables Freud to shame Otto before their medical circle for the kind of "incautious" injections and incautious use of toxic substances for which he seems personally to have suffered guilt and shame . And finally it may be worth noting that trimethylamin and Freud's linking of it with both cocaine and sexuality in his associations has a further significance that Freud reasonably enough chose not to disclose. Years after the publication of Freud's book, Karl Abraham wrote to him about his "suspicion of syphilitic infection in the patient: the spot in her mouth … the injection of trimethylamin which has been carelessly given, the dirty syringe (!!) … Is not this the organic illness for which you cannot be made responsible …?" (Abraham, Abraham, & Freud, 1965, p. 18). Freud replied: "Syphilis is not the subject matter … the three women are my daughters' three godmothers, and I have them all! There would be one simple therapy for widowhood, of course. All sorts of intimate things naturally" (Abraham, Abraham, & Freud, 1965, p. 20).

If we treat what Freud says here as further data, we have:

Data from associations	*Data from dream*
Freud had wished to have the widows in the dream	Otto gives the widow Irma an injection of trimethylamin with a dirty syringe
"There would be one simple therapy for widowhood"	As above
Trimethylamin is a sexual substance	As above

And again:

Data from associations	*Data that explains, unifies and predicts data*	*Data from dream*
Freud wished to have the widows in the dream	Freud manages conflict about his own guilt concerning sexual feelings towards Irma by wishfully/projectively but *symbolically* representing Otto as sexually invasive towards Irma	Otto gives the widow Irma an injection of trimethylamin with a dirty syringe
"There would be one simple therapy for widowhood"	As above	As above
Trimethylamin is a sexual substance	As above	As above

This takes us in the direction of sexual symbolism and the metaphor of the mind as a container, as noted above, and adds to our complex but pervasive sense of the emotion of guilt, and the range of projection, depicted in the dream. Taking this into account, moreover, enables us to see—and more or less automatically to participate in—the way the understanding of motive in dreams complements the understanding of action in waking life.

We have seen that Freud found Otto's remark annoying, and sat down to write up Irma's case history to show to M to discuss his treatment of her. In this his feelings and actions were those of a normal man and responsible physician. But we may wonder why, exactly, Freud found Otto's remark annoying, and why he responded to it in such a way ("… to justify myself …"). Prior to his analysis of the dream neither he nor we (his readers) had any particular understanding of this response. After his analysis, I think, we take ourselves to understand better. We think (hypothesise) that both his annoyance and his going over the case with the aim of justifying himself were caused by (non-conscious) stirrings of the guilt and desire to avoid shame that his analysis the next day revealed so clearly.

This is an hypothesis that readers will naturally entertain and try to test further as they read further, both in this dream and in Freud's book.[13] This kind of connection between the understanding of motive gained by the interpretation of dreams and that gained by the interpretation of action is an important part of the inferential engine of Freud's radical but step-by-step extension of common-sense psychology; and we see these two factors at work in the way Freud's analysis of his dream alters our sense of why he felt and acted as he did on the day before he had it.

Also in this we can see the importance of free association, in enabling a person who practises it to gain access to causes of his thoughts and feelings of which he would not otherwise become aware. Consider Freud's associations to the patient he had accidentally killed:

> My patient—who succumbed to the poison—had the same name as my eldest daughter. It had never occurred to me before, but it struck me now almost like an act of retribution on the part of destiny. It was as though the replacement of one person by another was to be continued in another sense: this Mathilde for that Mathilde, an eye for an eye and a tooth for a tooth. (Freud, 1900a, pp. 111–112)

That is: not only did Freud find in the course of his associations that a part of himself "had been collecting all the occasions which I could bring up against myself as evidence of lack of medical conscientiousness" (p. 112); but also this part of himself seemed somehow to menace him with terrible retribution—eye for eye and tooth for tooth, this Mathilde for that Mathilde—in the form of the death of his own daughter.[14]

This is a kind of deep but significant feeling that becomes available in free association, but rarely emerges in other frames of mind. In the context of Freud's thinking we can see that this process is particularly revealing, since we could scarcely ask for a clearer example of what Freud was later to call the harsh and moralistic superego or ego-ideal (e.g., Freud, 1923b, 1933a). Freud was later to study the working of this faculty in severe depression: "We see how [in severely depressed individuals] one part of the ego [*das Ich*] sets itself over against the other, judges it critically, and, as it were, takes it as its 'object', so that they direct ferocious moralistic anger against themselves, regarding themselves as 'worthless' and 'morally despicable'" (Freud, 1917e, pp. 246–247).

A characteristic example is provided by Elyn Saks' (2008) recent account of her own breakdown into depression and schizophrenia, which began with her attacking herself by saying: "I am not sick. I'm just a bad, defective, and evil person. Maybe if I would talk less I wouldn't spread my evil around" (p. 58). As time passed her self-reproaches became more constant, violent, and repetitive: "I am a piece of shit and I deserve to die. I am a piece of shit and I deserve to die. I am a piece of shit and I deserve to die" (p. 58). When medication temporarily lessened her depression she told her doctor *that she felt less angry*, and remarked on "how much rage I had felt, directed mostly at myself ..." (Saks, 2008, p. 69).

Freud's associations indicate that a similar but unconscious process of aggressive and menacing guilt had been at work in the formation of his own dream, and we have seen that he dealt with it by projecting the things he was guilty about into Otto. By the end of his dream, Freud could take the role of superego to Otto's ego and condemn Otto as a giver of the kind of thoughtless ("incautious") toxic injections that he regretted in his own case.

This is partly comparable to the way Neurocritic projected his own pain into another in the simple dream we discussed above, and Freud was later to find that such guilt—or pain-relieving projection was one of the main ways by which people seek to mitigate internal conflict involving guilt or shame. In particular he was to find that:

i. Many individuals deal with internal conflict that might cause guilt or shame by projecting what they unconsciously feel to be bad parts of themselves into others. In this way they can identify with their own moralistic superegos, by condemning or attacking what they feel to be bad aspects or parts of themselves as these appear in other persons.

This kind of projection-driven moralistic condemnation is common enough to be the target of the biblical imperative not to condemn the mote in another's eye while ignoring the beam in one's own; and it serves not only for the maintenance of individual self-esteem, as we see in Freud's dream, but also in fostering group-on-group aggression. Thus consider two fairly recent experimental studies of homophobia (Adams, Wright, & Lohr, 1996; Bernat, Calhoun, Adams, & Zeichner, 2001). In both, the experimental subjects were men who identified themselves as heterosexual, and were divided into homophobic and non-homophobic subgroups. In the first experiment both groups were shown homosexual pornography while their erectile responses were monitored. The most homophobic men were also the most likely to be aroused by watching homosexual acts, and to deny this arousal despite ongoing physiological measurement. This would be consilient with the idea that these men were condemning things in others that they unconsciously condemned in themselves, as Freud was doing in his dream.

In the second experiment the groups administered shocks to a (fictitious) opponent, as part of what they took to be a competitive examination of reaction times to explicit sexual material—which again was a male-on-male pornography. The homophobic group reported more negative affect, anger and hostility while watching the video; and in administering shocks they were significantly more aggressive towards opponents they took to be homosexual as opposed to heterosexual. This would fit with the idea that members of gay-bashing or other sexually prejudiced groups, who regard their activities as validating their masculinity, are maintaining idealised images of themselves by attacking what they unconsciously register as their own "bad" characteristics, as these have been located in others. Something similar seems to hold in many other cases—of sexual prejudice, or dehumanisation more generally—in which the same mechanisms of (identificatory) in-group idealisation and (projective) out-group contempt and denigration seem to operate.[15]

Taking Freud's dream in this light we see that his analysis here also looks forward to the work in which he founded psychoanalytic group psychology. As he was later to argue, human groups often establish in-group moral cohesion and cooperation for out-group conflict by identifying with idealised leaders or creeds, and thereby locating deviation from these in members of out-groups, against whom moralistic aggression becomes morally mandatory. We can see this pretty clearly in the idealisation of Hitler and anti-Semitism fostered by the Nazi party, in accord with which both Roosevelt and the Jews were represented as parties to a Jewish conspiracy of world domination, for which the only remedy was their extermination. So Freud's projection into Otto also exemplifies the mechanism that establishes the pattern of "good us (in-group) against bad them (out-group)" that underpins much human group conflict (for a fuller discussion of the working of identification and projection in group psychology see Hopkins, 2003, 2004, 2013b).

Freud also explained later how such projection can operate in severe mental illness:

> ii. Schizophrenic individuals often project their superego/ego-ideal itself, thereby creating a virtual world of moralistically threatening ("eye for an eye … tooth for a tooth") presences. Thus as Freud says "the voices, as well as the undefined multitude [of potentially critical psychological presences embodied in the superego/ego-ideal] are brought into the foreground again by the disease" so that the sufferer's superego/ego-ideal "confronts him in a regressive form as a hostile influence from without". (Freud, 1914c, p. 96)

We can see something closely comparable in Saks' (2008) account, in which lost was her sense that *she* was engaged in self-reproach, and that *her own* thoughts were involved. Rather, she came to feel that she was "receiving commands" from "shapeless powerful beings that controlled me with thoughts (not voices) that had been placed in my head" (p. 84). Thus she was commanded: "Walk through the tunnels and repent. Now lie down and don't move. You are evil" (p. 84). And as was appropriate to her evil, she also received commands to injure herself, which she obeyed by burning herself with cigarette lighters, electric heaters, or boiling water.[16] Likewise Freud was later to hold that:

> iii. Individuals suffering from mania are identifying or 'fusing' with their own superego/ego-ideal. While 'the misery of the melancholic' results from a 'sharp conflict' between the ego and the superego/ego-ideal, in mania the ego and the ego-ideal have fused together, so the individual is "disturbed by no self-criticism" (Freud, 1921c, p. 132). And here we can compare Freud's dream above, at the end of which he was "disturbed by no self-criticism" but was rather engaged in criticising Otto.

Freud's early formulations of these ideas have been improved by his successors in many ways, but the notion of projection that he first detailed from the inside in the Irma dream remains central to all accounts. Earlier I stressed that it is difficult to represent psychoanalytic clinical data in ways that are effective for scientific communication, and this is particularly well illustrated by the response of philosophers of science to the data and hypotheses we have been discussing here. As we saw above, Popper regarded Freud's analyses of individual dreams as cogent, and as constituting "a great discovery". Adolph Grünbaum and Clark Glymour also regard it as cogent, with Grünbaum (1984) saying that "this is a case in which commonsense psychology regards a dream as patently wishfulfilling" (p. 221) and Glymour (1983) that "the interpretation offered is enormously plausible" (p. 63). But in contrast to Popper, neither sees Freud's use of free association or his analysis of this dream as containing any kind of discovery at all.

Glymour (1983) opines that "the Irma dream is one whose interpretation can be read almost on its face, and the elaborate 'analysis' Freud offers us contributes virtually nothing" (p. 64); and Grünbaum (1984) says that although "the aggressive conscious wishes that Freud had on the day before the dream were then patently realized in its manifest content, free association played *no excavating role* in his recall of these wishes after the dream, since he had been avowedly conscious of them in the day before" (p. 222, his italics). Despite the intelligence, expertise and authority of their authors, these comments are clearly mistaken.[17] As we have seen, Freud's explicit references in his dream to toxins, injections, and trimethylamin, and particularly his closing reproaches to Otto, cannot be understood without considering his associations to his own killing of a patient by toxic injections; to his role in the death of a friend from cocaine injections, nor to the reproaches and guilt he suffered in relation to them.

Although these things figure prominently in Freud's associations *after the dream,* he was by no means "avowedly conscious" of them on the day before. Quite the opposite: Freud was then avowedly conscious only of "a disagreeable impression" that "was not clear to me" (1900a, p. 106); and he says that it was only after analysing the dream that he was able to put retrospectively into words "the obscure disagreeable impression I had had when Otto brought me the news of Irma's condition" (p. 120). And whatever Freud's conscious reflections after the dream there is no reason to suppose that they involved trimethylamin, or the incoherent idea that it would somehow set things right if Otto were to be shown to have made Irma very ill by giving her a toxic injection that Freud could triumphantly diagnose in front of M and the other members of their medical circle. On these topics, his associations—beginning with his noting that his reproaching Irma for not having accepted his "solution" indicated that he was "especially anxious" not to be blamed for her condition—clearly played an excavating role, and one that went further than Freud could then gauge.

Grünbaum and Glymour seem to me not to have understood many aspects of Freud's analysis, let alone the way it served not only as a specimen of his work at the time but as one of his first steps in the direction of many of his later discoveries. They might well disagree—after all these are matters of interpretation. But if Grünbaum were to have accepted the cogency of Freud's analysis while failing to appreciate the many discoveries it contains, it would be expected that he would likewise not appreciate the role of such analyses in extending common-sense psychology generally. Such disagreements therefore also underline the importance of Grünbaum's own argument that to carry conviction Freudian clinical claims require to be linked to fields of enquiry that are less dependent on interpretation. So let us turn to these.

Consilience: psychoanalysis, attachment, and neuroscience

Attachment

The process of attachment—the forming of basic emotional bonds as between infants and their mothers and others who care for them—is particularly relevant for psychoanalysis, and also a bridge between psychoanalysis, experimental developmental psychology from infancy, and neuroscience.[18] The founder of modern attachment research, John Bowlby, was trained in the British object-relations school of Melanie Klein—one of the pioneers of the psychoanalysis of children—and had been supervised by Klein herself. But he disagreed sharply with Klein on the role of events in the first year of life.

Klein had extended Freud's thinking about "the earliest parental imagos" (Freud, 1933a, p. 64), which they both thought constitutive of the superego/ego-ideal into an account of infantile phantasy in the first months of life. In retrospect we can see this account—in accord with which infants naturally imagine that good experiences (beginning with feeding at the breast) are caused by very good figures whom they seek to incorporate and identify themselves with, but that bad experiences are caused by very bad or figures from whom they seek to dissociate themselves, and who are the object of projections—as a specification of the operation of the innate conceptual equipment in terms of which infants initially attempt to make sense of postnatal experience. Taken in this light, the Kleinian notion of infantile phantasy also coheres with the group psychology of *good us* as opposed to *bad them*, as sustained by identification with good objects and projective dissociation from supposedly bad objects that we considered in connection with Freud's dream above.

Bowlby, however, saw Klein's emphasis on phantasy not as specifying innate mechanisms by which the infant makes sense of his early postnatal experience, but rather as indicating a neglect of the infant's actual and veridical experience of parenting, both in infancy and later childhood, which he had begun to study by empirical means. This criticism was also made from other analysts, as well as by empirical developmental psychologists of the time.

To render the issues involved more testable, Bowlby recast some of Klein's hypotheses about the "internal objects" of infantile phantasy as claims about the infant's "internal working models" of himself in relation to the mother (or other carers) to which the infant became attached. As he had intended, this facilitated the reformulation of psychoanalytic hypotheses in alternative theoretical vocabularies, and rendered his and Klein's conflicting claims amenable to more empirical investigation. (And as we will see later, the notion of an internal model of the things we experience, including our own bodies and those of others, has become central for neuroscience generally.)[19]

Bowlby's colleague Mary Ainsworth devised an empirical procedure, the "strange situation", that proved capable of assigning infants from about twelve months (shortly before the onset of speech) to a set of different but statistically reliable categories of emotional relationship. This was a striking and seminal intellectual advance, and was to render attachment theory capable of many kinds of empirical investigation. But it also rapidly brought Ainsworth's and Bowlby's perspective closer to Klein's, since it indicated that infants' internal models had already developed so far as to attain a life-influencing form of stability by twelve months. Such a role for the period prior to twelve months was what Klein had emphasised in the work with which Bowlby had disagreed; and such rapid postnatal development might be thought to presuppose an unlearned framework for the understanding of emotional relationships such as Klein had described. And Klein had also described the effects of parenting in this early period in terms similar to those Ainsworth and others were to use.

In setting out her hypotheses about what she called the paranoid-schizoid and depressive positions of infancy (1952), Klein had emphasised her agreement with the conclusions of Margaret Ribble's observational (and EEG) studies of attachment in infancy, published in 1944. She had stressed that "[m]uch of the quality and the cohesiveness of a child's personality depends upon an emotional attachment to the mother" because "the infant is, by its very incompleteness of brain and nervous system, continuously in potential danger of functional disorganization." This meant that there was particular danger for the infant in "the sudden separation from the mother who either intuitively or knowingly must sustain this functional balance". Also the delicacy of the balance entailed that "[a]ctual neglect or lack of love may be equally disastrous" so that "irregularities in the personal care and handling of the baby, such as too little care, too little handling of the baby" can "permanently alter the organic and psychic development" (pp. 88f).[20]

The idea was not, of course, that such alterations determined future development; rather only that they might contribute to its course, and in ways that Ribble, and later Bowlby, Ainsworth, and their colleagues, set out to measure. While emphasising these effects of parenting Klein also insisted that they were mediated by imagination or phantasy on the part of the infant, particularly concerning "the earliest parental imagos", whose role in shaping postnatal experience she had attempted to describe. The "early imagos" thus became the targets of Bowlby and Ainsworth's investigations as well, and with a growing awareness that there was no inconsistency between Klein's claims about early unlearned phantasy and Ainsworth's empirical discoveries about the formative role of experience in the first year.

Embodiment and identity

Klein's hypotheses about prior development, moreover, turned on a particular conceptual change, the importance of which all developmental psychologists were starting to acknowledge. This was the infant's coming to regard the mother (and by extension other persons and himself) as "whole objects"—that is, as distinct embodied individuals who maintained their identity in space and time. This same conception, as applied to the numerical identity of everyday material objects, was also a main focus of the researches of Jean Piaget, one of the leading cognitive psychologists of the time. Piaget did not investigate the concept of an object as it applied to the infant's mother, but rather to nonliving objects that could be readily manipulated and used in his informal but replicable experiments; but these indicated that ability to use the concept progressed with experience in stages from early infancy onwards.

Klein held that the infant's coming to grasp the numerical identity of the mother was particularly important for infantile emotional and mental life, since it went with the infant's coming to think and feel that both his mother and himself were single, unique and enduring beings. This required the baby to distinguish more clearly between its fleeting internal subjective experiences and the lasting external objective things, including himself and mother, that these experiences represented. Also it entailed that infant and mother endured separations from one another that might be sources of pain, particularly to the infant, and that while they were separated the infant might feel that he risked losing a relationship that was both indispensable and irreplaceable.

In this case, as Klein thought, the infant might seek to minimise pain by denying distress at separation, and also by denying dependence on the mother and/or her irreplaceability and significance in his life. But also the pain of separation, if acknowledged with a growing degree of realism, could evoke anxious but empathic concern for the mother; and Klein regarded this as the root of later sympathy, empathy, and care. Ainsworth's colleague Sylvia Bell began to espouse similar ideas in 1970, via notions of object—and person-permanence derived from the work of Piaget (Bell, 1970).

Other psychoanalytic schools also developed analogous views, cast in terms of a "pre-objectual" or "pre-ambivalent" stage of infantile mental life, before the notion of the mother as a single enduring object took hold (see Kumin, 1996). So over time, and despite other disagreements, psychoanalytic and empirical research, including that of cognitive psychologists influenced by Piaget, had started to focus on the infant's conception of the identity of persons *as embodied*, and on the emotional consequences that this might have.

Research would subsequently indicate that the infant's understanding of his mother as a single enduring object of emotion unfolded on a distinct development track from its understanding of objects that were merely physical. The process began as the infant's emotions were focused on the mother in nursing and care, and became increasingly interactive and social, taking the form of playful, rhythmic and turn-taking exchanges of expression of feeling ("protoconversations") by two months. At four months, however, a baby made angry by an experimenter's impeding hand would direct anger at the hand itself, as if still conceiving the world (including the mother, her breast, eyes, face, etc.) as consisting of anatomically incomplete part-objects, as psychoanalytic accounts had held (on the regulation of anger see Campos et al. (1983) and Stenberg, Campos, & Emde (1983)).

Sometime around the fifth month babies seemed to start to think of their mothers as single, unique, and lasting, as Klein had hypothesised;[21] and as we shall see, this period seems particularly important in a number of ways. Following it, by seven months babies direct anger at an offender's face, and can be seen to regulate it on the basis of their experience of the person concerned. A baby is especially angry if his mother annoys him *after* a stranger has done so, as if he expects comfort in such a situation and this expectation has been betrayed. And around this time, often by eight months, a baby will start angrily protesting mother's leaving his presence, and become fearful of strangers, although he had readily tolerated these things before—the difference, it seems, being made by the baby's increasing understanding of the nature and possible consequences of separation, and of his relation with the mother as uniquely valuable and important.

These protests and fears seem to lessen towards ten months, with the observable development of intersubjectivity. The infant becomes aware not only that he and mother are aware of one another—such mutual awareness seems already a part of the two month "protoconversations"—but also that each is aware of the other as attending to some third thing or person. This mutual awareness is naturally used to exchange information about these other things, so that, for example, the infant may come to welcome or to fear petting a dog, touching a snake, or ringing a bell, depending on the attitude mother communicates. This seems to be the point of intersection of the infant's growing conception of persons—who feel, think, and communicate—on the one hand, and inanimate objects on the other. And while the latter leads to our later conceptualisation of the realm of merely physical objects, and hence to the cultural development of the physical sciences, the former leads to our very different later ways of thinking of the realm of persons (including ourselves) and their minds (for recent discussion see Trevarthen (2009) and Ammaniti & Trentini (2009)).

The strange situation and infantile attachment

The consolidation that prompted focus on the first year apparently concerned the infants' emotional bonds with both parents and other carers; and Ainsworth's "strange situation" can be used to assess and classify any of these. Since the theoretical claims the procedure was initially designed to address turned mainly on infants' models of themselves in relation to mothers, we will take things in these terms, while bearing in mind that such research investigates the role of fathers and other carers (e.g., in adoptive and/or gay couples) as well.

The strange situation consists of eight episodes, the first lasting only thirty seconds; the rest were originally set for three minutes, but with the proviso that they would be shortened in response to infants' distress, which means that in practice the upsetting episodes (3) and (4) and (6) and (7) often last thirty seconds or less. In (1) mother and infant settle in an unfamiliar but comfortable situation in which (2) the mother is able to sit while the infant can explore the new place and play with toys that have been provided there. The real work of the procedure begins with episode (3) in which when the mother is settled and the infant (hopefully) at play a stranger enters and attempts to play with the infant (e.g., by offering a toy), thus activating the infant's recently mastered fear of strangers. Then in (4) the mother leaves the infant alone with the stranger, so triggering the infant's (usually angry) protests, and his recently mastered distress at separation from her, as well.

She comes back again in (5), so giving the infant an opportunity to relieve the anger and distress related to her going away and also the fear caused by the stranger, and with this to facilitate a return to exploration and play. But after three minutes, in (6), she leaves the infant entirely alone and then (and as if this was not already bad enough) in

(7) the stranger enters and again attempts to play. Thus in (6) and (7) the infant's distress at separation and his fear of strangers are activated, still more strongly, together with his anger at the mother for having left it in such a situation, and despite protests, yet again. (These phases, like (4) and (6), are shortened if they prove too distressing for the infant.) In (8), the final reunion, the mother returns with the opportunity again to relieve separation distress, anger, and fear, and to enable the infant to return to exploration and play.

Classification turns on how the infant copes with all this, and particularly on how it resolves conflict between the "negative" and "positive" emotions activated by the procedure. The negative emotions include anger at the mother—caused by her ignoring protest on leaving, and inflicting separation distress and fear of strangers in doing so—and the positive emotions include those roused by the mother's coming back, receiving comfort from her, and returning to exploration and play. Hence the classifications overall—as shown in the table below—relate to conflicts between feelings and emotions related to maternal care, exploration and play on the one hand, and anger, distress at separation and fear on the other. Roughly, the infants classed as secure at twelve months show less conflict among these emotions and resolve these conflicts more readily than those who are classed as insecure—that is, as ambivalent/resistant, avoidant, or disorganised.

This last classification turns on signs of conflict too severe for the infant to resolve—conflict that renders coherent feeling and behaviour impossible. Infants classed as disorganised at twelve months seem to manage a fully organised resolution of their emotional conflicts only by three; and the resolution often takes the form of a permanent predisposition to *coerce* and *control* what they seem to regard as perpetually untrustworthy objects of emotion. This they often achieve by violent means, or again by forms of helpfulness that are also coercive and intrusive. (For more on insecure and disorganised attachment and their later consequences see Howe (2011), particularly chapters 12 and 13. For disorganised attachment in particular see Solomon & George (1999) and Lyons-Ruth & Jacobovitz (2008)).

Correlation between infant and adult measures of attachment: the strange situation and the adult attachment interview

The strange situation has since been correlated with a range of other procedures to measure attachment in childhood, adolescence, and adulthood (see Crowell, Fraley, & Shaver (2008); Hesse (2000, 2008); Howe (2011, p. 50ff) and Magai (2008)). The longest established of these is the adult attachment interview, which consists of a series of questions designed to elicit interviewees' current thoughts, feelings and other states of mind with regard to their attachment relations as children. Thus the interviewer asks the interviewee "to describe your relationship with your parents as a young child, starting as far back as you can remember"; and again asks "Could you give me five adjectives to describe your relations with your mother (father) during childhood? I'll write them down and when we have all five I'll ask what memories led you to choose each one".[22] Answers to these questions support assignment to four adult categories that are closely comparable to the infant categories determined by the strange situation.

These comparisons have now been made over three generations of parents, and show impressive continuities between infant and adult forms. Some of these appear in the table below, taken from the more fuller accounts in Cassidy and Shaver (2000, 2008):[23]

Infant's attachment-related behaviour, as classified during the strange situation procedure	*Adult states of mind with respect to attachment, as measured by discussion in the adult attachment interview*
Secure	**Classifications**
Secure	Secure/autonomous
In pre-separation episodes explores room and toys with interest, with occasional returns to, or checks with, parent. Shows signs of missing parent during separation, often crying by second separation. Greets parent actively on return, often initiating physical contact. Usually maintains contact after second reunion but then settles and returns to play.	Coherent collaborative discourse about attachment with ready flexibility of attention. Avows missing, needing and depending on others. Explicit or implicit forgiveness of, or compassion towards, parents. Accepts imperfections in the self, ruefully describes own untoward flawed behaviour despite conscious efforts to the contrary. Sense of balance, proportion, or humour.

(*Continued*)

Continued.

Insecure	**Classifications**
Avoidant	Dismissing
Little flexibility of attention: focuses on toys or environment and away from parent, whether present, departing, or returning. Does not cry on separation, response to parent appears unemotional, but actively avoids and ignores parent on reunion (i.e., by moving away, stiffening, turning away, or leaning out of arms when picked up).	Discourse not coherent. Attention inflexibly focused away from attachment history and its implications. Makes positive or idealising generalisations about attachment history ("excellent, very normal mother") that are unsupported or actively contradicted by episodes actually remembered. Describes self as strong, independent, normal, with little or no acknowledgement of hurt, distress, or feelings of needing or depending on others. Repeated insistence on absence of memory or brief contemptuous derogation of, or active contemptuous refusal to discuss, a particular event or figure, so responses are often excessively short.
Resistant or Ambivalent	Preoccupied
Little flexibility of attention, may be wary or distressed even prior to separation, and focuses on mother and is preoccupied with her throughout. Upset by separation, fails to settle and take comfort in parent on reunion, usually focuses on parent and cries. May alternate bids for contact with signs of angry rejection or tantrums, or efforts may be weak. Does not explore during separation or after reunion.	Not coherent. Either passive or angry preoccupation with experience of being parented. Responses persistently and inflexibly tied to experiences with, or influence of, the parents even when this is not the topic of the question. Brings past into discussion of the present and vice versa. Sentences or conversational turns taken are often excessively long.

(*Continued*)

Continued.

Infant's attachment-related behaviour, as classified during the strange situation procedure	*Adult states of mind with respect to attachment, as measured by discussion in the adult attachment interview*
Disorganised	Unresolved/Disorganised
Infant displays disorganised or disoriented behaviour, inexplicable in terms of an overall strategy or goal. Criteria include simultaneous displays of contradictory behaviour patterns, such as very strong attachment behaviour followed by avoidance, freezing or dazed behaviour; strong avoidance with strong contact-seeking, distress or anger; extensive expressions of distress, with movement away from, rather than toward, the mother; indices of apprehension toward the mother, such as hunched shoulders or fearful facial expressions; multiple rapid changes in affect. Likely to show "disorganised controlling behaviour" by pre-school and elementary school age.	During discussion, particularly of loss or abuse, individual shows striking lapses in the monitoring of discourse (e.g., indicating a belief that a dead person is still alive, or was killed by a childhood thought). May lapse into prolonged silence or eulogistic speech.

Attachment, psychoanalysis, conflict, and identification

The table above illustrates how the criteria for insecure classifications turn on signs of conflict between "positive" and "negative" emotions, with the "positive" being those involved in maternal comfort, exploration, and play, and the negative those of anger, separation distress, and fear. Thus in infants both ambivalent/resistant and avoidant behaviours manifest anger at the mother for imposing the distress of separation, with both distress and anger amplified in those classed as avoidant/resistant, and suppressed in those classed as avoidant. Some infants classed as ambivalent/resistant also show fear of the mother, as do many classed as disorganised, and in both this fear seems to inhibit the expression of anger towards her. In the case of disorganised infants, such anger and fear are later shown in coercive relationships, both with the mother and playmates and others. Conflicts similar to those shown in infancy are found in the adult categories, with anger and fear again amplified and explicit in those classed as preoccupied, and suppressed (and idealised) in those classed as dismissing. The emotional conflicts of those classed as disorganised in adulthood also show the kinds of incoherence in thought and imagining that are found in mental disorder (e.g., in Freud's (1909d) patient the Rat Man).

As well as these comparisons, the table represents two directions of developmental correlation. First, infants tend to develop forward from twelve months in accord with their original classification, so that being a secure or insecure infant is a start towards having secure or insecure states of mind in regard to attachment as an adult—together with a range of related consequences for relationships, and life more generally. Second, research by Peter Fonagy and others (Fonagy, 2000; Fonagy, Gergely, & Target, 2008) has shown that there are relatively strong correlations between the categories assigned pregnant women via the adult attachment interview, and those to which their as-yet-unborn infants will later be assigned, in the strange situation from twelve months after birth.

These predictive relationships seem mainly determined by the experience that unfolds between mother and infant after birth, as opposed to their genetic overlap (see Howe (2011), chapters 14 and 15; van Ijzendoorn (1995); Vaughn, Bost, & van Ijzendoorn (2008)), although genetic factors may be more important in disorganised attachment than in the other categories.[24] Taken broadly, these data seem as we should expect them to be, given the psychoanalytic hypothesis that bear on them. In the case of the forward correlations from twelve months the psychoanalytic hypotheses would be: (i) that mental disturbance or disorder is characteristically rooted in emotional conflict, and; (ii) that later conflicts are underlain by conflicts about parental figures that can be traced back into infancy. Conflicting emotions towards the mother seem to have been shown clearly in the strange situation, and by further research, to be important for later relationships and development generally.

Likewise the correlations between maternal and infant categories are as would be expected, given the psychoanalytic hypothesis that infants learn their basic ways of coping with emotion by identifying with their parents. In this, as we saw earlier, identification is understood as "the assimilation of one ego to another" (Freud, 1933a, p. 63); and in post-Freudian (e.g., Kleinian) theory the most basic and formative identifications are assumed to be established during the first year, and via the nursing and caring relationship between mother and infant. Such identificatory mechanisms may help explain not only likenesses between infants and mothers, but also many other kinds of assimilative learning (e.g., of language). And with the discovery of mirror neurons and other neurological mechanisms that seem to enable identification, this notion has now come generally to be assigned the kind of importance in development that it was originally given by Freud.[25]

Infantile disorganisation and childhood determination to control

To see more of the importance of this let us take two examples of the transition from infantile disorganisation to childhood "disorganzied controlling behaviour" (from Solomon & George, 1999). Thus consider a little girl in the strange situation at eighteen months:

> In the second reunion Kate approached her mother with her arms outstretched towards her mother. When she was about two feet away from making contact, she moved her arms to the side and abruptly circled away from her mother like a banking airplane. As she moved away she had a blank, dazed expression on her face. (p. 131)

And then at thirty-two months with her mother helping her to complete a series of tasks:

> ... on three different occasions when Kate completed the tasks incorrectly, her mother moved a piece to illustrate the correct procedure. Each time Kate screamed "No!" and ordered in a threatening tone, "Put it back!" On each occasion her mother obeyed. (p. 139)

And finally at forty-two months with a boy called Trey:

> Pretending to bake a cake in a toy oven, Kate said in a very loud, bossy tone, "You can't have cake now! Go away: you can't have cake 'till I call you!" She then ordered Trey to get some dishes for her. She frowned when she saw what he brought and scolded him, shaking her finger with her hand on her hips. Trey pretended to eat ... Kate yelled "No! It's not done!" ... She ordered him to go away ... when he didn't move she pushed him roughly, and he fell to the floor .... (p. 150)

Again, consider a boy in the strange situation at eighteen months:

> In the first reunion, Sam approached his mother with his eyes cast down. When he was about two feet away he looked up at her, rising suddenly and making gasping noises with his breath as he did so. He quickly looked down again, bared his teeth in a half-grimace/half-smile and turned away. Hunching his shoulders and holding his arms and legs stiffly, he tiptoed to the other side of the room. He sat motionless in the chair for 30 seconds, grasping the armrests and staring straight ahead with a dazed expression. (p. 131)

Then at forty-two months with a friendly little girl called Jenny, who tries to interest him in playing with dolls:

> At first he ignores her overtures but finally he takes the doll she offers … [and] alternates between brushing its hair tenderly and smashing it against the floor. Jenny tries to integrate Sam's behavior into her pretend play … she pretends the doll is saying in a squeaky voice 'Ow, don't do that!' … Jenny tries again, making her doll say 'I'm going on the bus.' Sam grabbed the toy bus before Jenny could put her doll in it, crammed his doll in, and drove the bus away. Jenny gave up trying to play with Sam. (p. 153)

And finally, playing with a boy named Davy:

> Sam (54 months) grabbed a syringe from the toy doctor's kit Davy was holding and gave him a "shot". When Davy ignored this, he shined a flashlight right in Davy's eyes, while making strange whooping sounds. Davy also ignored this and suggested that they play with puppets. Sam took a puppet that Davy offered and then made his puppet "bite" Davy's nose while Sam grinned and giggled. He continued even after David repeatedly told him to stop … Davy finally ignored Sam and turned his back on him. (p. 153)

These last instances were more strange than aggressive, for they seem to have been done without focused intent to cause pain or discomfort. They may indicate how difficult it is for a child with such conflicting emotions—see the alteration between tenderly brushing the doll's hair and smashing it against the floor above—to find a coherent way of behaving and feeling towards others. But Sam was also aggressively controlling with his father, as we will see below.

Identification, aggression, and sexuality

Further points emerge as we consider the period that leads up to the twelve month consolidation. Wittgenstein (1998) once remarked that "[a]nyone who listens to a child's crying with understanding will know that psychic forces, terrible forces, sleep within it, different from anything commonly assumed. Profound rage and pain and lust for destruction" (p. 4e). Although it can seem sacrilegious to mention infancy, aggression and mothers in the same breath, we should expect the infant's learning to regulate his own anger towards his mother, which seems so important a feature of attachment, to be an important part of his learning to regulate his anger towards persons more generally. The idea that infants base later relationships on earlier paradigms in this way is one of the main findings of attachment research.

Such self-regulation seems particularly important in light of agreement among researchers on aggression that, as Tremblay (2008) reports, children use physical aggression naturally and spontaneously from when they are first able to do so, and such aggression is at its most impulsive and forcible early in life, and tends to decline thereafter. Here is one of the tables with which Tremblay (2002) illustrates his claims. As Tremblay says, children "have the physical, cognitive and emotional means of being physically aggressive towards others by 12 months of

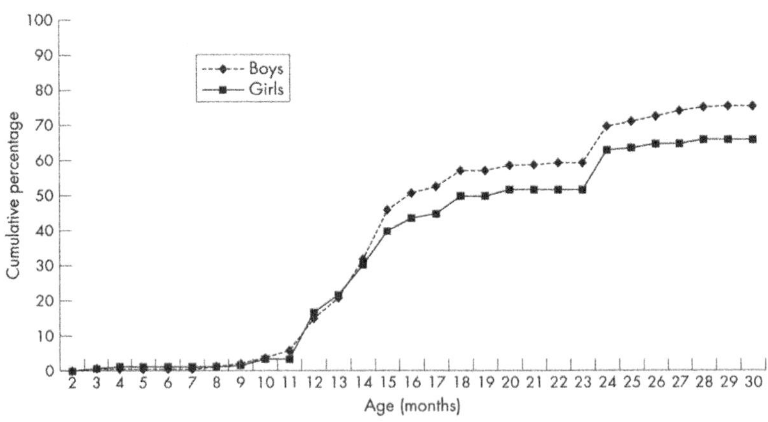

Figure 2. Pushes others to get what she or he wants.
Reproduced from "Prevention of injury by early socialization of aggressive behavior", Tremblay, R. E., *8*, iv17–iv21, 2002 with permission from BMJ Publishing Group Ltd.

age ... most children will 'onset' hitting or biting or kicking another child or even an adult before their second birthday" (p. 2617). In light of this, and the way such violence declines later, we should conclude that from infancy onwards "rather than to physically aggress" children "learn not to physically aggress".

But then why do some children *fail* to learn "not to physically aggress", and when does such failure in learning begin? Tremblay discusses this via individuals who show *chronic physical aggression*; and here again early experience, particularly in relation to the mother, seems important. One of the most important predictors of chronic physical aggression is the behaviour of chronic aggressors' mothers, particularly antisocial behaviour in adolescence. And assessments from the fifth month after birth—that is, some seven months *prior* to the twelve month consolidation discussed above—indicate that family dysfunction, and coercive-hostile parenting by mothers, are particularly significant (see Tremblay, 2002, 2008).

Above we reflected on how mother-infant correlations in attachment data might be understood in terms of "the assimilation of one ego to another" in infantile identification with maternal ways of regulating emotional conflict. Clearly, Tremblay's data on chronic physical aggression might be understood in the same way—that is, as involving identification on the part of infants or children with parents in dysfunctional relationships, including their own hostile-coercive mothers. (And of course Anna Freud regarded identification with an aggressor as a particularly important mechanism of defence (see A. Freud, 1968).) We see something that may be related to this, and that is also related to what might be regarded as dysfunction in the family relation between child, mother, and father, in the cases of Sam and Kate discussed above.

Sam's mother behaved towards him in ways that might be considered as showing dissociated anger or hostility. Once when he was doing badly in an intellectual task, she:

> ... became visibly tense, her voice harsh. Sam's voice softened. His shoulders tensed as he said to his mother in a soft, pleading tone, "I don't know any more Mommy. I don't know any more, Mommy." His mother stared ahead and stilled for a full 42 seconds. Sam twisted his foot and arm, appearing anxious, and he repeated over and over in the same soft, pleading voice, "I don't know mummy", while leaning up against her and patting her knee

> several times to more her out of what appeared to be a dissociated state. Sam's mother did not respond at all .... (p. 137)

Again at fifty-six months his mother:

> ... asked Sam to bring over a box of dress-up clothes. She then proceeded to dress herself up ... asking Sam to help her, which he did. She said "I love this! How do I look?" When Sam just smiled, she took a duck puppet and made it bite his ear. (p. 137)

This last was a minor and playful bit of aggressive behaviour, and related to a kind of request for admiring flattery on the part of his mother that Sam was familiar with. Still her slightly aggressive response to not getting the kind of attention she wanted in this instance was the same that Sam had directed at Davy two months before, while seeming not to understand that it was unusual and unpleasant. And while Sam's mother might show hostility to him, he seems from early childhood to have directed his hostility elsewhere. While Sam was still disorganised in relating to his peers, he had settled strategies in relation to his parents. He attempted to control both of them, but his method was affectionate in relation to his mother, but hostile and punitive in relation to his father:

> At the family dinners observed when Sam was 44 and 56 months old ... while he was pleasing and caregiving towards his mother he was punitive and derogating towards his father. Sam and his mother ridiculed nearly everything his father said and did, speaking to him in a hostile and demeaning voice ... Many times during dinner, Sam's mother spoke to her husband through Sam, and Sam spoke to his father through his mother. Twice during dinner Sam ran over to whisper a secret in his mother's ear, and the two of them giggled. When Sam wanted something he asked his mother ... [using] a soft, sweet voice. In contrast, he made stern demands of his father, using a mocking, challenging, authoritarian tone ... "Don't you take that piece! It's for me!" (p. 141)

In this, Sam's identification with his mother, and hers with him, seems to have been enacted in an alliance to belittle his father. Each spoke to the father through the other, thus identifying him- or herself with the other in delivering the current message, whatever it happened to be. Something similar could be observed in Kate's family, but with father and daughter in alliance against Kate's mother:

> Kate's father said to Kate, "Mummy is trying to be so polite, eating her eggroll with a knife and fork. We don't do it that way, do we Kate?" Kate says "No!" and they both laugh derisively at her mother. Later Kate purposely opened her mouth full of chewed food to show her mother. Her mother said seriously "Don't show food." Her father smiled and said "Hey Kate show food!" He then said "Eww!" and laughed appreciatively at her display .... (p. 141)

Beatrice Beebe and her colleagues (2010) have demonstrated that disorganised attachment of the kind shown by Sam and Kate in the strange situation can be predicted from microanalyses of videos of mother–infant interactions from as early as the fourth month—that is, from the beginning of the change from the paranoid/schizoid to the depressive position discussed above. These reveal, among other things, a range of fleeting expressions of emotion on mothers' and infants' faces that include anger and fear, as well as others that might be hypothesised to contribute to later disorganisation or aggression. The ability to form such facial expressions seems to develop prior to birth, and independently of experience; and such expressions can be detected from early infancy, and are particularly evocative and imitable in face-to-face contact.[26] So this seems a plausible locus for the infant–mother identifications that will be apparent from something like twelve months, as well as for the incipient disorganisation that face-to-face interactions can be used to predict.

But as the vignettes above suggest, the disorganised infants' relationships with others develop within and are shaped by their parents' relations with one another. The infantile feelings of anger towards the mother, distress at separation and fear that were so prominent in the strange situation at eighteen months in Kate and Sam seem to have been shaped and focused as part of what Freud would have regarded as a triangular oedipal relationship. Although attachment research has not focused on the development of these aspects of early internal models, the general perspective of attachment gives such development a readily intelligible place in empirical developmental psychology.

A main thrust of attachment research has been to show how emotional relationships in infancy, beginning with those to the mother's breast, face, body and voice in the first months of life, serve for *learning*, and as *precursors* and *developmental bases* for behaviour in later relationships. This is consistent with the understanding of Kleinian phantasy in terms of unlearned modes of representation that enable infants to make sense of their postnatal experience of persons, as sketched above; and we should expect such early preparation and learning to extend to behaviour in relationships that contribute directly to later reproductive success, namely those of courting, mating, and procreation.

In this connection, and as we shall consider further below, we should remember that such reproductive relationships are systematically interwoven with aggression. Aggression between members of the same sex—males against males, and females against females—commonly plays a role in competition between members of the same sex for reproductive opportunities with members of the opposite sex, and in relation to the fate of offspring conceived in such relationships. Thus males of many species not only fight one another over reproductive access to females, but also kill the offspring of other males, the better to mate with their bereaved mothers. The same patterns also appear among females (e.g., with meerkats the dominant female kills the offspring of subordinate females).

Human patterns are far more socially cooperative but nonetheless show similar male-male and female-female rivalries for which we might expect the experience of emotion in infancy to provide preparation. Taking Kate and Sam's behaviour in play together with their alliances as shown at the dinner table, we can see something of how their initially disorganised infantile feelings seem to have developed in this respect. Both appear to have focused their early patterns of affection and aggression in accord with, and as preparation for, later adult patterns connected with courting, mating, and child-rearing. Each had formed an affectionate alliance as small but active partner of the (dominating) parent of the opposite sex, and a corresponding aggressive attachment to the parent of the same sex—as if in preparation for later relationships with members of the opposite sex and later rivalries with members of their own sex.

This cluster of object relationships seems also to have been enacted in their play as prospective members of reproductive partnerships in later life. Kate's play as a housewife with Trey, for example, suggests that her present alliance with her father in dominating her mother may also play a role in preparing her for adult relationships of domination and/or submission with later partners; and one might think likewise in considering Sam in his still disorganised play with Jenny and the doll she put into his care. Such connections, although not recorded in these cases, would be concordant with other research on the relation of infant and childhood attachments to later sexual and romantic relationships (see Berlin, Cassidy, & Appleyard, 2008; Feeney, 2008).

As these examples indicate, the relationship between mother and infant is only one factor—although one that may be partly measureable—in the generation of disorganised attachment and the coercive behaviour that often follows it. The same would seem to hold for the fostering of chronic physical aggression that Tremblay traces to family dysfunction and hostile-coercive parenting. If these forms of aggression in relationships can be taken to originate in identification with hostile or coercive mothers, or in the kinds of face-to-face mother–infant interactions that enable Beebe et al. to detect incipient disorganisation from the fourth or fifth month of life, this will be because the patterns of emotion discernable in these interactions are themselves supported and shaped, both earlier and later, by triangular relationships in the family.

Attachment and neuroscience

So far we have been linking aggression and sexuality—two main themes in Freud—with early emotional conflict via attachment. There seems a good prospect that connections made in this way will also be investigable by neuroscience, and in ways that link with a broadly psychoanalytic conception of the mind. For according to an increasingly influential view in neuroscience, human beings are born with their cerebral cortices as yet undeveloped, but with the subcortical neural mechanisms, now thought to generate motivation and consciousness, intact and ready to function, and wired for communicative expression in the baby's voice, face, and hands.

In consequence the infant's cerebral cortices, and the nascent systems of conceptual thought and memory realised in them (short- and long-term procedural memory, semantic memory, episodic experiential memory) develop under the impact of experience, including experience of the infant's already active emotions and the things and persons at which they are directed. Foremost among these, normally, are the infant's mother, and presumably also his own self, which requires to be learned about via perception and emotional interaction as do other things. So these relationships are begun in a context provided by the activation of the infant's subcortical mechanisms of motivation, and his mother's and hisown responses to these activations, from before the infant becomes able to think about his mother, himself, or the relationship between them that is already in train. The earliest and most basic memories may thus be the pre-conceptual embodied "memories in feeling" about oneself and others that Klein took to be active in infantile phantasy.

As a number of neuroscientists have observed,[27] these basic mechanisms correspond to what Freud described in terms of the drives, or again the part of the id that was present from birth. By contrast the role of the cerebral cortices, as the infant comes gradually to know him- or herself, mother, and their relationship, and so to regulate emotions accordingly, is that which Freud assigned to the ego. So we can say that as development proceeds, and the infant begins to gain voluntary control over bodily functions and activities, cerebral cortices come to stand as ego—as top-down integrator, conflict resolver, and regulator—to the infant's already active subcortical id. We have already seen the importance of the resolution of motivational conflict in attachment, and noted that infants seem initially to identify with their mothers in doing so, and perhaps by mechanisms that neuroscience is starting to specify. This accords with Freud's account of the ego as formed via identification; and if choices among possible courses of action are made by a process like affordance competition (see Cisek & Kalaska, 2010), then the resolution of conflict among desires rooted in the basic mechanisms will be intrinsic to decision itself.

In his early attempts at a neuroscience of motivation and emotion, Freud described the basic mechanisms of motivation as rooted in "endogenous stimuli" that "gave rise to the major needs ... hunger, respiration, sexuality" (Freud, 1950a[1895], p. 297). These "endogenous stimuli" are now often seen, in Antonio Damasio's phrase, as "part of a multi-tiered and evolutionarily set neural organization aimed at maintaining organismic homeostasis" (Damasio et al., 2000, p. 1049). The tiers include inbuilt mechanisms that generate distress at hunger, thirst, excessive heat or cold, lack of oxygen, or other situations that threaten basic bodily equilibrium; and also "emotional command systems" that generate motivated behaviour, as well as the conscious experience by which it is regulated. Research on these mechanisms has recently been collated, summarised and advanced by Jaak Panksepp in a number of influential publications.[28]

Watt and Panksepp (2009) describe these "prototype emotional regulatory systems" as "sitting over homeostasis proper (hunger, thirst, temperature regulation, pain, etc.)" and as "giving rise to attachment", which establishes "the massive regulatory-lynchpin system of the human brain", exercising "primary influence over the prototype systems below" (p. 93). As this entails, the cortex—or again the cortical ego—develops at first as a regulator of attachment, and thereby of the emotions and experiences involved in the process. The same basic systems seem to generate the subcortical components of emotion and consciousness in all mammals,[29] and Panksepp describes them in capital letters to indicate their status as subcortical and experimentally defined, and hence also their status as prior to the working of the cortex, which in the course of development comes increasingly to regulate them. But as the cortical ego enlarges its role over the course of development—so that the generation of desire and action is increasingly regulated by learning and memory as these are routinised and distributed throughout the cortex—the role of the basic mechanisms becomes progressively more complex and less salient.[30]

The main systems include generators for the "negative" affects of RAGE (related to anger and affective attack), FEAR (related to fear, freezing, flight), and SEPARATION DISTRESS/PANIC/GRIEF (hereafter SPG, and related to onsets of panic as well as distress at separation, grief in loss of attachment and mourning, and also to the pain of social exclusion, social loss, and depression), and to the "positive" affects of LUST (related to sexuality, courting, and copulation), PLAY (related to mammalian play, and human social pleasure and enjoyment more generally) and CARE (maternal and paternal nurturance, and the infant's or child's actions or identifications that accord with these). These are integrated with a general SEEKING system, which drives foraging and exploration, and (given cortical guidance in the form of desire) reward-anticipating intentional action.

These systems have built-in relations of competition and co-activation, and so can conflict with one another, or again work in harmony. Thus RAGE and FEAR tend to be partly co-activating, as they prepare for both fight and flight; but are also partly competitive, as the balance between fight or flight is determined. Likewise SPG tends to activate RAGE and FEAR, preparing a separated creature for the worst, but can also deactivate SEEKING, producing a depression-like motivational inertia. Similarly FEAR and RAGE compete with PLAY, whereas SEEKING, PLAY and CARE may all be components of interactions between parents and offspring. Also of course, SPG operates to keep parents and offspring, or again (more or less monogamous) parents together, and so, despite the painfulness of activation, regulates LUST as well as CARE, and thereby attachment generally. They can be activated either by the exteroceptive sensory systems (such as sight, touch, or hearing), or again by the interoceptive systems that monitor the interior of the body.

This role of these systems in relation to attachment emerges particularly clearly in Ainsworth's strange situation, for every phase in the procedure—from the exploration (SEEKING) and play (PLAY) with which it begins, through to the anxiety (FEAR) produced by the entrance of the stranger, the angry protest (RAGE) of the infant at the mother's impending departure, the anxiety endured (SPG together with RAGE and FEAR) while she is away, and the relief (from SPG, RAGE, and FEAR) produced by her return, which otherwise remains in opposition to the evoking and receiving of CARE, and therefore also to the infant's return exploration (SEEKING) and play (PLAY)—keyed to one or more of the subcortical systems Panksepp describes. This consilience was of course unknown to Bowlby, and to Ainsworth when she devised the strange situation, and it remains unknown to researchers uninterested in neuroscience. But it suggests that in setting out to test psychoanalytic ideas experimentally, Ainsworth was particularly prescient.

In less complex animals the activation of these systems can be total and frightening, as indicated by Panksepp's description of stimulating the RAGE system in a cat. Within seconds the cat:

> ... lept viciously towards me with claws unsheathed, fangs bared, hissing and spitting. It could have pounced in many different directions but its arousal was directed right at my head. Fortunately a Plexiglas wall separated me from the enraged beast. Within a fraction of a minute after terminating the stimulation the cat was again relaxed and peaceful, and could be petted .... (Panksepp, 1998, p. 194)

In our far more social and cooperative species, however, and as between parent and child, they clearly serve the complex social functions. Thus Vasudevi Reddy describes an experience known to many a parent:

> Shamani ... had become hungry quickly and had wanted another feeding for some time. At first Shamani remained quiet, then became restless, and then, after some fussing, she frowned. Then she yelled—a furious-sounding shout. Louder in volume than any other vocalization I had heard, and clearly filled with rage. Then she made no other sound, although the look on her face remained angry. I was taken aback, and felt almost guilty. (Reddy & Trevarthan, 2004, p. 11)

Shamani was a five-week-old baby, who may already have begun the rhythmic face-to-face interactions of turn-taking smiling, vocalisation and mutual recognition that developmental psychologists call "proto-conversations", and so was already aware of her mother's caring presence. So by this time she will have learnt how the expression of anger can serve as a mother-mobilising form of communication.[31] Reddy describes this kind of interaction as familiar between her and Shamani at six weeks, when she saw how upset Shamani became when she interrupted such an exchange with a still face.

> In the midst of a good smiley "chat", when she was lying on the bed and I was leaning over her, I stopped, with my face pleasant but immobile, and continued looking at her. She tried to smile a bit, then looked away, then looked back at me and tried to chat, then looked away again. After maybe 30 seconds I couldn't stand it any longer and, smiling, I leaned forward and hugged her, saying "Oh you poor thing!" At this, she suddenly started crying ... I was shocked, and very moved. I didn't know she cared. Neither reading about [still face] research, nor even subsequently watching Lynne Murray's videos of still face experience, told me quite as much as this experience. (Reddy & Trevarthan, 2004, p. 11)

As Reddy says:

> If you allow yourself to be similarly engaged by a 2-month infant—especially an infant whom you know well and who knows you—it is impossible to resist becoming involved and talkative. It is impossible, then, to doubt the baby's communicative intent, or to argue that the baby's acts merely *appear* to be responses to yours. We cannot assume that the babies' actions are merely some kind of biologically programmed reflex behavior lacking appropriate feelings.

> Similarly we cannot assume that the baby is merely appreciating and testing the "mechanical" contingency of your behavior in time, with no appreciation for its affective or companionable content. (Reddy & Trevarthan, 2004, p. 12, their italics)

Interactions like these, and also the more complex examples of social behaviour discussed by Reddy in the article from which these quotations are taken, may make it more understandable that research such as that reported by Beebe et al. (2010) should detect signs of incipient disorganisation—and hence of the later need to control others, as was shown by Sam and Kate—in face-to-face exchanges between mother and baby during the fourth month. But then in the case of a newborn baby, who has as yet no such experience of interactive communication and the forms of homeostatic and emotional relief they can bring, we should expect more primitive expressions not only of RAGE but also of FEAR and SPG, as a newborn's particularly riveting and compelling cry seems to contain.

This is because alerting the mother's CARE system is a continual matter of life and death for the helpless human infant, not only in the period immediately after birth, but over the whole of the first year and beyond. The expression of such basic "negative" emotions, and in their earliest and rawest form, would seem to be the newborn infant's only way—particularly in the case of a preoccupied or inattentive parent—of coercing or compelling the nutrition, comfort and other expressions of maternal CARE without which he or she would waste and die. This is presumably also why infants are so upset by an unresponsive face, as Reddy found to her surprise. (And her responses to her own child's distress indicate how, even in mild instances, the infant's arousal of care can cause anxiety, guilt and remorse in a mother, as presumably evolution has shaped it to do.) The baby's nascent awareness of these contingencies, and its utter dependence on maternal care and solicitude, show even earlier than Reddy records, since the baby begins to connect mother's face and voice, and visual and tactile input from her breast and body, from almost immediately after birth; and by two or three months a baby is acutely distressed, evincing what seems an early version of a later fear of strangers, in experiments in which it encounter's mother's face but speaking with another's voice (on this see Carpenter, 1975, p. 134).

The infant's other means of securing these resources is via the activation of the systems Panksepp describes in terms of SEEKING, PLAY, and LUST, and so engaging the mother via the sort of affectionate (and in the case of sucking at the breast, often intensely sensual) interactions that Reddy describes in terms of protoconversation above. But then, as this makes clear, the inevitable early activation of *all* the systems of basic emotion—positive and negative alike—towards one and the same person, the nursing and caring mother, must constitute a source of emotional conflict that is inherent in the long and helpless infancy of our species.

This seems particularly clear in the context of attachment, for the conflicts aroused in the strange situation put RAGE, FEAR and SPG into conflict with evoking and accepting CARE, and with it SEEKING and PLAY. The former are components and precursors of later hatred and enmity, and the latter, together with LUST, are components and precursors of later affection, nurturance, and love. These are clearly the kinds of conflicts that will be important in later life. We have already seen, as exemplified in Sam and Kate, how these precursors may be transformed in the family into post-disorganised strategies of control. Thus Sam and Kate co-operated with their parent of the opposite sex, were in control of their parent of the same sex, but were controlling or hostile to playmates of the opposite sex. Similar precursors, as shaped by parental dysfunction and hostile-coercive parenting, were also predictors of chronic physical aggression.

The basic mechanisms and clinical psychoanalysis

We can also see the working of these mechanisms—and the conflicts among them—in clinical data. For example, the particular emotion of distress at separation, and the anger this was liable to arouse, played an important role in Freud's patient the Rat Man (Freud, 1909d). In his preliminary consultation with Freud, this patient described "compulsive impulses to cut his throat with a razor" and mentioned also his "impulse to commit a crime against the lady he venerates" (Hawelka & Hawelka, 1974, p. 1).[32] As Freud recorded, "this impulse [to commit a crime] remains silent when she is present; it arises in her absence"—that is, his impulse to commit a crime against his lady, like the angry protests and crying of infants in the strange situation, seemed to originate in his angry distress at his object of attachment leaving him alone. Again in the Rat Man's eighth session (Freud, 1909d, p. 260) he described how when his lady went away to visit her grandmother he received an imaginary command to cut his own throat, and as he went to get his razor to carry this out he received another command, saying "No it's not as simple as that: you must kill the old woman". As in the case of his impulses to commit a crime against his lady, these impulses to kill himself, and then to kill the old woman he took to be responsible for his lady's absence, seem to have arisen from his distress at separation. In Freud's account the impulses showed first the anger against himself and then the anger against the old woman that the separation roused in him.

This cluster of emotions was tacitly emphasised by Klein (e.g., in her emphasis on interpreting the analysand's reactions to separations at weekends and holidays), and also in attachment research, where protest at separation from the mother, and the grief-like pain of missing her and fearing her loss (as well as mourning, depression, etc., related to this), were part of Bowlby's original framework for understanding the role of attachment over the lifetime. As realised by Panksepp's SPG, which is liable in turn to activate both RAGE and FEAR, these emotions play a role that seems to accord with the general idea of a cortical ego regulating subcortical drives that we have been considering.

The same emotions were particularly clear in Elyn Saks' case, in what Kleinian analysis would regard as her infantile transference to her analyst. As her analysis progressed her psychotic thoughts grew more violent during her sessions, and her relationship to her analyst became suffused with three partly contradictory currents of imagination and feeling, in which we can recognise the triad of RAGE, FEAR, and SPG, and in conflict with CARE, as described in connection with both the strange situation and Panksepp's neuroscience above. So, for example, Saks (2008) associated to her analyst: "You are an evil monster … a witch … you are trying to kill me … Don't cross me. I've killed hundreds of thousands of people with my thoughts …" (p. 97). Or again she thought to herself: "She is evil and dangerous … She is a monster. I must kill her, or threaten her, to stop her doing evil things to me" (p. 98).

The closer Saks felt to her analyst the more terrified she became. She perused shops for weapons, and for a period brought a box-cutter or serrated knife to her sessions (which of course she never had occasion to use). As with the appearance of the superego in Freud's dream, we could hardly ask for clearer evidence of emotions related to Panksepp's systems of RAGE and FEAR, as related to malevolence projected into the figure of the analyst, and in this, again, comparable to the lack of conscientiousness projected into Otto in Freud's dream. But this was also regulated by emotions related to SPG, and in relation to what Saks regarded as a profound and healing form of CARE:

> At the very same time as I was terrified of Mrs. Jones, I was equally terrified that I was going to lose her, so much so that I could barely tolerate weekends when I would not see her for two days. I would start to unravel on Thursday and be nearly inconsolable until Tuesday. In the intervening time it took everything I had to protect myself ... all the while plotting ways to keep Mrs. Jones from abandoning me. *I will kidnap her and keep her tied up in my closet. I will take good care of her ... She will always be there to give me psychoanalysis ...* her steady and calm presence contained me, as if she were the glue that held me together. I was falling apart, flying apart, exploding—and she gathered my pieces and held me. (Saks, 2008, pp. 97–98, italics in original)

As well as providing examples of the kinds of conflicting emotions activated in the strange situation, and of Panksepp's RAGE, FEAR and SPG in conflict with the receipt of CARE, Saks' phantasies instantiate the kind of conflicting motives directed at one and the same person, originally a parent, that Freud hypothesised to be formative for the superego, and also active in neurosis and psychosis. Also they exemplify the states of mind that Klein described in terms of the paranoid/schizoid and depressive positions, in which the same person (originally, in Klein's account, the mother, or the part of her that was the most important early sensory focus, her breast) is felt either as extremely bad and threatening or as extremely helpful, good and liable to be lost owing to one's own aggression. So on their hypotheses—as indicated by Freud's remarks on the regressive fragmentation of the superego/ego-ideal in schizophrenia—the passage from depression to schizophrenia considered earlier would represent a reversal of the process by which the self-condemning part of herself manifest in her depression was originally formed.

On this kind of account the gathering together of her fragmenting self that Saks gratefully ascribed to her analyst would represent a partial reworking in the present of basic processes of integrating the self that take place during the initial consolidation of attachment between an infant with its mother (and other carers) in the first year of life. Likewise, the pain of separation that Saks found so intolerable at weekends, and the grief and phantasies of control that it evoked, would partly repeat those of an infantile self-suffering SPG, threatened with the loss of the parental presence that seemed the source life and coherence for the self. On these points attachment theory and Panksepp's attachment-related neuroscience would seem broadly consilient with Kleinian (and other Post-Freudian) claims.

The hypothesised reactivation of infantile conflicts in Saks' transference, and the consequent extension of the role of her cortical ego in regulating them, seems to have been therapeutic. Although she remained liable to hallucinatory presences, she found that as she:

> … became accustomed [in analysis] to spooling out the strange products of my mind my paranoia began to shift … the actual daily people in my comings and goings seemed less scary and more approachable … slowly I made one friend, then two … I began to move back into the world again … Blinking and shaky (as though I'd been in a cave, and the light, as welcome as it was, was something I had to get used to) I began to move back into the world again. (Saks, 2008, pp. 93–94)

Also it seems that such a result might fit with the recent work in the neuroscience of dreaming and memory we noted above. If we suppose—as Hobson and Friston (2012; Hobson, Hong & Friston 2014) hypothesise, and as is extensively borne out in Cartwright (2010) and more recent literature on memory consolidation—that the powerful emotional activations and vivid hallucinatory experiences of REM dreams serve to consolidate memory and optimise the models of the world by which we live, then we should also consider that the emotions and fictitious experience involved in mental disorders may arise from the same processes. This hypothesis—that emotional activation and fictitious experience in mental disorder result from attempts at consolidation, optimisation and complexity reduction on the part of a disordered brain—would explain the extensive similarities between dreams and mental disorder noted above.

In these terms the projective reduction of guilt and conflict with the superego that seems to have taken place in Freud's dream could be seen as one form of simplifying optimisation; another, Saks' projective transition from painful internal conflict to externalised conflict with shadowy presences; a third, the arousal and reconsolidation of early memories and conflicts in her analysis. Although this claim is now speculative, it indicates the kind of theoretical unification in accord with Freudian claims that current neuroscientific hypotheses might support.

Evolution

We have noted that Freud's division of the mind into ego, superego and id seems to correspond with the notion of an action-directing and conflict-resolving cortical ego, as recently elaborated via neuroscience. We have also noted that emotional conflicts involving deep sources of motive such as RAGE, FEAR and SPG seem a natural liability of human infancy. Deep connections of this kind suggest that the types of emotional conflict considered in psychoanalysis may have roots in the same evolutionary processes that have lengthened the helpless period of human infancy while enlarging the cortically immature brains that are shaped by experiences of attachment over its protracted course. And as regards evolutionary sources of conflict, psychoanalysis indicates an obvious place to look.

Hostility to siblings and parental sexuality

From the time Freud wrote *The Interpretation of Dreams* (Freud, 1900a) he argued that everyday rivalries between brothers and sisters were underlain by deeper unconscious hostilities. This was later borne out by Klein's analyses of children, who often played out astonishingly hostile phantasies towards siblings, but in the context of intense hostility directed at the mother and father and their sexual and procreative relationship (for recent discussions see Edwards (2011) and Mitchell (2003)).

We can illustrate this by some clinical material, starting with an example from Klein's (1932) work with a girl of six, who was anxious, depressed, and obsessional. She expressed her depression by brooding with a suffering expression, saying sadly that "there is something about life that I don't like" (p. 67). She defended herself from such feelings, among other ways, by the excitement of masturbating, which she did in front of strangers and almost continuously at her kindergarten. She regarded her mother as fond of her, never criticised her, and was, if anything, overly affectionate towards her. But a quite different aspect of her feelings emerged in her play. Thus in her first session:

> Erna began her play by taking a small carriage which stood on the table and letting it run next to me. She declared she had come to fetch me. But she put a toy woman in the carriage and added a toy man. The two loved and kissed one another and drove up and down all the time. Then a toy man in another carriage collided with them, ran over and killed them, and then roasted them and ate them up. (Klein, 1932, p. 67)

Here the man and woman who loved and kissed one another, and in consequence were killed, roasted, and eaten up, could be identified as the parents.[33] The same theme showed more explicitly in other material, as the child re-expressed the preoccupations with which she began. For example, Erna played a queen who married a king, and when she:

> ... had celebrated her marriage to the king, she lay down on the sofa and wanted me [Mrs. Klein], as king, to lie down beside her. As I refused to do this I had to sit on a little chair by her side instead and knock at the sofa with my fist. This she called 'churning' ... Immediately after this she announced that a child was creeping out of her, and she represented the scene in a quite realistic way, writhing about and groaning. Her imaginary child then shared its parents' bedroom and had to be a spectator of sexual intercourse between them. If it interrupted it was beaten ... If she, as mother, put the child to bed it was only in order to get rid of it and to be united with the father all the sooner. (Klein, 1932, p. 71)

Freud often described how the parents are represented in dreams by Kings and Queens. Here Klein understood her little patient as using the same symbolism, to represent her phantasies about parental intercourse. Since her ideas about this were immature and incomplete, she represented it by the parents lying in bed with something knocking, and "churning"; and she represented the connection between intercourse and pregnancy by giving birth immediately after the "churning" had taken place. In this, however, she represented herself and her parents as in deep conflict about sex and procreation, with her mother constantly neglecting and abusing her to get on with making babies. Thus conflict about procreation had affected her attitude towards her parents, and towards people in general, in a deep and pervasive way. As Klein recorded:

> Erna often made me [Klein] be a child while she was a mother or teacher. I then had to undergo fantastic tortures and humiliations. If in the game anyone treated me kindly, it generally turned out that the kindness was only simulated. The paranoid traits showed in the fact that I was constantly spied upon, people divined my thoughts, and the father or teacher allied with the mother against me—in fact, I was always surrounded by persecutors. I myself, in the role of the child, had constantly to spy on and torment the others. Often Erna herself played the child. Then the game generally ended in her escaping the persecutions (on these occasions the "child" was good), becoming rich and powerful, being made a queen and taking a cruel revenge on her persecutors. (Klein, 1929, pp. 199–200)

In her hostility to parental intercourse Erna was characteristic of most psychoanalytic patients. Freud (1895) had recorded the impact of this on his patients from the beginning of his clinical practice, when a patient had told him "how I came by my attacks of anxiety when I was a girl ... I saw my father get into bed with my mother and heard sounds that greatly excited me. It was then that my attacks came on" (p. 127). Later he described it as "the primal scene", and came to regard it as a topic of universal "primal phantasies" that were important sources of psychological disturbance. We can see another example in what Freud described as "a turning point" in his analysis of the Rat Man (Freud, 1909d).[34] This came after he had become very anxious about the way his free associations brought sexual and aggressive thoughts about Freud and his family. Despite Freud's reassurances, he felt that Freud would "turn him out" for reporting these thoughts. (Freud's actual attitude seems to have been quite different: when the Rat Man reported imaging copulating with Freud's daughter "by means of a stool hanging from his anus" Freud recorded this as a "wonderful anal phantasy" (p. 287).)

At one point he became so anxious that he got up off the couch, as if he feared remaining near Freud, and walked around the room. As Freud (1909d) recorded the episode in his notes from the time:

> He agreed that his walking about the room while he was making these confessions was because he was afraid of being beaten by me. The reason he had alleged was delicacy of feeling—that he could not lie comfortably there while he was saying these dreadful things to me. Moreover, he kept hitting himself while he was making these admissions which he still found so difficult.
>
> "Now you'll turn me out." It was a question of a picture of me and my wife in bed with a dead child lying between us. He knew the origin of this. When he was a little boy (age uncertain, perhaps 5 or 6) he was lying between his father and mother and wetted the bed, upon which his father beat him and turned him out. The dead child can only be his sister Katherine, he must have gained by her death. The scene occurred, as he confirmed, after her death.
>
> His demeanour during all this was that of a man in desperation and one who was trying to save himself from blows of terrific violence; he buried his head in his hands, rushed away, covered his face with his arm, etc. He told me that his father had a passionate temper, and then did not know what he was doing. (p. 284)

The patient had previously told Freud that all his childhood he had been terribly afraid of blows, and was grateful for his father for never having beaten him, at least so far as he could remember. So it seems that in this episode he recovered a previously repressed memory—and one inconsistent with the conscious image he had previously maintained—of his father as a fearsome punisher, beating him for fouling the parental bed. The particular image that went with the Rat Man's memory was one of Freud and his wife in bed with a dead child between them. Freud related this to his rivalry with his sister, who had died before this time. And his fears had mounted because of other images of Freud's family that related to childbearing. In the session prior to remembering his punishment he had told Freud about imagining:

> My [Freud's] mother's body naked. Two swords sticking into her breast (like a decoration, he said later …). The lower part of her body and especially her genitals had been eaten up by me and the children … The two swords were the Japanese ones of his dreams: marriage and copulation. (pp. 282–283)

This imagined attack on the mother's organs of procreation—including special and sexualised violence (stabbing by the patient's own swords, representing marriage and copulation) to the breast—was a variant of the anal attack the Rat Man regularly imagined on his father, with Freud and his children in place of the rats (or alternatively, with the Rat Man's hostile sexual and aggressive feelings projected into them in his phantasy). This version is comparable to the hostile phantasies Klein's little patients regularly played out, as when Erna imagined the parental couple killed and eaten, for loving and kissing one another and driving up and down all the time. Freud did not report this material in his case history, but it illustrates the kind of continuity of data and hypotheses mentioned earlier in connection with projection and projective identification in his Irma dream.

Here again, however we may suppose Freud's hypotheses to have influenced the Rat Man we cannot take data such as this as produced to confirm them. And in the instances we have been considering, the data are related to a potentially deeper source of consilience between psychoanalysis on the one hand, and attachment and neuroscience on the other. Evolutionary biologists have come to recognise that aggressive attitudes towards parental procreation, as well as hostility towards siblings, may be predicted by Darwinian theory; and these topics have recently been discussed in terms of the interrelated notions of parental investment, sexual conflict, and parent-offspring conflict.[35]

Evolutionary conflict and emotional conflict

Some relations among these concepts are depicted in the diagram below, which is based on that of Mock and Parker (1997, p. 41). The developmental arrow at the right has been added for the present discussion. In considering these forms of conflict we move away from individual psychology to the very different theoretical framework of natural selection. The notions of sexual conflict and parent-offspring conflict are specified in terms of probabilities for the replications of genes. The notion of parental investment is intended to encompass the provision by a parent of anything that contributes to the thriving of a particular offspring where this is done at a cost to the parent in contributing to the thriving of any other offspring (or at a cost to the parent's fitness more generally). This means that parental investment coincides with whatever activities on the part of that parental genome contribute to its replication in one child as opposed to any other, and hence to its overall effect on parental fitness as this would be measured in genetic terms. In

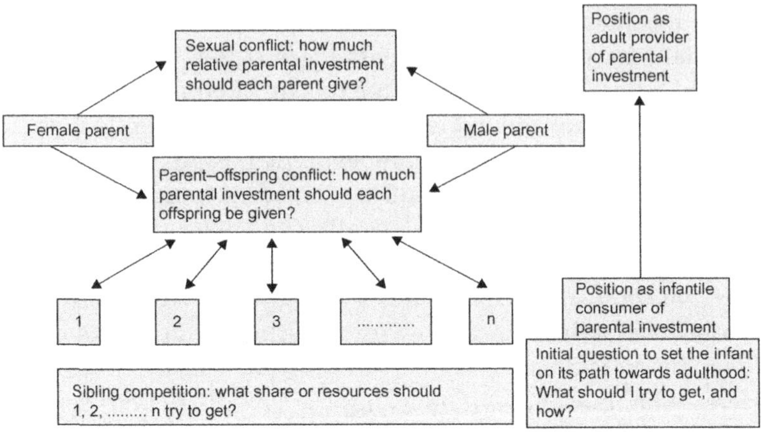

Figure 3. Relationships between parental investment, sexual conflict, and parent–offspiring conflict. Adapted from Mock, D. and Parker, A. (1997). *The Evolution of Sibling Rivalry*, p. 41 © 1997, Oxford Univeresity Press, with permission.

this broad role, the genes are hypothesised to function so as to yield a co-evolving pattern of adaptation and counter-adaptation that encompasses both physiology and psychology, such as the conflicts around weaning that are to be observed between mothers and infants.

So, for example, the working of these conflicts can apparently be observed from conception, in the invasion of the mother's body by the placenta. This organ is constructed via the activity of the father's genome to extract maternal investment on behalf of the fetus, and discount, in accord with the abilities of fathers to invest elsewhere, other children the mother might have. The placenta has thus evolved as "a ruthless parasitic organ existing solely for the maintenance and protection of the fetus, perhaps too often to the disregard of the maternal organism" (Hrdy, 2000, p. 433). In this it bores into the mother's blood vessels, secreting hormones that raise her blood pressure and sugars in ways that benefit the fetus but may injure her. The mother's body, in turn, has evolved to produce hormones that counteract these; and so on. In this we can see how sexual conflict between the genes of the parents, as carried forward in countervailing physiological adaptations over many generations, takes the form of physiological conflict between a pregnant mother and her unborn child (for further discussion see Haig, (1993, pp. 495–532)).

The physiological investment of females in many species—and particularly in mammals—evidently outweighs that of males. By contrast with the work of a female, who carries offspring in the womb, gives birth to them, and feeds them by producing milk for months afterwards, what males do, and even more what they can get away with doing, seems paltry. Even the most dedicated of human fathers often invest in their offspring by working to provide opportunities for others to provide hands- and mind-on care, and these others are often women.

Female fecundity and rate of reproduction thus sets a limit to the reproductive success of males, which the latter often try overcome by reproducing with more than one female partner. As this indicates, where the nature of parental investment systematically differs between reproductive partners, so too must many aspects of reproductive behaviour related to it—the partner's (conscious or unconscious) strategies in courting and choosing those with whom they mate, the conditions in which they would attempt or avoid intercourse, the ways they view conception and pregnancy, their attitudes towards rearing children once they are born, and so forth.

Such differences generate sexual conflict, for they entail that different patterns of behaviour, or different motivational structures that produce such patterns, will result in the replication of a mother's, as opposed to a father's, genes (thus see Gegestand (2007), chapter 23). So if female reproduction limits that of males, we should expect males to compete for access to females, and so to advertise themselves, fight among themselves, etc., in order to obtain it. Likewise, if females must incur unavoidable greater costs in investing than males, they have more to lose in indiscriminate mating, and more to gain by careful choice—say in the likely capacity for cooperation in parental investment, or again simply in the genetic quality, of those with whom they mate. So, and as in many other species, human females tend to copulate more selectively than males, at least when pregnancy is a possible outcome. This pits female selectivity against male opportunism in the forms of sexual conflict that are still referred to as the battle of the sexes.

Part of this battle stems from the fact that there are many circumstances in which it is in the genetic interests of either member of a reproductive partnership to shift the burden of investment to the other. These are a familiar source of domestic discord. Also, either partner can secretly invest with someone else, and to the disadvantage of the other. This gives rise to infidelity, deceit, betrayal, and as these indicate, both men and women can shift investment to future offspring, where the future can include other reproductive partners. The means for this include the abandonment of partners and children, as practised by men who leave to set up another family, and occasionally also by women, although in this case a reason for abandonment is often anger at the failure of the male partner to do his share.

Limitations in parental investment set the stage for sibling rivalry, which we see even in domestic pets. Newborn kittens or puppies often crowd one another out in getting to the mother's teats, and some ("the runt of the litter") are disadvantaged, or even die, as a result. Likewise, as the evolutionary literature reports, some pigs are born with tusks to slash competitors for sucking, birds in the nest peck weaker siblings to death, bird parents toss superfluous nestlings away, and so on (for examples and discussion see Mock & Parker (1997) and Mock (2005)). Sand tiger sharks are particularly impressive in this respect. The female has two uteruses, and economises parental investment by providing the fetuses in each only themselves to eat. The siblings accordingly devour each other until only a single pair remains, each safe from the other in their separate domains of conquest. After this prenatal compression of development and learning they are born into the sea, as well-nourished and practised predators (see Eilperin, 2012).

Parental investment and sibling rivalry take very different forms in human beings, for we are born into the seas of the family and other social groups. Our "group-oriented hypersocial" species naturally shares out the burden of infant care, with kin such as grandparents, uncles, aunts, and elder cousins often taking part; parents in different families exchanging help with one another, and other helpers available via other exchanges. In this as in many other things we cooperate far more extensively than other primates, who generally do not allow others even to hold their infants; and the fact that grandparents provide resources that enable their grandchildren to survive, thereby assisting the carrying of longevity-promoting genes into a third generation, may be among the causes of our increased span of life.

Still this cooperation is underlain by conflict. In hard times—as seem often to have obtained in human history—the disposal of one child may be an important means to ensuring the survival, or alternatively the later conception, of others. This gives rise to abortion, infanticide, orphanage and other kinds of abandonment, as well as many forms of selective neglect. These practices reflect parent-offspring conflict—conflict between the interests of the genes of parents, as opposed to those of their offspring, who may be neglected, abandoned, or killed.

Although we tend steadily to ignore the possibility of such conflict, it is often not far from the surface. The demands of feeding and caring for a baby are so great that they cannot be met by a lone mother, or even by a single couple, in the absence of help from others. Given the precariousness of motherhood, these seem to be alternatives that people who live by hunting and gathering, or near subsistence levels for other reasons, must often have to consider; and they seem to have a natural place in maternal psychology. Even in contemporary affluent societies the number of babies abandoned, or left anonymously at hospitals or orphanages, is liable to increase with unemployment or recession. Sarah Blaffer Hrdy has long stressed the evolutionary importance for babies of being able to evoke love and care (see Hrdy, 2000, 2009), and I have been urging the importance of their also being able to coerce it by rage, pain, and the infliction of anxiety, guilt, and remorse. From the perspective of the infant, securing parental investment is in part a continual matter of life and death.

Like sexual conflict, parent-offspring conflict seems intrinsic to sexual reproduction. Evolution prepares infants to secure a maximum of parental investment for themselves, as was illustrated by the way infants' early natural expressions of emotion elicit investment via both affectionate cooperation and angry coercion. But evolution also adapts parents to apportion investment over more than one offspring, lest their genotypes pass less than a single copy into the next generation. So newborns seem fated naturally to seek more in the way of parental investment than parents are naturally prepared to give—and at the expense of siblings, whether actual or only potential.

A newborn's parents are also subject to sexual conflict, even from shortly after birth. The genetic interests of a father are likely to be served by getting the mother pregnant again quickly, since males in general have been able easily to invest elsewhere. By contrast the genetic interests of a mother—her body having been given over to housing this particular infant during months of prenatal development, the resources for which have been provided at physiological loss to herself, and then gone through the wear and tear of giving birth—are likely to be best served by getting this particular and already costly infant well established, and allowing her body to recover and repair itself; and this would be better for this particular infant as well.

In this, evolution has cast its lot with the interests of newborn infants and their mothers by binding them in the relationship of nursing. This activity is contraceptive, and so aligns the genetic interests of mother and baby against those of the father, at least until after the baby is weaned. This, however, means that by sucking at the breast—beginning the first and most formative of its emotional relationships, and one that is both pleasurable and life-giving—the infant perforce casts itself as the mother's ally, and the father's opponent, in sexual conflict; and likewise that by nursing and sustaining her infant, the mother becomes its ally in preventing the conception of rival siblings. (On the role of nursing, and such factors as intensity of nursing and metabolic load see Ellison (2001), particularly Chapter Four.)

We have seen that the infant's use of incompatible emotions in securing parental investment early in life naturally puts him or her at risk of later emotional conflict; but emotions related to affection on the one hand, and hostility on the other, would seem to unite in opposition to the production of rivals. Infants (and little children) stand to increase their share of parental investment by using their abilities to engage their parents affectionately, or again to coerce them by rage, fear, or SPG, in a single simple way—that is, in any emotional or other manipulation that makes it less likely that the parents will conceive another child. Any such disposition to limit further parental reproduction would apparently render infants more likely to secure parental investment for themselves, and so more likely to reproduce in their turn, and so to perpetuate that disposition together with others of the same kind.

These dispositions would be continuous with, and successors of, the conception-preventing rivalry with both the father and potential siblings that infants enact in nursing at the breast. Freud regarded nursing as part of establishing "the first and strongest love-object and as the prototype of all later love-relations—for both sexes" (Freud, 1940a, p. 188). Darwinian theory, it seems, obliges us also to recognise it as the first prototype of unknowing engagement in sexual, parent-offspring and sibling conflict.

Reflecting on parent-offspring, Trivers remarked that "all the machinations Freud imagined going on in early life had a reality … which I had formerly disbelieved …" (cited in Hrdy, 2000, p. 430) and he was later to develop an account of self-knowledge according to which we systematically deceive ourselves about our own desires and intentions in order better to deceive others. Yet despite the findings of attachment research, neither he nor other evolutionary psychologists have faced the implications of this idea—and the kind of early formative and pervasive suppression of self-understanding that might be involved—in the context of the first year of life. If Trivers had considered that the attitudes that the infant had naturally to suppress in order to deceive others might include those involving the direction of sensual affection, as well as RAGE, FEAR and SPG towards the mother and father during the first year of life, his account might well have resembled the psychoanalytic ones we have been considering.

So I think that taking explicit account of these evolutionary conflicts may enable us to better understand why the infant's relation to the mother at the breast is regarded as the inception of the developments that Freud described in terms of the oedipus complex, and also the far-reaching significance that these have in human life. There is good reason to hold that infants have precursors of adult sexual experience (in addition to their observable oral and anal pleasures, male babies are capable of erection, females of vaginal lubrication, and both of what seems to be orgasm without ejaculation (Gray, 2013)). But the development of the cortex seems to combine and distribute the basics of motivation over the whole range of our actions and projects, and in such a way that assigning an intrinsically sexual or non-sexual nature to any activity or experience becomes at best a matter of degree.

Freud was one of the first to draw attention to the spreading and blending of sexual significance in the form of sexual symbolism, which as noted above can often be understood as conceptual metaphor.[36] It has been made clearer by work in evolutionary psychology, which indicates how much of everyday life involves the signalling of information (or again forms of false advertising) relevant to procreation (see, for example, Seabright, 2012, Chapter Three). But the same spreading means that the deeper importance of sensual experience in nursing and attachment pertain to a very wide range of effects throughout infants' more general dispositions to affection and cooperation, as opposed to hostility and conflict, as these develop over the course of life in our ultrasocial group cooperative, and often violently group-conflicting species.

As the arrow inserted at the right of the diagram above illustrates, we can see individual development as involving a transition from infantile to adult positions in respect of parental investment and sexual and parent-offspring conflict. Although the infant may start postnatal as a thoughtless placenta-like extractor of parental investment on its own behalf, and regardless of others, this situation changes very rapidly with development. By the end of the first year it has become a fully conscious, cooperative, thinking and soon-to-be-speaking member of a family, whose aggression has already come to be regulated in interactions with its mother or other carers. Regulation of this kind will enable infants, as Tremblay says, to "learn not to aggress" (unduly) in later childhood, and so to negotiate later sexual and other conflicts to become mature and relatively unselfish providers of parental investment to children of their own.

From the perspective of both evolution and attachment, this seems one of the most significant of human psychological developments. This in turn suggests that we should consider how the infant's early experiences of parental investment, sexual conflict and sibling rivalry are used during development to prepare him or her for later conflicts of the same kinds—and hence for conscious choices not just about killing or stealing but also about truth and realism as opposed to phantasy and deception in courting, in what circumstances and with whom to have sex, when and with whom to seek or risk conception, and whether and how the needs of children will be met.

Choices of these kinds involve the moral conflicts that Freud took to be regulated by the superego/ego-ideal, and so by guilt and shame; and his analysis of his dream, like Saks' experience of psychosis, enables us to see something of the internal working of this regulation and how it extends beyond the family. Even the few associations we considered above provide a glimpse as to how Freud's feelings about his own daughters were extended outside the family to his patients and friends, and others show the same for the rivalries he experienced in childhood. So we see small but real mental particulars of the working not only of projection as this imaginarily dissociates Freud from Otto, but also of identification (this Mathilde with that Mathilde) as this linked members of morally comparable groups (children and patients) in Freud's unconscious mind.

As this indicates, the infant's development from consumer to provider of parental investment is also one of moral character;[37] and the same range of conflicts that determine madness or sanity (as shown in the material from Saks above) are also those with which morality is concerned (and one of the most striking parts of Saks' disorder was her imaginary fascination with killing babies, as apparently derived from early sibling rivalry). If the line of thought we have been following is correct, all these conflicts—sexual, emotional, and moral—are inescapable consequences (but ones we can work to alter and mitigate) of our evolutionary heritage.

This whole topic remains to be scientifically explored. But we can see something more of the nature and scope of these conflicts by using further concepts from evolutionary and social psychology. In these terms infantile experience is a formative starting point both:

i. For what will become sympathetic male-with-female cooperation in courtship, mating and child-rearing on the one hand, and what will become antipathetic male-against-male and female-against-female competition in these same activities on the other, and also, at the same time;
ii. for what will become sympathetic ingroup-with-ingroup cooperation (family with family, kin group with kin group, tribe with tribe, etc.) on the one hand, and what will become antipathetic ingroup-against-outgroup competition and conflict (family against family, kin group against kin group, tribe against tribe, and nation against nation) on the other.

In (ii) the mother–infant couple is taken as the first of a series of nested ingroups, and the father the first of many potentially alien outgroup figures—to be rapidly succeeded by strangers at seven months—that the infant will encounter as it extends its horizons to the rest of the family and then beyond. Darwin and many of his successors have taken the cooperative and competitive activities of tribes with tribes as important drivers of a process that combines natural selection with social or cultural evolution (for a recent discussion see Mesoudi, 2011). Still, the human fusion of (i) and (ii) should be as evident as the fact that adolescent male muscular strength is as often devoted to forms of group conflict (real or imaginary gangs, team sports, etc.) as it is to individual sexual competition, and that effectiveness in such activities is often registered in courting. And as in the other cases we have considered, this familiar feature of human life goes deep into our psychobiological, as well as our social, nature—here, perhaps, into a genetically prepared lateralisation in the cortical elaboration of RAGE that may distinguish adolescent male from female brains, and may in our present cultural circumstances also be related to "mental disorders" most frequent in adolescent males (i.e., conduct disorder; see Schneider et al., 2011).

At present, such topics, and others linked in (i) and (ii), are studied in fragmentary ways across the human sciences. Psychoanalysis connects and unifies them, and it does so by linking them directly with psychological processes that we can see clearly in individual cases, understand in near common-sense terms, and extend in the ways we have been considering. Thus we can study the working of identification and projection in ideographic common-sense detail in examples like Freud's dream, or again in experimental conditions like those of the homophobic men discussed above, or via possible physiological mechanisms such as mirror neurons.

These mechanisms, as preliminarily specified Freud and his successors, enable us better to understand the regulation of affection and aggression in the family, and the extension of this to successively larger cooperating or competing groups. Thus the regulation of aggression within the family is developmentally rooted in the infant's ability to identify himselfand his mother as anatomically and psychologically coherent individuals in a cooperative relationship; and as we have seen, the formation of this first mother-infant *good us* goes with the development of fear of strangers as imaginary *bad them*.[38]

Prospects

An interesting range of these phenomena are caught in a proverb that has many versions:

> Myself against my brother
> My brother and I against the family
> My family against the clan
> All of us against the foreigner

This represents sibling rivalry and parent-offspring conflict as in (i) and (ii) above—that is, as part of a larger pattern of cooperating to compete, sustained by the dialectic of identification and projection, so as to encompass successively larger cooperating and competing groups. Hypothesising such a structure, even in this simple schematic way, may help us in understanding how we have come to be as we are, and also some of the difficulties we seem clearly to face. Insofar as we naturally employ identification and projection in this way, we cannot mobilise identification in the service of cooperating as a single non-competing group—the human species—even when very common interests (removing the threat of nuclear weapons, seriously mitigating global warming) would be served by doing so. Insofar as this suggests an explanation of our situation, we should surely investigate it. Since such an investigation would concern how emotional conflicts within individuals drive social conflicts of many different kinds, it might offer a prospect of scientific unification that is individual and social as well.

Notes

1. Here it may be worth noting that since H and not-H are contradictory, P(H and not-H) = 0 and P(H or not-H) = 1. This being so, P(H) = 1–P(not-H), and so approaches 1 as P(not-H) approaches 0, and vice versa. This makes clear, as we should expect, that whatever D confirm H thereby disconfirms not-H and vice-versa. This is also indicated by taking not-H as the hypothesis under investigation (as of course it is whenever H is) and the evidence as not-D. This transforms the predictive condition of probabilistic relevance for H by D [P(D given H) > P(D given not-H)] into the predictive condition for not-H by not-e [P(not-D given not-H) > P(not-D given H)].
2. This image is gratefully reproduced from the Wikimedia commons, as described at http://en.wikipedia.org/wiki/File:Belon_Oyseaux.jpg. [last accessed 22/12/2014]
3. Thus Darwin (1903) wrote "I have always looked at the doctrine of natural selection as an hypothesis, which if it explained several large classes of facts, would deserve to be ranked as a theory deserving acceptance" (pp. 139–140); and on the role of probability: "Mere chance ... alone [i.e., probability taken in the absence of the causal mechanisms he had hypothesised] would never account for so habitual and large an amount of difference as that between varieties of the same species" (Darwin, 1859, p. 111).
4. This website illustrates both the scope of Darwin's account and, at the level of particular species, some of the many divergent hypotheses that it encompasses. So, for example, there have been many disputes about the evolutionary lineage of homo sapiens. Compare the tree of life on homo sapiens with Lordkipanidze et al. (2013).
5. Thus, for example, Jung's "compensation", as defined in rebellious opposition to Freud's account of wish-fulfilment, appears on inspection to be almost indistinguishable from that notion, particularly in empirical consequences. (There is little difference between saying that in the dream of Irma's injection Freud nocturnally compensates his annoyance at Otto by the experience of dreaming that Otto has given Irma a thoughtless dirty injection of trimethylamin and saying

that he fulfils his nocturnal wishes in doing so.) The same applies to more global disputes. Thus while all schools emphasise the role of aggression, conflict about aggression, and aggression turned against the self, followers of Klein argue that infantile aggression is an innate expression of a drive, whereas followers of Kohut hold that infantile narcissism means that narcissistic rage is easily aroused in an infant. So disagreement becomes crystallised around clinically irresoluable verbal differences—whether infants are innately aggressive or innately, exclusively concerned with themselves, and so liable to be aggressive—that have closely similar observable consequences. Among groups that are in regular communication—such as followers of Freud, Klein, Winnicott and Jung in London—there is a sense of general clinical agreement, fostered by each school's ability to understand its concepts in terms of the others'. For a Jungian note about Jung in this connection see: www.thesap.org.uk/michael-fordham.

6. As in the case of Darwin, one may wonder how Popper can accept explanations in a theory he is discussing as confirmed "beyond reasonable doubt", without withdrawing his claim that the theory does not really explain and cannot really be confirmed. Grünbaum (1989) reasonably criticises Popper for inconsistency on this point, and I am inclined to think of his incoherence as follows:

> From the beginning of his work Popper focused on the fact that open generalisations like "all swans are white" could be conclusively falsified but never conclusively verified by observation. At first he took this to mean that we could never confirm but only falsify such statements. But it seemed inadequate to hold that we could never have reasons for accepting general beliefs or theories, but only for rejecting them. So, consistently with his fixation on conclusive falsification, Popper held that instances *had they been different would have falsified* a belief or theory could also be taken to confirm it. (Taking the account we have been using this is like thinking that since P(not-H given not-D) approaches 1 as P(D given H) does, the latter is the *only right condition* in which to hold that P(H given D) > P(H)—although if one is not so focused on conclusive falsification, this is an arbitrary restriction on the more general [P(H given D) > P(H) if and only if P(D given H) > P(D given not-H)] mandated by Bayes' theorem.)

This restricted account enabled Popper to accept confirmation of instances of "all swans are white", and hence for the kind of strict generalisations he favoured. Still he provided no account of confirmation or disconfirmation for the particular *instances* on which such generalisations are based—no account, that is, of the way in which we confirm or disconfirm "this is a swan and it is white", in the case of "all swans are white". This vacancy, where the foundations of his account should have been, left Popper free open-mindedly to accept as confirmed individual instances of whatever explanations he appreciated, such as Freud's explanations of particular dreams, or Darwinian explanations of the adaptation of particular populations of bacteria to penicillin.

But then Popper could hold, consistently with his account, that Freudian or Darwinian *generalisations* from these cases remained unable "*really* to predict" and so "*really* to explain", despite the cases he accepted. Here his use of "really" could be seen as indicating that P(D given H) approaching 1 was required for "real" prediction or explanation. He could have dispensed with such verbal manoeuvres by abandoning his criterion of conclusive falsifiability in favour of the more flexible Bayesian account, and could have applied this to observational data as well. But although many of his followers seem to have done this, Popper himself did not.

7. The fullest treatments are in Hopkins (1999a), but see also Hopkins (1996, 1999b) where the role of wish-fulfilment in Freud's work more generally is sketched out; Hopkins (2012) where the role of wish-fulfilment is compared with projection and integrated, together with repression and the superego, into Friston's Freud-like "free energy" neuroscience; Hopkins (2013a) in which Freudian claims are discussed in terms of the Bayesian sketch above; and Hopkins (2013b) where implications of this for psychiatry are discussed. These and other papers are also available online at jimhopkins.org.
8. I speculatively traced how this practice might have evolved in Hopkins (2000a).
9. As Coren (1998) reports, two men known to have endured long-term sleep deprivation voluntarily, Randy Gardner and Peter Tripp, both developed paranoid symptoms, despite (probably) getting short, unobserved bits of sleep during their periods of deprivation.
10. There is a particularly approachable discussion on the role of dreaming in memory consolidation in Cartwright (2010), and the claims there are coherent with those in Hobson, Hong and Friston (2014). These claims have also been borne out by more recent work. See also among others Payne (2011; especially Fig 1 p. 273); Lewis and Durrant (2011); Dudai (2012); Inostroza and Born (2013). On preparation for future activity see also van Dongen et al. (2013); Diekelmann, Wilhelm, Wagner, and Born (2013).

11. The Neurocritic, http://neurocritic.blogspot.co.uk/2011/09/neurophysiology-of-pain-during-rem.html [last accessed]. See also the articles cited in this blog entry, particularly Bastuji et al. (2012). As the Neurocriti reports, this would seem to be just the kind of functional dissociation required to protect sleep, since their effect was that activity "decreased dramatically in the cingulate. Recall that the medial mid-anterior cingulate cortex (ACC) is associated with the attentional and affective components of pain, while the lateral opercular and insular cortices are more related to the sensory aspects of pain. The authors suggest that this dissociation between the lateral and medial pain systems is what allows the experience of pain in dreams without being alerted enough to wake up".
12. Thus Howson and Urbach (1989) explain how in this context only a few data presenting what Bayesians sometimes call "suspicious coincidences" can give powerful support to causal hypotheses predicting them.

    > ... The distinguished scientist, Charles Babbage, examined numerous logarithmic tables published over two centuries in various parts of the world. He was interested in whether they were derived from the same source, or had been worked out independently. Babbage (1827) found the same six errors in all but two, and drew the 'irresistible' conclusion that, apart from these two, all the tables originated in a common source ... In fact scientists seem to regard a few shared mistakes in different mathematical tables as so strongly indicative of a common source that at least one compiler of such tables attempted to protect his copyright by deliberately incorporating three minor errors as "a trap for would-be plagiarists" .... (p. 87)

    The same principle is frequently used in neuroscience (e.g., to establish conclusions about causal relations between non-coincidental patterns of neural firing by means of data coming from a small number of implanted electrodes).
13. This hypothesis would be sharpened by considering that the sexual "solution" to Irma's problems that Freud blames Irma for not accepting at the beginning of the dream and the toxic sexual solution thoughtlessly injected by Otto into Irma at the end of the dream were linked in his mind. As he explained later in a letter to Karl Abraham, he understood the dream as also expressing his own sexual desires: "there would be one therapy for widowhood ... all sorts of intimate things, naturally" (Freud & Abraham, 2002). This may also have reflected his

unconscious feelings about his own therapeutic practice, which was focused on sexuality at the time.

14. And here as in the case of "solution" above the dream expresses deep emotional connections by use of the same word ("solution"/"solution", "Mathilde"/"Mathilde").
15. For recent work on dehumanisation, and on sexual prejudice, see Haslam and Loughnan (2014, advance online posting) and Herek and McLemore (2013). The mechanisms discussed in these essays are compatible with the use of ingroup-idealising and outgroup-denegrating projection, as described in the text, and in the essays cited below.
16. I have discussed this further in Hopkins (2013b). For recent discussion of further similar examples see, for example, Maltsberger (2008).
17. There is a fuller account of this, as well as citations to the quotations above, in Hopkins (1988).
18. The whole field of developmental psychology from infancy, including parts of psychoanalysis, is reviewed in Bornstein (2014, advance electronic publication). A good overall recent account of work in attachment, from infancy over the lifespan, is Howe (2011), which can be consulted on almost all the topics discussed in the text. For more detailed (but not quite so up-to-date) information and citation of sources see Cassidy and Shaver (2008). As regards psychoanalysis and infancy, Kenny (2013) seeks to integrate a range of materials from psychoanalysis, developmental psychology (including attachment), and neuroscience. See particularly the discussion "Integration of neuroscience, psychoanalysis, and attachment theory" (pp. 251ff). For discussion of psychoanalysis and attachment generally see Fonagy (2000) and Fonagy, Gergely, and Target (2008). There is now a vast literature on attachment, neuroscience, and psychotherapy. For a recent overview of his own work see Schore (2012); see also Hart (2008), as well as the text below. In what follows, however, we will be linking attachment with psychoanalysis and neuroscience via the notion of a cortical ego in relation to a subcortical id or family of basic drives or generators of motivation, as developed in the work discussed and noted below. I think this provides the neuroscientific context that best integrates attachment and psychoanalysis.
19. For Bowlby's conception see Bretherton and Mullholand (2008). For contemporary neuroscience see below.
20. Ribble's (1944) abstract describes her pioneering work as:

> A Freudian analysis of the significance of infantile experience in the formation of personality is followed by a discussion of direct observations in this area, most of it based on unpublished

studies by the author. Important topics deal with the child's emotional relation to the mother, oral experiences, the effect of experiences related to elimination, and experiences related to affectional needs. There is a brief review of related studies of animals.

21. The main non-interpretive evidence for this is an experiment performed by Thomas Bower, (Bower, 1977). He describes:

> A simple optical arrangement that allows one to present infants with multiple images of a single object … If one presents the infant with multiple images of its mother—say three "mothers"—the infant of less than five months is not disturbed at all but will in fact interact with all three "mothers" in turn. If the setup provides one mother and two strangers, the infant will preferentially interact with its mother and still show no signs of disturbance. However, past the age of 5 months (after the co-ordination of place and movement) the sight of three "mothers" becomes very disturbing to the infant. At this same age a setup of one mother and two strangers has no effect. I would contend that this in fact shows that the young infant (less than five months old) thinks it has a multiplicity of mothers, whereas the older infant knows it has only one. (p. 217)

   There is also some evidence from more recent eye-tracking studies: see Bertenthal, Gredeback, and Boyer (2012).
22. For more information about Adult Attachment Interview (AAI) see for example http://www.psychology.sunysb.edu/attachment/measures/content/aai_interview.pdf [last accessed] and Hesse (2000, 2008). For an in-depth study see Steele and Steele (2008).
23. Phrases in the discussion and the first table are taken from Howe (2011, pp. 48–49); Solomon and George (2000); Hesse (2000, table 19.2, p. 399), and Hesse (2008, tables 25.3 and 25.4, pp. 568–569). Data about disorganisation and 3 + year development of disorganised coercive strategy from Solomon and George (2000, table 14.3), and Lyons-Ruth and Jacobovitz (2008, particularly pp. 681–685). The final table is taken from Howe (2011, p. 49).
24. On genetic factors see Howe (2011, chapter 14); van Ijzendoorn (1995); Lyons-Ruth and Jacobovitz, (2008, particularly pp. 681–685). Recent results, not yet consolidated, suggest that although the distributions among categories remain stable as measured at different periods of life, in the case of individuals the strong early influence of experience with

the mother may tend to give way to genetic or epigenetic factors over time. It may well be, as in the case of language, that evolution prepares the infant to learn as much as possible about currently useful modes of coping by identifying with relevant persons in the environment; but then for emotion and motivation also permits genetic or epigenetic factors to reassert themselves over time.

25. See Rizzolatti and Sinigaglia (2010), and Gallese, (2009).
26. On the unlearned and early-developing nature of the facial expression of emotion see Matusomoto (2009) and Reissland, Francis, Mason, and Lincoln (2011). For face-to-face salience and imitability see Wang, Ramsey, and Hamilton (2011). New research reveals more about how the brain processes facial expressions and emotion.
27. The general idea of a cortical ego as developing to regulate subcortical drives or sources of excitation, as well as associated claims about cortical secondary and subcortical primary processes, was advanced independently by Richard Carhart-Harris and Karl Friston (2010), and by Mark Solms and Jaak Panksepp (2012), and has recently been espoused by Rizzolatti, Semi, and Fabbri-Destro (2014).

    Carhart-Harris and Friston presented a range of Freud's theories, originally cast in terms of a conception of free energy partly isomorphic to Friston's, as consilient both with Frison's overall programme, and with a large range of data drawn from neuropsychology, neuroimaging, and psychopharmacology. I followed this in Hopkins (2012), developing a Bayesian account of repression and the superego, and again in connection with psychiatry and neuroscience in Hopkins (2013c). These papers provide more detailed discussion of some of the ideas in this essay.
28. For Panksepp's most detailed discussion and delineation of these systems, which contains many subtleties not reflected in this telegraphic discussion, see Panksepp (1998). This work has recently been updated and presented for general readers and therapists in Panksepp and Biven (2012) and celebrated and discussed in a special edition of *Neuroscience and Biobehavioral Reviews* (vol. 35, Issue 9, pp. 1789–2044; October 2011).
29. For discussion of the idea that both motivated behaviour and the conscious experience that accompanies and regulates it originate in the same subcortical regions and via the same or closely coordinated mechanisms see Damasio, Damasio, and Traniel (2012); Solms and Panksepp (2012); and Solms (2013), with replies by a range of neuroscientists and others such as my "Repression creates an unconscious id" (Hopkins, 2013c). The claims by Damasio, Panksepp, and Solms about the role of the cortex are assessed in the perspective of the

Helmholtz/Bayes neuroscience discussed below, which places greater emphasis on top-down cortical processing, in Gu, Hof, Friston, and Fan (2013). Their claims about the cortex, as well as the work on the insula by Craig that they cite, seem to me to be consistent with the overall picture of subcortical generation and cortical elaboration they are discussing.

30. See Lindquist, Wager, Kober, Bliss-Moreau, and Barrett (2012), for a "psychological construction" account emphasising the cortex. They contrast their view with Panksepp's by saying (p. 138) that:

> A locationist approach has linked the PAG to distinct circuits corresponding to several emotion categories: rage, fear, joy, distress, love and lust (Panksepp, 1998). In a psychological construction approach, the assumption is that a given dedicated circuit for a specific behavioral adaptation (e.g., withdrawal) will be active across a range of emotion categories (e.g., a person can withdraw in instances of both fear and anger), and different dedicated circuits within the PAG (e.g., fight, flight) will be active within instances of a single emotion category depending upon which behavioral adaptation is more relevant for the immediate context.

This, however, is quite consistent with the role Panksepp assigns to the cortex in constructing the more complex "tertiary" emotions required for human social life. See, for example, Panksepp and Biven (2012, p. 16, Fig. 1.6).

31. The regulation of infantile anger in relation to the mother is discussed in more detail in Hopkins (1987) and related to neuroscience in Hopkins (2012).
32. This and the following quotation are from Freud's notes from the first seven sessions, which were not published in the *Standard Edition* because they were reproduced almost verbatim in the case history. They were published in Hawelka and Hawelka (1974).
33. Here the relations of the parental couple are expressed in a familiar metaphorical structure, in which being together in a vehicle represents being in a relationship, and the fate of the vehicle and of the relationship go together. For example the relationship may be *taking off* (airplane); *on the rocks* (boat); *off the rails* (train); or again *in the slow lane, at a crossroads, stalled, stuck,* or *at a dead end* (car). Taking a lyric from a popular song, we recognise instantly that in singing "we're driving on the fast lane in the freeway of love" the singer is referring to a relationship that is exciting, risky, etc. This is the same system of metaphor that the little girl is naturally using, in representing the couple as loving and kissing

one another and "driving up and down all the time". The relation of psychoanalytic symbolism to conceptual metaphor—another consilience with cognitive science—is discussed in more detail in Hopkins (2000b). There I emphasise the metaphor of the mind as a container. This is relevant both to projective identification in general and to the fate of Freud's "solution" in the Irma dream.

34. This case as well as the dream of Irma's injection considered in detail below is discussed in the context of a fuller account of the superego, ego and id in terms of Bayesian neuroscience in Hopkins (2012) and in connection with psychiatry and neuroscience in Hopkins (2013b). It is worth noting that Freud's (1909d) description of the "turning point" in his case history at p. 205ff can very usefully be compared with his much fuller description of the episode in his own notes at p. 281ff (The crucial "he agreed that his walking about the room while making these confessions ..." appears at 283). It appears from Freud's notes that the punishment the Rat Man remembered was not, as Freud had hypothesised, a result of masturbation, but rather for something that could be regarded as much more specifically Freudian, but upon which Freud was not focusing at the time. The actual punishment was for a symbolic attack on the parents and their sexual intercourse, and enacted by the child's lying between the parents and peeing in the parental bed. And the Rat Man's feelings about this were reflected in his imagining Freud and his wife with a dead baby lying between them. As noted below, the Rat Man's memory of this attack and the punishment it produced were preceded by expressions of destructive hostility to Freud's mother that are readily understood as projected versions of his own. So it appears that this episode should be understood in terms of the deeper issues of parent-offspring conflict and sibling rivalry considered later in the text.
35. Robert Trivers' pioneering essays on these topics are in Trivers (2002): see particularly "Parental investment and reproductive success" and "Parent-offspring conflict". The latter is linked in detail with sexual conflict in Mock and Parker (1997) and both are illuminatingly discussed in Hrdy (2000). The linked topics of parental investment and parent-offspring conflict are related briefly to psychoanalysis in Hopkins (2003) and (2004).
36. See note above, and consider also the sexual "solution" first proposed to Irma by Freud, then physically injected into her by Otto. In this the dream draws on the network of conceptual metaphor that relates mental to physical concepts via the metaphor of the mind as a container.
37. This is also why considering parental investment and sexual and parent-offspring conflict have led evolutionary theorists to argue that the genetic interests of offspring would best be served by what they describe as "true monogamy" (Mock & Parker, 1997, p. 222), which corresponds

to the human moral ideal of lifelong faithful marriage centred on the rearing of children.

38. This is discussed in more detail in Hopkins (1987) and in relation to neuroscience and the gene-culture evolution mentioned above in Hopkins (2003, 2004).

CHAPTER THREE

Freud's aesthetics: artists, art and psychoanalysis

Michael Levine

> Freud's studies of ... artists are primarily analyses of behaviour and inner motivations. The focus is ... not upon problems of art ... the artist is a gifted and sensitive person, sometimes neurotic and sometimes not, but governed by the same inner forces that rule the rest of mankind.
>
> —Fraiberg, 1956, p. 87*

Introduction

In part one of this chapter, preliminary issues concerning "Freud's aesthetics"[1] are discussed. What is it that he is trying to do and how does he go about it? Freud's basic ideas about understanding art and the artistic process in relation to the artist's psychology are explained and a few common criticisms and misconceptions are examined. Here are two. The first is that if there are exceptions to Freud's claim that art is orectic, driven by desire and wish-fulfilment and functions so as

---

*From "Freud's writings on art" by L. Fraiberg, *International Journal of Psycho-Analysis, 37*: 82–96, reprinted by kind permission of John Wiley & Sons Ltd © 1956.

to satisfy certain psychological needs of artists (and audiences), then one will have shown Freud's views about art to be mistaken (even outrageous). The second objection is based on the assumption that we need to take artists at their word. Thus, if artists tell us that the reason why they pursue art is not to fulfil unconscious wishes, negotiate the demands of reality, and satisfy other desires they would not otherwise be able to satisfy, then it is not. Were these objections raised by those with little more than a passing interest in psychoanalysis then perhaps they wouldn't be interesting. But when professional philosophers (e.g., Grünbaum) and distinguished art critics and curators (e.g., Fry) raise a version of these, then a response may be called for—even if the objections remain superfluous.[2]

The second part of this chapter continues the account of art and the artist in relation to central features of psychoanalysis such as dream analysis.[3] This part is largely reiterative of Freud's views and those who have exposited, elaborated upon and critiqued them. Freud's views on art, artists and the nature of artistic creation are intrinsically connected to psychoanalysis. His discussion of the meaning of an artwork is virtually always cast in terms of psychoanalytic theory. For example, Shakespeare's plays *Hamlet*, *Macbeth*, and of course Sophocles' *Oedipus Rex*, are explained in terms of the oedipal complex. Details of Leonardo da Vinci's art, as well as his artistic nature and motivation are accounted for in terms of his psychosexual development—especially in relation to his two mothers.

The third part of the essay seeks to locate these psychoanalytic views about art and the artists in terms of key long-standing questions in philosophical aesthetics. Psychoanalysis has something distinctive to say about: (i) the nature (or definition) of art; (ii) the value of art: is it extrinsic or intrinsic, and does a distinctively "aesthetic pleasure" give an adequate explanation of the value of art, and; (iii) the purpose and function (which are not the same things) of art, as well as how these fundamental questions in aesthetics are related.

Additionally, as informed by psychoanalysis, aesthetics has a unique—though by no means univocal or thoroughly articulated—set of insights and answers to the question of how art is to be judged; good art *vs.* bad art; low art *vs.* high art; the possibility of objective aesthetic judgement; and the relation of ethics to aesthetic value ("ethicism" or moralism *vs.* "aestheticism"). In general terms, aestheticism holds that the aesthetic value of an artwork is independent of its moral value, while moralists (or moderate moralism) hold that the moral value of an aesthetic object may at times and to some degree impact on its aesthetic value. On Freud's account, to understand art it is necessary to focus on artists and the artistic process as psychoanalytically conceived. And in view of all of the aforementioned issues, the scope and significance of Freud's aesthetics (suppose he is right?), as opposed to certain other philosophical accounts of art, is also remarkable and worth reflecting upon. This constitutes a direction for future research for philosophers of art as well as psychoanalysts.

Part I

The term "Psychoanalysis" refers to (i) a theoretical account, based originally on Freud's, of the structure and workings of the mind, and (ii) the psychotherapeutic method employed in clinical practice. Freud thought that both aspects of psychoanalysis, though particularly theory, are useful in understanding the nature and meaning of art—visual art, literature, and theatre—generally, as well as specific works of art.[4] Furthermore, art could be used, much as the psychopathology of everyday life, to further support the validity of psychoanalysis. Theoretically and practically speaking, understanding art on the one hand and psychoanalysis on the other are seen to be mutually supportive.[5]

Wollheim (1970, p. 214) claims Freud's "essay on Leonardo—and much the same sort of claim could be mounted for the essay on Dostoievsky—is primarily a study in psycho-analytic biography: and the connexion with art is *almost* exhausted by the fact that the subject of the biography happens to be one of the greatest, as well as one of the strangest, artists in history". Fraiberg (1956, p. 87) agrees: "Freud's studies of these individual artists are primarily analyses of behaviour and inner motivations. The focus is upon these and not upon problems of art, with the single major exception of the reasons why the artist elects to treat certain themes".

This is not, in my view, a correct let alone useful way of looking at the matter. It could at least as insightfully be said that the essays are primarily an account of art and artistic process and that the connection with psychoanalytic biographies of Leonardo da Vinci and Dostoievsky is *almost* exhausted by that account. Understand their art and psychoanalytically speaking you understand the artist. Freud's focus in these essays is art—not psychoanalytic biography as Wollheim suggests. Freud's interest is in the content in artwork, and that content is revelatory of the biography. But Wollheim, and of course many others, are often more interested in form and technique and the place of a work in historical/cultural development. Freud does not have much to say about these things.[6]

The following quotation lends some support to the view that Freud's concern was not biography of any kind. Gombrich (1987) says:

> It is true, of course, that Freud invited one great artist of the past into his consulting room. His monograph of 1910 on Leonardo da Vinci approaches at least two of Leonardo's paintings, the *Mona Lisa* and the *St. Anne,* as if they were the phantasies of a patient. A large bibliography criticizing or defending Freud's use of the evidence has grown up round this venture … which has, perhaps, coloured the popular image of Freud's approach to art more than any other of his publications. It comes as a relief to the sceptical historian to read in Freud's letter to the painter Hermann Struck (7 November 1914) that he regarded it as "half a novelistic fiction"—"would not want you to judge the certainty of our results by this sample". (p. 227)

But to see that Freud's concern is with art rather than psychoanalytic biography one just has to step back from the admittedly unsubstantiated biographical details and ask what it is that Freud is trying to establish. Freud's concern is with what psychoanalysis can tell us about artists and practice of art, and also how such findings can bolster the scope of psychoanalysis while further supporting it.

However from a psychoanalytic view, to say that psychoanalysis is useful to understanding art, artists and the artistic processes (or vice versa) is a misleading understatement. While particular psychoanalytic interpretations may be mistaken—Freud may after all have completely misunderstood the smile on the Mona Lisa—the relevant psychoanalytic claim is that in general it is not possible to understand any of these aspects of *some* art (more on "some" later) apart from psychoanalyses. In a letter to the actress Yvette Guilbert (quoted in Gombrich, 1987, p. 237), who questioned the idea that acting involved psychological self-expression, or the extent to which it did, Freud says: "The idea that an artist's achievements are conditioned internally by childhood impressions, destiny, suppressions and disappointments has yielded much enlightenment to us … I once ventured to approach one of the very greatest … Leonardo da Vinci. I was able at least to make it probable that his *St. Anne* ... would not be intelligible without the peculiar childhood story of Leonardo. Nor, possibly, would other works".[7] The claim that it is not possible to understand art—understand it—that is, not completely but more or less adequately—apart from psychoanalysis is not meant to be an analytic truth (true by definition). It is meant to be an empirically grounded theoretical discovery.

The claim that such a theoretical framework is necessary to understanding art does not mean that other things (experience, appreciation of historical circumstances, theory, patience, exposure to art) may not also be useful or at times necessary to understanding or appreciating art. Nor does it mean that art is wholly or solely expressive of an artist's internal psychic states apart from external influences on such states. Gombrich (1987, p. 236) claims that Freud's theory of art encompasses both "the centripetal force of traditions and trends" on artists and art as well as self-expressive "centrifugal forces". These forces are mutually interactive and influence each other: "Even Byron's art is not all 'self-expression'. Nor, if it is not, need it therefore be an empty pose". Gombrich (1987, pp. 238–239) also thinks it important to stress the mastery of skills involved in (good) art—implying perhaps that Freud somehow underestimated this. Freud, however, was neither concerned with nor qualified to discuss intrinsically technical aspects of art—whether in painting, sculpture, literature, or performance. In any case, the idea that Freud underestimated the significance of technique in good, let alone great, art, if this is what Gombrich is claiming, seems difficult to sustain given that Freud at times seems virtually in awe of artistic ability (e.g., Michelangelo's). Contrast Freud's views on art, and appreciation of art, with those on philosophy. He never appears to be in awe of philosophical ability.

Art, on Freud's view, is not all about or all a matter of self-expression, and so understanding art cannot be just about such expression either.[8] Nevertheless, on Freud's account, a great deal of art can only be understood in terms of sublimated sexual desire, and art generally is the result of sublimated libidinal energy and desire. The artist seeks satisfaction, frustrated by the real world, in phantasy and wish-fulfilment.[9] In doing so, a certain amount of satisfaction and success in the real world may also be obtained. These satisfactions include "honour, power and the love of women" (Freud, 1916–1917, p. 377). However, Segal (1991, p. 63) believes that "[t]his ... leaves Freud open to attack, since it is well known that true artists often sacrifice money, power, position, and possibly love of women, for the sake of the integrity of their art". But even if it were true that artists often do make those sacrifices (and it probably isn't), it would not conflict in the least with Freud's claim. Artists, like academics, may like to *believe* that they are sacrificing money, power, and prestige, etc. for the integrity of their art or intellectual pursuits. But that is another matter. Segal also does not appear to take into account when Freud talks about seeking honour, power and women that he is talking about internal ends, satisfying narcissistic needs, the internal mother, etc.

Contrary to what one might initially think, Freud did not like surrealism or abstract expressionism—though both are allegedly concerned with the unconscious. In a letter about Dali, whom he met in London and whose work he appears to have thought well of if not liked, Freud writes that "the concept of art resisted an extension beyond the point where the quantitative proportion between unconscious material and preconscious elaboration is kept within a certain limit" (Gombrich, 1987, p. 239). Gombrich takes this as indicative of Freud's conservative tastes in art. But it can also be that Freud is here calling attention to the very same thing Gombrich is. Art requires skill. It isn't all about spilling (excavating or expressing) one's unconscious. Gombrich (1987, p. 235) says, "The artist who thus experiments and plays—who looks for discoveries in language if he is a writer or a poet, in visual shapes if he is a painter—will no doubt select in that preconscious process of which Freud speaks the structures that will greet him as meaningful in terms of his mind and conflicts. But it is his art that informs his mind, not his mind that breaks through in his art".

It is not clear what Gombrich has in mind with this distinction (art informing mind or mind informing art) or whether Freud would even recognise it. Just as unconscious and preconscious processes mutually affect and influence each other, so too are mind (conscious, unconscious, and preconscious) and art linked in artistic process. As Gombrich (1987, p. 232) says: "Far from looking in the world of art only for its unconscious content of biological drives and childhood memories he [Freud] insisted on that degree of adjustment to reality that alone turns a dream into a work of art". Segal (1991, p. 63) echoes this view with her distinction between the daydreamer and the artist: "[T]he artist differs essentially from the day-dreamer. Where the day-dreamer avoids conflict by a phantasy of omnipotent wish-fulfilment and a denial of external and psychic realities, the artist seeks to locate his conflict and resolve it in his creation. He does not look for easy solutions".

Freud's views on art are not reductive. He is not offering a single explanation of art, nor is he giving a univocal account of the artistic process. However, the claim that it is not possible to understand art apart from psychoanalysis does mean that if psychoanalysis is (broadly) correct, then it is also essential to anything even approaching an adequate understanding of art. The same, of course, will be true of anything else for which the explanation is not overdetermined—that is, for which there is only one correct explanation or which essentially requires reference to that explanation if it is to be minimally adequate as an explanation. But the point is worth making in relation to psychoanalysis and art, precisely because so many post-Freudian accounts of art (its nature, function, value) omit psychoanalysis altogether. It might seem that the problem in the background here is that both the notion of art and of "understanding art" are so open-ended, but I doubt that is the case. Some (indefensibly) narrow notions may rule out the applicability of Freud's views, but most will not.

Art is by no means the only thing to which psychoanalytic interpretation is essential—if psychoanalysis is more or less right. (The question of just how right psychoanalysis has to be in order to be more or less right is left to one side—for example, see Chodorow, 1989.) Consider racism for example; cognitive models hold racism and other prejudices to derive largely from ignorance and false consciousness. Racist hatred, so the story goes, stems from a cognitive defect of sorts. It is a matter of false beliefs personally and socially grounded in mistaken facts and flawed reasoning. On a psychoanalytic account, however, the varieties of prejudice (different kinds of racism, misogyny, homophobia, etc.) and the forms they take are partly a function of different character types and the processes undertaken by these types to defend themselves—their ego and self-image—from imaginatively perceived (and often projected) threats. This account of prejudice is called the psychological defence model.[10] The point here is that, as in the case of art, there is no chance of adequately understanding the nature of the prejudices, their sources and how they function, apart from a psychoanalytic account if such an account is basically right. Such an account is not only essential, it is also central.

Part II

Even when discussing particular works of art, it is no surprise that Freud's account of art focuses on the artist. He does so for reasons obviously based in psychoanalysis, and to an extent that few, if any, other overarching theories match. The fact that his account is artist-centric, though not in ways that all artists would either identify with let alone endorse, does present some reason for artists in particular, though others as well, to regard such an approach seriously. It underlies an opportunity by artists for self-reflection and understanding with regard to themselves, other artists, and the nature and significance of the artistic process generally.

To adequately understand or *in some ways* even appreciate a work of art, a person, including the artist, must know something about the artist from a psychoanalytic perspective. This does mean that we need to know personal details about artists in order to appreciate a work of art. We can appreciate African masks and ancient and medieval works without such knowledge. But if Freud is right, then in many cases such knowledge will aid understanding and appreciation and in other cases will be indispensable to any adequate—let alone complete—understanding. From this epistemological standpoint an artist may not be particularly privileged, or privileged at all, in terms of interpreting their work, since they may not necessarily be cognisant—not consciously at least—of some significant or crucial aspect of what their work is expressing or indeed what they intend to express. As Sayers says, for instance, "The analysand's use of symbolism in their dream-work disguise of their unconscious wishes proves that the analysand has, Freud argued, 'a symbolic mode of expression at his disposal which he does not know in waking life and does not recognize'" (Sayers, 2007, pp. 25–26). Whether or not Leonardo da Vinci knew, or was consciously aware, that the smiles on the Mona Lisa and Saint Anne were essentially the same—his own mother's, and that St. Anne and St. Mary were representative or expressive of his childhood experiences with his real mother and his father's wife—*if they are*, then one needs to know this to understand the paintings, as well as other important features of Leonardo's childhood experiences—real and imagined.

As Fraiberg (1956) says:

> [Freud] … pointed out the likelihood that it [Mona Lisa's smile] was a reminder to Leonardo of the smile of his own mother, which appeared again in the picture of Saint John and on the faces of both women in the painting of Saint Anne, Mary, and the Holy Infant. Freud interpreted the latter as an unconsciously motivated representation both of Leonardo's real mother, the

> peasant woman ... and of his father's barren wife ... The childhood group of two mothers and infant son was an idealization of Leonardo's own history, both real and fantasied—the father is conspicuously absent. (p. 87)

And if the smiles are the same and do relate to his mother then he would have had to have been at least unconsciously aware of this. Fraiberg (1956, p. 86) says Freud "restricted his aim to demonstrating connections between the artist's outer experiences and the paths of his instinctual activity ... But he could not resist the temptation to remark ...'It does seem, however, as if only a man with Leonardo's childhood experiences could have painted Mona Lisa and Saint Anne.'"

Without meaning to be, and despite the fact it is often seen as derogatory (e.g., by Fry, 1924), Freud's account of art and artists is extraordinarily favourable. Artists are, no more than the rest of us, generally happy, untroubled, or neurosis free. But they are, at least in some respects, lucky—luckier, that is, than most. As Fraiberg (1956) says:

> [T]o those who are not artists the gratification that can be drawn from the springs of fantasy is very limited; their inexorable repressions prevent the enjoyment of all but the meagre day-dreams which can become conscious. A true artist has more at his disposal. First of all he understands how to elaborate his daydreams so that they lose that personal note which grates upon strange ears and become enjoyable to others; he knows too how to modify them sufficiently so that their origin in prohibited sources is not easily detected. Further, he possesses the mysterious ability to mould his particular material until it expresses the ideas of his fantasy faithfully; and then he knows how to attach to this reflection of his fantasy life so strong a stream of pleasure that, for a time at least, the repressions are out-balanced and dispelled by it. (pp. 94–95; cf. Freud, 1943, p. 328)

The pleasures art affords both the artist and their audience are, it should be remembered, temporary. "Art affects us but as a mild narcotic and can provide no more than a temporary refuge for us from the hardships of life; its influence is not strong enough to make us forget real misery" (Freud, 1930a, p. 34. Quoted in Fraiberg, 1956, pp. 93–94).

Whether or not emulating artists psychically—or emulating the artistic temperament—is even possible, there is little doubt that on Freud's account most people would be better off if they were more like artists—by being either less repressed, better at more positively engaging with repression, and ultimately obtaining a level of satisfaction through their work in terms of psychically satisfying unconscious wishes and desires, and thereby avoiding the quite different substitutive satisfaction neuroses brings;[11] but also in obtaining a degree of satisfaction (recognition, sense of accomplishment, reward, admiration, pleasure) in the real world that would otherwise be unavailable to them.

Sterba (1940) similarly describes the source of artistic impulse as psychoanalytically conceived as follows:

> At the basis of artistic creation we find the same instinctual forces which are effective as components of intrapsychic conflicts ... The work of art is therefore the product of psychic forces that are in opposition to each other, such as desire and inner prohibition. It represents reconciliation between these conflicting forces and has therefore the character of a compromise, as have also those psychopathological formations—errors, dreams and neurotic symptoms—which are well known. The fundamental dynamic force at the root of a work of art is an unfulfilled wish of the artist; just as in dreams and fantasies, the work of art represents this wish as fulfilled ... The artist is an introvert. Since he is unable to satisfy his overpowering instinctual needs in the world of reality, he is obliged to turn away from the real world to the realm of phantasy thus taking the way which leads to neurosis. But it is here that the creative process sets in, enabling him through discharge of instinctual energy and the effect of the work of art on the outside world to save himself from neurosis and to regain contact with reality. He is able through the creation of a work of art to obtain sufficient gratification of his intense childhood wishes which he represents as fulfilled in his creation ... His particular method of representation, possible to the artist on account of his talent, enables him in a certain measure to find a way back from fantasy to reality, obtaining in this roundabout way a means of gratifying actual wishes and of achieving success for which, in a direct way, his forces would never have been adequate. (pp. 257–260)

On this point about art being used as a way of returning to reality—or satisfying wishes in reality—Wollheim (1970, p. 224) says that: "In a number of celebrated places Freud equated art with recovery or reparation or the path back to reality: in the case of Leonardo, as we have seen, he attempted to document this moment. But nowhere did he indicate the mechanism by which this came about". Just what sort of mechanism Wollheim is looking for, or what he means by it, is unclear. Why, for instance, or in what way, is Sterba's succinct but standard psychoanalytic account of the process (rather than mechanism) above insufficient? The mechanism Wollheim may have in mind is that referred to by Freud in his famous pronouncement "before the problem of the creative artist analysis must, alas, lay down its arms" (Freud, 1928b, para.1).[12]

Towards the end of his essay on Freud's aesthetics, Wollheim appears to suggest that infantile wish-fulfilment does not play the central role in understanding and interpreting art or the artist on a psychoanalytic account that most claim it does; or at least the part it does play is not as straightforward as in Sterba's account (above). Wollheim (1970) asks:

> Is there, according to Freud, anything parallel in the work of art to the purpose that finds, seeks, expression in the work of art? An understanding of psychoanalysis should warn us that this question is unanswerable. For outside the comparative inflexibility of the neurosis, there is no single unchanging form that our characters or temperaments assume. There are constant vicissitudes of feeling and impulse, constant formings and reformings of phantasy, over which it is certain very general tendencies pattern themselves: but with a flexibility in which, Freud suggests, the artist is peculiarly adept. The artist expresses himself in his work—how could he not? But what he expresses has not the simplicity of a wish or impulse. (pp. 223–224)

What sort of "parallel" thing—that is, parallel to the purpose that finds expression in a work of art—is Wollheim referring to? Isn't it Freud's view that the work of art results from, expresses and in a sense embodies such purpose (e.g., wish-fulfilment)? Wollheim claims that because "there is no single unchanging form that our characters or temperaments assume", what the artists expresses in a work of art, and what the work satisfies, may frequently not involve infantile wish-fulfilment.

He may mean only (and if so, there is no disagreement with Wollheim here) that what the artist expresses cannot "simply" be reduced to such wishes and impulses, and, along with the idea that wish-fulfilment may at times play virtually no role in an artwork, this is worth keeping in mind. But, not only may variations in the modes of expression of infantile wish-fulfilment (variations in forms of art themselves) take account of such "vicissitudes" of feeling and impulse. Accommodating such changes is quite consonant with the view that works of art express such wishes. What is "parallel in the work of art" to the purpose that finds expression in the work of art is the embodiment of what may be a quite complex wish-fulfilling expression, (or the expression of a wish-fulfilling phantasy) itself—one (or more) such expressions tinged with changeable feelings and impulses. This does not make them anything other than wish-fulfilling phantasies. It does, however, suggest that understanding a work of art may also, or even sometimes primarily, require understanding and otherwise accounting for these other feelings and impulses involved. (A parallel might be the dream in which there is always the fulfilment of some infantile wishes but compounded with the day residues and other circumstantial material.) Freud would never have denied that and psychoanalysis has no need to do so.

Like many other theories of art, Freud not only accounts for the function of art (in terms of the satisfaction of unfulfilled wishes), but also how and why a work of art is able to elicit the audience response it does. Sterba (1940, p. 262) says: "The disclosure of the fact that unfulfilled wishes, originating in the unconscious, are satisfied in the work of art, and that it is possible through analysis of the work of art to discover these; that, furthermore, the enjoyment of the work of art derives principally from the satisfaction of these infantile wishes, is Freud's most important contribution to the psychology of the work of art". According to Freud (1911b, p. 224) "[a]n artist is originally a man who turns away from reality because he cannot come to terms with the renunciation of instinctual satisfaction … [The artist] finds his way back to reality, however, from this world of phantasy, by making use of special gifts to mould his phantasies into truths of a new kind, which are valued by men as precious reflections of reality" (quoted in Sayers, 2007, p. 23). Relatedly, Sterba (1940, p. 266) notes that, "[t]he mutual permeation of the fields of domination of the pleasure and reality principles led Freud to call art a *kind of reconciliation between the two principles in mental functioning*".

The wishes that the artist temporarily and transiently satisfies in a work of art mirror the audience's own wishes and satisfies them as well.[13] The satisfaction is not vicarious but direct—though it is dependent on recognising their satisfaction in the work of art. Some wishes will be more or less specific to individuals with certain character types and contoured to them. But others, like those wishes associated with the oedipal complex, Freud takes to be universal. It is because Oedipus's wishes are also our own that we can obtain a satisfaction much like that of the artist when they are represented as fulfilled in a work of art. Hence, Freud explains the appeal of not only Sophocles' *Oedipus Rex* but also Shakespeare's *Hamlet* and *Macbeth* in terms of the expression and satisfaction of oedipal wishes.

Before continuing it would be useful to consider a far too common objection to Freud's view on art—one raised at the start of this essay. If Freud indeed means that unfulfilled wishes are satisfied in the work of art, and this is to be taken as universal rather than significantly general, then it seems plainly false. It is implausible to suppose that *every* work of art is to be understood in this way.[14] Here Fraiberg (1956, p. 82) is correct: "What Freud did was to establish the principle that evaluations of art fall within the purview of psycho-analysis only as they reveal the psychic needs out of which art arises, the psychic materials which it uses, and the psychic purposes it serves".

But the fact that artists produce artworks in which no unfulfilled wishes are satisfied—in which they consciously address an issue, or seek to express emotion, a moral point of view, or further some cognitive goal—does nothing to undermine Freud's claims regarding the role of the orectic and the unconscious in much art—good and bad art, high and low art—and how such art is related to wish-fulfilment, dreaming and the like, and how psychoanalysis is therefore essential to understanding a great deal of art and also what is important about artists and art. Why be procrustean? A simple unified theory is desirable if and when it can be shown to be correct. But the fact that *some* art falls outside the purview of psychoanalysis—as it most certainly does—does nothing to show that *all* art does. Why would one think that it does?

The same can be said of virtually every other theory of art in philosophical aesthetics. For example, expressivism is the view that the nature or value of art is to express or transmit the artist's emotion to the viewer by means of a work of art. A cognitivist account claims that nature (value or purpose) is to further our understanding—perhaps in some unique sort of way. There are theorists that interpret these views and hence art/artists reductively. In order to be a work of art the work must, for instance, necessarily express emotion. But interpreting any of these theories (or others) as universally valid general accounts is problematic. None can encompass and account for all forms of art and for what all artists *always* do. This is just as true with regard to art preceding Marcel Duchamp's *Fountain* as it is now.[15] The point is this: one cannot refute or even criticise psychoanalytic explanation generally, including Freud's theory of art or any other theory for that matter, by showing it not to be universally true. Genuine criticism would have to show it to be insignificant—substantively—in terms of explaining what it attempts to explain.

The same strategy Sterba cites above as "Freud's most important contribution to the psychology of the work of art" has been used to explain why people watch horror films given that the experience of fear, disgust and the like seems to be intrinsically unpleasant and un-pleasurable. This is the puzzle that is sometimes called "the paradox of horror" (see Carroll (1990); Cox and Levine (2012); Levine (2004)). It isn't a paradox as there is nothing essentially paradoxical or contradictory about the notion that one may enjoy experiencing negative emotions. What may be unpleasant to one part of the personality may be quite pleasant to another. Negative emotions aren't *necessarily* unpleasant; they are *usually* unpleasant.[16] People watch horror films because they get considerable pleasure from them: "The dynamic effect of the work of art upon those who enjoy it consists in the fact that through the hallucinatory participation in the artist's infantile fantasy, the wishes of the person enjoying the work of art are at the same time also satisfied, the reason being that such wishes are common to us all" (Sterba, 1940, p. 263).[17] Audiences at first resist works of art—and not just disturbing works such as horror films—and so for a work of art to be enjoyed, barriers between the ego of the artist and the egos of the audience must be overcome. Wollheim (1970) compares the "diversion of attention" need to appreciate a joke with that of a work of art:

> [T]he "diversion of attention" required of the spectator of the work of art is far more thoroughgoing than the corresponding demand made on the hearer of the joke. For the spectator not merely uses what we may call the scenario of the work of art to divert his attention from the element of play, he may also have to use the element

> of play to divert his attention from the more disturbing content of the work of art. In this respect he combines in himself the roles of the maker and the hearer of the tendentious joke. (p. 222)

What kind of pleasure do those who enjoy horror films get? What kind of pleasure is there to be had from something that provokes negative emotion in an especially intense way? What makes the revulsion and fear typically generated by horror films a reliable source of pleasure? Horror films in particular, though the same may apply to other genres and artworks as well, are able to satisfy certain fantasies by transiently invoking and imaginatively satisfying sadistic, masochistic, fetishist, voyeuristic, vengeful and other largely unfulfilled infantile wishes. This does not make the viewer who experiences satisfaction in this way a sadist, masochist or any of the other things listed. It means that infantile wishes and fantasies remain active and are capable of being invoked and satisfied, as well as frustrated, in different ways and degrees throughout life.

As Sterba (1940, p. 261) says: "Analysis maintains that the immense dynamic effect of the work of art, the satisfaction which it brings not only to the artist, but also to the spectator, is produced though the fulfilment of the repressed infantile wishes: that the latent part, as Freud calls it, of the pleasure of art is in the opinion of psychoanalysis far greater than the manifest and aesthetic part". This is a remarkable claim. The source of a great deal of intense aesthetic pleasure is discovered to be other than what it may appear to be or what others—aesthetic theorists—have taken it to be: "The amount of pleasure radiating from these unconscious sources is automatically [and incorrectly] ascribed to the processes which bring about pleasure consciously, that is, to the aesthetic features of the work of art. The result of this is the overestimation of the aesthetic side" (Sterba, 1940, p. 268).

Part III

Elaborating Freud's views on artists and art (i.e., his "philosophy of art") takes us further into psychoanalytic theory generally rather than in the direction of his specific views on art. In any case, given the account above, we can turn to the more original contribution of this essay; the question of where that account fits with some of the central questions in philosophical aesthetics. These include (i) the nature or definition of art;

what makes something art? Is art, for example, intrinsically related to pleasure, and if so is there a distinctively aesthetic experience or pleasure that art must somehow give rise to in order to be art? (ii) The value of art; is the value of art fundamentally intrinsic, extrinsic or both? Does the value of art reside in its ability to encapsulate and somehow transfer an artist's emotion to those experiencing the artwork? Is the value of art largely cognitive; residing in its ability to reveal certain truths about the world and ourselves? Alternatively, perhaps it is both—and more? Does the conceptual content of representational or non-representational art affect aesthetic value? There are good grounds for supposing that for Freud it must, and in a way directly, relate to psychoanalysis. The value of art, or at least a good deal of art, must be regarded as connected to its function although not reduced to it. The orectic nature of art is, after all, bound up with such content even if the artist and audience are not consciously aware of it.

These are just a few of the questions about the value of art that are addressed in philosophical aesthetics. As is likely, there is no reductive account of art or its value that can come close to capturing all kinds of art—not even classical art let alone contemporary art—and its values. Thus far we have considered the implications of Freud's aesthetics for two contemporary issues in philosophical aesthetics. A final central question in philosophical aesthetics is (iii) the purpose and function of art. Any account of the function of art is going to be closely aligned with—even intrinsically connected to—the answers one gives to (i) and (ii)—that is, the nature of art and its value. Additional interrelated issues include how art is to be judged and the possibility of objective aesthetic judgement; good art *vs.* bad art and low art *vs.* high art; and the relation of ethics to aesthetic value.

As described above, Freud's focus is largely on (iii) the purpose and function of art; how art functions for the artist and audience, and also on why and how it is attractive and made attractive to audiences. But it is easy—and interesting—to extrapolate and see how Freud's understanding of art as wish-fulfilment is integral to what he sees as (ii) the value of art, and also of course to (i) the nature of art.

Freud's theory concerning the nature of art avoids reductionism in that it does not claim that all art is the product of wish-fulfilment. His account of the function and value of art also avoids reductionism in ways that much aesthetic theory often does not. Thus, for example, it would reject Bell's (1914) and Fry's (1924, pp. 2–3) simple formalism; the view that the "contemplation of formal relations constitutes the distinctive aesthetic activity", without denying that understanding and employing such relations is often an important part of the artist's craft, or that in some cases such relations account for an object's beauty and aesthetic value. But so too does Freud's account reject expressivism, cognitivism, mimesis and other essentialist accounts—insofar as they are taken as reductive accounts about the true essence of art and artistic practice as such.[18]

A psychoanalytic account that focuses on wish-fulfilment and sublimation easily accommodates the insights of these other far more exclusivist accounts—in part because it is not offering an alternative definition or even an account of the nature of art. But also because it need not, and, as far as I can tell, it does not deny significant aspects of these aesthetic theories regarding the value, purpose or function of art, or even the criteria for judging art that may be ingredient in such theory. It augments and supplements these theories and at times—and with regard to particular works of art and artists—alters their focus or offers an incompatible account. However, as psychoanalytically understood, art does (at times) embody and express the emotion of the artist and is meant to convey it to its audience as expressivism holds. And sometimes the nature or value of a work of art is to be found primarily in the way it furthers our understanding of the world—as aesthetic cognitivism maintains. Fraiberg (1956) explains Freud's account of the value of art in relation to how art works:

> ... it stresses the value of the social function of art, its communication of mind with mind and psyche with psyche. This involves the transmission of the artist's ideas and psychic states by the use of symbols capable of carrying both conscious and unconscious stimuli which together evoke in the appreciator a combined intellectual and emotional response. Their power is enhanced by their patterns (artistic form), especially when these approximate the patterns of the basic human experiences which both artist and audience have as their common heritage ... this experience includes the response to similar material in mythological or other form, and so there has been established an almost universally favourable predisposition towards artistic representation of the same themes. (p. 94)

A psychoanalytic view of the nature and value of art may be encompassing and ecumenical but it is also distinctive. It gives a special account of the kinds, types and origins of emotion that artists at times seek to express in art and that may at times be necessary to understanding, experiencing or appreciating a work of art. It gives a unique account of ways in which art furthers our understanding of the world and ourselves in *some* art. And it gives a distinctive account of aesthetic pleasure in terms not only of wish-fulfilment, but also as related to other satisfactions and as a prophylactic to neuroses and neurotic behaviour, in a way that at least partly (not universally) accounts for or explains other significant aspects of the value of art.

This, however, does not make Freud's account all things to all people. And if the account is correct then it remains true (as above) that one cannot understand art or artists—that is, a great deal about art and artists and their significance—apart from psychoanalytic theory. Philosophically or strictly speaking it remains the case that the psychoanalytic theory of art is incompatible with, for example, formalism, expressivist or cognitivist accounts narrowly understood—though not just as essentialist accounts. The incompatibility, however, is largely generated not by psychoanalytic understanding but by the myopic or reductionist views of such aesthetic theory. But one thing that becomes clear in reading competing accounts of, say, the value of art (even before Duchamp's *Fountain*) is that no single theory can account for the nature, value or purpose(s) of all art. Duchamp's *Fountain* called into question the nature of nature by conceptually challenging and expanding upon received notions of what constitutes art.

Insofar as Freud is concerned with aesthetics at all, the concern is subsidiary. He is not concerned or bothered with questions about the nature of beauty (but see his paper "On transience" (1916a)), though what he says about infantile phantasy generally—the "oceanic feeling" and the like—can be usefully compared with, for example, Kant's account of the beautiful and the sublime.[19] Nor is he concerned with the question about whether art is intrinsically or extrinsically valuable. The value of art would, I imagine, be seen by Freud as largely, but very importantly, instrumental. Look at the role it plays in the life of the artist. It's a prophylactic and a form of sublimation, to be sure. It eases and at times overcomes repression (the artist's and the audience's) and provides the artistically competent and aesthetically attuned with meaning, solace, and at times even a degree of "real world" success otherwise unattainable. (Compare it with the ways in which Nietzsche or Schopenhauer took art to be functionally significant—even salvific.) It also enables the audience certain vicarious wish-fulfilling pleasures in measures and forms that would otherwise be personally unpalatable and socially unacceptable. I doubt, however, that Freud would have trouble with the claim that "the inherent value of art is a distinct form of instrumental value" (Kieran, 2005, p. 295)[20]. Indeed, he is able to explain just what is inherently distinct and valuable about art generally as well as specifically—but only from a psychoanalytic perspective. Any psychoanalytic account of art, certainly Freud's, is inseparable from an account of art's psychological function and how it fulfils it. Psychoanalysis is also necessary to adequately understand certain works of art. There is no psychoanalytic account or judgement of art apart from this. Freud, however, says nothing that implies a denial of the entertainment value, or other values of art. To the contrary, he explains how and why art entertains and engages its audience; and he does so in ways that arguably undermine or pre-empt expressivist or cognitivist accounts—particularly as reductively conceived.

Consider too the question of how art is to be judged. Given the kind of value he attributed to art—a value based in the artistic process but one that ultimately resides in the functions it performs—it is likely that one criterion for judging art would be how well it functions to satisfy repressed wishes, overcome neurosis, and bring together the reality and pleasure principles and so on for the artist and audience (see Pataki, 1997b). Some functions will be specific to artists and some to audiences or viewers. But this functional criterion is by no means coincident with or identical to that of an aesthetic criterion for what constitutes good art in some objective sense. Or it shouldn't be. The criterion might well overlap, and on Freud's account there is good reason to assume that they would (e.g., as in *Oedipus Rex*, *Hamlet*, or the Mona Lisa). But there is no reason to think that the picture of the wolves in the trees that Freud's patient (the "Wolf Man") presented him with was regarded by Freud as good (let alone great) art, despite the fact that it performed many of the psychological functions Freud sees art as fulfilling. In fact, Freud's aesthetic taste—his aesthetic judgement—was, as one would expect, rather independent of his judgements regarding their nature, function and, even to some extent, their value as art.

What might Freud say about the aestheticism *vs.* moralism debate? It isn't straightforward, partly because his account of aesthetic value does not fit easily into the philosophical accounts that the debate is couched in. Another aspect of his account that needs to be kept in mind is that the aesthetic pleasure of the viewer (audience) arises in part from their identification with the wish-fulfilling phantasy constitutive of the artwork.

If his account of aesthetic value remains unclear (does psychoanalysis need an account?), then Freud's views on the morality of artworks are even more problematic. There is a great deal that can be said about this. From one perspective, artworks may serve an ethical purpose. For example, art may relieve unnecessary and potentially unhealthy repression, and otherwise promote the wellbeing of the artist and audience alike by temporarily satisfying wish-fulfilling phantasies—even if it does so by means of engaging "illicit" phantasy (scenarios that would be clearly immoral were they to occur in reality) and satisfying real but transient vengeful, sadistic, masochistic, voyeuristic, etc. impulses.

If one conceives of aesthetic value psychoanalytically (largely in functional terms) then it seems that the ethical nature of an artwork is going to be integrally related to its aesthetic value—though not as ordinarily conceived. That is, if an artwork embodies something unethical (a perspective, message, or understanding) its aesthetic value, psychoanalytically speaking, might conceivably be enhanced (functionally speaking) rather than lessened or undermined. The kind of release from repressive forces provided by a nasty (morally offensive) artwork may enhance its value as a work of art. Freud's theory could conceivably align the overall aesthetic value of an artwork with its moral value as closely as the philosophical view ("radical moralism") that aesthetic value is determined solely by moral value does. If it did, however, it would be for reasons rather different from this position as conceived in philosophical aesthetics—a position, probably incorrectly, attributed to Tolstoy (*What is Art?* (1896)).

Alternatively, there may be grounds (aesthetic, psychoanalytic, common sense) on which Freud could distinguish between the aesthetic value of a work of art on the one hand and the functional/ethical roles such works may perform on the other. There is nothing in Freud's account of the nature and function of art in relation to artist or audience that prevents him from holding the view that at least in some cases the immoral content of a work of art may undermine it aesthetically ("moderate moralism")—even if and when it serves some psychologically beneficial end for the artist and audience. Alternatively, moral content may at times be seen as enhancing a work's aesthetic value. A work of art that is both morally repugnant and of little if any aesthetic merit, no matter how these two are taken to be related, may still be beneficial, psychoanalytically speaking, to artist and audience. The aestheticism *vs.* moralism debate might better be reconfigured, if it is to be meaningful, from a psychoanalytic perspective. Indeed, because psychoanalysis alters our understanding of art and its moral content—and of art in relation to its moral content—the debate as currently conceived is likely to be seen as inconsequential and even otiose.

Did Freud, by means of psychoanalysis, make a distinctively new and noteworthy contribution to philosophical aesthetics and our understanding of art? Suppose his account of what is going on in the creation of (some) art and how it serves both art and audiences is roughly right. Though there are important aspects of aesthetics his explanations leave virtually untouched—including a more detailed picture of what we do learn from art and additional grounds for supposing art to be valuable—it profoundly engages with others (symbolism is not the most important) and with our understanding and even appreciation of art and artists. Did Freud's views on art make a distinctive contribution to psychoanalysis? You bet. But it does not have to be the whole story in order to do so and Freud never claimed it was. He led us right out of Plato's minimalist crib (no painting in that cave—no music either) and into the world of art, the real world, as it is.

A final point: this chapter is largely about Freud exegesis but it is worth noting that a great deal of psychoanalytic commentary on art has moved away from a focus on wish-fulfilment to Kleinian themes about reparation (which isn't far from wish-fulfilment)—as in Segal (1991), Winnicottian ideas about transitional objects, and various other things as well.[21] It remains the case, however, that from a psychoanalytic perspective there is no chance of adequately understanding art apart from psychoanalysis.

Notes

1. I refer to Freud's aesthetics, but it should be noted that he does not have a theory of aesthetics; he has a psychoanalytic view about the nature, purpose and value of art.
2. Objections at times serve a purpose because of the responses elicited. Thus Hopkins's (1988, 1982) discussion of Grünbaum's view is useful

not so much because it refutes Grünbaum, though it does, but because it is an insightful explanation of Freud's views.

3. Sayers (2007, p. 23) says: "Freud … allied the artist's transformation of their wishful fantasies into art with our dream-work … our wish-fulfilling, sleeping hallucinations into the pictures and stories we tell as dreams. Freud also allied art, by implication, with the neurotic's transformation of their repressed unconscious wishes into bodily symptoms as mnemic images of what they repress. Indeed, he mused, the conversion or transformation of their fantasies into bodily symptoms could be regarded as 'a caricature of a work of art'".

   Segal (1991, p. 61) says "… nearly all of Freud's papers on art precede his structural theory of mind … his notion of working through an unconscious conflict would have enabled him to think of art as work rather than day-dreaming or play. Also it would illuminate the question of the socalled wish-fulfilment, because the question would be, also, which wish is fulfilled—that of the id, the ego, or the superego, the aggressive or the libidinal?"
4. "Strachey lists no fewer than twenty-two papers of Freud dealing directly or indirectly with artists' individual works of art, themes reflected in literature, or general problems of artistic creativity. And in his books and papers references to works of art abound" (Segal, 1991, p. 57). Fraiberg (1956, p. 88) notes that, "Only twice did Freud essay such detailed analyses of painting and sculpture [Leonardo da Vinci's paintings and Michelangelo's sculpture *Moses*]; most of his application of psycho-analysis to art was in the field of literature". Important additional information regarding Freud's view of art is found in his correspondence (Freud, 1960a). See Gombrich (1987, p. 221). Freud's principal writing on art and literature is collected in Freud (1997).
5. See Sterba (1940, p. 257): "The … complemental relationship between the two sources of information consists then in the theoretical enlightenment about art and the artist to be found in papers devoted to the psychoanalytic theory of neurosis, while in those papers devoted to an examination of specific objects of art and artists we are given insight into more general analytic theories and methods".
6. My thanks to Tamas Pataki for his account of this issue.
7. Freud continues:

   > Now you will say that Madame Yvette has more than a single role, she embodies with equal mastery all possible characters; saints and sinners, coquettes, the virtuous, criminals and *ingénues*. That is true and it proves an unusually rich and adaptable psychic life. But I would not despair of tracing back her whole

repertory to the experiences and conflicts of her early years. It would be tempting to continue here but something keeps me back. I know that unsolicited analyses cause annoyance and I would not like to do anything to disturb the cordial sympathy of our relationship. (26 March 1931) (quoted in Gombrich, 1987, p. 237)

8. Fry (1924, pp. 2–3) at first appears to grant that some art involves wish-fulfilling phantasy—seemingly simply reminding his audience (psychologists) that this is not the whole story. Art is also "concerned with the contemplation of formal relations ... as much detached from the instinctive life as an human activity that we know". This, he says, "I consider ... the distinctive aesthetic activity". In seeking to avoid one form of reductionism Fry substitutes an equally indefensible and false one. Further in the essay it becomes clear he doesn't think the wish-fulfilling theory about art is of any significance, and that it is presumptuous of psychoanalysis to tell artists what art is about (p. 1). Roger Fry (1866–1934) was an artist, art critic, member of The Bloomsbury Group and curator of paintings at The Metropolitan Museum of Art in New York. His simple version of formalism appears to follow that of Clive Bell's (1914), whereas "Sophisticated aestheticists, such as Beardsley (1958), recognise that form is not necessarily wholly independent of content" (Kieran, 2005, p. 296). But it is Fry, not Freud, who presumes to speak on behalf of all art and all artists. Fry's own account of the nature of art is elitist (see pp. 12–14 and his account of "the real artist"). There is also little indication in the essay that he understands Freud's account of art, what he was trying to do, or the supporting psychoanalytic theory. For example, Fry seems unaware (or just ignores the fact) that on Freud's account artists are not generally conscious of the wish-fulfilling aspect of their work or that their activity is a form of sublimation.
9. See Levine (2005). Fraiberg (1956, p. 94) notes: "Generalizations are risky here, but as Freud points out, the relation between possible sublimation and indispensable sexual activity naturally varies very much in different persons, and indeed with the various kinds of occupation. An abstinent artist is scarcely conceivable: an abstinent young intellectual is by no means a rarity. The young intellectual can by abstinence enhance his powers of concentration, whereas the production of the artist is probably powerfully stimulated by his sexual experience ..." [cf. "'Civilized' sexual morality and modern nervousness". Freud (1908d, p. 92)]
10. Young-Bruehl (1996). The account is basically [essentially?] Freudian, although the basic structure of psychological defence can be

maintained in non-Freudian ways; without assuming a Freudian model of psychosexual development, for example. The most thorough and careful development of the psychological defense model has been undertaken within a psychoanalytic framework. See also Pataki's essay "Psychoanalysis, Racism and Envy" (Levine and Pataki (Eds.), 2004, pp. 179–205) and his introduction (pp. 1–23).

11. Fraiberg (1956, p. 94): "Neurosis is not a condition of artistic creativity ... In Freud's view the artistic gift is as likely to be used for the purpose of avoiding neurosis as it is for augmenting it. In fact, both uses may occur simultaneously, the preventive function usually being the dominant one. For the artist, with his extraordinary psychic sensitivity, the regulatory devices which society furnishes (education, convention, certain socially approved activities like business, politics, and war) are not enough. He achieves his best results in the transformation of his instinctual impulses through artistic activity. If this fails, as it sometimes does, he crosses the border into neurosis".
12. For details of publication see Jones (1957, pp. 142–143, 426–427), Frank (1976, pp. 379–385), Rice, 1985, pp. 210–223) [cf. (Rosen, 1988)].
13. Freud (1914b, p. 212): "[W]hat grips us so powerfully can only be the artist's *intention* in so far as he succeeds in expressing it in his work and in getting us to understand it. I realize that this cannot be merely a matter of *intellectual* comprehension; what he aims at is to awaken in us the same emotional attitude, the same mental constellation which produces in him the impetus to create". Fraiberg (1956, p. 95) says, "They become a work of art through alteration which softens objections to them, disguises their personal origin and, by observance of the principles of aesthetics, offers the onlookers or hearers attractive pleasure-premiums".
14. See Adolf Grünbaum's (1988) discussion of Freud's so-called "tally argument". According to Grünbaum (1988, p. 18) "even if the clinical evidence could be taken at face value, Freud's principal clinical arguments for his entire cornerstone theory of repression (the 'Tally Argument') still turns out to be fundamentally flawed". According to the tally argument (Clark and Wright 1988, p. ix) "a patient will experience a lasting cure only if the psychoanalytic interpretations achieved in therapy tally with something real in him". The objection is similar to the one about art discussed here. The critique rests on taking Freud's claim concerning a ground for validating psychoanalysis to be universal. No one suffering from neurosis could be cured unless the psychoanalytic interpretation "tallied" with the nature of the complaint. Grünbaum sees Freud's claim as falsifiable and indeed falsified if one allows for cases of spontaneous remission or remission of symptoms due to suggestion (a placebo effect) by the psychoanalyst, effects of transference,

etc. (See Hopkins, 1988, p. 34). Yet as Grünbaum acknowledges—and how could one not—Freud was well aware of the problem of contamination and the vicissitudes of analysis. In *The Psychotherapy of Hysteria*, Freud (in Breuer & Freud, 1895d, p. 305) says "No doubt fate would find it easier than I do to relieve you of your illness". Freud did not rest his case for the validation of psychoanalysis exclusively on clinical data rather than on such data along with evidence gleaned from wider experience (as in *The Psychopathology of Everyday Life* (Freud, 1901b)). Psychological factors that one may be unaware of are virtually always present in determining how neuroses play out; whether they will be permanent and the like. The short and simple refutation of Grünbaum's critique of the tally argument is to deny that Freud meant it to be taken as universally valid, literally at face value, as Grünbaum's argument peculiarly insists it should be.

15. http://philosophynow.org/issues/67/Did_Duchamps_Urinal_Flush_Away_Art [last accessed]

    Kieran (2005, p. 304) says "Perhaps the real problem concerns the ways in which two rival but partial accounts [aestheticism and cognitivism] have attempted to generalize indiscriminately over all the arts to give an account of the value of art. Hence it would be more informative to concentrate on such questions in relation to particular art forms and genres. After all, to think one of the two rival traditions could hope to capture everything that is valuable about art, ranging across forms such as pure music, abstract art, sculpture, dance, literature, and film and down to genres within a particular form such as light comedy, satire, tragedy and documentary, would appear hopelessly ambitious".

16 This is Gaut's (1993) way of dissolving the paradox of horror. But if Freud is right, then insofar as the source and nature of the pleasures involved remain unexplained or unaccounted for, such an explanation is superficial. It remains descriptive rather than explanatory.

17. See Freud's (1908e) "Creative writers and day-dreaming" for an account, in terms of artistic technique, of how we are able to share in the artist's gratification of wish-fulfilment. Sterba (1940, p. 264): "The possibility offered by the work of art of an identification with the hallucinatory wish fulfilment—on the basis of kindred wishes—one can even say, the urge of the work of art to this identification, must be considered as a condition of the work of art". Part of what takes place in the artistic process is very much like what goes on in "dream work". See Sterba's (1940, pp. 264–268) summary.

18. There are many recent philosophical introductions, guides, companions and handbooks to aesthetic theory. See for example Graham (2000); Gaut and Lopes (Eds.) (2005); Davies, Higgins, Hopkins, Stecker, and

Cooper, (Eds.) (2009); Kieran (Ed.) (2006), Lemarque and Olsen (Eds.) (2004).

19. "Kant distinguishes two notions of the sublime: the mathematically sublime and the dynamically sublime. In the case of both notions, the experience of the sublime consists in a feeling of the superiority of our own power of reason, as a supersensible faculty, over nature … We have the feeling of the dynamically sublime when we experience nature as fearful while knowing ourselves to be in a position of safety and hence without in fact being afraid". (Ginsborg, 2013; §28, p. 261). Compare with Freud (1930a): "I can imagine that the oceanic feeling became connected with religion later on. The 'oneness with the universe' which constitutes its ideational content sounds like a first attempt at a religious consolation, as though it were another way of disclaiming the danger which the ego recognizes as threatening it from the external world" (p. 72).
20. Kieran (2005, p. 294) says: "For something to possess inherent value it must not only be the means to a valuable end, but also the means must partly constitute and thus be internal to the ends involved". Kieran is discussing the views of Stecker (1997), who claims that the value of art is not intrinsic, and Budd (1995).
21. Pataki (1997b, p. 48): "Heinz Kohut [1978, pp. 821–822] has put forward the idea that the work of art is an extension of the self, more specifically of the perfect or ideal self. We create for ourselves idealised representations of how we would like to be, using the material of admired or envied others, and in fantasy elaborating our own features. Such representations, because they are often radically incompatible with reality, are largely unconscious, but nevertheless play a very important part in the regulation of self-esteem. Falling short of the ideal self in appearance, action or virtue, causes pining and suffering; approaching it enhances self-esteem and the sense of well-being".

My thanks to Tamas Pataki for his insights, and to Oenone Rooksby and Joely-Kym Sobott for their assistance.

CHAPTER FOUR

Beyond the philosophy of the (unconscious) mind: the Freudian cornerstone as scientific theory, a cult, and a way of talking

Vesa Talvitie

The scientific status of psychoanalysis may be approached from numerous perspectives—methodology, empirical studies supporting and contradicting psychoanalytic claims, the relations between psychoanalytic and other theories, and so on. In terms of the philosophy of mind, the unconscious is a self-evident and actually rather appealing viewpoint: on one hand Freud's idea(s) about the unconscious, "the cornerstone of psychoanalysis", still characterises the theories and practice of psychoanalysis. On the other hand we find that from the 1980s onwards there has been extensive research around the topic of the unconscious (unconscious processes, implicit memory, procedural knowledge, etc.), outside the scope of psychoanalysis. It has been argued that those studies both support (for example, Westen, 1998) and contradict (for example, Talvitie, 2009) Freud's insights. This kind of situation indicates that there is not only room for philosophical considerations but also a real need for them.

Around the turn of the millennium I spent some years writing a doctoral thesis on the relation between the "psychoanalytic" and the "cognitive-neuroscience" unconscious. For the most part I focused on empirical research on unconscious matters, and topics falling in the domain of the philosophy of the mind. I wrote "Freudian unconscious and cognitive neuroscience: From unconscious fantasies to neural algorithms" (Talvitie, 2009), basing this on my dissertation, and the main points can be presented as follows.

Freud made certain very interesting observations, and created explanations that reflected the prevailing state of art in science. (When talking about science, I'm referring to both natural science and the human sciences.) A century later we find that issues and topics relating to the Freudian unconscious have been studied; actually studied a lot, both in terms of empirical research and philosophy of the mind, which enables us to present an up-to-date formulation of the "Freudian unconscious". By leaning on views shaped into such general presentations as, for example, Wilson's (2002) *Strangers to Ourselves: Discovering the Adaptive Unconscious*; Mlodinow's (2012) *Subliminal: How Your Unconscious Mind Rules Your Behavior*; and Hassin, Uleman, and Bargh's (2005) *The New Unconscious*, it is rather easy to reformulate Freud's ideas (concerning the unconscious determinants of our behaviour) in a manner that is in line with present-day views of behavioural sciences.

When reflecting on my conclusions and the impact of my doctoral thesis some years later, I find that the world has remained the same: folks in the psychoanalytic and cognitive camps (still) do not care much how the issues around the term unconscious are seen on the other side. I have also found that my viewpoint was somewhat restricted: I now believe that one should not remain in the domain of philosophy of mind, but also study the psychoanalytic view of man as a metaphysical conception. Thus, I wrote with (my former supervisor) Juhani Ihanus an article focusing upon the metaphysical issues.

In that article (published in *The International Journal of Psychoanalysis*—Talvitie & Ihanus, 2011a) we argued that neuropsychoanalysis—an endeavour that appeals to some people as an exciting and modern branch of psychoanalysis—is incongruent with both traditional Freudian viewpoints and basic tenets of modern neuroscience. The article was accepted, despite bringing bad news both to the advocates of neuropsychoanalysis and its opponents representing the traditional reading of psychoanalysis, and the journal also published three comments concerning it. As far as I know, the rather serious problems we introduced have still not been treated in depth, and especially conspicuous is the seeming neglect of our arguments from the realm of neuropsychoanalysis.

Researchers quite often complain bitterly that their findings do not enjoy the attention they deserve, and the above reflections of mine are by no means an exception. But, researchers' self-centredness aside, the psychoanalytic community does possess an exceptional relation to Freud's opinions concerning the unconscious mind as well as other matters. Some outsiders even consider psychoanalysis as a cult. On this basis, we might presume that the characteristics of psychoanalysis as a community affect how the unconscious is conceptualised in psychoanalytic theories. However, it is difficult to argue on this ground without falling into the ad hominem fallacy.

Regardless of the characteristics of the psychoanalytic community and the scientific status of Freud's theories, discussions about defences and unconscious wishes and fears enjoy a rather significant role in the folk psychology of our times. People conceptualise their states of mind as well as their acts in terms of unconscious wishes, fears, and memories, and this way of talking is also echoed in psychotherapists' consultation rooms—even those therapists who are not psychoanalytically oriented. From this perspective psychoanalysis is a profession that has a special relation to folk-psychological talk of the unconscious. In some contexts that relation is a stigma; in others it may provide a competitive edge.

Below I will connect together rather disjointed aspects of the Freudian unconscious, presenting frameworks in which the scientific and ideological issues, as well as those relating to psychoanalysis as a profession, should be set. In the opening section I study the Freudian idea of the mental unconscious from the viewpoints of philosophy of mind and metaphysics. In the next two sections I will go beyond that perspective and approach the cult and profession aspects of the psychoanalytic community in terms of social epistemology, sociology of professions, and philosophy of language.

Before going to those issues, let me, however, present a suggestion about how the diversity of psychoanalytic theories might be seen. The suggestion is crucial for the current topic, since it presents the unconscious as the common denominator of different psychoanalytic theories and schools. Laymen talk about psychoanalysis as a unitary doctrine, but actually psychoanalysis consists of several theories, which possess rather complicated interrelations. Psychoanalysis is—understandably—often equated with Sigmund Freud. When we consider psychoanalytic *clinicians* in particular, however, Freud's (clinical) ideas dominated the field in Europe only for a relatively short period, ending around the year 1918 (Makari, 2008, p. 299), and in America such a hegemony has never existed (Makari, 2012). Thus, we might even state that in (present-day) *clinical* psychoanalysis, Freud is a relatively peripheral figure.

I have argued elsewhere (Talvitie, 2012, pp. 1–15) that the field of psychotherapy inevitably exists in the post-Tower of Babel era: psychological terms are constructs, with infinite possibilities to conceptualise human patterns of feeling, thinking, and reacting. Thus, the diversity of psychoanalytic theories reflects the state of the art typical not only for psychotherapies, but in various fields within the humanities. The theoretical diversity seen in clinical psychoanalysis is by no means exceptional. There are hundreds of different psychotherapy schools, and, for example, cognitive psychotherapy contains branches such as cognitive therapy (CT), cognitive behavioural therapy (CBT), cognitive constructivist psychotherapy, cognitive emotive narrative therapy (CENT), post-rationalist cognitive therapy, rational-emotive behaviour therapy, mindfulness-based cognitive therapy, and so on. Thus cognitive therapies also lack a consistent theoretical core that all cognitive therapists would accept. Perhaps only a young, authoritative school of psychotherapy could possess a coherent theoretical basis (whether or not it had "scientific" standing). Thus, when studying cognitive, psychodynamic, or family therapy, researchers often merely select one theory as representative of the orientation, and then focus upon it. In the case of psychoanalysis both critics and advocates of psychoanalysis most often choose Freud's theories.

Freud's theories are at the same time a justified and problematic choice. In any case it is plausible to state that certain presuppositions concerning the unconscious are an important part of the shared foundation of different psychoanalytic theories: both theoretical and practical focus is upon repressed desires and fears, and defensive operations. On this basis, my suggestion is the following: in academic contexts it is (often) reasonable to treat diversity in psychoanalysis as a *research programme* (instead of a theory or -ies) grounded on shared ideas about the unconscious.

The unconscious as a scientific theory: from the philosophy of the mind to metaphysics

The Freudian unconscious and philosophy of mind

Freud called his ideas concerning the unconscious the cornerstone of psychoanalysis, and they set the logic of psychoanalytic thinking: psychic disorders as well as slips of tongue are caused by repressed ideas located in the unconscious part of the mind. Repressed contents may be brought (or transformed) into the domain of consciousness, which is the goal of classic psychoanalysis, since once these contents are conscious the disorders are alleviated. A popular version of this logic has spread widely around Western culture, appearing as an appreciation of self-reflection. In the scope of science and humanities, however, Freud's logic faces serious difficulties in terms of ontology and causal power of the unconscious. Below I present the problems of the Freudian cornerstone as a chain of questions.

How and where do repressed wishes, fears, memories and ideas exist? Freud stressed the mental essence of the unconscious, which means that repressed contents lie in the mind but nevertheless outside consciousness. On this basis it is very unclear what a repressed mental content is, and where and how it exists. Freud does give us some hints on the essence of it: it cannot be observed directly, but only through its consequences (dreams, slips of tongue, psychic disorders); unconscious contents are like conscious ones, just lacking the property of consciousness (Freud, 1915e, p. 168). But in my view these sorts of hints are not informative at all, and in some cases they sound like the oracle's or a Zen master'scomments. Freud's assertive and self-confident style may make one forget that he had not perceived the unconscious either—he just created a theory about it. Anyway, as far as the unconscious is able to affect phenomenal states and bodily ones, one has to account for its existence somewhere, somehow.

How do repressed contents become conscious? Freud used the so-called perception metaphor in order to illustrate the logic of the repressed becoming conscious (see, for example, Talvitie & Ihanus, 2003a). He stated that similar to physical objects, mental contents may or may not be perceived—and if a content is not perceived, this is not an argument against its existence. However, it is very unclear where the non-perceived (and also perceived) mental contents lie, and what sense-organ is used to perceive them; we see with the help of our eyes, hear with ears, but *what is the organ that perceives mental contents*?

As we can see, the cornerstone is surrounded by a web of very difficult questions, and thus it is not surprising that there is a lot of criticism toward the psychoanalytic idea of the unconscious (see, for example, MacIntyre, 1958; O'Brien & Jureidini, 2002; Searle, 1992; Talvitie, 2009; Talvitie & Ihanus, 2011a; Uleman, 2005). Psychoanalysis has not been able to give satisfactory answers to these tricky questions during the past century, and it may be the case that answers will not be forthcoming in the next hundred years either—many psychoanalysts are more fascinated by the mysterious nature of the cornerstone concepts than about the scientific status of psychoanalysis.

In order to slide smoothly into the domain of metaphysics, let us present one further question: *How are unconscious repressed contents able to cause disorders?* Psychic disorders often possess a bodily aspect: when having a panic attack the heart beats faster and the hands tremble. However, if the unconscious is mental, how is it able to possesses causal power over the physical body in this way? Now we are in the domain of metaphysics, as is also the case when we add the question concerning free will. Thus it seems clear that the cornerstone concept of psychoanalysis is not restricted to the domain of the philosophy of mind, and therefore we should take up something larger—the *psychoanalytic conception of man*—and put this under scrutiny. Such a move implies a reformulation of the fundamental common denominator of psychoanalytic theories: it is not merely the Freudian unconscious, but rather this larger concept—the psychoanalytic view of man.

Painting a bigger picture—metaphysics

What is a "conception of man"? It is reasonable to approach the question through two tightly intertwined issues: first, what man is (supposed to be) "made of", and second "what makes him tick" (how the reasons and/or causes behind human behaviour are sketched). The candidates for the constituents of man are body (and brain), mind, and soul. Regarding soul (or the spiritual aspect of man), in our times it is considered a religious concept rarely taken seriously as an object of scientific study. Contrary to that, the existence of the body and the brain has been denied by only some idealistic philosophers living hundreds of years ago (Bishop Berkeley (see Berkeley, 1988; originally published in 1710 and 1713) being the only one commonly known). Thus, so-called *immaterialism* is a peripheral metaphysical option for present-day research—both laymen and (especially neuro-) scientists do think that our bodies and brains exist outside our imagination.

Some contemporary philosophers (eliminative materialists like Paul Churchland (1988) and John Bickle (2003)), for their part, have denied the existence of mind. Apart from philosophers, empirical researchers rarely follow that path. As far as a researcher is acquainted with philosophical topics, he or she usually advocates some kind of "realism", and calls him or herself, for example, an emergent materialist or a (dual-aspect) monist. Thus, regarding the "made of" or constituent aspect of the conception of man, the above exclusions and inclusions lead to the conclusion that for most present-day researchers man consists of body (and brain) and mind (often equated with consciousness—see Strawson, 1994).

For psychiatrists, psychotherapists, and other clinicians, eliminative materialism (i.e., denying the existence of the mind) is simply absurd—if we did not possess minds, what are the grounds for aiming to relieve suffering? We argued (Talvitie & Ihanus, 2011a) that all psychotherapies have to rest upon the conception we termed "ordinary mentalism". Similar to folk psychology, that conception presupposes that mental matters like contents of consciousness, feelings and mental images have causal power over other mental states and behaviour—for instance, a certain belief or desire may make me go to the shop or practise guitar. A clinician also presumes that his or her clients (as well as him- or herself) possess free will. Thus, without these metaphysical presuppositions behind ordinary mentalism there is simply no rationale for clinical work.

When considering the above terms "causal power" and "free will" we move from the question of "what is man made of" to that of "what makes us tick". The presupposition of free will, in particular, constitutes not only our foundational institutions, but also our very interactions among people: a judge cannot help from presupposing free will; it is inescapable to think that an unfaithful spouse could have done otherwise; a clinician would lack rationale for his or her work if we did not possess such free will and the concomitant mental states of anguish and anxiety that often accompany such choices (see Pockett, Banks, & Gallagher, 2006; Talvitie & Ihanus, 2011a).

It is important to be explicit that there is a clear tension between ordinary mentalism and a scientifically based materialism. One may try to represent (I would say camouflage) ordinary mentalism as a type of property dualism or an emergent materialism (which are commonly accepted positions in the academic community). However, the ideas of free will and causal powers of the mind often contain at least a flavour of Cartesian soul and dualism, the problems of which are commonly known (at least among philosophers—see, for example, Kim, 2005).

As such, it is important to bear in mind that the one who claims something, has the burden of proof. Thus, when someone claims that it is reasonable to explain mental characteristics or mental disorders by referring to brain, mind, mental unconscious, demons, birth order, or astronomical phenomena, the burden of proof is on the side of that "someone" making the claim. But how do the advocates of ordinary mentalism (i.e., all of us at least in daily, real-life situations) carry it off?

We do this mostly by referring to our inner feelings (i.e., presenting a first-person point of view argument) along with commonly held intuitions: don't you feel hurt if I prick your finger with a needle? If someone steals your car or violates your relative, don't you think he or she should be punished (which implies that he or she possesses free will)? These kinds of arguments are insufficient in academic contexts, but very persuasive in daily life situations. When it comes to the causal power of the brain, new technology and equipment has enabled neuroscientists to generate studies on how a certain part of the brain or a certain neurotransmitter possesses a crucial role in a certain mental or behavioural phenomenon. Thus, hardly anybody dares to doubt that the brain possesses causal power.

To conclude, the existence and causal power of the mind, as well as free will, are from the perspective of science very dubious presuppositions. Ordinary mentalism is nevertheless an unavoidable presupposition (or a constituent) of psychotherapy and actually of most human activities. All kinds of psychotherapies are tied to these particular metaphysical conceptions of man.

Psychoanalytic mentalism—could the mental unconscious make us tick?

Above I have argued that when the scientific status of psychoanalysis is considered, one does not get anywhere by studying numerous individual psychoanalytic theories. Instead, it is reasonable to focus on their common ground, which in my view is the psychoanalytic conception of man. The origin of the conception—which we (Talvitie & Ihanus, 2011a) termed "psychoanalytic mentalism"—can be tracked to Kant's philosophy and positivism (Tauber, 2010; Talvitie, Ihanus, & Kaitaro, 2013).

Psychoanalytic mentalism can be summarised in two presuppositions: first, man has an unconscious (part of the) mind (the "what man is made of" aspect), and second, that the unconscious possesses causal power over consciousness and behaviour (the "what make us tick" aspect). I demonstrated above how difficult it is even to conceive of how the mental unconscious might exist. Below, we shall see that psychoanalytic mentalism has also considerable problems with forming a coherent picture on the "what makes us tick" aspect.

Nobody has succeeded in explaining how the immaterial mind—unconscious or conscious—is able to move material body. Advocates of ordinary mentalism are apt to think that mental phenomena (feelings, ideas, etc.) have neural correlates, and thus that the causal power of mind becomes somehow realised via the brain (this view can be problematic in that it easily leads to epiphenomenalism). But over and above these problems, what happens with respect to the mental unconscious—are there neural correlates for it?

It is difficult to see how this issue might be studied empirically, but anyway both "no" and "yes" answers are troublesome (for a detailed study, see Talvitie & Ihanus, 2011a). If the mental unconscious does not have neural correlates it is difficult to see how it might affect the body—the Freudian cornerstone appears as a "ghost in the machine", or a doctrine based single-handedly on faith in psychoanalytic concepts. If one presumes that there are neural correlates for the mental unconscious, the first task is to pinpoint them. But on what grounds could one argue that a certain neural network was a neural correlate for the mental unconscious (or a certain content of it)?

It is difficult to sketch a reasonable answer to this. But if a neural correlate could be somehow determined, does one need the idea of the *mental* unconscious anymore? For if a certain neural network—a correlate of the mental unconscious or one of its contents—is found to cause a slip of tongue or a psychic disorder, the mental unconscious itself does not possess an explanatory role anymore (i.e., it is just an epiphenomenon): if the brain (i.e., neural networks as the neural correlates of the mental unconscious) does the job, why should we talk about the mental unconscious? It seems that the Freudian cornerstone is doomed to be either a ghost in the machine or a needless presupposition.

On the past, current and forthcoming scientific status of the cornerstone

Science has not proved that people *do not* possess souls; that astronomical phenomena *do not* affect our personality; that demons *do not* cause serious psychic illnesses; or that somewhere in the universe there *does not exist* a planet made of cheese. However, as far as the above more or less absurd ideas have not (and more strongly cannot have) generated credible research projects, they are not scientific. Theories are never proven true in the strict sense of the word; one of the important measures of the success of a theory or conception appears rather in its ability to generate research projects (see, for example, Laudan, 1996). Consider Darwin's theory of evolution: it has inspired research in, and received support from, many domains of research.

The psychoanalytic research project, explaining disorders and other mental and behavioural phenomena by referring to the mental unconscious, did have a rather successful run from about the 1920s to the 1980s. In many countries even psychoanalytic clinical training was (in the domain of psychiatry) well thought of in the academic world (Paris, 2005; Stepansky, 2009). The situation has changed, however. The research project based upon psychoanalytic mentalism has become restricted to the scope of the psychoanalytic community. We might even say that from the 1980s the presupposition of the unconscious mind has moved from the field of science toward the category of alternative medicine.

The rather new endeavour of neuropsychoanalysis presents itself as bridging the views of neuroscience and psychoanalysis. Thus, it might be thought to be able to restore scientific credibility to the psychoanalytic cornerstone. However, neuropsychoanalysis has carefully avoided addressing the incompatibilities between cognitive neuroscience and psychoanalytic mentalism. Further, it seems that neuropsychoanalysts have not cared to inform their non-psychoanalytic collaborators about their own inherent metaphysical background assumptions. As far as I know, only Juhani Ihanus and I (Talvitie & Ihanus, 2003a, 2003b, 2006, 2011a, 2011b) have explicitly addressed the incompatibility question. In this light it is difficult to see neuropsychoanalysis as a saviour of psychoanalytic mentalism.

Restoration of the psychoanalytic cornerstone can be sought in a different direction from that of neuroscience, via philosophy. Psychoanalytic texts treating philosophical issues in the past focused mainly on themes of continental philosophy—the heroes of that philosophical tradition include Martin Heidegger, Edmund Husserl, Emanuel Levinas, Jean-Paul Sartre, Søren Kierkegaard, Jürgen Habermas, and Hans-Georg Gadamer. The cognitive revolution in the 1970s brought out a new generation of philosophers representing (mainly) analytic philosophy: Jerry Fodor, Daniel Dennett, Paul and Patricia Churchland, Hilary Putnam, John Searle, Fred Dretske, Hubert Dreyfus, Jaegwon Kim.

When the essence of the mind and its relation to the brain is studied from the philosophical viewpoint, the writings of the latter group of philosophers form the modern context of the discussion. The crucial thing for our topic is that these philosophers are hardly ever cited in the psychoanalytic literature. Thus, although the relations between the psychoanalytic conception of man and continental philosophy has been widely studied, psychoanalytic writers have not been interested in exploring the relation between psychoanalysis and modern philosophy of mind and analytic philosophy in general.

Let us note that above I have *not* argued that psychoanalytic mentalism and the presupposition of mental unconscious are wrong or untrue. Instead, I have shown how badly these views fit with the background assumptions of current-day behavioural sciences. Consequently, the foundations for genuine collaboration with academic psychology, philosophy and neuroscience are, for the present, unfortunately quite weak.

The problems with the Freudian cornerstone imply that when one is interested in finding out what lies behind particular phenomena—like, for example, a certain psychic disorder—psychoanalytic mentalism is not a promising foundation for the study. For the psychoanalytic community this problem seems to necessitate adopting the following strategy: as far as psychoanalysis aims at being an academic discipline, it would be rational to abandon the cornerstone concept and embrace, instead, recent views concerning unconscious matters. However, it is clear that the psychoanalytic community is not willing at all to make this strategically wise move. Why? Here we can hear relentless Freud bashers whispering, "As I have told you for years, psychoanalysis is not science but a cult formed by father Freud". To put it a little less degradingly, in psychoanalysis there is an ideological element that affects its theory formation, too. Below, our sight is turned to that aspect of psychoanalysis.

The cult of the unconscious: from the secret rings to the epistemic machinery

Let us begin with some examples, the first two from the United States. David Levy commented in 1939 about the disputes in the American psychoanalytic communities as follows: "The old-timers from Vienna are a good example of the danger of starting with holy writ … [T]hey never ask themselves the question 'What is the truth?' They ask rather 'Does he agree with Freud?' implying 'There is no truth but Freud.' And that is why the discussions are so little grounded in empiricism, so thoroughly dialectic" (David Levy to Lawrence Kubie, 14 November 1939, David Levy Papers; cited in Makari, 2012, p. 118). More than forty years later, Heinz Kohut, one of the big names in American psychoanalysis, claimed that psychoanalysis should "make the decisive developmental step of the full transmuting internalization of the great parental self-object of its past—it must turn from the study of Freud to the study of man" (Kohut, 1982, p. 405).

When looking for the source of this kind of problem, Freud's setting of the cornerstone concepts is, of course, crucial: "The assumption that there are unconscious mental processes, the recognition of the theory of resistance and repression, the appreciation of the importance of sexuality and of the Oedipus complex—these constitute the principal subject-matter of psycho-analysis and the foundations of its theory. No one who cannot accept them all should count himself a psycho-analyst" (Freud, 1923a, p. 247). Freud's behaviour toward non-conformist members of the early psychoanalytic community on one hand, and loyal ones on the other, is also revealing. Freud even formed a secret committee (equipping its members with rings) in order to safeguard the dogma after his death (Grosskurth, 1991). It is obvious that Freud had a rather vigorous desire to control the future of psychoanalysis—he wanted to tie the hands of his followers (or rather their minds). One may look at the psychoanalytic communities of the post-Freud era and ponder whether he could have succeeded better.

Present-day psychoanalytic communities are of course not forced to follow Freud's authoritarian suggestions. Everybody with some knowledge of psychoanalytic communities (others may study psychoanalytic politics, for example, Grosskurth (1991), Makari (2008, 2012) and Reeder (2004)) knows that Freud's legacy (not withstanding differing ideas on what it actually is) is still alive. The tension described in the first part of this chapter is a consequence of this state of affairs.

Ideology in science and clinical practice

Science is value-free—or at least it is held important that it should be. However, ideological elements are by no means absent within psychology and other disciplines. Behaviourism's denial to talk about inner mental states clearly has an ideological slant, and, for example, Kurt Danziger (1990, pp. 136–155) has talked about *methodolatry* (method-fetishism would be a more powerful expression): namely that psychologists' interest to mirror natural-science methodology has occasionally been stronger than the interest toward the objects of study. Brain study and biological psychiatry, for their part, are affected by strong economic interests (see, for example, Kirsch, 2009). In the domain of psychotherapy research, researchers have often found that those therapies that reflected their own orientation were more effective (Luborsky & Barrett, 2006). George Stricker states that "[w]e can assume that every practitioner has a strong allegiance to his or her own treatment approach" (Stricker, 2006, p. 286).

Values, or "ideologies", are also a crucial part of professions. The Hippocratic oath represents an ideological aspect of a physician's profession, and an antiquarian bookseller may or may not cherish his profession's cultural value of old literature and old things in general. Freidson (2001, p. 122) states, "[t]he professional ideology of service goes beyond serving others' choices. Rather, it claims devotion to a transcendent value which infuses its specialization with a larger and putatively higher goal which may reach beyond that of those they are supposed to serve". Psychoanalytic clinicians' communities share the general ideological components with other psychotherapists and health professionals. The distinctive ideological component concerns Freud's theories.

As we can see, although psychology of science has been rather uninterested in the researchers' non-epistemic motives (see, for example, Feist, 2006), it is commonplace for researchers as well as clinicians to possess emotional and ideological bonds to the theories they apply. That said—what bearing, after all, does the ideological component have on the scientific standing of psychoanalysis? Talk about the ideological component might seem like a social version of (the fallacious) ad hominem argument—since one's personal characteristic do not affect the truth-value of his or her claims, we might think that the communal or institutional characteristics of psychoanalysis should likewise not affect the scientific status of psychoanalytic theories. Whatever happened between Freud and Adler a century ago, and/or whatever conflicts take place in present-day psychoanalytic institutions, should have no bearing on the scientific status of psychoanalytic theories.

It seems that we have arrived at an ambiguous situation: on one hand it is intuitively evident that when a discipline possesses cult-like aspects it is better to be cautious toward its "truths". On the other hand, scientific disciplines often possess ideological undertones, and the argument "but psychoanalysis is too ideological to be a scientific discipline" does not sound like a strong one.

Freud-bashing as well as the cult around Freud's legacy represents an equally personifying approach to science. Popular scientific writings in the past have supported that kind of approach by telling stories about (solitary) scientific masterminds making respectable discoveries by unveiling the truths of nature. However, we do not get science right by thinking in terms of geniuses and collections of truths—rather, science is characterised by (empirical and logical) procedures, through which the grounds of different beliefs, claims and suppositions are studied (see, for example, Chalmers, 1990; Kitcher, 1993; Laudan, 1996; Ziman, 2000).

In order to lay the groundwork for studying psychoanalytic communities, let us take a closer look at the characteristics of scientific community. The following description on the functioning of the scientific community is quite near to Alvin Goldman's (1999, pp. 244–271) views (or his so-called *comparative scientific superiority thesis*).

On the dynamics and structures of academic community

The academic community surely attracts intelligent and creative people. But the reason(s) why beliefs generated in the domain of science should be taken as more trustworthy than other beliefs should not be a function of the quality of persons. The power and competencies of science are based on the structure, norms and dynamics of the academic community.

The aim of scientific activities is to "change the picture": to present new explanations for a phenomenon (the more undisputed and/or far-reaching the explanation, the better), or to challenge the prevailing explanation (the more commonly accepted the prevailing explanation is, the better). Our only way to study whether an idea is true is to evaluate empirical data and arguments speaking both for and against it. Thus, the ideas that we consider as true are at best only well founded. And it may occur that new evidence changes the picture (again).

Researchers' aims are generally realised in articles, being published in scientific journals. Publication of an article, however, is as such not the crucial issue, but the (possible) discussion after that—the more the article is cited, the better. Fame and success of a researcher or a group of researchers depend on how well they succeed in the game of argumentation and critique. That way scientists' personal "nonepistemic motives" (Goldman, 1999, pp. 260–263) contribute to serving the aims of science.

Over and above whatever commitment individual scientists (as persons) have toward supporting the critical evaluation of ideas, the dynamics of scientific community strongly advocate for just such evaluations. Crucial for these dynamics is that the scientific community consists of agents—journals, universities, faculties, funds—that are relatively independent from each other. If a researcher has enemies in one direction, or surrounding people seem to be too "stupid" to understand his or her revolutionary ideas, it is always possible to move to another university, or try to get the manuscript published in another journal. The power of science to generate well-founded beliefs is due to these kinds of dynamics and structures of the scientific community. Let us also remember the significance of the practical aspect of the academic community: the researchers are, for the most part, working full-time with science.

When approaching the scientific status of psychoanalysis from the social perspective, we are led to ask what the psychoanalytic community is like, and especially what it is like compared to the scientific community. By elaborating the above characterisation of the nature of the scientific community we get a preliminary conceptualisation of the weakness of the psychoanalytic community: it lacks mechanisms for controlling its members' non-epistemic motives.

Is the psychoanalytic community scientific?

A century ago Sigmund Freud succeeded in "changing the picture" in a quite dramatic manner. Following this for some decades, psychoanalysis was undeniably part of the scientific community, and thus was in a social sense "scientific". Kitcher (1992) holds that in terms of the standards of his time, Freud's ideas were scientifically sound. About a half century later in America the status of a slightly different kind of psychoanalysis was even higher. The core term was "narcissism", which enjoys only a minor role in classical psychoanalysis. Lunbeck (2012, p. 216) states, "Christopher Lash's *Culture of narcissism*, published in 1978, positioned psychoanalysis at the center of a long-running conversation about the failings of the modal America". Lunbeck (2012) continues, "Lash skillfully—if promiscuously—mined the discipline, fashioning a contradictory theoretical hodgepodge of Kohut, Otto Kernberg, and Melanie Klein, among other analysts, into a manifestly convincing and rhetorically persuasive account of precipitous national decline" (p. 216).

Success of a discipline or a theoretical orientation depends on its relation to the surrounding world. It should possess shared foundations with other disciplines in order to be taken seriously; it should be able to provide fresh viewpoints for study and allow the changes of the surrounding world to promote change in itself. The unapologetic, confident and somewhat arrogant ethos of psychoanalysis was successful during its first seven decades: psychoanalysis became the leading paradigm of psychiatry, and Freud was commonly considered a genius.

In the 1950s and 1960s the so-called cognitive revolution took place, and psychoanalysis began to recede and resign from the core of the academic world. By protecting the cornerstone concepts psychoanalysis slowly drifted away from the discussions taking place in academic forums, turned its back to progress taking place in the domain of behavioural sciences, and lost the ability to generate fresh ideas. The discipline moved in the direction of a heritage society. Psychoanalytic mentalism is currently a problematic foundation for scientific study, but it is important to note that when the efficacy of psychoanalytic therapies and the related parts of psychoanalytic theorising—for example, ideas concerning defence mechanisms and transference—are considered, there are no notable problems regarding the scientific standing of the discipline.

Lash's eclectic contribution is rather exceptional in the field of psychoanalysis. The history of psychoanalysis is characterised by processes in which disagreements lead to breaches and formations of new schools of psychoanalysis. Thus, we have currently Freudian, Jungian, Kleinian and Lacanian object relations, and ego psychology schools of psychoanalysis. Behind those historical processes lie authoritarian structures, psychoanalytic politics, and difficulties in investigating ideas and theories critically (see, for example, Grosskurth, 1991; Reeder, 2004; Makari, 2008, 2012).

We find similar processes and dynamics from scientific communities and other psychotherapists' communities. Above I reviewed the characteristics of the scientific community. The crucial characteristic was that its rules, conventions and dynamics harness human tendencies in the service of trustworthy belief formation. Conventions and dynamics of psychoanalytic (as well as other psychotherapy schools') communities seem to lack such a function. Similar to the players in the scientific fields, psychoanalytic organisations and journals are independent from each other. However, they are independent in another way, and to the extent that the different psychoanalytic schools are not *interdependent* on one another anymore—journals and organisations of one school need not care about the views of the others. When in, say, a Kleinian organisation or journal Anna Freud's ideas are criticised, Anna Freud-based organisations do not necessarily find compelling reasons to react.

When the dynamics of the psychoanalytic community are considered, psychoanalytic journals and associations are the most significant platforms. When it comes to the former, I can attest from my own experience that it is very difficult, but nevertheless possible, to get manuscripts challenging Freud's legacy published. When a psychoanalytic clinician challenges the psychoanalytic view of man (especially the existence and role of mental unconscious) in his local community, he or she is in danger of becoming labelled, for example, a "behaviourist" or "positivist" by his or her fellows, and becoming excluded from the community. When exclusion means that the rebellious clinician is not recommended as a therapist or supervisor anymore by colleagues, the exclusion is reflected also in his or her earnings. From the viewpoint of sociology of professions, self-regulation is one of the functions of professions, and colleague boycott is an informal mechanism to maintain norms and codes of ethics (Freidson, 1970, p. 162).

There is also no pressure for the psychoanalytic community (as a whole) to react to criticism presented in academic forums. Consider, for example, Renee Smith's (2010) article "Against treating introspection as perception-like". Already the title indicates that Smith's article challenges the cornerstone of psychoanalysis. In the academic world such a paper would lead to a debate. However, according to *Psychoanalytic literature search* (www.pep-web.org/) Smith's article has not been cited in the psychoanalytic journals.

As a whole, the psychoanalytic community simply does not care what happens in the domain of science, and even the pressure of psychoanalytic sub-communities to react to what is taking place in other psychoanalytic sub-communities is weak. These matters are serious obstacles for the accumulation of knowledge. All in all we must draw the conclusion that the psychoanalytic community lacks the self-corrective nature of belief formation characterising the scientific community. However, we should not blame the psychoanalytic community for this state of things. Psychoanalytic communities consist (mainly) of clinicians, and clinicians' communities (and professional communities generally) function differently from the scientific community. Only a community structured in a certain way can possess the properties of scientific community. The crucial implication is that psychoanalytic community cannot be scientific in itself—as far as psychoanalysis is a scientific endeavour it is a consequence of being a part of the academic community.

Behind the problematic parts of psychoanalytic theories and the marginalisation of psychoanalysis there seems to hide a common figure—the charismatic founder Sigismund Schlomo Freud and his bold legacy. But how has Freud's (scientific and personal) qualities and the dynamics between Freud and his collaborators succeeded in holding such a tight grip on psychoanalytic endeavour for a century? This questions remains outside the scope of this chapter. However, I would like to mention one constituent of the phenomenon: the members of the psychoanalytic community share the experience of their own psychoanalytic cure. That experience has remarkable personal significance, and it is surely reflected upon in the work of psychoanalytic clinicians and in the interactions between the members of the community, as well as in their theoretical preferences, and ideas concerning the human condition and meaning of life. The shared experience surely strengthens the cohesion of psychoanalytic community, but it also adds a very personal aspect to theoretical topics. Namely, if my analyst was Kleinian and someone states that Kleinian theories and therapeutic techniques are inappropriate, the claim implies that my past therapy as well as my current understanding concerning myself, the therapeutic process and the world around me should also be considered as inappropriate.

Ideology in terms of social epistemology

Science can be taken as an object of study, too. In the first half of the twentieth century the studies were characterised by (mainly positivist philosophers') search for the scientific method common to all disciplines. Currently the majority of philosophers of science (for example, Godfrey-Smith, 2003; van Fraassen, 2008) hold that there is no general method of science—characteristics of the object of study determine how it may be studied scientifically. The turn can be tracked to Thomas Kuhn's revolutionary *The Structure of Scientific Revolutions* (Kuhn, 1962). This work triggered a process that led sociology to partly displace philosophy as the leading paradigm of science studies (strictly speaking this expression is anachronistic, since the term "science studies" emerged only after the Kuhnian revolution). Post-Kuhnian, sociologically oriented science studies take into account also the *cognitive and social processes* leading to beliefs and theories, and *social systems* in which those processes take place.

When researching the scientific method, philosophers did not care a lot about what researchers actually did. Sociologically oriented science study has focused upon this matter in particular. In the introduction of their classical study *Laboratory Life: The Social Construction of Scientific Facts* Bruno Latour and Steve Woolgar (1979) stated prominently that they studied scientists in their laboratories "… as if they were a colony of ants in a maze …" (Latour & Woolgar, 1979, p. 12). The Kuhnian revolution contains significant implications for the discussions concerning the scientific status of psychoanalysis.

Freud, the neurologist, sketched his theories in the era of early, positivist philosophy of science. Not surprisingly, Freud tried to describe the functioning of the mind in terms of laws (of nature). From the viewpoint of present-day behavioural sciences and post-Kuhnian philosophy of science this is a hopeless project. Thus, we must abandon the fantasy that the background theory of psychotherapy might resemble the theories of natural sciences. Psychoanalysis has to be set in an appropriate context, and the criteria of science sketched on that basis.

Psychoanalytic theories have been applied in many domains: those of psychotherapy, psychiatry, film study, anthropology, and literature study, among others. In the positivist frames of thinking, the underlying presupposition is that there is just one correct answer to the question concerning the scientific status of psychoanalysis. In the post-positivistic times, however, we have to take into account the possibility that the answer depends more or less on the branch of study. In the "Freud wars" considerations are sometimes restricted to the domains of psychiatry and psychotherapies. Clinical topics can be seen as the core of psychoanalysis, and on that basis such a restriction is justified.

The Kuhnian tradition of science studies provides tools for conceptualising the ideological aspect of psychoanalysis too. Karen Knorr Cetina has introduced the term *epistemic machine* (Knorr Cetina, 1999), which refers to people's, organisations' and groups' ways of forming beliefs, or "constructing knowledge". Through that term, Freud's legacy appears as casting doubt on the trustworthiness of the epistemic machines of the psychoanalytic communities. The epistemic viewpoint applied below serves as a bridge from the world of science (focused on above) to that of clinical practice of psychoanalysis (the third part of the chapter).

Epistemology is the study of knowledge and the justification of beliefs. In the scope of the philosophical branch of epistemology, the typical epistemic agent is an individual, and the analysis is focused on, for example, the trustworthiness of perceptions—considering that there are perceptional illusions, how might one know that the perception "it rains outside" is accurate and reliable? Now as science studies increasingly focus on social contexts of scientific research, social systems are often considered as epistemic agents, too. Knorr Cetina's studies on epistemic machineries and cultures fall in the domain of so-called social epistemology (see Goldman, 1999; Goldman & Whitcomb, 2011).

In her work *Epistemic Cultures: How the Sciences Make Knowledge* Knorr Cetina (1999) reports the results of a fifteen year ethnographic study that took place in biology and high energy physics laboratories. One might think that all laboratories function in a basically similar manner. It turned out, however, that due to the differences concerning objects of studies, there were non-trivial differences between the epistemic cultures and epistemic machines of those two laboratories.

We will not dive deeper into the worlds of biology and theoretical physics. Instead, let us note that the studies of Janet Malcolm (1980), Jurgen Reeder (2004), and especially James Davies (2009) on psychoanalytic organisations come quite close to the work of Knorr Cetina and Latour and Woolgar. For us, the crucial thing is Knorr Cetina's notion that the epistemic machines of the non-academic organisations can also be compared and evaluated.

In both academic and practical affairs, persons and groups collect data or acquire knowledge relevant for the task at hand. In each affair—or *epistemic context*—a certain kind of knowledge/data is relevant, and there are specific ways to collect such knowledge and data. However, there are differences in the agents' ways of doing that (i.e., in their epistemic machines) and that makes a difference in terms of success. Practical affairs—psychotherapy among them—are not scientific disciplines. However, by applying the viewpoints of social epistemology, it is possible to compare and evaluate different agents' ways of forming and testing beliefs. Thus, luthiers, firms, news teams or meteorologists, religious communities, folk healers and doctors, among others, can be compared by focusing on their particular epistemic machines. The news reports of one TV channel may be more trustworthy than that of another, and the same holds with the weather reports.

Beliefs and presuppositions in general may be based, for example, on scientific studies, intuition, divine revelation, methods like chemical analysis or tarot cards, or authorities. Scientific methods are respected in many domains and by many people. This is reasonable, since science represents the most serious, profound and persistent human effort to make sense of things. Scientists as people, or the respectability of the institution in which the research is taking place (university), is of secondary importance. In terms of social epistemology, the problem with the ideological component is that it makes the epistemic machinery less trustworthy.

Considering the epistemic context of psychotherapy, there is an important question about which matters are of significance: about what issues should an organisation training therapists possess trustworthy beliefs? I think the following issues cannot be ignored: what are the causes of psychic troubles; What are effective therapeutic techniques (or curative factors of therapy)?; How do you organise a community around the school of psychotherapy?; Which therapists' personal skills or characteristics affect the therapy process and how?; What are the best methods to teach the psychotherapist candidates?

On a general level we may say that schools of psychotherapy that are aware of research concerning the above matters should be seen as more trustworthy. In practice this means that such schools will have close relations to universities, some of the teachers will demonstrate academic merits, and scientific literature from several domains of study will be applied in training. As mentioned, organisational (or community) dynamics of a psychotherapy school is an aspect of its epistemological machinery, and—when it comes to the Freudian legacy—it is not a surprise that authoritarian structures have been found to affect the epistemic machinery of an epistemic system (for example, see Goldman, 2011; Sunstein, 2011).

As a conclusion to this middle part of the chapter, I want to stress that I'm *not* claiming that due to its ideological aspect psychoanalysis is non-scientific, or less scientific than other schools of psychotherapy. The above considerations illustrate the difference between the traditional philosophy-driven study of science and the more recent sociological approach. In terms of the former, references to Freud's legacy and the dynamics of psychoanalytic communities are nothing more than ad hominem arguments and gossip. Social epistemology provides a more practical viewpoint to science, and also to the questions concerning the scientific status of psychoanalysis. In terms of social epistemology the ideological aspect of psychoanalysis is a threat to its epistemic trustworthiness.

In the first part of this essay psychoanalysis and its cornerstone concept (the mental unconscious) was studied as a scientific theory; in the second part in terms of a community and a cult, and below I will treat it as a profession and a way of talking.

Folk psychology and psychoanalysis as a profession

When, for example, Karl Popper, Edward Erwin, and Adolf Grünbaum, the great critics of psychoanalysis, approach psychoanalysis in terms of philosophy of science, the starting point is science, universities, and the academic institution in general. That tradition is interested in how things are *in principle* and, consequently, the connection between scientific theories (of psychoanalysis) and (psychoanalytic) practice appears as solid and logical. The clinical reality of psychotherapy is outside the scope of philosophical interests, and the implicit logic seems to be that "scientific-ness" of the academic world might somehow accrue to the clinician's practical affairs. When we take the perspective of the sociological study of professions and expertise (see, for example, Abbott, 1988; Freidson, 1970; Freidson, 2001; Selinger & Crease, 2006), the picture is rather different.

Setting the stage: psychoanalysis and the markets of inter-professional competition

A clinician's life and the life of other experts would be quite easy if there were scientific theories that could somehow reveal a solution to a client's problem, or contain complete instructions on how to "treat" the client. However, it seems that the distance between researchers and clinicians is greater than has been recognised in the wars around the question concerning the scientific status of psychoanalysis. In his classical work from the 1970s, *Profession of Medicine: A Study of the Sociology of Applied Knowledge*, Eliot Freidson (1970) studied the differences between clinicians' and researchers' basic orientations, and summarises the clinical mentality with five points (Freidson, 1970, pp. 158–184):

1. Clinicians' interest is primarily not in knowledge, but in action.
2. For a clinician it is personally important to believe in the work that he or she does.
3. Clinicians are pragmatists who rely on apparent results rather than theories.
4. A clinician is prone to trust his or her personal experiences on what is of help to clients.
5. A clinician does not live in the world of (scientific) laws or general principles, but that of uncertainty; individual cases; personal judgements he or she is responsible for; and the pressure to act even when there is not appropriate knowledge and methods available.

Freidson's characterisation is illuminating, and gives rise to a plethora of questions: to what extent, how, and for what issues is it possible (and not possible) to base clinical pragmatism on academic research (and what kind of research)?; If faith in his or her methods and personal experience is crucial for a clinician, does this create a barricade between science and clinical practice?; Are psychoanalysts less theoretical in their work than we have been led to think, or are psychoanalytic clinicians exceptions, who blindly believe in Freudian theories and laws even when they contradict clinical reality around them?

Historically, psychotherapy deals with issues that were conceptualised as "personal problems" in the latter part of the nineteenth century (Abbott, 1988, pp. 280–314). At first they fell into the domains of clergymen, doctors, and lawyers. In the 1880s "nerves" were recognised as a major cause for those problems, and neurology became the profession that was held competent to cure them. The neurologists' conception proved not satisfactory, however: their diagnostic system was very complex and the treatments were not especially effective. And yet, the neurologists' "general nervousness" had been the first alternative for the clergy's conceptualisation. Their system of knowledge was "powerfully scientific in the academy but profusely idiosyncratic in practice" (Abbott, 1988, p. 288). Thus, talk about "nerves" was *the* scientific approach to personal problems at the end of the nineteenth century, but its scientific status collapsed rapidly when psychotherapy developed. Abbot's study illustrates how the scientific status of methods and theories is a historical issue. The hegemony of the neurologists waned due to the emergence of alternatives, and that of psychoanalysis has waned for similar reasons: there has been considerable development in the domains of biological psychiatry and other branches of psychotherapy.

There is a vast body of sociological literature on professions (see, for example, Abbot, 1988; Freidson, 2001; Macdonald, 1995), claiming that professions are closely tied to markets (and clients) on one hand, and to the state on the other. In *The Sociology of Professions* Macdonald (1995, pp. 1–35; see also, for example, Freidson, 1970, pp. 3–84) holds that "professional projects" contain four core issues:

1. Professions are interest groups that aim at achieving a monopoly or at least licensure. In order to do that, they must make a "regulative bargain" with the state.
2. Professions have to compete in the market against other professions.
3. Professions are not entirely self-seeking, they also aim to provide services to their clients.
4. Social closure is a central strategy for professions: professions attempt to control who has access and permission to apply the methods and knowledge of the discipline.

Psychoanalytic clinicians operate in the market in which several professions compete for clients. The potential clients of psychoanalytic clinicians choose between psychiatrists, psychoanalysts, psychoanalytic psychotherapists, other psychotherapists, naturopaths, exorcists, fortune tellers, and so on. For us the interesting issue concerns the role of science, or scientific status of a profession in this competition.

Science and inter-professional competition

There are different kinds of institutions, societies, endeavours, groups, and movements, and we hold (on different grounds) that the epithet "scientific" characterises some of them. For certain communities the views of science are, for the most part, simply irrelevant. For example, golf clubs, fan clubs and steel guitar associations do not care about science (although a golf club may ask a professor to lecture on golf swing mechanics), but usually it makes no sense to claim that these organisations are non-scientific or would contradict the views of science.

We might say that some other communities and endeavours are non-scientific "by definition". They do not try to be scientific, although they are also seeking truth in their own way. Religious communities and fortune tellers may serve as examples of this kind of community. Other groups such as Christian Science, creationism, homeopathy, and The Flat Earth Society represent endeavours that they consider scientific, but possess no foothold in the academic world. For several decades, in my view, psychoanalysis has been moving from the domain of science and into the direction of these kinds of groups.

When one faces a practical problem and needs an expert's help it is rational to consult those relying on scientific research in his or her domain. Let us consider some cases:

A. You have inherited a valuable violin that needs some restoration. How do you find a luthier who is able to repair the instrument without spoiling it?
B. You have a summer place on a lakeside in Finland. During the past five years or so the lake has become eutrophic and in the water there is a sickening smell. You and your neighbours claim that the change is due to the farm (or factory) on the opposite side of the lake, and you bring a lawsuit against it. The juries have to listen to expert testimony on whether or not the process is due to the farm/factory. How do they choose the experts—how do they determine the appropriate discipline (of the experts)? And, on what basis do they determine which of the disagreeing experts to trust?
C. You are going to surgery due to problems with your heart. You are given an opportunity to choose between a traditional licenced surgeon and one representing an alternative school known for its innovativeness. Which one do you choose, and why?
D. Mr. X is an engineer whose sixteen-year-old daughter has lately become melancholic and isolated from her friends. Mr. X ponders whether he should consult a family therapist, a cognitive psychotherapist, a psychoanalyst, a psychiatrist (representing biological psychiatry), an exorcist, or a healer representing alternative medicine. On what basis should he make the choice?

As we see, practical challenges of ordinary life, like the above, contain an epistemic aspect: there are facts concerning the characteristics of different words, clues (which ones did Antonio Stradivari use?), and luthiers' techniques; processes leading to the pollution of water; human physiology and surgical techniques; and there are personal problems and their cure, etc. When science is seen as representing the most serious, profound and persistent human effort to make sense of things, we are self-evidently cautious toward experts that are arrogant toward science. A very rough way to evaluate an expert's competence is to look at his or her bookshelf: if it contains mainly centuries-old books, the expert is not interested in the progress taking place in his or her professional field.

Psychoanalysts sometimes claim that there is a significant difference between psychoanalysis and other forms of psychotherapy: while other psychotherapies and other branches of behavioural sciences focus on behaviour and consciousness, the object of study of psychoanalysis is the unconscious. On this basis, psychoanalysts (and perhaps also psychodynamic therapists) might be seen as forming a profession of their own. This kind of distinction is, however, very abstract; theoretical, philosophical, and we might also say metaphysical. From the perspective of markets, psychoanalysis does not appear that way. Instead, psychoanalysis' focus on the unconscious should be seen as a distinctive conception of the causes of the clients' problems.

The explorations of the first two parts of this chapter appear in the context of the inter-professional competition as follows: considering that psychoanalytic clinicians are reluctant to study critically the Freudian cornerstone concept of causative unconscious content, and the community possesses cult-like aspects, should one trust their thinking and methods? The public image of psychoanalysis has slid from the core of psychiatry toward the domain of alternative medicine, and this also affects the psychoanalytic clinicians' professional condition.

What makes psychotherapy "scientific"?

When the scientific status of psychoanalysis is studied from the practical perspective sketched above, it seems almost ridiculous to suppose that the psychoanalytic theories should resemble those of natural sciences. Psychiatrists and psychotherapists apply to real-life situations the (more or less scientific) background theories of the field. Therefore the scientific status of psychoanalysis should be studied using the same criteria we use to evaluate other practical affairs, for example, cognitive psychotherapy. When the scientific status of psychoanalysis is considered, the issue has to be set in an appropriate context: the criteria for science should be the same as those applied to other branches of psychotherapy.

However, it is rather unclear what those criteria actually are. Attempting to provide a benchmark, Aaron Beck and colleagues' work *Scientific Foundations of Cognitive Theory and Therapy of Depression* (Clark, Beck, & Alford, 1999) sounds promising. Interestingly, the criticism presented against Beck's theory might sound familiar to psychoanalytic folks: Beck's theory is said to be impossible to disconfirm, it does not have adequate theoretical basis, and it does not meet the criteria of scientific theory (Clark, Beck, & Alford, 1999, p. 54). Beck and co-authors focus very strictly on therapy and its effectiveness, and only on disorders of depression. As everybody knows, the aims and scope of psychoanalysis is much wider, and thus Beckian therapy is rather limited in providing a useful benchmark—Beckian and Freudian theories clearly being at different levels of abstraction.

Abbot (1988, pp. 102–108) has presented some interesting ideas on this issue. He states that when abstract knowledge of a profession is at a low level, the profession appears to just follow rules of thumb without being able to formalise its knowledge. A very high level of abstraction, on the other hand, means that the relation between the abstractions and the experts' interventions and working models is weak. In cases of both high and low level abstractions, a profession is actually weakened. Hence, the optimal level of abstraction is in the middle. In psychoanalytic models in general, and in Freud's metaphysical ideas in particular, the level of abstraction is very high. While Clark, Beck and Alford carefully avoid even making claims concerning the causes for depression, from psychoanalytic theories we find general principles and laws, phylogenetic phantasies, and metaphysical speculations. The aims of psychoanalysis are bold, and this makes it a too easy target for criticism.

The idea behind "scientific" (or science-based) psychotherapies might be something like this: academic study equips therapists with theories that have been proven right, objective data about the phenomena relevant for a therapist, and methods that have proven effective. On this basis "scientific" therapists are supposedly more useful than their non-scientific rivals. But this kind of thinking is imaginary in many ways: in science, theories are never proven right; the question concerning evidence-based methods is very complicated (see Norcross, Beutler, & Levant, 2006); academic education does not consist of learning lists of good and true things. In short, the above sketch reflects a very mechanical view of psychotherapists' work. I'm afraid it is waste of time to search for a strict definition of the criteria for scientific psychotherapies.

The prevailing views concerning the effectiveness of psychoanalysis and other psychotherapies can be summarised as follows: psychotherapy in general is a rather effective method of cure; it is not known where its curative power lies; psychodynamic therapies are not more effective than other forms of psychotherapy (see, for example, Cooper, 2008; Lambert, 2004; Shedler, 2010). These facts possess a significant implication for our topic: the effectiveness of psychotherapy does not derive from the theories therapists apply. According to Norcross and Lambert (2006) psychotherapy outcome studies explain only 40–50% of the outcome variance. According to these authors the factors concerning the patient accounts for 25% of the outcome, the relationship between the patient and the therapist 10%, and the treatment method only from 5% to 8%.

Experts' knowledge is often seen as based for the most part on implicit "know-how" rather than explicit "know-that" (see, for instance, Bengson & Moffett, 2011), and it looks like psychotherapists are no exception. The above implies that neither the successes nor failures of psychoanalytic therapies are due to Freud's theories or those of other psychoanalysts. In so far as psychoanalytic therapy works, it works for similar reasons as other therapies. This kind of conclusion is a disappointment to those engaged in Freud wars on both sides.

From the viewpoint of the sociology of professions, the connection between science and practice has to be sketched on a much more general level than that of single theories and methods. Abbot, who recognises the discontinuity between academic abstract knowledge and experts' interventions (Abbott, 1988, pp. 52–58), states the significance of universities for professions in the following way: "They [universities] can serve as legitimators, providing authoritative grounds for the exclusive exercise of expertise. They can house the function of knowledge advancement, enabling academic professionals to develop new techniques outside of practise. They can train young professionals, often in conjunction with the function of research. Finally, universities, like states, may become another arena for interprofessional competition". (Abbott, 1988, p. 196)

The cornerstone concept as providing a competitive edge: the unconscious and layman psychology

The considerations made so far make the Freudian cornerstone concept of the mental unconscious appear to function as a straitjacket for psychoanalysts. However, we must not forget that Freudian ideas as well as the Freudian "label" still enjoy considerable popularity among laymen (i.e., clinicians' potential clients). Antiquarian booksellers like to purchase psychoanalytic books for resale, academic people enjoy Woody Allen-style humour, psychoanalytic notions still provide the most interesting psychological viewpoints to movies, and Western people in general talk about repressed wishes, Freudian slips, and traumatic memories. This kind of popularity does not reflect merely a superficial and erroneous habit of talk. Psychological concepts—for example, intelligence, personality, narcissism, and self-esteem—are not anchored to reality in a similar fashion to those of natural sciences. Another difference with natural sciences is that the terminology of academic psychology is to a great extent based on folk psychology. Psychological terms are constructs (and thus psychology might be said to have (partly) created its own object of study) (Danziger 1997; Talvitie, 2012, pp. 1–30).

From the Wittgensteinian viewpoint, words in general are tools of communication rather than labels of things. Thus, the psychological concepts like "mind", "representation", "soul" or "unconscious" do not refer to a mental thing (Bouveresse, 1996; Sluga, 1996). In the Wittgensteinian framework the expressions "I was not conscious that X" and "I became conscious of X" do not imply that the mental unconscious existed and contained X's desires and memories, for example. Instead, those expressions mean that, at first, one did not articulate his or her condition as envy or rage, for example. When the cornerstone concept is looked at in a Wittgensteinian light, Freud appears to have introduced a point of view and vocabulary, and extended and enriched our folk psychology. Due to Freud's contribution, thinking in terms of unconscious matters is a crucial part of the self-understanding of the Western man. Furthermore, many people—considerable numbers of therapists of other schools among them—still see the psychoanalytic method and its theories as the route to oneself. Thus, one cannot deny that psychoanalysis still has a strong identity as a form of psychotherapy and still possesses a competitive edge.

It is also important to remember the valuable and unique consequences of the psychoanalytic ethos. The therapist's epistemic machinery is his or her own mind, and due to a long and intensive personal therapy, psychoanalytic clinicians are well acquainted with its functioning and biases. The psychoanalytic ethos is also careful to avoid manipulative techniques and is sensitive in promoting personal growth and self-understanding (instead of just being restricted to treating disorders). Thus it is the case that, for many people, commitment to such foundational humanistic values makes psychoanalytic therapy single-handedly superior to its rivals.

CHAPTER FIVE

Unconscious knowing: psychoanalytic evidence in support of a radical epistemic view*

Linda A. W. Brakel

Introduction

In most standard contemporary work in philosophy of mind and epistemology, knowledge is considered some form of true belief. (See Armstrong, 1973, p. 137; Goldman, 1975, p. 111; Margolis, 1973, p. 3; and also Williamson, 2000, p. 2, who emphatically does not share this view but notes it historically.) Until the publication of the Gettier cases (Gettier, 1963) this issue seemed largely settled with justified true belief regarded as the type of belief that simply *was* knowledge.

*This chapter is a slightly revised version of two earlier works, first an article: Brakel, L. A. W. (2008). "Knowledge and Belief: Psychoanalytic Evidence in Support of a Radical Epistemic View", *American Imago* 65: 3 (2008), 427–471, © 2008 by The Johns Hopkins University Press, reprinted with permission of The Johns Hopkins University Press; second, a chapter in Brakel, L. A. W. (2010), "Unconscious Knowing and Other Essays in Psycho-philosophical Analysis" (pp. 9–50), Oxford, Oxford University Press, reprinted by permission of Oxford University Press, www.oup.com.

(See Danto, 1968, p. 73; Shope, 1983, pp. 10–11). After Edmund Gettier (1963) presented cases in which even justified true belief could not suffice for knowledge,[1] the status of justified true belief *as* knowledge did indeed change. But, interestingly, the quest to explain knowledge in terms of belief did not change. Belief continued to be held among the conditions necessary, but alas not sufficient for knowledge (Goldman, 1975, pp. 111–112; Margolis, 1973, p. 3). Thus, according to Timothy Williamson (2000), for the last four decades many epistemologists "have expended vast efforts attempting to state exactly what kind of true belief knowledge is" (p. 2).[2] Williamson holds that philosophers of mind similarly "marginalize the category of knowledge" insofar as "belief is what matters for the understanding of the mind"—belief being the mental attitude that aims at the truth, and truth obtaining only when the truth conditions of the belief match those of the world (p. 2).[3] For these philosophers too, then, knowledge not only entails belief but is also "merely a peculiar kind of true belief" (p. 2), one requiring at least two additions to the mental state of belief—first, truth, as is needed also for true belief, and then "other more elusive features" (p. 3).[4] Thus both for epistemologists attempting to specify the essence of knowledge and belief, and for philosophers of mind attempting to gain knowledge of the mind, belief is maintained as the foundational attitude, conceptually prior to knowledge.

Does this have to be the case? Or, are there arguments and evidence for the reverse: that it is knowledge that comes first, conceptually and ontologically, with belief dependent on knowledge, and not vice versa? In other words, what if the standard view has it backwards; that it is belief (justified or not; true or not) that is always predicated on, built upon, and entailing knowledge? What would be implied?

In this chapter, I will advance this "radical view", presenting data derived from the central psychoanalytic assumption of a meaningful unconscious—data both from psychoanalysis and from close cognate areas, including subliminal research, cognitive psychology, and cognitive neuropsychology—all in support of philosophical arguments (due largely to Williamson, 2000, but including a few others) for this position. In so doing I hope not only to provide converging evidence for the radical view, but also to illustrate a) the strength of psychoanalysis as an "evidence-provider" and b) the importance of interdisciplinary approaches to questions that can only be properly located at an interface between or among disciplines—in this case epistemology, psychoanalytic theory, cognitive psychology and neuropsychology, and philosophy of mind.

So to begin I will present a case in which the agent in question has much knowledge but amazingly no belief at all about what he knows. This case comprises the section called "Knowing without seeing or believing: A very striking negative hallucination", which follows immediately below. The subsequent sections are: "Differences between knowledge (knowing) and belief (believing)"; "Similarities between knowledge (knowing) and belief (believing)"; "First and second order knowledge and belief: Believing what one knows, knowledge without (any sort of) belief"; "Unconscious knowledge and unconscious belief"; "The priority of knowledge"; and finally "Psychoanalysis and the priority of knowledge". Indeed there is much ground to cover. Thus without further introduction, here is the clinical backbone of this chapter: the negative hallucination.

Knowing without seeing or believing: a very striking negative hallucination

Many years ago when I was a resident in psychiatry, and consequently often sleep deprived, I fell asleep for about ten seconds during a session with a patient (Dr. N) in psychoanalytic psychotherapy. He had to have been aware of my closed eyes and nodding head, as we faced each other directly and our chairs were no more than six feet apart. Through the rest of that session, as I'd been taught to do, I listened and looked carefully for any sign of his reaction, direct or derivative. However, there were no allusions to careless doctors, sleepy people, inappropriate activities, consumers not getting what they pay for, inattentive women, etc. and no physical changes in Dr. N—not in that session.

But at the start of our next meeting Dr. N recounted the following dream: "I (Dr. N) fell asleep in our session. You (Dr. B) didn't seem to notice". He added that, "there was not much feeling in the dream". I told Dr. N that his dream must be a reaction to his noticing my having fallen asleep in front of him during our previous session. He reacted as if I were crazy, saying with much animation: "What are you talking about? You didn't fall asleep here last time! If you had, I'd be really furious". Now, *I* was incredulous. It seemed impossible that he hadn't seen me. I was right in his line of vision, the lighting was not unusual, and certainly I was a salient stimulus object. True, he had, in his brief associations, provided a "reason" for not seeing me—he'd be furious with me; and Dr. N was a man who was quite afraid that he could not adequately control his rage. But how could he not have had full conscious awareness of something that he recaptured so accurately in his dream? Obviously (to me) the thin disguise of reversing our roles did not obscure the contents—identical in dream and waking life—that one person, A, fell asleep right in front of the other person, B; yet person B hadn't seemed to notice.

Dr. N, in a) not observing my falling asleep, b) dreaming the unseen content in thin disguise, and c) not recapturing the percept, had had an instance of what is known as a negative hallucination. This particular psychological event had pivotal psychoanalytic significance in two ways: 1) Clinically, Dr. N was forced to confront the fact that I had fallen asleep in his session, and that despite his robust defensive efforts to feel very little, both in reality and in the dream, he was in fact furious. 2) Theoretically, the event was instructive regarding the limits of psychoanalytic explanation. *Why* my patient would have had a negative hallucination given his conflicts and character; this type of question could (and can) be adequately addressed in terms of psychoanalytic clinical theory.[5] But the *how*—how he could not see something he had to have seen—this type of question was (and remains) unanswerable by psychoanalytic theory alone. Yet once one observes that the responses of subjects in subliminal experiments are structurally analogous to those of patients with negative hallucinations (see Brakel, 1989), answers to questions of this sort can begin to be addressed through research into the processing of subliminal stimuli. The sort of research involved—cognitive and neuropsychological—is cognate to, but is outside and independent of, psychoanalysis.[6]

Beyond their psychoanalytic clinical implications, for our present purposes it is the philosophical importance of negative hallucinations that is of greatest interest. Negative hallucinations can help illuminate aspects of the complex interrelationships among seeing, not seeing, believing, and knowing; these last two being of special relevance here. Dr. N claimed not to have seen me fall asleep. Although he ultimately did not doubt my account of what transpired—after all, his own dream provided confirming evidence—he never did recapture the experience of having seen me nod off right in front of him. Consequently, before my explanation, Dr. N had *no beliefs* at all about the incident he did not see. But would it be plausible or even coherent to say that he had *no knowledge* of it? Defending the position that he lacked knowledge would be difficult. For if indeed he had no knowledge of my sleeping, how would he have dreamt and reported the particular dream contents he did, given that they mirrored so precisely what happened? Dr. N had *knowledge*, more specifically *unconscious knowledge*, of the contents in question without the conscious experience of seeing anything, and without any sort of belief, justified or not, true or false, about the matter. This case suggests that knowledge is dependent neither on beliefs nor on seeing. Dr. N did not see anything about my sleeping; he had no beliefs about it; and yet, as his dream showed, he knew all about it, *unconsciously*.[7]

Dr. N's negative hallucination clearly raises a number of issues concerning knowledge and belief at the intersection of philosophy of mind, epistemology, and psychoanalysis. The case certainly seems to lend support to the radical view that knowledge, rather than belief, is the more fundamental and foundational mental state. Let us proceed with our exploration of the relations between belief and knowledge to see if that view holds up.

Differences between knowledge (knowing) and belief (believing)

The relations between knowledge (knowing) and belief (believing) are of central import in determining whether or not knowledge is merely a type of true belief. If knowledge is only some type of true belief, on this ground, belief should be considered foundational and conceptually prior to knowledge. The opposite case—knowledge being prior to belief—must also rely on the relations between these two mental states. Hence, in this section, the differences between knowledge and belief will be explored, and in the section to follow I shall explore their similarities.

General differences

To introduce the notion of a significant difference between knowledge and belief, let me start with H. A. Pritchard (1950), a philosopher who was so convinced of important general differences, that he asserted "dogmatically ... [and without] ... offer of reasons" (p. 87) the following:

> Knowing and believing differ in kind ... Their difference in kind is not that of species and genus, like that of a red colour and a colour [simpliciter]. To know is not to have a belief of a special kind,

> differing from beliefs of other kinds; and no improvement in a belief and no increase in the feeling of conviction which it implies will convert it into knowledge. Nor is their difference that of being two species of a general genus. It is not that there is a general kind of activity ... which admits of two kinds, the better of which is knowing and the worse believing. (pp. 87–88)

Another philosopher, J. J. Macintosh (1979–1980) does offer an interesting reductio ad absurdum argument for the general difference. He starts with the counterargument that the mental state of knowing really is just the mental state of believing, because when we find out that what we thought we knew is wrong, "what we replace it with is not a claim that we used to know (though we now no longer do) but rather a claim that we used to *believe*, though we now no longer do. But our mental state was what it was ... all along: and if we are now correct in speaking of ourselves as having a *belief*, then a belief it also was [before]" (p. 171). However, Macintosh continues, if knowing is thereby accepted as a kind of believing "... by the same argument we can show that seeing is a kind *of* ... hallucinating; that being awake is a kind *of* ... dreaming, and so on" (p. 180).

Both philosophers allude to what is probably the most important general difference between knowledge and belief, and certainly the most obvious: namely, that whereas what is believed can be either true or false, what is known is either true or it is not knowledge. This is reflected in Robert Shope's (1983) statement, "We may say that what is false is what we believed (but not what we knew)" (p. 173). One way of understanding this difference is to suggest that a strictly internalist[8] account of knowledge as a mental state cannot possibly work, whereas for belief such an account could suffice.[9] Thus, on the internalist view all that is needed to have identical beliefs about X are identical *internal* mental/brain states. So given whatever is needed neurologically to qualify as identical mental/brain states, S's belief that "*p* is q" when *p is* q, is identical to S's belief that "*p* is q" when *p is not* q. In other words, S's belief that "that ball is in that corner" when the ball is there in that corner, is identical to S's belief that "that ball is in that corner" when someone (unbeknownst to S) has moved the ball from the corner. This clearly will not work for knowledge. S's knowledge that "*p* is q" when *p is* q, cannot be identical to S's ~knowledge[10] that "*p* is q" when *p is not* q. While S can know that "that ball is in that corner" when the ball is there, S cannot *know* that "that ball is in that corner" when it is not. Facts about the world, facts *external* to S's brain states, must contribute to the mental state of knowledge.

Another general difference between knowledge and belief, widely agreed upon, is that whereas there are degrees of belief, there can be no degrees of knowledge. Regarding knowledge as a psychological state, Joseph Margolis (1973) states, "that someone knows that *p*—is an all-or-nothing affair; this is not true … of such psychological states as beliefs: one may half-believe, half-disbelieve" (p. 35). Roderick Chisolm (1957) puts it like this: "A man can be said to believe firmly, or reluctantly or hesitantly, but no one can be said to know firmly, reluctantly or hesitantly" (p. 18). Relatedly, one can even evaluate beliefs, but not knowledge, as "silly or sensible; or as mature versus childlike" (Shope, 1983, p. 176). (See also Ring, 1977, p. 57 for a similar account of the general differences.)

Because of this difference between them, although both beliefs and knowledge are regulated by truth conditions in the world and therefore sensitive to evidence, beliefs are much more apt to be changed given new evidence, whereas knowledge is much more stable and sturdy. This is a point made by Norman Malcolm (1952, p. 80), Arthur Danto (1968, p. 108), who cites Malcolm, and Williamson (2000, pp. 7–8, 62–63) who states: "Although knowing is not invulnerable to destruction by later evidence, its nature is to be robust in that respect. Stubbornness in one's beliefs, an irrational insensitivity to counterevidence, is a different kind of robustness … those who know *p* often lack a stubborn belief in *p*" (p. 63). Williamson (2000, pp. 7–8, 62–63, 86–87) takes a further step, linking the robustness of knowledge with persistence in the carrying through of actions. "Action typically involves complex interaction with the environment; one needs continual feedback to bring it to a successful conclusion … Attributions of knowledge often explain the success of these interactions better than do the corresponding attributions of belief, even true belief" (p. 8). Thus whenever Bob *knows* that a certain puzzle can be solved, he will devote whatever time it takes to solve it, but not so when Bob (merely) *believes* that some puzzle has a solution.[11]

Various types of knowledge

Another important distinction between knowledge and belief is that knowledge, but not belief, comes in different kinds.[12] Aside from the most frequently dealt with *knowing that Z*, there is *knowing-how*, in the sense of having an ability, *knowing Y*, in the sense of being familiar with Y, and *knowing X from Y*, in the sense of being capable of making a discrimination.

Gilbert Ryle (1949, pp. 28, 59–60) made what has become the classic distinction between *knowing that* and *knowing-how*. Knowing that Z pertains to one knowing that Z is the case, while knowing-how to R, means that one has the ability to R. So, for example, Ann *knows that* the answer to a particular problem involving solving certain types of equations is 4.00076. She knows because she looked it up in the index. However, she looked it up in the index because she does not yet have the *know-how* to solve that sort of problem. Cindy, on the other hand, does have the know-how to solve that sort of problem, but when she arrives at her answer, she is not ready to say that she knows it to be the case, as she realises that she might have made an error in one of the many steps in carrying it out.

There have been attempts to demonstrate that all knowing-that actually reduces to knowing-how. John Hartland-Swann, (1958, esp. p. 58) for example,[13] argues that every knowing that X can be construed as an ability or a knowing-how to answer a particular question to which X is the answer. Oppositely, there have been arguments that knowing-how is a subspecies of knowing-that. Jason Stanley and Timothy Williamson (2001), for example, hold that knowing-how—while neither fully defined by nor reducible to terms applicable generally to knowing-that (pp. 433–434)—is essentially involved with knowing "ways of engaging in actions" (p. 431). And for Stanley and Williamson, to know a *way* is a form of knowing that is "no less propositional" than other examples of knowing-that (p. 431); indeed for them "… to say someone knows how to *F* is always to ascribe to them knowledge-that" (p. 426).

Other philosophers have extended the know-that/know-how distinction in interesting ways. David Lewis (1983, 1990), for instance, asks what sort of knowledge is needed to *know what it is like*. He answers (1983), regarding the taste of Vegemite, "knowing what it is like is not the possession of information at all … Rather knowing what it is like is the possession of abilities: abilities to recognize, abilities to imagine, abilities to predict one's behavior by means of imaginative experiments" (p. 131). He concludes (1990), "… knowing what an experience is like … is not knowing-that. It's knowing how" (p. 516). David Armstrong (1973, p. 177) finds that know-how is the sort of knowledge needed both for the capacity to discriminate X from Y, and for the ability to be acquainted or familiar with Z, where Z in Armstrong's example is someone, or something, about which one could have mental content.

E. J. Lemmon (1967), while agreeing that there is a distinction to be made among different types of knowledge, contends that knowing-how and knowing-that are actually closer than either is to *knowing how to*. Using the example of driving a car, Lemmon explains that someone can know how it is done without knowing how to do it, concluding that the main difference is between "*practical* and *theoretical* information" (p. 59).

Knowing X in the sense of being familiar enough with X to be able to make a discrimination between X and Y, leads to a consideration of perceptual knowledge. Here the work of Alvin Goldman figures prominently. Speaking of his own goals, Goldman (1976) says:

> I am trying to fashion an account of knowing that focuses on more primitive and pervasive aspects of cognitive life, in connection with which ... the term "know" gets its application. A fundamental facet of animate life, both human and infra-human, is telling things apart, distinguishing predator from prey, for example, or a protective habitat from a threatening one. The concept of knowledge has its roots in this kind of cognitive activity. (p. 791)

For Goldman, a reliablist[14] knowledge (perceptual knowledge, but pointing the way toward knowledge in general) involves discrimination such that one must not only be able to differentiate between incompatible but relevantly alternative states of affairs, but do so non-accidentally through appropriate causal connections such that knowledge of X is *reliably* produced when X is present, and knowledge of X *reliably* denied when X is not present (pp. 771–772, 790). Although he does not reduce all types of knowledge to either knowing-that or knowing-how, Goldman implies that, at least in some cases, by having the kind of *reliable* ability or know-how necessary to be familiar enough with X to discriminate it from Y, one is in effect also demonstrating knowing-that. In his words (1976, p. 772): "I suggest that a person is said to know that *p* just in case he *distinguishes* or *discriminates* the truth of *p* from relevant alternatives".[15]

Similarities between knowledge (knowing) and belief (believing)

Knowledge and belief are mental states

A mental state is a state of mind of an agent. Mental states come in various forms. The ones under discussion here are called mental or psychological attitudes—attitudes toward contents—and mental attitudes also come in various forms. There are conative attitudes, like desire, in which the content is *to be brought about*, and cognitive attitudes, like belief, in which the content of the attitude is regarded as *having come about*. (See Velleman, 2000, pp. 9–10, 111–112.) When I desire *d*, a cool drink of water, I would like *d*, my having a cool drink, to be made the case. The direction is from my psychological state to the world. When I believe *w*, that there is a water fountain twenty feet from here, it is the case (from my point of view) that *w*, a water fountain, exists twenty feet from here. Here the direction is from the world to my mental state. And then there are also *factive* mental attitudes, of which knowing is the most basic[16] (Williamson, 2000, p. 21). Contents of factive mental states also have the world-to-mind direction, but whereas I can believe *p* even if *p* is not true, I can know *p* only if *p* is true. There is a tricky aspect to this. For belief, although I can believe *p* even if *p* is not true, I cannot believe *p* if I find out that *p* is not true. For knowledge, I can never be in the mental state of knowing *p* if *p* is not true—even if I am not in possession of the relevant facts. I can think I know *p* at time *t* (before I've learned the facts); but if *p* is not true, I was mistaken at time *t*, no matter when or if I learn the facts. If at time *t+1* I learn the facts and now know I was mistaken, I can correctly assert that at time *t* I thought I knew *p*, but that I was wrong.

Internalist accounts do not suffice for knowledge or belief

Not all philosophers agree that knowledge is a mental state (see, for example, Hintikka, 1962, esp. p. 82). Part of the difficulty comes from the notion that with regard to the internal psychological aspect of both belief (true and false) and knowledge, both are identical; whereas the truth aspect necessary for knowledge comes externally, from the world. On this view knowing is a mixture of mental and non-mental parts and therefore not a true mental state. Williamson (2000, pp. 55–56) discusses the problem thus: "The idea that the mental (or psychological) component of knowing is simply believing seems to be expressed in a remark by Stephen Stich, endorsed by Jaegwon Kim: 'what knowledge adds to belief is psychologically irrelevant' (Stich, 1978, p. 574 quoted in Kim, 1993, p. 188) …" To the contrary, in the view held here (following Williamson), knowledge is a distinct mental state; not a conjunctive amalgam of belief plus something else. That is: "To know is not merely to believe while various other conditions are met; it is to be in a new kind of state, a factive one … [which implies] the rejection of a conjunctive account of knowing" (Williamson, 2000, pp. 47–48).

The challenge conjunctive accounts of knowing present to the view of knowing as a singular factive mental state will be taken up later. (See the subsection "The case for belief entailing knowledge", and footnote 36 below.) But for now it is of interest, and counts as a point of similarity between knowledge and belief, to hold (as I do) that a strictly internalist account won't suffice for knowledge or belief. The case is straightforward with knowledge, as has been discussed above. The mental state of knowing "p is q" when p *is* q, cannot be identical to the mental state of ~knowing "p is q" when p *is not* q. Knowing as an attitude is partly determined by truth conditions in the world external to the subject.

On the other hand a belief that "p is q" when p *is* q can seem identical to a belief that "p is q", when p *is not* q. The content of the true belief and that of the false belief can appear to be the same. Nonetheless, many hold that the content of beliefs cannot be fully determined internally, any more than can the contents comprising attitudes of knowledge. This is readily demonstrated with the famous twin earth cases (Putnam, 1975) in which some earthling's belief about water—water is wet—is not the same as his or her twin earth doppelganger's belief—twin earth-water (t-water) is wet—no matter how identical the content seems and even if the neuronal firing patterns are identical. The earthling's belief is about *water*, while the twin-earthling's belief is about *t-water*, and since they are not having beliefs about the same content, the beliefs are different.[17] Thus on this view internalism is insufficient both for knowledge and belief. Hence Williamson's statement (2000, p. 6): "If the content of a mental state can depend on the external world [in the belief case], so can the attitude to that content. Knowledge is such an attitude".[18]

The proper causal chain

As was discussed above (see footnote 1) both knowledge and justified true belief must arrive at their content in appropriate ways to count as instances of knowledge or justified true belief. So, for example, suppose I had a dream that my favourite uncle would call me in exactly one week. Then, exactly one week later, owing to the dream, when I heard the phone ring I had the belief that it was my favourite uncle. Now suppose further that it was in fact my uncle on the phone. Concerning his call, I would have had a true, but unjustified belief. Hallucinations that happen to contain content that is accurate—veridical hallucinations (see Armstrong, 1973, p. 171)—can be understood in the same way. The hallucinator hears a voice saying, "Come here now" and believes that there is an external person saying, "Come here now". If on some occasion there *is* a person telling the hallucinator, "Come here now", the hallucinator's belief in this case will be true but unjustified to the extent that it is still predicated on the hallucinatory, rather than the external voice.

Knowledge too must be obtained with the right "pedigree". Some years ago I was running an experiment in which stimuli were presented subliminally, at the objective threshold for vision. This means that participants' conscious visual experience of the presented stimuli was nil. One task that participants were asked to perform was to indicate whether on a particular trial they thought a stimulus item or a blank was being presented, this after being informed that in this portion of the experiment they would receive blanks half the time and stimulus items half the time, and that they should try to respond with that information in mind. Most participants dutifully attended to the stimuli and found reasons or intuitions to give approximately half of their responses as "blank" and half as "stimulus item". One subject refused to participate (although he only told the experimenter this after the fact). He did not really pay an attention to the stimuli, but said "blank" on every trial. Later he revealed his reasoning: "Since I never saw anything, anyway, I *know* that actually they were all blanks no matter what you said". He was right exactly fifty percent of the time—but he had no knowledge—neither on those trials on which he happened to be correct nor on those about which he was wrong.[19]

Anti-luminosity: belief and knowledge are not transparent mental states

A luminous condition is defined as one in which whenever it obtains in an agent, the agent knows that it obtains. The conditions of being in pain and having things appear to us in whatever ways they do are examples used to demonstrate conditions considered luminous, transparent, and directly accessible first-personally to the agent in question. (This definition is from Williamson, 2000, pp. 95–96). The case for anti-luminosity with regard to both knowledge and belief is perhaps most simply stated thus: we can believe things and we can know things without believing, knowing or being aware that we believe or know them. We have no privileged access; not to the proper category typing of the mental states we are in, nor to the content of these mental states. Taking a strong anti-luminosity position, Williamson (2000), without denying that there is much that we can know, calls us "cognitively homeless" (p. 94), claiming that there is no central core of transparent mental states about which we can't go wrong (pp. 93–113).

The position that knowing is non-luminous seems most obviously true about performances—that is, knowings-how, as for example A. D. Woozley (1953, p. 152) states: "[Take] A claiming that he doesn't know how to do something, and B replying that he (A) knows perfectly well how to do it … B can often follow up … by showing A that he (A) does know". (See also Ryle, 1949, p. 53.) But Woozley himself adds that this is no less true for knowings-that (p. 172): "knowing is not self-certifying, as you can know but not know that you know, just as much as you can wrongly think you know and not know that you're wrongly thinking it". Along these same lines Armstrong (1973, p. 146) explains that: "… it is logically possible to be mistaken about, or unaware of the existence of, any of our current mental states just as much as any other state of affair in the world". Moreover (p. 212): "It is possible … for A to know that p and disbelieve he knows it". (See also Danto, 1968, p. 153, and Margolis, 1973, p. 15 who also hold this view.)

As for mis-typing one sort of mental state for another, this everyday occurrence stands out even more clearly when working with psychoanalytic patients. (See Brakel, 2001, 2009, especially Chapters Seven and Eight.) Conative attitudes (mental states) such as desires and wishes not only color beliefs but can also be mistaken for beliefs. The trope of the parched desert traveller's oasis mirage is made real by patients who, for example, are so hungry for love from indifferent persons, that they take neutral (or even frankly negative) facts as positive indicators. Thus spouse A, desiring love from spouse B, interprets B's phone call telling him that she will have to cancel their plans as a sign that she really loves him. A says to his analyst, "Yes, she cancelled, but she called first, she really cares". This suggests that he experiences his desire for her to love him as a belief that she does.

Patients in analysis even more frequently confuse distinct cognitive mental states, one for another. For example, certain phantasies—attitudes with content that one phantasises or imagines to be the case—are often regarded, expressed, and in some important ways serve to function as beliefs. But clearly they are not beliefs; they are not regulated by evidence and do not aim at the truth. Take for instance a patient, who despite his own ample evidence to the contrary, fixedly believes that no one likes him, and in many ways acts as though it is the case that nobody does. I have termed these fixed phantasy-laden mental states "neurotic-beliefs" (Brakel, 2001, 2009, especially p. 384), maintaining that in part the most troubling, life disturbing, pathological nature of neurosis is caused by this very mis-categorising; for example, when these phantasy-like neurotic-beliefs are mistaken for beliefs-proper and thereby used to guide (really misguide) the patient's real world actions.

Other patients make an even more serious categorising mistake, confounding phantasies with knowledge. There are, for instance, patients who engage in physically self-mutilating behaviours such as cutting themselves. These are most often very complex patients, and yet one common "reason" for their physically self-destructive behaviour often emerges: cutters cut because they "know" that this is the only way that they can feel better. That this sort of mis-typing (mistaking phantasies for knowledge) often contributes to more severe psychopathology derives from one of the important differences between beliefs and knowledge discussed above, namely, that knowledge, more so than belief, resists change and leads to persistence in acting in accord with its content.

For our current purpose, what follows is perhaps the most important implication of knowing as a non-transparent, non-luminous mental state about which we have no privileged access, either in terms of content or mental state attitude type: if there is no luminosity there can be no necessity that knowing p entails knowing that you know p or even believe that you know p. Three vital questions follow:

1. What is the nature of the relation of first order knowledge (knowing p) to second order knowledge (knowing that you know p, KK) and second order belief (believing that you know p, BK)?[20]
2. Must one believe what one knows (BK)?
3. Can one have knowledge without any belief at all—that is, with neither subsequent nor prior belief? In other words, must knowledge entail belief (K→B)?

These matters are so fundamental that they warrant a section of their own, which follows forthwith.

First and second order knowledge and belief: believing what one knows, knowledge without (any sort of) belief

Background

Chisholm (1957, pp. 17–18) warns that even if there is a sense that knowing does entail believing: "... we must not think of knowing as being, in any sense, a 'species' of believing ... The relation of knowing to believing ... is not that of a falcon to bird or airedale to dog;[21] it is more like that of arriving to traveling. Arriving entails traveling—a man cannot arrive unless he has traveled—but arriving is not a species of traveling". Merrill Ring (1977) argues that Chisholm cannot have both that 1) knowing entails believing and that 2) knowing is not a species of believing. Ring explains that Chisholm wants to "save" the thesis that knowledge entails belief, but that the example of travelling and arriving "... is so far from upholding his view that it belongs to mine" (p. 59). Ring's view uses the very same example to demonstrate that knowledge cannot entail belief (p. 59): "Arriving does not entail traveling—it entails having traveled. When one has arrived, one is no longer traveling. Similarly, when one does come to know what was previously believed, the believing like the traveling is over". Ring (1977, p. 59) goes on to describe that in knowing something the knower cannot be trying to find out what is already known, as distinct from believing something in which the believer will be trying to find out what is merely believed.

And yet Ring's position, although an emphatic denial that knowledge entails belief, is an equally strong avowal that knowing entails having believed. Obviously, looked at from the account I am trying to advance here about the primacy of knowing, this temporal entailment is no improvement. So, here for instance, is some evidence against Ring's view. In the negative hallucination case presented above, Dr. N had no prior beliefs regarding the content that he both knew but didn't know he knew. Further, prior to his state of knowledge he made no attempts to gain the knowledge, in fact he tried to not-know it. On the other hand, take a case of someone knowing the answer to something but not being able to bring it to mind. The agent in this situation knows that he or she knows. Yet the content of the knowledge remains unconscious. The agent tries hard to bring the answer to consciousness but experiences difficulty in retrieving the unconsciously known content. Again, no prior beliefs are involved.

Others, despite having views largely similar to Ring's, agree with me (to an extent) regarding the problem with knowing necessarily entailing having believed. Pritchard's (1950) account, for example, first makes a claim identical to Ring's that knowing, as a mental state, entails "not-believing", in the very particular sense of not currently believing. He then argues that because knowledge and belief are both irreducible mental states, knowledge can neither be a species of belief, nor entail ongoing belief, even though "... believing is a stage we *sometimes* [my emphasis] reach in the endeavour to attain knowledge" (p. 88).[22]

Still, Pritchard's account is problematic in another way. He holds that the very separateness of knowledge from belief is predicated on complete transparency or luminosity of each of these mental states: "... whenever we know something, we do, or at least can, by reflecting directly know that we are knowing it, and that whenever we believe something, we similarly do or can directly know that we are believing it and not knowing it" (p. 86). Transparency, just like luminosity, of course amounts to knowing that you know and knowing that you believe; epistemic capacities that are far from established.

Clearly then, the position I take in this chapter is far different from those of Chisholm, and Pritchard and Ring, and it includes the following: 1) knowing and believing are each separate mental states 2) knowing and believing are not luminous or transparent, meaning there is no privileged access. Thus neither KK (knowing that and what you know) and KB (knowing that and what you believe) nor BK (believing what you know) obtains routinely. And 3) Knowing does not imply ongoing or prior believing, not conceptually and not temporally. Can this view hold up? In the words of the title of this section, can a case be made for:

1. First order knowledge without second order knowledge (K but not necessarily KK);
2. Knowing without second order believing what you know (K but not necessarily BK), and finally;
3. Knowledge, without knowledge entailing belief of any sort, including prior belief (K, but not K→ B)?

The following subsections present examples that argue for one or more of the above claims. (Negative hallucinations warrant such a subsection, but are not included here as they were described at length earlier in the chapter.)

Savant syndrome

Savant syndrome (this term replacing "idiot savant") represents a disorder marked by any one of a group of unusual cognitive abilities, usually associated with autism or related disturbances:

> Savant Syndrome … can also be acquired in an accident or illness, typically one that injures or impairs the left side of the brain. There is some research that suggests that it can be induced, which might support the view that savant abilities are latent within all people but are obscured by the normal functioning intellect … Most autistic savants have very extensive mental abilities, called splinter skills. They can memorize facts, numbers, license plates, maps, and extensive lists of sports and weather statistics. Some savants can mentally note and then recall perfectly a very long sequence of music, numbers, or speech. Some, dubbed mental calculators, can do exceptionally fast arithmetic, including prime factorization. Other skills include precisely estimating distances and angles by sight, calculating the day of the week for any given date over the span of tens of thousands of years, and being able to accurately gauge the passing of time without a clock. Usually these skills are concrete, non-symbolic, right hemisphere skills, rather than left hemisphere skills, which tend to be more sequential, logical, and symbolic.[23]

When persons with savant syndrome are asked to perform any of their splinter skills—say picking out the day of the week for several dates in different years across thousands of years—assuming that the savants get the answers right, they clearly know the answers. That this ability involves first order knowledge is clear. But what else does such a splinter skill entail? Certainly there seem to be no beliefs necessary to arrive at these answers; the savants know the right answers without any prior beliefs about which days of the week fall on particular dates. Further, when savants demonstrate their skill for the first time, as far as experimenters can tell, these savants have neither secondary knowledge nor even secondary belief as to whether or not they can perform this task. Likely, after many flawless performances a secondary belief in their own ability to know grows; but this is conceptually trivial.

A (fictional) French Canadian who claims to know no English history

Colin Radford (1966, pp. 2–7) introduces Jean, a fictional French Canadian who claims to know no English history. After all, Jean explains, this is not what is taught at French-Canadian schools. Nonetheless, he gets involved in trying to answer questions on this subject for cash, and he misses a few. Then he's asked when Queen Elizabeth died. He responds, "Ohh … Mmm … Sixteen-oh-three?" To which his questioner replies, "Yes! Now tell me you haven't done any history! … (sarcastically): That was just a guess, was it" (p. 2)? Jean then proceeds to answer when Elizabeth's successor, James I, died, "Oh … Ah … James the First. So he's sixteen-oh-three to … to … sixteen twenty-five" (p. 3)? Now the questioner, affirming that Jean's answer is correct, is more emphatic that Jean must have learned these English history dates. Jean says, "Well, I certainly don't remember. As far as I can tell I'm just guessing" (p. 3). Finally, after getting a few more questions right about Tudor and Stuart royalty, Jean himself is impressed by the detail of his own correct responses, and realises that he must have learned these things. He then comes up with the occasion; it was as a punishment that the dates of particular kings and queens had to be memorised. But Jean comments that he'd completely forgotten, and his questioner believes him, "Freudian forgetting, I expect" (p. 3).

Radford (1966) analyses the case as one in which Jean knows P (the dates he got right), but "was not certain, or sure, or confident that P. Indeed he was fairly certain that his answer … was wrong, i.e. that not-P, since he believed it to be a pure guess" (p. 4). Radford continues that if the case of Jean "… is a possible one … it shows that a man may know that P even though he is neither sure that P, and indeed is fairly sure that not-P, nor justified in being sure, etc., that P" (p. 4)! Further, Jean did not know that he knew until the questioner told him that his answers were correct. For Radford this means "Jean knows at the first level—even though he is not sure … and that these considerations do not exist or operate at the second level" (p. 6). In other words, "… he is not aware, does not realize, i.e., he does not know, that he knows any [English] history" (p. 7).

Jean, like people with savant syndrome, can have 1) knowledge without belief prior to or about that knowledge, and 2) first order knowledge without second order knowledge or belief. Further, not only is it possible for Jean to know P without believing P, he can in fact believe not-P.

The chicken-sexer and horserace picker

Goldman (1975, pp. 114–116) presents the case of a professional chicken-sexer who despite having the know-how to distinguish between male and female chicks with remarkable accuracy, has no idea how he does it. A similar case is offered by D. S. Mannison (1976, pp. 142–147)—that of Jones the picker of horserace winners. Jones too has predictive know-how; he can choose the winning horse with great consistency, but like the chicken-sexer is mystified by his own technique. Both men clearly have know-how, and regarding each of many individual situations they show that they know-that too. The chicken-sexer knows for instance that chick X is female, chick Y is male; and Jones knows that Fleetfoot will win race 1, Firefly race 2, etc. But do they have second order knowledge? Can Jones know that he will know the outcome of an upcoming race?

The answer for Mannison (1976) turns on Jones' experience. If it is 1950 and Jones has just started the winning racehorse-picking business, he cannot know that he will know, even though he indeed does know that Sure Thing will be the winner. But if it is 1974 and he's been selecting the winning horses for every race for more than two decades, he can know that he will pick the winner of a specific upcoming race. Further for Mannison (1976), Jones would be justified in claiming to know solely on the grounds that he always does pick the winner of a race. This second order knowledge is based on knowing of one's know-how or "knowing that I can and shall" (p. 144), and it is not the same as know-how. Wittgenstein (1953) in *Philosophical Investigations* (section #324, p. 106) advances the same position: "… I am as certain that I shall be able to continue the series, as I am that this book will drop to the ground when I let it go; and that I should be no less astonished if I suddenly and for no obvious reason got stuck … than I should if the book remained hanging in the air … What could justify the certainty better than success?"

But let's return to Jones in 1950. Here Mannison (1976) describes him as having neither second order knowledge nor second order belief about his knowing that a particular horse, No. 4, will win; and in fact disbelieving what he knows. Speaking for Jones, Mannison (1976, p. 147) writes: "As there are twelve horses in the race, and I have no horseracing expertise, I have no reason to believe that No. 4 will win ... the odds against No. 4 winning are eleven to one. As these are formidable odds, I would only be reasonable in holding that some horse other than No. 4 will win". So the case of Jones, like that of Jean, also demonstrates that one can have knowledge of P without second order knowledge or belief of P, and in fact with belief of not-P.

What about second order knowledge and belief and the chicken-sexer? In the natural course of events it would seem that the chicken-sexer, once he became established, would form beliefs that the chicks he "knew" to be males really were males and those he "knew" to be female really were female. These beliefs and their justification, like those of Jones and his horserace predictions, clearly would be entirely predicated on the success of his chicken-sexing know-how and the many resultant instances of his demonstrating that he knows-that.

But then Goldman (1975, p. 115) sets up an interesting case: suppose the chicken-sexer is persuaded that his performances lately have been bad. Assuming his abilities are intact, he would still be correctly sexing chicks—that is, still possessing his know-how, so that the resultant instances of chick-sexing (knowings-that) would still be correct. The chicken-sexer, under these conditions, would still have first order knowledge. But now he would be without any true and justified second order beliefs a) about his know-how, b) about the individual cases, and c) about the knowing that he can and shall, described by Mannison. In fact he would have false beliefs about his outcomes.

Although Goldman (1975) seems to agree regarding the first order knowledge, he introduces confusing belief-talk where it is most inappropriate:

> Why ... do we credit knowledge to the chicken-sexer ...? The answer ... is given by the causal theory of knowing ... there is a certain kind of causal connection between the fact that p and S's *belief* [my italics] that p ... In the chicken-sexing case the fact that the chick is male causes S to *believe* [my italics] that it is male. (p. 116)

Actually his belief (second order) about the sex of the chick can be distorted by what he is falsely told about his performances, but not his knowledge (first order) about its sex. Assuming he is still sexing the chicks correctly, he still knows that a male chick is male, even if he can no longer believe in his knowledge. Thus, emending Goldman's statement above, without contesting the causal theory of knowing, and in fact repeating most of his own words, I hold:

> Why ... do we credit knowledge to the chicken-sexer ...? The answer ... is given by the causal theory of knowing ... there is a certain kind of causal connection between the fact that p and S's knowing that p. In the chicken-sexing case, the fact that the chick is male causes S to know it is male.

And let's add that this is the case no matter what he is told and subsequently falsely believes about the matter and/or if he has no beliefs about the matter whatsoever![24] Thus whether the chicken-sexer has false second order beliefs, predicated on the false information given him, or true second order beliefs, predicated on his experience and memories of his remarkable record of successful instances of correct sexing of chicks, his first order knowledge is intact and not reliant on beliefs of any sort.

The winning racehorse picker and the chicken-sexer are examples of know-how leading to instances of first order knowing-that, all requiring no prior (or concomitant) belief. Further, both cases demonstrate that such first order knowledge can exist without second order true belief or second order knowledge about what is known, and indeed with false belief about what is known.

The duck/rabbit dual figure and dream drawing

The duck/rabbit dual figure (see Figure 1) and other such ambiguous figures have been used in many psychological experiments. Although the psychologists did not set out to explore first and second order knowledge, there is one group of experiments that bears on this matter. Following earlier work (see Reed & Johnsen, 1975), David Chambers and Daniel Reisberg (1985) presented the duck/rabbit stimulus figure to subjects who were unfamiliar with it. After the subjects had had enough time to form a mental image, the figure was removed. Subjects were asked what they had seen. All of the subjects who reported both a duck and a rabbit were excused from the rest of the study. The remaining subjects were asked to consider the other ambiguous stimulus figures they had worked with in practice sessions and then to internally re-examine their mental image of the figure (the duck/rabbit) they had been presented. Still they reported only the single original animal; duck or rabbit. Next they were given hints about the missing answer, and again asked to review their mental image. And, again, most gave just the unitary response. Finally the subjects were asked to draw their mental image. Now, in looking at their drawings both duck and rabbit emerged for all of the subjects.

The question bearing on first and second order knowledge concerns the status of the duck or rabbit figure that could not be recognised until the subjects drew the mental image of the presented stimulus figure. Take Subject A who immediately reported that in her mental image she saw a duck. But nothing else; she saw no rabbit—not until the very last step in the experiment, when she was asked to draw her mental image of the figure originally presented. At this point, and with some surprise, she looked at her own drawing and saw not just a duck, but also a rabbit. What can be made of this? It is uncontestable that throughout the process Subject A had both first and second order knowledge of the duck. She not only knew that a duck was presented, she knew that she knew. But the more interesting matter is: what did she know about the rabbit and when? For most of the experiment it seemed that she had no knowledge about the rabbit. However, when she was asked to draw her own mental image—presto—a rabbit emerged. Once she recognised the rabbit, she had second order knowledge of it. I maintain that all along she had first order knowledge of the rabbit; but this first order knowledge was unconscious. This is strikingly like the negative hallucination case presented at length at the beginning of the chapter. Dr. N had unconscious first order knowledge of my having fallen asleep. Only after reporting his thinly disguised dream did he have conscious second order knowledge; and he never recaptured his first order knowledge that I had fallen asleep. Subject A, after she drew her mental image could see and know both duck and rabbit, at which point she had both first and second order knowledge of both of the figures.

Consistent with these experimental findings are some examples from clinical psychoanalytic work. Although these data are of necessity more complex than those from psychology experiments, it has been found that certain patients in analysis, when asked to draw particular elements from their dreams, can sometimes discover (un-cover) something they had known but not wanted to know. (See Fisher, 1957; Slap, 1976; and Brakel, 1993.) In other words patients can, after viewing their drawing of a dream element, arrive at first and second order knowledge

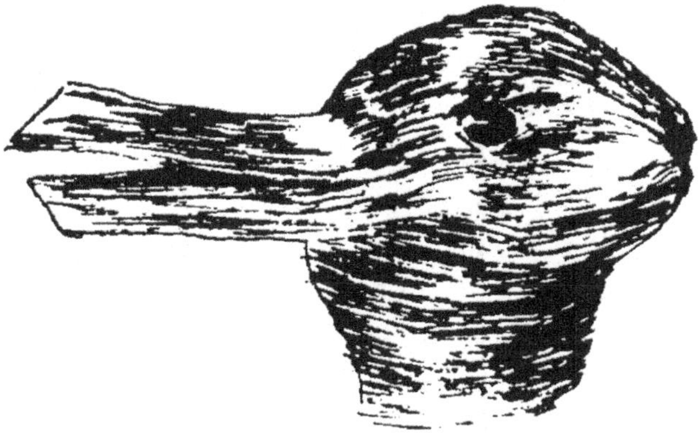

Figure 1. Duck/Rabbit stimulus.

of something that had been repressed and therefore known only in an unconscious first order way. This resembles closely the situation just described in the duck/rabbit drawing experiment.

For an example, consider my patient Ms. P.[25] She remembered that her father had been physically abusive to her mother and her brothers. She remembered that he killed two family pets. But after three years in analysis she was struggling with whether or not she had been physically abused or perhaps sexually molested by her father or someone else. Ms. P reported the following dream: "It is a life-or-death situation. Either kill or be killed. I'd never shot anyone before, but I shot this guy. I had a weird gun with itty-bitty tear drop bullets". She associated to several elements, but said nothing about the gun. When I pointed this out to her, she said: "It was a weird gun, lots of bullets, like a machine gun, but it didn't look like that, more square, like a hand-held fertilizer or a sifter with a handle; squeeze it and shoot all the bullets. I can't describe the gun". At this point I asked Ms. N to draw the gun. (See Figure 2.) As soon as the drawing was complete she said, "Now the handle looks like a big limp penis. And the tear-drop bullets something reproductive—sperm. But I don't want it to be; I'd rather bury it. I think something really did happen and I say I want to remember but I really don't [want to]".

Note that I am not suggesting that Ms. N, on the basis of this dream, could now know whether or not she was abused. My clinical epistemological claims are far more modest. All I am saying is that when

Figure 2. Ms. P's drawing of dream elements.[26]

Ms. N dreamt of guns and associated to handheld fertilisers, she had penises and sperm on her mind. She knew in a first order and unconscious way of her worries about the aggressive and sexual misuse of penises and sperm. Penises and sperm were then disguised through the dream-work to guns and bullets, and then in her associations to sifters and fertilisers. Although both guns and fertilisers were rather thin disguises, it took the drawing of the dream element for Ms. N to know about her unconscious first order knowledge in a second order and conscious form.

Before the subjects and patients were asked to draw their mental or dream images, they had both first and second order knowledge of some things—for example, the duck, and the gun in the dream. But they had only first order unconscious knowledge of some other things—the rabbit, and the penis and sperm. Note that this first order unconscious knowledge was unaccompanied by beliefs of any sort, and, as is true for all knowledge that is first order only, no knowledge of what they knew. When we add that this knowledge was not only just first order but also unconscious, we add that the subjects and patients did not even know that they knew. They had no awareness that there was anything to know beyond the duck, and beyond the gun.[27]

Subliminal experiments

The examples in this section should make it even clearer that one can have first order knowledge without any sort of belief—no prior belief, and no second order belief—and no second order knowledge about what is known. In subliminal experiments, subjects are presented stimulus items in such a way that they can have no conscious awareness of what has been presented. In some circumstances, namely under conditions that are at the objective threshold for detection, not only are subjects not aware of what item has been presented, they cannot even determine that an item has been presented. And yet, such experiments demonstrate that subjects can gain what can best be considered first order knowledge even under these stringent conditions.

For a first example take a well-known phenomenon in psychology called the mere exposure effect. In a classic experiment, William Kunst-Wilson and Robert Zajonc (1980) presented subjects a series of irregular polygons subliminally under subjective threshold conditions. (This means that subjects had no subjective awareness of seeing the polygons.) Next, each of these polygons was presented supraliminally (in full conscious awareness) and paired with an irregular polygon that had not been presented before. For each pair, subjects were asked two questions: one question concerned which of the two polygons they recognised, and the other asked which of the two they liked better. The recognition results were at chance; subjects were not aware of seeing the polygons, so they did not recognise them. But when subjects were asked which of the two polygons they liked better, the results were significantly in favour of the polygon that had been presented previously. Though the subjects did not know that they knew the polygons that had been presented to them, they knew them in the sense of discriminating them from those that had not been presented, by liking them better. The subjects had first order unconscious knowledge but no second order knowledge of (nor beliefs about) the polygons they had been presented earlier.

In another experiment, this one done at the objective detection threshold, subjects were not even aware that a stimulus was presented, much less what it was. The subjects were all social phobics. Researchers (Shevrin, Bond, Brakel, Hertel, & Williams, 1996) presented two sets of words to each subject; one set representing the subject's unconscious conflict and another set representing the subject's conscious symptom.[28] Each subject had his or her own individualised sets of words. Both sets of words were presented to each subject both subliminally (at the objective threshold) and supraliminally (in full awareness). Evoked response potentials (ERPs), which are electrical measures of brainwave activity, were recorded during the presentations.

Using a mathematically sophisticated time-frequency information analysis, whereby certain features of the ERPs can be used to test how well the ERPs to a certain class of stimuli can themselves be classified, we found the following. Across subjects, the time-frequency features classified the ERPs to the subliminally presented unconscious conflict words significantly better than they did the ERPs to the subliminally presented conscious symptom words; whereas supraliminally the reverse was true—ERPs to the supraliminally presented conscious symptom words were classified by the time-frequency features significantly more successfully than the ERPs from the supraliminally presented unconscious conflict words. Later in the experiment, when subjects were given a list of all of the words presented and asked to put them in categories, the conscious symptom words were placed in a single category, while the unconscious conflict words were dispersed over three or more categories. Both sets of results suggest that words associated with the subjects' symptoms and words representing their unconscious conflicts were experienced quite differently. Unlike the case with their conscious symptom words, subjects did not have second order conscious knowledge of the words representing their own unconscious conflicts. And yet their brain responses gave evidence of first order unconscious knowledge in that when these words were presented outside of consciousness (subliminally), they cohered very well for the subject's brain, just as they had for the psychoanalytic clinicians.

A final example comes from an experiment done with spider phobics. Howard Shevrin, Michael Snodgrass, James Abelson, Ramesh Kuswaha, and L. A. W. Brakel (in preparation) presented spider-phobic subjects subliminal stimuli consisting of line drawings of spiders and drawings of rectangles. All the stimuli were delivered at the objective detection threshold, meaning that subjects had no conscious awareness when and even that stimuli were presented, much less of their contents. ERPs were collected during eighty presentations; forty of spiders and forty of rectangles delivered in randomised orders. Before and after the presentations subjects rated their fear of spiders on several dimensions on an instrument called a visual analog scale (VAS). The findings of interest for our purposes concern an early component of the ERP, called N100. A negative-going (hence the "N") wave form in the ERP occurring 100 milliseconds after the presentation of stimuli, the N100 is associated with attention. The bigger a spider phobic's N100 response was to the spider pictures compared to that of the rectangle pictures, the greater was his/her VAS improvement. This means that the more a spider phobic's brain behaviour indicated discrimination between the spider pictures and the rectangle pictures (and in this sense knowing spiders from rectangles), the more improved was the phobic response. But all of this was entirely unconscious. No subject had any notion of whether a spider or rectangle stimulus was presented on any trial. No subject had any notion that they were making this discrimination. And finally subjects were not even aware that they were giving responses that indicated a lessening of their phobic symptom. In a later debriefing it was clear that they believed that their response to spiders was unchanged. No second order knowledge was available, even though there was brain and behavioural evidence of first order unconscious knowing of (in the sense of discriminating) spider from rectangle stimuli. Subjects did not know that they knew, they did not believe what they knew, and no prior belief formed the foundation of their knowledge.[29]

Neurotic-beliefs

The phenomenon of neurotic-belief (which I've discussed at length elsewhere; see Brakel, 2001, 2009, Chapter Seven) demonstrates another way in which one can know without believing what one knows. Most neurotic persons (and patients) have central phantasies, which are nonetheless treated as beliefs, and have some of belief's causal and functional roles—this despite the important fact that unlike beliefs, neurotic-beliefs are phantasies and as such do not aim at the truth and are not regulated by evidence.

Take for instance Mr. R, who was brutally beaten many times by his father as a child. Now a very successful business man, middle aged and homosexual, he behaves in ways seemingly designed to never attract any man, even as he longs for sex, marriage, and male companionship. Through work in analysis, Mr. R first came to see that his characteristic overly dramatic style alternating with cool indifference was not likely to attract any of the men he was interested in attracting. We then began to understand the purpose of these behaviours. Over the decades he had developed a complex phantasy (partly unconscious and partly conscious but irrational) that worked to explain his past problems and prevent future ones. The phantasy as we constructed it looked like this: Mr. R held the neurotic-belief that his father's damaging acts had been largely caused by his own lively (and very normal) little boy activities directed toward his father. So he maintained the neurotic-belief that as long as he was the opposite of normal—either too histrionic or too cold—not only would this sort of thing never happen again, it would also undo the past. Now, Mr. R was not a psychotic person; he was competent and sophisticated and functioned well in the world. Clearly he knew that his father's sadistic, physically damaging behaviour owed mostly to his serious psychopathology and moral turpitude. He knew that behaving either with outrageous flamboyance or with cold self-containment could not guarantee future safety. And of course he knew that the present cannot effect the past. And yet his neurotic-belief interfered with his rational capacities to believe what he knew. Mr. R had knowledge without believing what he knew.[30]

Non-human animals

Several authors grapple with the notion of animal knowledge. Shope (1983, p. 182, n.10) states: "We may say of a dog that it knows which bag holds the meat or knows that there is meat in this bag, without thereby implying that the dog accepts propositions". But Shope acknowledges that for some authors, granting that animals have knowledge implies attributing beliefs to them. Armstrong (1973), in talking of animal knowledge starts out directly claiming that if there is knowledge then there is belief (p. 27): "If A [an animal] perceives that something is the case … then it is entailed that A knows that that thing is the case. And 'A knows that p' entails 'A believes that p' … Now it seems obvious that the dog perceives that a cat is streaking across the lawn … So the dog acquires knowledge and, if he acquires knowledge, acquires beliefs". But later Armstrong leaves room for another interpretation, one more congenial to the view taken in this chapter, that knowledge precedes belief (p. 63): "If things of the sort X act upon an animal's sense organs, and, as a result, the animal proves able to act in a discriminating way toward the object which acted upon it, differentiating it from something which is not X, the animal can be credited with at least a simple concept of X".[31]

Goldman (1975, p. 118) describes the behaviour of ticks as "believing" that a certain odour (butyric acid, a component of human sweat) and a certain temperature (37 degrees centigrade) are indicators of a good place to suck blood. He goes on to describe an appropriate natural-selection based causal connection between these "beliefs" of ticks and the fact that these conditions are good for sucking blood. Because there is this appropriate causal connection, Goldman states (p. 118): "The causal theory of knowing, therefore, would vindicate the claim that the tick not only has innate true belief, but that it has innate knowledge". I am convinced about knowledge: beyond the know-how involved in sucking, ticks discriminate good targets from not good ones, knowing-that this one or that one is worth the energy investment. But why do beliefs have to be a prior part of this picture? On my view they do not; and Goldman once again (as above with regard to the chicken-sexer) talks of beliefs, instead of knowledge. Tick knowledge accounts for the phenomenon in question more elegantly. (See the next section on "Unconscious knowledge and unconscious belief" for the argument supporting this claim against Goldman's move and others like it.)

Conclusions on first and second order knowledge and belief

These cases demonstrate several classes of counter-examples to KK and BK (second order knowing and believing) and thereby to luminosity. They also show various disconnects between knowledge and belief (prior, concomitant and subsequent belief). In fact, in none of these examples does knowledge entail belief; rather we have many cases with knowledge but no belief. Savants, and Jean the French Canadian quizzed on English history, do not have any beliefs at all about what they know[32] at least until after the fact of the performance. Likewise, people with negative hallucinations have no beliefs about what they unconsciously know until someone reveals the content of the negative hallucination to them. The chicken-sexer and winning racehorse picker early in their careers might even disbelieve what they know. The duck/rabbit subjects, until they have made their drawings, believe only half of what they fully know unconsciously. Participants in the subliminal experiments never believe anything about the contents of the stimuli they are presented, as they never consciously experience these contents. Yet they demonstrate that they have considerable unconscious knowledge of these contents. Patients with neurotic-beliefs have knowledge that they just do not (cannot/will not) believe. And as for non-human animals, despite some claims to the contrary, it is more parsimonious to allow that they have first order knowledge simpliciter, without entailed belief and without knowing or believing that they know.

But these cases raise two vital questions, which I will take up one at a time. First, why are we willing to attribute knowledge to these agents, but not beliefs? Are they meeting sufficient conditions for knowing, while they do not meet certain necessary conditions for believing? Velleman (personal communication, 2007) suggests an answer regarding cases such as those detailed in this section:

> The subject's subjective probability for p is greater than his subjective probability for not-p, and this differential is reliably linked to the fact that p; but 1) subjective probability for p is not great enough to satisfy our intuitive threshold for all-out belief; and in some cases also 2) he misjudges the differential, claiming that he has no more credence in p than in not-p (a false second order belief) … [Thus] we are willing to credit someone with knowledge on the basis of small differences in his cognitive states that are reliable indicators of the truth; but [these] are not sufficient [for the subject him or herself] to qualify [for him or her] as beliefs.

While this answer does help to some extent, one is still left wondering why it is the case that when one's subjective probability for p is greater than for not-p, and this differential is reliably linked to the fact that p, our intuitive threshold for all-out belief is higher than that for knowledge. One possibility concerns the nature of belief, a cognitive attitude that aims constitutively at the truth (Velleman, 2000, p. 16), in contrast to the nature of knowledge, a factive attitude that could well be characterised as constitutively registering a truth rather than aiming at it. Understanding belief and knowledge in this way strongly suggests the possibility that some sort of registering of truth is an ontologically necessary precursor to aiming at the truth, as after all, one must have some particular truth at which to aim.[33]

The second important question raised by the analyses of these cases is: why is it that the standard view in epistemology has been that knowledge entails belief, and that knowledge entails second order knowing (both knowing that you know and knowing what you know)? It is because this dual entailment thesis, according to Jaakko Hintikka (1962, p. 30), "… presuppose[s] a certain amount of rationality in the people whose attitudes are being discussed". David Annis (1977) agrees that to hold that knowledge entails belief presumes rationality. But Annis (p. 223), unlike Hintikka, finds this view highly problematic: "[W]e cannot define knowledge by including rationality. Nor can we conditionalize the entailment thesis on the assumption of rationality". To support his view he gives a counter-example in which rationality is not expected, and yet knowledge is still attributed (p. 223): "If we are told that the idiot savant does not believe, our reaction is not: 'If he does not believe, he must not really know; otherwise why would he not believe?'" Rather, Annis points out, it is granted by many philosophers[34] that "… in such a case the person has knowledge" (p. 223). Therefore, he concludes, if, in cases such as this, knowledge does not entail belief, knowledge need not entail belief.

By adding many different cases to that of the savants, including the instances of unconscious knowledge that arise in the real-world settings of subliminal research, cognitive psychology experiments, and the clinical psychoanalytic situation, the premise that there are instances of knowledge without entailed belief is broadened and strengthened. And if this premise is strengthened, the conclusion that knowledge can and does exist without belief becomes all the more difficult to resist.

Unconscious knowledge and unconscious belief

Unconscious knowledge without unconscious belief

In the section just above I presented several types of examples demonstrating first order knowing without second order knowing. In order to avoid later misunderstanding, and because it is a topic of general interest, let's at this point consider whether (and how) the phenomena of first and second order knowledge are related to those of first and second order consciousness.[35] Almost immediately it can be appreciated that although there is some area of overlap between first and second order knowledge and first and second order consciousness, there is no perfect one-to-one mapping. When, for example, the winning horserace picker selects a winning horse, he is fully conscious of his choice: he is conscious of the specific horse he selects (first order consciousness), and he can reflect both on the fact that he did make a choice and on his having chosen this particular horse (second order consciousness). But he has only first order knowledge that the horse he picks is a winner. He does not know how he has made his choice, and especially early in his successful career he does not know that he knows the winner. He has no second order knowledge. This obtains for the chicken-sexer too. But the situation is different for Jean (the French-Canadian "student" of English history), the subjects in the subliminal and duck/rabbit experiments, the analytic patients drawing their dream elements, people with negative hallucinations, and savants. While these people also had first order but no second order knowledge, here even their first order knowledge was unconscious.

But isn't it the case that beliefs can be unconscious too? This leads to a very interesting set of arguments that developed among several philosophers, concerning Radford's (1966) claim that Jean, his fictional French-Canadian English history "student", unconsciously knew. Essentially Keith Lehrer (1970, 1974), Annis (1969), and Armstrong (1969–1970, 1973) all argue that while Radford (1966) properly allows that Jean had unconscious knowledge, he illegitimately denies that he also had unconscious belief. Armstrong (1969–1970, p. 26) puts it thus: "... the case is a case of knowledge ... But ... on the very same grounds that lead him to say it is a case of knowledge, he should say it is also a case of belief". Lehrer (1970, p. 137) further holds that Radford takes "conscious conviction and a readiness to report as a condition of the application of the epistemic term [he] wish[es] to prove not to apply [i.e., belief] while rejecting these as conditions of the epistemic term [he] wish[es] to assume does apply [i.e., knowledge]".

Radford (1970, p. 107) addresses his critics: "Having shown that Jean does not consciously believe that P, we are still, however, left with the possibility that he unwittingly, unconsciously believes this ... But if our only reason for saying that Jean unwittingly believes that P were that he unwittingly knows that P, we should be assuming what is in question, viz., that if someone knows that something is the case he therefore believes that something is the case". Thus, unless it is accepted that knowledge necessarily entails belief, there is no reason to assume that Jean's unconscious knowledge entails his unconscious belief.

Next, Radford (1970, pp. 106–107) gives a positive reason for denying that Jean has unconscious beliefs. He contrasts Jean's unconscious knowledge—immediately and simply obvious from his correct answers—with his putative unconscious belief, which as a "theoretical construct" requires another level of inference.

Note that if Radford's argument about Jean having unconscious knowledge without unconscious belief holds, it will work for the other types of cases too. This is important because just as there are significant differences between knowledge and belief, there are also significant differences between unconscious knowledge and unconscious belief, the topic of the next subsection.

Unconscious knowledge and unconscious belief

As is true regarding knowledge coming in many varieties (see the subsection on "Various types of knowledge" above), there are several sorts of unconscious knowledge. On the simplest level, one can unconsciously discriminate between or among stimuli, as is true in the subliminal experiments. Also one can unconsciously know content, in the sense of being acquainted with it, as is demonstrated by the mere exposure effect and duck/rabbit experiments. Then there is unconsciousness with regard to know-how, both not being conscious of having know-how, and being unconscious with respect to how the know-how works. Savants, the chicken-sexer and the winning horserace picker demonstrate both kinds of know-how unconsciousness; with consciousness of having the skill developing only with experience, while access to the nature of the skill remains unconscious. Finally, one can be unconscious of knowing-that p in two different senses; unconscious about the knowing-that, and unconscious about the content, p.

Unconscious belief does not come in many types, only two. One can be unconscious of one's mental state of believing, perhaps miscategorising it as some other mental attitude. And one can be unconscious about the contents of one's belief. Suppose that my mother is ill and I want very much for her to recover. At some point I might have a realistic belief that she is in fact dying. But as this belief is one that is very painful, it might be the case that I repress this belief (i.e., its contents) and render it unconscious. Or, it might be that I am still conscious of the contents, but mis-type the mental attitude convincing myself that it is just a baseless fear that she is dying, a fear I can dismiss.

The priority of knowledge

The case for belief entailing knowledge

Much space in this chapter has been devoted to undermining the claim that knowledge entails belief (K→B). What if the entailment thesis went the other way, such that belief entails knowledge (B→K)?[36] Peter Unger (1975) makes such a claim, maintaining that for someone to have a reasonable belief one must have a reason for that belief, and this comes down to knowing something; minimally a) some fact(s) and b) that the reason is connected to the belief (p. 37). Oliver Johnson (1979, p. 379) in a discussion of Unger's (1975) view elaborates: "If anyone gives, as his reason for believing X, some proposition 'p', then for us to count p as a reason for him, and therefore to count the person reasonable in believing X for the reason p, he must know that p. Reasonable belief, it follows, entails knowledge". Put another way, believing X (for any X) entails knowing that p (for some p related to X in the right way).

Zeno Vendler (1975) defends what at first glance seems to be a very specific, narrow and limited case of belief entailing knowledge. Referring to the attitudes of a listener after a speaker has spoken, Vendler states (pp. 372–373): "The knowledge of what one said does not imply belief, but the belief of what one said presupposes the knowledge of what one said". In other words, if Z says, "I'm going to stop doing A right now", in order for me to begin to assess whether or not to believe him as to whether or not he'll stop doing A—that is, to have a belief about this content—I have to know the content. While one might think that this pertains only to speech acts, upon reflection Vendler might have hit upon a general epistemological fact: in order to have any belief at all about some X, it is the case that X (or something non-trivially and predictably related to X) must be known, even if that knowledge is in the truth-registering sense of acquaintance or discrimination knowledge. Thereby belief entails knowledge, and not vice versa.

Samuel Guttenplan (1994) extends the idea of belief entailing knowledge to the idea that belief originated from knowledge. Like Williamson (2000) Guttenplan sees knowledge as a factive state that cannot be described as belief plus some other things. Instead, knowledge is central with belief "as knowledge minus something" (p. 297). To demonstrate this point, Guttenplan (p. 298) tells what he admits is a "just so story" about some very early propositional attitude-using ancestors:

> [O]n seeing a spider, and also seeing A's extremely anxious-to-leave sort of behavior, it was natural to connect the two. What was said was that A feared the spider. And this kind of talk was itself built out of other kinds of relation between A and the spider: there was the "seeing" relation ... and of course there was the knowing relation. This latter was central to the functioning of the whole scheme: A had to be in that relation to the spider's presence for fearing ... to so much as make sense. Now ... this scheme had one great drawback: there were times when ... a shadow on the wall provoked the [spider] response ... But of course this happened when in fact there was no spider ... It was at this point that ... someone suggested that a new attitude be invented, one which was exactly like knowledge in all but one respect: the requirement that things actually be as described ... the new attitude was ..."quasi-knowledge"... [i.e., knowledge minus the spider's actual presence] ... belief.

The relationship of evidence to belief and knowledge

On the standard account, knowledge is belief plus something else. The view described in the story above reverses this, holding that belief is knowledge minus something. Where does evidence fit in this equation both with respect to belief and knowledge? The standard analysis has it that belief plus evidence yields knowledge. But what if this were reversed too? Williamson (2000, pp. 8–11, 184–186, 203–208) argues for this strongly, equating "... S's evidence with S's knowledge ... E = K" (p. 185). When it is the case that E = K, that one's evidence is equal to one's knowledge "... all one's knowledge serves as the foundation for all one's justified beliefs" (p. 186). Filling this out: it is belief that gains grounds in its aim at the truth, by adding evidence, and evidence is in the form of knowledge (p. 208). Clearly, on this account (and related to Unger's claim described just above), a new equation: Belief plus Knowledge/Evidence yields Justified Belief, (B + K/E = Justified B), replaces the standard view equation: Belief plus Evidence yields Knowledge, (B + E = K).

The new equation fits the savant, chicken-sexer and winning horse picker cases quite naturally. The agents in these circumstances do not have beliefs about their capacities or about the outcome of a particular instance until they have established, through experience, that they know how to make these selections. On the basis of this K/E, namely their experiential evidence that they have the know-how; they can form justified beliefs about their abilities and about the particulars of a specific chick or race.

The developmental priority of knowledge

Wimmer and Perner (1983) did a classic experiment that can be interpreted in a variety of ways, including one which suggests that children are demonstrably capable of knowing things before they can be shown to have beliefs. In the experiment, children were shown a puppet play in which a puppet boy named Maxi first puts some candies in a box and then goes out to play. While he is out playing, the mother puppet moves the candies to the cupboard. Children are asked where Maxi will look for the candies on his return. Five-year-olds have no trouble indicating that Maxi will look for the candies in the box where he left them. But three- and four-year-olds more often indicate that Maxi will look for the candies in the cupboard. These children, by virtue of their watching the play and seeing the puppet mother move the candies, *know* that the candies are in the cupboard, and this fact seems arresting. In the face of their own knowing, they seem unable to grasp that the other children could in fact not-know and thereby merely believe falsely.

This interpretation of this experiment may in itself not be convincing. But let's add an evolutionary perspective here by returning to findings from non-human animals. Animals, functioning in ways that are adaptive, clearly possess knowledge, at least in the acquaintance, recognition, discrimination and know-how senses, and probably in terms of knowing-that too. (For example dogs know-that certain sounds are often associated with certain outcomes—cabinet door with dog biscuits, leash noises with going outside—and we can tell they know-that by their responsive behaviours.) But couldn't one then assume that dogs (and other animals) also have beliefs? The answer is no. As Radford's argument made clear, regarding inferring unconscious beliefs as well as unconscious knowledge in the case of Jean the French Canadian, positing animal belief requires an additional level of inference over and above that which will suffice for animal knowledge.

Conclusions on the priority of knowledge

Each of the foregoing subsections takes up a different aspect of the priority of knowledge over belief. The subsection on belief entailing knowledge makes a case for knowledge being conceptually and ontologically fundamental. The subsection on the relationship of evidence to belief and knowledge presents the view that knowledge constitutes the evidence for belief, rather than the standard notion that in order to arrive at knowledge one needs belief plus evidence. Knowledge providing evidence for belief, and not vice versa, amounts to a claim for knowing as an epistemologically prior state. Finally, the subsection on development considers that knowing is a state of mind available evolutionarily and developmentally earlier than believing.

Psychoanalysis and the priority of knowledge

This chapter has provided psychoanalytic data and theory in support of a radical view in epistemology and philosophy—that knowledge, rather than belief, is the fundamental epistemic mental state. Psychoanalytic data and theory have helped in two ways. First, to the question "but isn't it the case that knowledge entails belief?", psychoanalytic data provide answers favouring the independence of knowledge. Patients with negative hallucinations, for instance, clearly have unconscious contentful knowledge without any prior or concurrent beliefs about what they know. Further, neurotic patients (and most "normal" people) have neurotic-beliefs. These are actually phantasies, regarded as beliefs. And yet neurotic-beliefs, unlike beliefs-proper are not evidence sensitive. In fact neurotic-beliefs interfere with patients' use of knowledge as evidence. For example, some patients who are smart have neurotic-beliefs that they are dumb. Consequently, without outright denial of obvious evidential knowledge (such as IQ tests and school performance) that confirm above average intellect, these patients isolate these facts. The knowledge of objectively measured intelligence, as is indicated by the IQ tests, etc., is intact but inert; it is simply not believed. Thus, instead of having second order true beliefs about knowing their intelligence, such patients continue with neurotic-beliefs about being dumb. The realm of their knowledge on this matter and the realm of their beliefs are not just independent but disconnected. Finally, the dream drawing case illustrates another psychoanalytic situation in which contents are known in a first order unconscious fashion without beliefs having played any role at all. In these ways psychoanalytic data help defeat the idea that knowledge entails belief (K→B).

Second, and perhaps more important, psychoanalytic theory has added something to the debate concerning first and second order knowledge—a debate compressed into the single question: "if one knows mustn't one also know that (and what) one knows?" Unconscious knowing, the existence of which is one of the most important assumptions of psychoanalysis, is also evinced in several of the cases demonstrating that one can indeed know without knowing one knows. It is unconscious knowledge that explains how Jean the French Canadian knows but does not know he knows some English history. Unconscious knowledge also determines how the chicken-sexer can know males from females, and how the winning horserace picker can choose the winners, with neither practitioner having a clue how he knows, and, at first, even that he knows. When we move beyond the constructed cases, unconscious knowledge figures just as importantly. The performances of savants, and the responses of subjects in mere exposure, subliminal, and duck/rabbit experiments, all illustrate agents knowing without knowing they know, all necessitating the posit of unconscious first order knowledge. Finally, in examples involving actual psychoanalytic data too—cases such as negative hallucination and dream drawing—again first order knowledge is shown to exist without second order knowledge or second order belief, with the first order knowledge quite unconscious.

In closing I shall remark that there is a significant way in which this chapter's contribution goes the other way too—by which I mean that the radical philosophical view that knowledge is the fundamental epistemological mental state points to a new understanding of the psychoanalytic endeavour itself. In order to illustrate this, let's return to Dr. N's negative hallucination. As he demonstrated with his manifest dream content, Dr. N had unconscious knowledge of my falling asleep. But he had no conscious knowledge of my lapse. Even after I showed him the evidence of his dream he said, "You did not fall asleep here last time! If you had, I'd be really furious". But I did, and so we have to assume that he was really furious, and that he rendered his fury unconscious too. What is the analytic task here? Certainly it is to make the unconscious conscious; to make content pertaining to my having fallen asleep and his feelings about it available to examine. This is vitally important. But alone this account is incomplete, and construes the analytic task too broadly and without the proper emphasis. More specifically, the analytic task goes deeper than generally facilitating a patient's gaining the possession of certain contents. In Dr. N's case it involves helping him know that he knew I fell asleep; helping him understand why, fearing his furious feelings, he had to try to un-know that knowledge. The compromising of one's knowledge and one's capacity to know—seen so clearly in negative hallucinations as a paradigmatic neurotic symptom—is arguably the most deleterious aspect of any neurosis; and it is present in every one. Keeping in mind the philosophical view of the primacy of knowledge can help analysts go beyond making the unconscious conscious toward making what must be kept un-knowable ultimately known.

Notes

1. The purpose of this long footnote is to illustrate: a) justified true beliefs that seem to constitute knowledge, b) justified true beliefs that do not constitute knowledge (Gettier-like cases), c) unjustified true beliefs, and d) justified false beliefs. To begin with take the following five facts as true: 1) It is Friday evening at 5pm. 2) Our front doorbell is broken. 3) Vic, a punctual visitor at 5pm each day, arrives on this particular Friday at 5pm and presses the broken doorbell, but does not knock on the door. 4) Meanwhile, at 5pm I hear what sounds to be a knock on the door. 5) Also, there has been a strong wind blowing intermittently for hours, and at 5pm a medium-sized tree branch hits our front door just as Vic is "ringing" the broken doorbell. So with this in mind, here is a) an example of a simple justified true belief that is consistent with knowledge: I have the justified true belief/ knowledge that since the doorbell doesn't work, some other sound (like a knock) will be needed to signal a visitor's presence. Now, for b) a Gettier-like case, where justified true beliefs do not constitute knowledge: on the basis of the "knock" sound at 5pm, I believe that someone is at the door, especially as I am expecting Vic. Although this was a justified and true belief—justified as it is rational to think that when doorbells are broken people will knock to signal their arrival, and that knocking makes the type of knocking sound I heard; and true in that Vic truly was at the door at 5pm—still, I cannot be said to have had knowledge of Vic being at the door at 5pm, because the appropriate causal chain did not figure into my justified true belief. I believed Vic was at the door due to what turns out to have been the false belief that Vic had knocked on the door when really the "knock" was the sound of the branch banging against the door. c) An unjustified true belief is as follows: my husband, Art, was daydreaming at 5pm that someone was at the door. On this a-rational basis he believed that someone was at the door. Since there *was* a visitor at 5pm, this turned out to be a true belief. But this belief was true only by accident; Art arrived at it without sufficiently justifiable reasons. Finally to illustrate d) a justified

false belief, let's change one of the facts above. It is still Friday at 5pm, but Vic does not arrive until 5:30pm. At 5pm when I heard the knocking sound, expecting Vic at 5pm, I had the justified belief that it was Vic. As in the Gettier-like case above (example b), the knocking sound was really the branch hitting the door; but this time Vic was not yet present. My belief that it was someone at the door was equally justified, but under these circumstances it was false.

2. Williamson (2000) maintains that some have insisted "that knowledge *is* justified true belief on an understanding of 'justified' strong enough to exclude Gettier cases but weak enough to include everyday empirical knowledge" (p. 4). This is a view Williamson finds circular, lacking in a standard for justification sufficiently independent of knowledge.
3. Because beliefs (by definition) are those cognitive attitudes that aim at the truth, they are attitudes regulated by evidence. (See for example Velleman, 2000, p. 16.) Thus if Ari holds a belief B with the content that X is T, and this content is shown to Ari to be false, then Ari can no longer hold B as a belief. Ari can still have the content that X is T in other cognitive attitudes; for example as a supposition or a phantasy, but no longer as a belief. Note that in this chapter religious and cultural "beliefs", and the class of cognitive attitudes I have termed "neurotic-beliefs" (Brakel, 2001, 2009), will not be taken up as proper beliefs because none of these are evidence sensitive. Neurotic-beliefs will be discussed briefly in footnote 12, and in the subsection on "anti-luminosity" in this chapter.)
4. When a concept is a conjunction of two concepts it is not as foundational as the conjuncts. For example the concept "striped shirt" is a conjunction of the concepts "shirt" and "striped", both of which are more fundamental than striped shirt. Clearly, for the philosophers now under discussion, "knowledge" is conjunctive and not as fundamental as "belief", one of its conjuncts.
5. Note too, that negative hallucination do take place normally, or at least as part of the psychopathology of everyday life.
6. Later in the chapter I shall offer more examples from these areas. See the section "First and second order knowledge and belief: Believing what one knows, knowing without (any sort of) belief".
7. Furthermore, the dream content suggests that he unconsciously knew the further fact that he experienced himself as not having consciously noticed my falling asleep, for in the dream *I* do not notice *his* having fallen asleep. Could Dr. N have had an unconscious belief, instead of or in addition to his unconscious knowledge? The argument against this view will be developed in the later section, "Unconscious knowledge and unconscious belief".

8. Internalism will be briefly explained just below.
9. But see the next section "Similarities between knowledge (knowing) and belief (believing)" for the view that a strictly internalist account cannot work for belief either.
10. The symbol ~ is used to indicate "not".
11. Jim Joyce (personal communication, 2007) points out a problem with Williamson's view here. Joyce grants that knowing will produce persistence in action over and above believing—except in the following type of important case: since both the mental state of believing and that of knowing are not transparent, Joyce asks what happens when some agent has an internal mental state consistent with knowing, but actually is wrong? One must conclude that the agent's actions would be just as persistent. But since knowing is a factive mental state, regulated externally and therefore never false, one must also conclude that this type of persistence of action is due to what has turned out to be a false belief (albeit one experienced as knowledge). This argument is sound, but leads to a new problem, namely, the post hoc classifying of all mental states of failed knowledge as false belief. But how *is* one to classify them? Indeed, granting Williamson's externalist criterion—that knowing requires truth—such mental states clearly cannot be knowledge.

    Here is my proposed solution. Although admittedly it is not desirable to add entities to epistemic ontology, because neither "false belief" nor "knowledge" satisfactorily specifies these state types, I propose that a separate mental state for "knowing-that-turns-out-wrong" be considered. Animal actions argue in favour of such a proposal. Animals have mental states in which they have knowledge and they act upon these mental states. They are also wrong sometimes and, pace Joyce, they act in these cases with just as much vigour and perseverance. But does one want to claim that these animals had false beliefs? No, since this would necessarily imply that they have the sophistication necessary for having beliefs generally—beliefs, for example, that are not all or none, but inherently graded. (For more on animals, see the subsection on "non-human animals" in a later section of this chapter.)
12. Now it may be argued that belief also comes in different types. There are beliefs about facts like: "I believe that our dog is barking". And then there are beliefs like: "Z believes in God", and "Q believes you should always arrive at least ten minutes late for a dinner party". I have argued (Brakel, 2001) that these sorts of cultural and religious beliefs, as well as certain fixed phantasies of neurotic patients experienced and treated as beliefs, "neurotic-beliefs" (e.g., a good looking man who is convinced he is ugly) are not in fact beliefs-proper. These sorts of cognitive attitudes seem not to come in degrees, are often evidence insensitive, and

in the extreme admit of no evidence—for example, in the God case, what would count as evidence against God's existence for a believer? In short, since these "beliefs" are not evidence regulated and do not aim at the truth (the definition of belief operative here), they cannot be beliefs-proper. (See also footnote 3.)

13. And see Chisholm (1957, p. 15) for more references to such arguments.
14. Reliabilism is briefly explained below.
15. For Goldman (correctly in my view) the discriminator need have no concept of "truth". One can observe behavioural manifestations in which it is clear that an animal can reliably pick out that *p* (predator) is present, when *p* is present, and that *q* (prey) is not, when *q* is not. It is these behaviours, not the possession of a concept of truth, that constitute (as well as demonstrate) the "truth" of *p*, and the not-"truth" of *q* for that animal.
16. Other factive mental attitudes include perceiving and remembering.
17. If an earthling is on twin earth and thinks "I know this water is wet", pointing to some body of *t-water*, this does not constitute knowledge, but an unjustified true belief. The earthling is right but for the wrong reasons. He or she has taken the *t-water* sample, which happens to be wet, as *water*.
18. This is not to deny that internalism about beliefs *is* different from internalism about knowledge. Internalism about beliefs leads to problems individuating differing contents; but the different beliefs with different contents are still all beliefs, and a strict internalist account would still get that right. Strict internalism about knowledge, on the other hand, would have more profound consequences. External truth values contribute to the determination of whether a mental state is one of knowing at all; there is no mental state consisting in "false knowing"; knowledge that is false is incoherent. But see footnote 11.
19. Accounts of knowing the contents of subliminally presented items will be given at length in the section just below.
20. Clearly K stands for knowing; B for believing. What can be known or believed includes both content and mental state type.
21. Chisholm (1957, p. 18) attributes these examples of dis-analogy to Ryle.
22. Philosophers such as Ring and Pritchard endorse the "historical" position (i.e., knowing following after believing), a position that according to Williamson (2000, pp. 41–42) stands in sharp contrast to those embracing the "standard analysis" on which knowing entails ongoing believing.
23. From Darold Treffert MD, Clinical Professor of Psychiatry, University of Wisconsin: www.wisconsinmedicalsociety.org/professional/savant-syndrome/resources/articles/the-autistic-savant/ [last accessed March 9, 2007].

24. One might wonder about prior beliefs contributing to the successes of the chicken-sexer, in other words do prior beliefs contribute to his knowledge? But Goldman (1975, p. 114) has taken pains to specify that the chicken-sexer "... is ignorant of *how* he tells the sex of the chick"—that is, he has no idea of his technique. This implies that he does not have a set of consistent beliefs leading him to his ultimate conclusion. We have instead another case of knowledge without belief.
25. This material is taken from Brakel (1993, pp. 363–364).
26. The original version of this figure was published in the Journal of the American Psychoanalytic Association. Used with permission ©1993 American Psychoanalytic Association. All rights reserved.
27. One might ask: Why not infer first order unconscious beliefs as well as unconscious first order knowledge? Like the objection raised in footnote 7, this question will be taken up at length in the "Unconscious knowledge and unconscious belief" section below.
28. Two psychoanalytic clinicians interviewed each subject extensively while the text of the interviews was recorded. Psychological tests were also administered and recorded. The interviewers and the two other psychoanalysts reviewed the data from the texts of the interviews and the tests and then selected words that they all agreed best represented the subject's unconscious conflict, in other words the unconscious source of the subject's symptom. These words were unique and quite different for each subject. For example, the name of a subject's sibling could be one of the words, if that sibling was central in a subject's unconscious conflict. The clinicians also picked out the words from the interviews and tests that best represented each subject's conscious symptom. These words, while not uniform among the subjects, had much more in common. For example, words capturing one's anxiety would be present in the conscious symptom word set of many of the subjects.
29. For an opposing view to the one offered here with respect to the last two experiments, see O. R. Jones (1971, p. 23) who argues against "[a]ttributing knowledge ... on the grounds of certain suppositions about ... brain states".
30. Is there something similar, although highly rationally based and not psychopathological, in skeptics who systematically refuse to believe what they know?
31. Armstrong unfortunately (from my viewpoint) still stops short of equating having a concept with knowledge, and seems to leave open whether or not belief is entailed by this sort of discrimination as a function of concept possession.
32. Jean actually believed he had no knowledge of English history, making the knowledge he had in this sense unconscious knowledge.

33. But there are two important things to note in this last sentence. First consider that the phrase "registering of truth" is not very specific. This is intended as indeed I am not claiming that in order to have a belief that *p* one needs to know *p*; I am making the far weaker claim that in order to have a belief that *p*, one must have knowledge of some *q* that is related in some non-trivial way to *p*. (See more on this below in the subsection "The case for belief entailing knowledge".) Second, the phrase "some sort of registering" is meant to indicate that there are not only different levels of specificity of registration, but also different kinds of registerings. Do these match the different sorts of knowing?

    Certainly against the view that knowledge is constitutively the registration of some truth *p* or some truth *q* related non-trivially to *p*, one might contend that while it is plausible for knowing-that, and maybe even probable for the discrimination and recognition types of knowledge, how could this account work for know-how and knowing-how-to, the dispositional and ability types of knowledge?

    My reply must invoke truth registrations at the level of the brain—neuronal patterns involving motor and sensory cortical pathways interacting with 1) cerebellar input and feedback, and 2) brain areas associated with memory—along with more peripheral registrations at the level of spinal column, neuromuscular junction, and peripheral musculature. An example from baseball might help. What does it mean to have the know-how to hit a cut fastball? It means that one can reliably hit that type of pitch. Suppose B, after many failed attempts, finally does successfully hit a cut fastball. Consider this to constitute the first instance of truth registered; the truth in this case being the correct series of complicated perceptions and actions needed to accurately register and then respond to cut fastballs in order to hit them. Now, to the extent that B can repeat (perhaps tens of thousands of times) that particular complex entrainment of eyes, brain, hands, major muscle groups, in precisely the same truth-registering-and-reacting pattern that has resulted in successfully hitting the cut fastball, to that extent B will eventually have the ability, that is—the know-how, to hit that sort of pitch.
34. Annis cites Ayers (1956, pp. 32–35), Malcolm (1963, pp. 226–228), and Unger (1967, pp. 152–173), and states there are others who hold this view.
35. These two types of consciousness have been known by various terms. For just a few examples: Ned Block (1991) refers to phenomenal and access consciousness, Gerald Edelman (1989) to primary and higher order consciousness, and David Rosenthal (1986) talks of HOTs or higher order thoughts to describe the consciousness of being conscious

of something. Although I have lately favoured "primary consciousness" and "reflective consciousness", as this second term is quite descriptive, for the purpose of this chapter the terms first and second order consciousness work best as they avoid unnecessary confusion.

36. According to Williamson (2000, pp. 3, 41–48) even if knowledge does entail belief (and not vice versa), the conceptual independence of knowledge is not at stake. For example, even though every instance of being a dog entails having at least one dog-like quality, being a dog is conceptually prior to having at least one dog-like quality. (This example owes to Williamson, personal communication, 2006.)

    Nonetheless Williamson (2000) notes that the prevalent standard idea that knowledge is belief plus something else might in fact be due to the entailment thesis (K→B). And he maintains that the conjunctive view of knowledge must be defeated in order to grant that knowledge is conceptually prior (p. 48). He argues that this can be done rather simply. Just as red cannot be analysed as coloured plus something else because the something else must include some specification of redness, knowledge cannot be analysed as belief plus something else because the something else would have to include specifying knowledge in some way (Williamson, 2000, pp. 3, 32).

CHAPTER SIX

In defence of unconscious mentality*

Simon Boag

While no one would object to the claim that we may be ignorant of things in either the world or in the minds of others, the claim that we can be ignorant of our own mental processes seems to pose conceptual difficulties. The claim that we can *know unconsciously* appears to some to be self-contradictory: knowing entails consciousness, and so *unconscious knowing* appears to be an oxymoron. Accordingly, when nineteenth century writers began discussing unconscious mental processes, such views were met with scepticism and even derision (see Klein, 1977). Nevertheless, not only did certain theorists embrace unconscious mentality, they made it the centrepiece of their theories, and none more so than Sigmund Freud. Freud's approach to mentality, however, complicates matters further. Not only could mental processes be unconscious; mental processes could be prevented from becoming known, and once unconscious were believed to behave differently from conscious ones (Freud, 1912g, 1915).

*I would like to thank Linda Brakel, Agnes Petocz, and Vesa Talvitie for comments on an earlier version of this chapter.

It is perhaps due to the intricacies of Freud's theory of the "unconscious" that mid twentieth- century psychology by and large ignored Freud's contribution, and when the "new unconscious" emerged in the 1980s (e.g., Kihlstrom, 1987) it shared little with Freud's thinking, and wherever possible distinguished itself from psychoanalytic theory (e.g., Greenwald, 1992; Uleman, 2005). However, while modern psychology has (for the most part) outgrown the mistrust associated with postulating anything unconscious, there nevertheless remain difficulties in reconciling the term "unconscious" with "mentality". Recently, for instance, Talvitie and colleagues (e.g., Talvitie, 2009; Talvitie & Ihanus, 2003a, 2003b, 2005, 2011a; Talvitie & Tiitinen, 2006), following Searle (1992), argue that unconscious mentality is a contradiction in terms, and propose instead that unconscious processes must in fact be neural ones.

Clarifying what is meant by unconscious mental processes is not helped by the proliferation of associated terms intended to replace or approximate the adjective "unconscious" (e.g., non-conscious, a-conscious, implicit, etc.—see Erdelyi's 2004 discussion here), and instead what is required is both a coherent account of mentality and conceptual clarification with respect to what "unconscious" or "consciousness" is specifically referring to. While there is wide scope in matters of conceptualising "mentality" itself, a useful starting point is the position of the Austrian philosopher Franz Brentano (1874). Brentano, following the scholastics, believes that mental acts can be distinguished from physical processes by virtue of their *Intentionality*. Mental acts *intended objects*; they entail "direction toward an object" (p. 88) and so are always *of* or *about* something (e.g., a perception *of* light or a belief *about* the future).[1] This "of-ness" or "aboutness" means that mental acts always involve what can be generally described as awareness or consciousness *of* some state of affairs. Brentano, for his part, however, rejected the possibility of unconscious mental acts, and since a mental process is necessarily conscious *of something*, it would then seem that the critics of unconscious mentality may be correct.

However, despite these apparent grounds for dismissing the possibility of unconscious mental processes, what is easily obscured is the question of what precisely is said to be unconscious when discussing unconscious mental acts. The aim of this chapter is to mount a defence for unconscious mentality and the possibility of "unconscious knowing". To address this, I first discuss Searle and Talvitie's arguments against unconscious mentality based on the concept of

Intentionality. Brentano's specific thesis of the Intentionality of mental acts is addressed, and the chapter demonstrates that within Brentano's account there is scope for coherently conceptualising unconscious mental processes and thus providing a foundation for understanding psychoanalytically relevant phenomena, such as unconscious fantasies and repressed mentality. Nevertheless, recent critics of unconscious mentality (e.g., Talvitie, 2009, 2012) are correct with respect to recognising that a non-Intentional mental process is a contradiction in terms, and that some accounts of the unconscious found in psychoanalytic theorising are problematic (e.g., Gillett, 1988; Solms, 2003). Furthermore, elements of Freud's theory of unconscious processes require revision or even rejection. In particular, Freud's systemic view of unconscious mentality both reifies the cognitive relation and proposes a dualism between conscious and unconscious processes that cannot be coherently maintained. This notwithstanding, an account of both the descriptive and dynamic unconscious is defensible and provides a basis for understanding the unconscious in psychoanalytic theorising.

The problem of the mental unconscious

Talvitie (2009) believes that there is a fundamental distinction between the way cognitive researchers and psychoanalysts conceptualise unconscious processes:

> While a cognitivist holds that the unconscious is just the brain, psychoanalysts have stressed the unconscious is mental. In short, in psychoanalytic circles it is held that the mind has an unconscious part where repressed memories and desires lie, and whence they may be brought (or transformed) into the domain of consciousness. (Talvitie, 2009, p. xiii)

Part of the problem that Talvitie identifies here hinges upon the possibility of non-phenomenal "mentality": "As we know … psychoanalytically orientated people are deeply involved in the Freudian view that the mind refers also to non-phenomenal matters. This means that there is a *foundational* disagreement between psychoanalysis and present-day cognitive neuroscience" (Talvitie, 2009, p. 49, his italics). "Phenomenal consciousness", for Talvitie (2009), consists of all mental acts that are Intentional in so far as they are of or about something (e.g., perceptions of the world, fantasies about the future, memories of past events), and "the term 'mind' refers to phenomenal consciousness and characteristics of conscious states" (p. 48). Thus, a mental state is, by definition, a conscious one, and thus an unconscious mental state is, by definition, a contradiction in terms. Talvitie subsequently attempts to reformulate unconscious processes in biological, non-mental "cognitivist" terms, even if mentalising these for the sake of therapy. "Unconscious mentality" is at best a metaphor or tool actually referring to neural states (Talvitie, 2009, 2012).

Talvitie's (2009) position springs from the reasoning of the philosopher John Searle (1992, 1995). Searle (1992) distinguishes "non-conscious" states involving non-mental physical properties from conscious states that are Intentional (e.g., where *S* believes that *p*). A belief, says Searle, has Intentionality ("intrinsic mentality"), which qualifies it as a mental state, and since unconscious processes by definition do not involve awareness, then, according to Searle, we have a paradox:

> Once one adopts the view that mental states are both *in themselves* mental and *in themselves* unconscious, then it is not going to be easy to explain how consciousness fits into the picture. It looks as if the view that mental states are unconscious in themselves has the consequence that consciousness is totally extrinsic, not an essential part of any conscious state or event. (Searle, 1992, p. 170, his italics)

Searle concludes that since unconscious processes are non-Intentional (i.e., without objects) they must be brain states. Such brain states give rise to a "dispositional unconscious" whereby unconscious states are in fact neural states that are mental only by virtue of their power to bring about conscious mental states: "Unconscious beliefs are indeed dispositional states of the brain, but they are dispositions to produce conscious thoughts and conscious behaviour" (Searle, 1992, p. 161).

Talvitie (2009) extends Searle's argument to attack what he calls the traditional psychoanalytic three-sphere framework that proposes the existence of: (i) consciousness; (ii) a mental unconscious, and; (iii) neural processes. Talvitie argues that (ii) cannot be coherently formulated and his argument for this follows Searle's:

a. mental states, *by definition*, involve awareness;
b. unconscious states, *by definition*, do not involve awareness;
c. therefore unconscious states are not mental.

Talvitie's argument here is valid (all *A*s have *C*s; no *B*s have *C*s; therefore no *B*s are *A*s), and based on this deduction he instead proposes a "two-sphere" psychoanalytic approach, proposing only conscious (mental) states and neural processes and dispensing with unconscious mentality altogether: "the unconscious is only the brain and its neural processes" (p. 94). As a consequence, unconscious states are simply non-Intentional brain states, and to treat them as mental states is to propose a logically incoherent ontology:

> Because unconscious states are not experienced, and they do not—of course—appear in the scope of consciousness, the unconscious is not intentional. Thus, in terms of intentionality, the idea of mental unconscious is an oxymoron, and probably that is the reason why Freud never reflected (in public) his ideas in the light of Brentano's thinking. (Talvitie, 2009, p. 53)

Brentano and the Intentionality of mental acts

Given that Talvitie's argument above is valid, further inspection of Brentano's position is warranted so as to assess whether the premises are true. In particular, premise two (that unconscious states, *by definition*, do not involve awareness) requires scrutiny, since there is a distinction between: (i) not being aware of a mental state, and; (ii) mental states that do not involve awareness of something. As described earlier, Brentano distinguishes mentality from physical objects through the notion of Intentionality:

> Every mental phenomenon includes something as an object within itself, although they do not do so in the same way. In presentation something is presented, in judgement something is affirmed or denied, in love loved, in hate hated, in desire desired and so on ... No physical object exhibits anything like it. We can, therefore, define mental phenomena by saying that they are those which contain an object intentionally within themselves. (Brentano, 1874, pp. 88–89)

That is, all mental acts such as judgements and emotions take (or *intend*) objects. However, for Brentano, mental acts were also self-reflexively known insofar as any mental act was incidentally directed towards itself: a mental act not only intended its object but also itself, so that in knowing x a person also knew that x was known. This view is the orthodox Cartesian view whereby knowing necessitates knowing that we know:

> As to the fact that there can be nothing in the mind, in so far as it is a thinking thing, of which it is not aware, this seems to me self-evident. For there is nothing that we can understand to be in the mind, regarded in this way, that is not a thought or dependent on a thought. If it were not a thought or dependent on a thought it would not belong to the mind *qua* thinking thing; and we cannot have any thought of which we are not aware at the very moment when it is in us. (Descartes, 1641, p. 171; cf. Descartes, 1648, p. 357)

Consequently, Brentano (like Descartes) denies the possibility of unconscious mental acts, not because unconscious mental processes are without Intentionality but rather because mental acts were self-reflexively known. For example, according to Brentano, in the case of hearing a sound, both the sound and the act of hearing the sound are known simultaneously:

> the consciousness of the presentation of the sound clearly occurs together with the consciousness of this consciousness, for the consciousness which accompanies the presentation of the sound is a consciousness not so much of this presentation as of the whole mental act in which the sound is presented, and in which the consciousness itself exists concomitantly. Apart from the fact that it presents the physical phenomenon of sound, the mental act of hearing becomes at the same time its own object and content, taken as a whole. (Brentano, 1874, p. 129)

In fact, it is worth noting that Brentano himself did not draw the same conclusion as Searle and Talvitie with respect to "unconscious mentality" constituting an oxymoron. Instead, Brentano states that we need to carefully distinguish between the *object* of a mental act and the *mental act* itself:

> a person who raises the question of whether there is an unconscious consciousness is not being ridiculous in the same way he

> would be had he asked whether there is a non-red redness. An unconscious consciousness is no more a contradiction in terms than an unseen case of seeing. (Brentano, 1874, p. 102)

That is, while the mental act of being conscious of *x* necessarily involves knowing the intended object (*x*), it is of course logically possible for the mental *act* itself not to be known if not reflected upon (i.e., the act can be unconscious). Here Brentano clarifies the source of apparent confusion:

> We use the term "unconscious" in two ways. First, in an active sense, speaking of a person who is not conscious of a thing; secondly, in a passive sense, speaking of a thing of which we are not conscious. In the first sense, the expression "unconscious consciousness" would be a contradiction, but not in the second. It is the latter sense that the term "unconscious" is used here. (Brentano, 1874, pp. 102–103*n*)

Thus, Brentano did not seek to refute unconscious mental acts on the basis of a logical contradiction in terms. Instead, while we may be conscious of situations, we can be unconscious of that consciousness without compromising the position that the initial mental act is Intentional. Nevertheless, Brentano devotes a lengthy discussion to justifying his conclusion that mental acts were both conscious of objects and simultaneously self-conscious. His basic position here is to assume "that there is a special connection between the object of inner presentation and the presentation itself, and that both belong to one and the same mental act" (p. 127). For instance, in the case of sound he writes:

> The presentation of the sound and presentation of the presentation of the sound form a single mental phenomenon; it is only by considering it in its relation to two different objects, one of which is a physical phenomenon and the other a mental phenomenon, that we divide it conceptually into two presentations. In the same mental phenomenon in which the sound is present in our minds we simultaneously apprehend the mental phenomenon itself. (p. 127)

Hence, Brentano notes that we can distinguish between two different objects in the example above: (i), the *primary object* of hearing (the sound; a physical phenomenon), and; (ii) the *secondary object*, which is the mental *act* of hearing (i.e., a mental phenomenon). Consequently, what appears (according to Brentano) to be a "single mental phenomenon" actually includes two known objects occurring simultaneously, even if the sound must logically occur first:

> sound is the *primary object* of the *act* of hearing, and ... the act of hearing itself is the *secondary object*. Temporally they both occur at the same time, but in the nature of the case, the sound is prior. A presentation of the sound without a presentation of the act of hearing would not be inconceivable, at least *a priori*, but a presentation of the act of hearing without a presentation of the sound would be an obvious contradiction. (p. 128, his italics)

However, an immediate problem here for Brentano (and one that he was aware of) follows from claiming that knowing the primary object also involves knowing the secondary object (i.e., knowing x further involves knowing that x is known). This problem involves an infinite regress: if knowing p involves also necessarily knowing that I know it, then I would need to know that, too, ad infinitum (see Maze, 1983, p. 90; Michell, 1988, p. 236). Brentano is cognisant of this threatening infinite regress of knowing acts, and his response is simply to assert that "[f]ar from having to absorb an infinite series of presentations which become more and more complicated, we see the series ends with the second member" (p. 130). That is, Brentano makes an empirical claim that in knowing that x is known, the series simply terminates and the possibility of regress is thus avoided.

It is noteworthy, too, that Searle (1992) also appreciated a distinction between knowing and knowing that one knows, but that he was reluctant to fully consider the implications of this distinction for fear of an infinite regress:

> What about the act of perceiving—is this a mental phenomenon? If so, it must be "in itself" unconscious, and it would appear that for me to become conscious of that act, I would need some higher-level act of perceiving of my act of perceiving. I am not sure about this, but it looks like an infinite regress argument threatens. (Searle, 1992, p. 171)

Consequently, Searle appears to not have further explored the possibility of considering whether the distinction between "knowing" and "knowing that one knows" might provide a coherent account of unconscious mentality, even if making the sound, logical conclusion that the act is itself unconscious until it becomes the object of a second mental act. However, as I have noted elsewhere (Boag, 2012, pp. 82–84), Searle's concern here is unfounded. There is only the threat of an infinite regress if the first mental act by *necessity* entails a second, which is precisely the problem for Brentano's (and Descartes') position that knowing necessitates knowing that we know. Put differently, if we accept that mental states involve awareness (of something) it does not logically follow that that same awareness is itself known. Brentano even admits that logically unconscious mental acts could occur in principle (p. 128); he is simply proposing that phenomenologically we experience the object and the act simultaneously.

Consequently, the actual basis for Brentano's argument concerning awareness being self-reflexively aware is not made on logical grounds. At best it is an empirical claim that Brentano asserts from authority: "the characteristic fusion of the accompanying presentation with its object ... has indeed been recognized by the great majority of psychologists ..." (p. 130). Such a claim is easily refuted, though, since it only takes one case of a mental act that is not self-reflexive to disprove Brentano's point, and such examples are found in abundance. Talvitie (2009), for instance, uses the example of driving on "autopilot" where "we are able to drive a car without thinking of the pedals the whole time" (p. 3). That is, we can drive a car without needing to reflect on the fact that we are driving:

> When learning to drive a car, for example, we think all the time about such things as changing gears, braking, and keeping on the road. Gradually, those matters become automatic, and later such ideas do not appear in the scope of consciousness while driving. One may even be totally unaware later of what happened on a familiar journey from home to work. (Talvitie, 2009, p. 75)

When we drive on "autopilot" we are, of course, presumably aware of events around us, since we generally avoid accidents. What Talvitie is thus indicating is that it is possible to know events without concurrently knowing that we know them. Furthermore, there is no shortage of empirical research demonstrating that we can know without knowing that we know, such as occurs in the case with subliminal perception (see Brakel (this volume, 2010) and Boag (2008b) for a review of findings and further theoretical discussion).

To briefly summarise, then, we can conclude that although Talvitie's (2009) argument is valid (mental states, *by definition*, involve awareness; unconscious states, *by definition*, do not involve awareness; and so therefore, unconscious states are not mental) it does not follow that an unconscious mental act is a contradiction in terms. Instead, a perfectly sensible account of unconscious mentality can be provided by distinguishing between primary and secondary acts and objects. While mental acts, *by definition*, involve awareness of a primary object (e.g., where *S* hears a sound), it does not follow that the mental act as secondary object is itself known. That is, in hearing a sound, the act of hearing itself is not necessarily known (i.e., the *awareness of* the sound is not self-reflexive; *S* being aware of *p* does not necessarily entail *S* being aware of being aware of *p*). However, some clarification of this position is further required, and here, turning to the structure and ontology of mental acts is necessary.

Unconscious consciousness and the relational view of mental acts

As seen above, the apparent problem with postulating unconscious mentality arises from failing to recognise the distinction between the mental act of knowing *x* (where *x* is the primary object) and the mental act of knowing that one knows *x* (where the *act* itself is the secondary object of a second mental act). This is not a new distinction. As we have seen, Brentano was aware of it, and the position is similarly found in the distinction between first and second order knowledge (Brakel, this volume, 2010) and in accounts of metacognition ("knowing about knowing"—Metcalfe & Shimamura, 1994), amongst others. However, what is less explicit is the acknowledgement that mental acts are themselves *relations*. To state that a person is aware or conscious of some situation is to describe a *relation* between a cognising *subject* (the person, in this example) and an *object* of cognition (the situation known).[2] Cognition here refers to acts of *knowing*, such as believing, thinking, remembering, wishing, and desiring, which may either be veridical or non-veridical: "psychological processes are … typified by a kind of relation not to be found in merely physical interactions, and that is the relation of *knowing about* or *referring to*" (Maze, 1983, p. 83, his italics;

cf. Maze & Henry, 1996, p. 1089). Thus, cognition is used here to cover all mental acts that can be described as being conscious of, aware of, knowing of, etc.

Taken as a relation, cognition, then, cannot be reduced to anything less than a relation (i.e., mental acts cannot be reduced to either the subject or object term): "Knowledge being taken as a relation, it is thus asserted that, when I know this paper, 'I know' in no way constitutes this paper, nor does 'know this paper' in any way constitute me, nor does 'know' constitute either me or this paper" (Anderson, 1927, p. 27). That is, in any instance of knowing (where *S* knows *p*), there is: (i) a *subject S* that knows something, and; (ii) the something known (*p*). *S*'s knowing *p* is entailed by neither (i) nor (ii) alone (and thus any account of cognition thus requires stipulating the subject term (the knower) and object term (the known) involved in the cognitive relation). The cognitive relation itself "is not a kind of *stuff* that binds the terms. It is just how the terms are with respect to each other" (Michell, 1988, p. 234). Accordingly, as a relation, to be conscious of something is not to ascribe properties (qualities) to either the knower or the state of affairs cognised, and thus care is required when conceptualising mentality to avoid the possibility of reifying relations into qualities. For instance, while I am in broad agreement with Brakel's position regarding unconscious knowing (this volume), she refers to the terms *anti-luminosity* and *luminosity* that appear to be synonymous with *knowing* and *knowing that one knows* respectively. Luminosity, however, suggests that somehow consciousness is a quality of the mental act insofar as a mental process somehow radiates or shines some property of consciousness, and while luminosity is most likely used metaphorically, the term nevertheless lends itself to reification (treating consciousness as if a property of what is cognised).

On the relational view described here, however, being aware of something does not add anything to what is known—to know something is simply to stand in a particular (knowing) relationship to it. Accordingly, consciousness (or better, the relation of knowing some state of affairs) is not a quality of mental processes, and although mental processes involve knowing, they do not possess a quality of consciousness that makes themselves automatically known (see Boag, 2008a, 2008b, 2012; Maze, 1983; Michell, 1998; Petocz, 1999). Instead, while any mental act involves knowing or being conscious of *x*, a second mental act is required for knowing that *x* is known. More specifically, when *S* knows (or is conscious of, etc.) *p* (which can be signified as *SRp*), that relation of knowing *SRp* is itself unconscious and does not become conscious unless it becomes the object of a *second mental act* such that *S* knows *SRp*. For example, I may believe that the world is round (a primary mental act) and for the most part be unaware that I hold this belief (i.e., the belief is not presently attended to/unconscious). However, when I reflect upon what I believe, I can make the belief conscious (presently known) and this act of reflection constitutes a second mental act. Consequently, no mental act can be conscious without first having been unconscious and a second mental act is required for making any mental act known/conscious.

The position that primary mental acts are themselves unknown (unconscious) is implicated in Freud's repeated insistence that any mental act (which involves awareness of something) is initially unconscious because it exists logically prior to any reflection upon it. Freud writes: "Everything conscious has an unconscious preliminary stage: whereas what is unconscious may remain at that stage and nevertheless claim to be regarded as having the full value of a psychical process" (Freud, 1900a, pp. 612–613). Similarly, Freud writes that "every psychical act begins as an unconscious one, and it may either remain so or go developing into consciousness" (Freud, 1912g, p. 264, Freud, 1915e, p. 171, Freud, 1916–1917, p. 295). What Freud is proposing is the view that *psychical acts* exist unconsciously until attention is turned to them, which itself involves an act of perception. As Freud writes, coming to know our own mental acts involves turning our attention to them (coming to know what we know): "In psycho-analysis there is no choice for us but to assert that mental processes are in themselves unconscious, and to liken the perception of them by means of consciousness to the perception of the external world by means of the sense-organs" (Freud, 1915e, p. 171, cf. Freud, 1924f, p. 198; 1940a, p. 160).[3] Talvitie (2012) comments here, however, that Freud's metaphor is difficult to substantiate and raises further questions with respect to what is actually perceived:

> Sense organs are neural systems, but consciousness, if anything is mental. Each sense organ reacts to certain specific kinds of physical stimuli, but what are the stimuli that consciousness receives? We may perceive objects that exist in the outer world, but what is actually the world and the objects that consciousness perceives? These questions are hard to answer. (p. 87)

There are, however, two major issues here that require clarification. The first is with respect to the distinction between mental acts as relations and the terms of the mental act (i.e., the knower and known). Hearing, for instance, is a mental act that cannot be reduced to, or confused with, the ear (or neural system) alone, since a relation cannot be reduced to simply one term of the relation. Accordingly, hearing cannot be reduced to the ear, even if the ear is necessary for hearing. So, when Freud likens consciousness to "the perception of the external world *by means of* the sense-organs" he is simply indicating that the sense-organ allows hearing to occur (and the sense-organ is not the hearing itself). Nevertheless, Talvitie poses perfectly sensible questions when he asks: what is the sense-organ of consciousness and what are the objects that consciousness senses? In response to this first question, there is no need to postulate a specific sense-organ of consciousness, since, presumably, the general sense-organs are sufficient for being conscious of states of affairs in the world. However, whether this answer is satisfying will be determined by the matter of *what* is known when one knows one's own mental states. For instance, on the matter of ontology, Talvitie appears to treat mental acts as constructs (mental objects) of inner states, which requires asking where such states exist, what they consist of, etc. and thus a sense-organ of perception of inner mental states is required. There is, however, an alternative to this inner representationist position that he does not consider, viz. that mental acts are relations and that whatever is known (including mental acts) are states of affairs in the one and the same spatio-temporal universe. On the relational viewpoint, when one knows a mental act one knows a certain kind of relation between a subject and object (a cognising relation). A realist position proposes that both the knower and known exist in the one and the same spatio-temporal universe (obviating the problem of dualism). There are no inner mental objects cognised, only states of affairs in the world, and so no special sense-organ is required for attending to cognitive acts.

This distinction between knowing and knowing that one knows also helps clarify apparent contradictions in discussions of unconscious and conscious mentality. To say that a person S currently knows some state of affairs x is to describe a relationship whereby S currently knows x. Similarly, S's coming to know that x is known similarly describes a relation where S knows that S knows x. In both cases the cognitive act is a relation between a cognising subject S and some object of cognition (x or that S knows x). Nevertheless, these are distinct mental acts given that different objects are intended in each cognitive act (x or S knows *x* respectively). Focusing, then, upon what is or is not known in any situation allows clarifying discussions of unconscious processes and consciousness. Given that we only ever know more or less about what is known, there will always be aspects unknown or unconscious to us. Furthermore, the distinction between knowing and knowing that one knows is, in fact, implicit in Talvitie's (2009) account when he discusses consciousness and self-consciousness:

> There is also the distinction between consciousness and self-consciousness. A fish is conscious of another fish swimming in front of it, and an infant is conscious of the light being switched off. Fish and infants possess conscious states, but they are not self-conscious beings: they do not possess ideas on their personal characteristics (sex, age, unique life history, idiosyncratic ways of reacting to stimuli, etc.), do not know what their current feelings are compared to those they had yesterday, and they do not understand that their life is finite. (Talvitie, 2009, p. 96)

Leaving aside the terminology of "conscious" and "self-conscious" for the moment, Talvitie's account here can be recast in terms of mental acts that *know* and mental acts that are *known* (i.e., mental act reflected upon) (see Boag, 2012). It is clear that Talvitie's account above allows for *unknown* mental acts. More specifically, the "consciousness" of fish and infants, while of the world, is itself unknown (so occurs unconsciously since it is not reflected upon) whereas adults can generally reflect upon their mental processes and thus make those mental acts currently known. Thus, examining Talvitie's position reveals that a conscious mental act can itself nevertheless be unknown (i.e., be unconscious) insofar as it is not reflected upon. Consequently, what is proposed here is that Talvitie is correct in rejecting non-Intentional unconscious mentality, but we can nevertheless postulate unconscious (i.e., non-reflected upon) conscious processes that are the hallmark of psychoanalytic theory.

The relevance of the relational view of cognition for psychoanalysis

Admittedly, making sense of Freudian theory is not always easy. Freud's position on both the relation between brain and mind and unconscious and conscious mental processes is complex, since the influences upon his thinking were diverse and at times incompatible with one another. Petocz (2006), for instance, notes that "[i]t is possible to find in Freud's writings almost every major position on the mind-body relationship—from various Kantian 'veil doctrines' ... to psychophysical parallelism, ... non-reductive materialism, ... [and] neurophysiological reductionism ..." (p. 50). Freud's approach to mentality was similarly influenced by a number of sources (see Talvitie, 2012, pp. 71–72). For instance, MacIntyre (1958) identifies the influence of the British empiricist tradition's atomic view in Freud's treatment of ideas (e.g., Locke. 1690, p. 34), even if Freud appears to have adopted Brentano's concept of *Vorstellungen* ("presentations") (Brentano, 1874, p. 5), translated by Freud's editor Strachey as "idea", "image" and "presentation" (in Freud, 1915e, p. 174). Brentano's influence may also be apparent in Freud's attempt to capture the relationship between knowing and knowing that one knows in what he calls the *descriptive* view of mental processes. Freud writes:

> in support of there being an unconscious psychical state, that at any given moment consciousness includes only a small content, so that the greater part of what we call conscious knowledge must in any case be for very considerable periods of time in a state of latency, that is to say, of being psychically unconscious. When all our latent memories are taken into consideration it becomes totally incomprehensible how the existence of the unconscious can be denied. (Freud, 1915e, p. 167, cf. Freud, 1912g, p. 260, 1933a, p. 70, 1939a, p. 95)

As Freud above indicates, at any given moment a person holds numerous beliefs and memories, the vast majority of which are not presently known (or could be described as unconscious) but which are psychical nevertheless. One reason for why the vast majority of what a person knows and believes is generally unconscious (or not reflected upon) is simply because we do not have the cognitive capabilities for attending to everything we know, believe, think, desire, etc. at any given time. Furthermore, it is not the case that such unconscious knowledge, beliefs, etc. are thereby inoperative or uninfluential upon our behaviour simply because they are not presently known. Thankfully we can generally act in the world without having to bring individual beliefs to mind (which would otherwise make all activity exceedingly laborious).

To use an earlier example, while driving a car I know that I have to stop at red lights and have various beliefs about rules and road situations, none of which need to be presently attended to for the most part in order to drive from *A* to *B* (in fact, as is common experience, we can be currently attending to all manner of things unrelated to driving (e.g., the radio) and still stop for red lights, obey road rules and the like). Consequently, the psychoanalytic thinker will be concerned with the infantile unconscious desires, beliefs and conflicts that might be influencing behaviour 'automatically'. For example, transference behaviours exhibited in therapy may be interpreted as reflecting certain desires and beliefs towards the parents that a person holds unknowingly. However, as noted earlier, Freud also postulated that mental process could be prevented from becoming known via repression and that once unconscious, the repressed behaves differently to conscious processes (Freud's systemic position). The relational view helps clarify these two areas of psychoanalytic thinking by clarifying (i) what happens to mental content after repression, and; (ii) the distinction between primary and secondary processes.

Unconscious fantasies and the nature of the repressed

The relational view of cognition has implications for understanding the nature of the dynamic unconscious with respect to the inhibition of a second mental act of reflection. As Eagle (2000) states: "The essence of repression lies in its interference with one's ability to reflect on one's mental state" (p. 173). Repression could thus be understood in terms of preventing mental content from becoming the object of a second mental act. A person could, for instance, desire *x* but be prevented from knowing *x* is desired, or, as I have proposed elsewhere, repression could *prevent knowing (or acknowledging) that the repressed is known* (Boag, 2007, 2008b, 2012).

That some mental acts are easier than others to reflect upon is trivially true. For example, most of us would be familiar with "tip-of-the-tongue" experiences, which clearly demonstrate that it is possible to know something (say, a name) and yet be unable to reflect upon it in certain contexts. However, while it appears perfectly reasonable to say that we may be motivated to avoid knowing various states of affairs, Talvitie (2009) questions whether the repressed is banished to a location called "the unconscious", comparable to a "place, sphere, or space where repressed ideas lie, and from which they may be brought into the domain of consciousness" (Talvitie, 2009, p. 70). It is, of course, clear that Freud likened the unconscious to a spatial location, as seen in his discussion of the systems Unconscious (*Ucs.*), Preconscious (*Pcs.*), and Conscious (*Cs.*). There he likens the systems *Ucs.* and *Pcs.* to *two rooms*, with "consciousness as a spectator at the end of the second room" (Freud, 1916–1917, p. 296):

> The crudest idea of these systems is the most convenient for us—a spatial one. Let us therefore compare the system of the unconscious to a large entrance hall in which the mental impulses jostle one another like separate individuals. Adjoining this entrance hall there is a second, narrower room—a kind of drawing room—in which consciousness, too, resides ... We are therefore justified in calling the second room the system of the *preconscious*. (Freud, 1916–1917, pp. 295–296, his italics)

Taken literally, this spatial metaphor involves viewing unconscious mental processes as existing *somewhere* different from preconscious processes. Repression consequently entails "banishing" the repressed "into the unconscious".

The spatial view of the unconscious has been seized upon by critics with respect to locating the repressed. In the case of repressed unconscious phantasies, for instance, Talvitie and colleagues ask where such unconscious phantasies exist (Talvitie, 2009; Talvitie & Ihanus, 2003a, 2003b, 2005; Talvitie & Tiitinen, 2006). These authors believe that there is a fundamental problem here since no one has ever been able to satisfactorily address this question. Instead, these authors conclude that since repressed ideas are not stored in the brain (since the brain simply consists of physical properties), "[t]he obvious logical conclusion is that when ideas are missing from consciousness, they are not 'hiding' anywhere, but are prevented from being formed in the domain of consciousness" (p. 91). Thus, contra Freud, there are no repressed mental processes, and instead, at best, only neural ones.

Talvitie is making a fair point with respect to locating the repressed and unconscious mentality, and it is not difficult to find instances in the psychoanalytic literature where authors struggle with conceptualising and locating unconscious fantasies. For instance, Talvitie (2009, 2012) draws attention to the treatment of unconscious fantasies in Mark

Solms' (2003) account. For Solms, the term "unconscious" refers to an unknowable reality:

> there lies something else, *something which is independent of our perceptual modalities*, and which can, in itself, never be perceived directly. Our conscious perceptions of this underlying reality are, and can only be, indirect representations of it. In other words, behind the different varieties of conscious perception there lies the stuff of reality, which is itself non-perceptual, and therefore *unconscious*. (Solms, 2003, p. 97, his italics)

Consequently, unconscious fantasies are themselves unknowable: "Unconscious phantasies can … never be perceived directly; they can … only be *inferred* from the data of conscious perception" (Solms, 2003, p. 103, his italics). Talvitie (2009) correctly notes here that this would make a science of the unconscious impossible, and it is further unclear how either Solms, Freud or anyone else could make knowledge claims of anything that is literally unknowable (see also Boag, 2012, p. 77).

Talvitie thus poses a legitimate question for psychoanalysis to answer: if repressed mental processes exist, then where? Here the relational view clarifies matters in terms of what happens when we turn our attention to and away from objects and events. The key to understanding repression is in terms of interference of reflection rather than banishing the repressed into a location called "the unconscious". If I turn my attention towards or away from some state of affairs *x*, then *x* does not move anywhere: my attention changes but the objects that are either attended to or unattended to remain exactly where they are. Freud's likening of consciousness with an act of perception is instructive here in terms of the spotlight analogy: shining a spotlight onto an object does not change the object's spatial location, and, similarly, when shining the light elsewhere, the object does not shift spatial location either. Accordingly, if I turn my attention to my beliefs they do not "enter consciousness" as if entering a room, and when I am ignoring anything (whether it be an irritating person or my own beliefs) the things ignored do not change location as if sent into a dungeon. The shift is in the relation of attention. Consequently, there is no difficulty in locating the repressed, since the repressed exists in the same place as so-called conscious mental states. What occurs with repression is interference with turning our attention to the repressed. Thus a mental act, whether repressed or not, does not change location: only the second mental act of reflection is interfered with.

Mental acts and primary/secondary processes

As the preceding discussion indicates, the dynamic (repressed) unconscious can be coherently sustained in terms of interference with reflection (i.e., second mental acts). Nevertheless, there are apparent question marks over Freud's systemic view of mentality. Aside from the spatial implications above, Freud further proposes that each mental system possesses qualitatively distinct processes not found in the other systems. The system *Ucs.* is especially notable as "a particular realm of the mind with its own wishful impulses, its own mode of expression and its peculiar mental mechanisms which are not in force elsewhere" (Freud, 1916–1917, p. 212, cf. Freud, 1912g, p. 266, 1915e, p. 186). *Ucs.* characteristics include primary process mentation, exemption from mutual contradiction, timelessness, and replacement of external by psychical reality (Freud, 1915e, p. 187). Primary process psychical energy is highly mobile (Freud, 1900a, p. 600) and mental content ("wishes") are subject to "condensation" and "displacement":

> The cathectic intensities [in the *Ucs.*] are much more mobile. By the process of *displacement* one idea may surrender to another its whole quota of cathexis; by the process of *condensation* it may appropriate the whole cathexis of several other ideas. I have proposed to regard these two processes as distinguishing marks of the so-called *primary psychical process*. (Freud, 1915e, p. 186, his italics)

Ucs. processes subsequently possess an "irrational" character, since the meaning and relation of ideas to reality is neglected (Freud, 1900a, p. 597, 1915e, p. 187). Freud further depicts the system *Ucs.*'s operations as governing all that is irrational and illogical in the mind:

> The governing rules of logic carry no weight in the unconscious; it might be called the realm of the Illogical. Urges with contrary aims exist side by side in the unconscious without any need arising for any adjustment between them. Either they have no influence whatever on each other, or if they have, no decision is reached, but a compromise comes about which is nonsensical since it embraces

> mutually incompatible details. (Freud, 1940a, pp. 168–169; cf. Freud, 1900a, p. 598; 1905e, p. 61; 1915e, p. 186)

Secondary processes then develop after the primary process due to the need for attending to "indications of reality", which determine whether the wished for situation is in fact real or not, and inhibits hallucinatory satisfaction (Freud, 1911b, p. 219). This coincides with the development of the system *Pcs.* where the more reality-oriented *secondary* processes gradually replace or cover the earlier primitive primary processes. Secondary processes are said to follow the "reality" principle, a reality-tempered modification of the primitive pleasure principle, where actual conditions of satisfaction and frustration are taken into account before initiating action:

> Under the influence of the ego's instincts of self-preservation, the pleasure principle is replaced by the *reality principle.* This latter principle does not abandon the intention of ultimately obtaining pleasure, but it nevertheless demands and carries into effect the postponement of satisfaction, the abandonment of a number of possibilities of gaining satisfaction and the temporary toleration of unpleasure as a step on the long indirect road to pleasure. (Freud, 1920g, p. 10, his italics; cf. 1900a, p. 601; 1915c, p. 120; 1925i, p. 127)

The primary/secondary process distinction is championed by some as one of Freud's greatest contributions. For example, Ernest Jones (1953) believes that Freud's revolutionary contribution to psychology was "his proposition that there are two fundamentally different kinds of mental process, which he termed primary and secondary respectively, together with his description of them" (p. 436). The longevity of Freud's contribution here is also apparent within Linda Brakel's (2009, 2010, 2015) recent discussion of the distinction between primary processes a-rationality and rational secondary processes: "Secondary process thinking is the largely rational, rule following, ordinary logic of adults in the alert, waking state. Primary process thinking, in contrast, is a-rational and associatively based" (2009, p. 8). A-rationality here is similar to irrationality but is developmentally prior to rational thinking and lacks the constraints of logic and internal consistency: "[It] is a form of thinking that operates *outside* (rather than in violation) of rationality and its principles" (Brakel, 2010, p. 56). More specifically, whereas secondary process rational mentation is tensed (occurs in time), is reality tested, originates from a single agent's viewpoint,[4] and "tolerates no contradiction" (2015, p. 131), primary process a-rational mentation involves "only a tenseless and unexamined present", an absence of reality-testing ("no attempt to regulate representations for considerations of truth"), is developmentally prior to a stable self that is "capable of grasping (in any fashion) continuity-in-experience …" (p. 132), and is without the constraints of standard logic ("Most notably, contradictions are tolerated"—p. 132). Primary process thinking is nevertheless psychological insofar as it is Intentional (has "content") and primarily involves *phantasies*, whereas secondary processes involve *beliefs* (Brakel, 2015).

Problems with the systemic account of mentality

There are, however, several problems with the systemic account of mental processes that call into question the validity of Freud's approach here. The main problem is whether there is any basis for postulating qualitatively distinct types of systems and processes. As Petocz (1999) has cogently argued, if a quality of a process is unique to a particular mental system as Freud suggests, then such qualities should not be found in the other systems' processes. However, as many note, inspection of each system in Freud's account demonstrates that there is much overlap between the processes (Arlow & Brenner, 1964; Gay, 1982; Gill, 1963; Macmillan, 1991; Petocz, 1999; Weintraub, 1987; Westen, 1999). For instance, Freud's claim that illogical thinking and irrationality are the hallmarks of *Ucs.* processes (whereas the *Pcs./Cs.* is rational and logical) (Freud, 1900a, p. 65, 1915e, p. 187) is unsustainable since (pre)conscious thought activity may clearly also be illogical or irrational (Arlow & Brenner, 1964; Petocz, 1999; Weintraub, 1987). Similarly, "exemption from mutual contradiction" is not exclusive to the *Ucs.* since contrary impulses and wishes (a wish that *p* and that not *p*) can exist side by side consciously (Weintraub, 1987). Freud himself even notes that *Ucs.* processes could be retained in consciousness and that *Ucs.* processes could operate like *Pcs./Cs.* processes:

> certain modes of thought proper to the unconscious have also been retained by the conscious—for instance, some kinds of indirect representation, allusion, and so on—even though their conscious

> employment is subject to considerable restrictions. (Freud, 1905c, p. 204)
>
> Among the derivatives of the *Ucs.* instinctual impulses ... there are those which unite in themselves characters of an opposite kind. On the one hand, they are highly organised, free from self-contradiction, have made use of every acquisition of the system *Cs.* and would hardly be distinguished in our judgement from the formation of that system. On the other hand they are unconscious and are incapable of becoming conscious. Thus *qualitatively* they belong to the system *Pcs.*, but *factually* to the *Ucs.* (Freud, 1915e, p. 191, his italics)

This overlap between the systems also casts doubt on the explanatory role of repression whereby the repressed is banished into the *Ucs.* and then behaves according to primary process principles. For example, *parapraxes* (such as slips of the tongue) are said to be products of *Ucs.* processes (Freud, 1905c), and yet appear to be products of secondary processes, since they are highly organised, syntactically valid structures (Gay, 1982; Macmillan, 1991). Similarly, dreams appear to show that the *Ucs.* contains highly structured, repressed fantasies that should be antithetical to the system *Ucs.* Macmillan (1991) subsequently concludes that dreams require the existence of a class of fantasies that cannot exist according to the systematic theory:

> Repressed fantasies cannot exist in the *Ucs.* and cannot therefore be incorporated into dreams. Dreams incorporating such fantasies disprove the theory. Further, because fantasies well enough structured to resemble real memories of childhood seduction cannot exist in *Ucs.* they cannot explain hysterical symptoms. (Macmillan, 1991, p. 271)

The carry over of the systemic distinction into the id and ego (Freud, 1923b), whereby the ego is an organisation and the id is not, similarly creates problems, since the existence of organised repressed content (supposedly antithetical to the id) leads to the conclusion that the repressed must belong to the ego:

> If we assume that the fantasy which is unconscious retains its organization, to whatever degree, we must grant the continued

> activity of ego functions. 'The ego is an organisation', Freud has said, 'and the id is not'. An 'id fantasy', then, is by definition a contradiction in terms, and to speak of a fantasy being 'repressed into the id' is, in my opinion, a complex of logical fallacies. (Beres, 1962, p. 324; cf. Slap & Saykin, 1984, p. 110)

Consequently, it appears impossible to sustain the Freudian account of qualitatively distinct systems, each with their own specific processes not found in the other.

The problems identified in Freud's account similarly extend to Brakel's primary and secondary process distinction, and her own examples of a-rationality demonstrate that it is difficult to maintain a hard and fast distinction between primary and secondary processes. For instance, she provides an example of a speech *parapraxis* whereby after being frustrated with her partner's "disobedience" she accidentally refers to her husband by their dog's name. This, she believes, was based on an a-rational association between her "husband-who-does-not-respond" and the "disobedient dog" (2009, p. 8), which, she argues, demonstrates a primary process, a-rational condensation by "combining thoughts together that by ordinary logic do not belong together" (p. 8).

However, whether this example really demonstrates a-rationality (or any other kind of qualitatively distinct processes) is unclear. While it is true that by convention we do not ordinarily associate husbands (or perhaps more generally, men) with dogs, this does not seem to violate "ordinary logic", since there are nevertheless comprehensible (i.e., logical/rational) grounds for the association, given a variety of similarities (whether it be common behaviours, belonging to the class "mammal", genetic similarity, etc.). A truly a-rational association—that is, an association outside the boundaries of logic and rationality—would presumably be an association between two things that bear no similarity whatsoever and thus have no grounds for any association being made. Thus, Brakel's example, if anything, demonstrates a degree of logic and rationality even if such associations might not be the norm. Nevertheless, this is not to say that there is no merit to Brakel's position, since, like Freud, she draws attention to the meaningful connections that we make in mental life, which occur at a more affective and simple level rather than being cognitively complex (perhaps in a similar manner to the way we might compare the mental processes of a child with that of an adult). For example, her discussion of a-rational primary process thinking demonstrates that aspects of human mental life can be characterised by much simpler processes, such as perceiving similarity by contiguity, and that an understanding of psychodynamic processes can consequently reveal sense in apparent nonsense (cf. Petocz, 1999).

Can we rescue the primary/secondary process distinction?

Given the problems associated with the primary/secondary process distinction, Petocz (1999) advocates abandoning these terms altogether. She does, however, say that some sense of the distinction holds with respect to the infant's initial intolerance of frustration, leading to hallucinatory wish-fulfilment, before subsequent attention to reality for gratification. However, the distinction might also have some usefulness in the context of Brentano's distinction between primary and secondary mental acts discussed earlier. As developed before, a primary mental act is unconscious because it occurs logically prior to reflection of it (cf. Freud, 1900a, pp. 612–613, 1912g, p. 264, 1915e, p. 171, 1916–1917, p. 295). While any primary mental act (such as a belief) is either true or false, determining whether it is true or false, rational or otherwise, requires a mental act of examination. To examine something, then, is a secondary act of reflection that assumes there is something existing prior for the examination to occur. If one inspects the features of primary process mentation that Brakel uses to distinguish primary process from secondary process qualities, then it is apparent that the so-called a-rational primary processes for the most part lack examination and thus presumably occur prior to reflection. For instance, the apparent tenseless primary process cannot be literally timeless, since anything that exists occurs across time (and so must have a continuous past, present, and future). However, here Brakel's reference to an "unexamined present" (2015, p. 131) is noteworthy, since, as mentioned above, any "examination" would entail a second mental act reflecting upon the primary one (and thereby noting temporal characteristics). Similarly, "reality-testing"—examining veridicality—assumes that there is a mental act initially to be tested, since to "regulate representations for considerations of truth" indicates that such representations exist *prior* to their regulation. Accordingly, reality-testing must itself be a secondary mental act, subsequent to the occurrence of the primary mental act that is being tested. Again, the finding that standard logic is not followed and that "contradictions are tolerated" simply indicates that propositions have not yet been scrutinised for their coherency. All in all, Brakel's primary/secondary distinction (which follows Freud's) could be seen, then, as indicating that a distinction exists between unconscious primary mental acts and secondary mental acts reflecting upon and correcting these, rather than qualitatively distinct mental processes.

The apparent characteristics of the *Ucs.*, then, are explicable in terms of the lack of critical reflection: any primary mental act occurs prior to reflection and consequent regulation, reality testing, and scrutiny of logic.[5] A primary mental act is not initially judged to be either true or false, logical or otherwise: a second mental act needs to scrutinise this, and such scrutiny itself may fail. While for the most part secondary mental acts may help prevent errors and violation of logic, this is not necessarily so, and even Brakel (2009) notes that "[s]econdary process thinking is the *largely* rational, rule following, ordinary logic of adults in the alert, waking state" (p. 8, my italics). That it is "largely rational" suggests that there is no absolute distinction between primary and secondary processes in terms of a-rationality and rationality. Nevertheless, there is a basis for primary and secondary *mental acts*—not in terms of qualitatively distinct processes, but rather in terms of temporal order that Brentano identified. This might also be what Freud was trying to indicate when he proposes that the mental systems could be conceived of *temporally* rather than spatially:

> there is no need for the hypothesis that the psychical systems are actually arranged in a *spatial* order. It would be sufficient if a fixed order were established by the fact that in a given psychical process the excitation passes through the systems in a particular *temporal* sequence. (Freud, 1900a, p. 537, italics in original)

That is, a primary mental act must first occur unconsciously before being reflected upon by a secondary mental act. Prior to reflection, then, a mental act is not subject to reasoned correction or inhibition (repression), which requires examination before such correction or inhibition can occur. Such correction is essentially an act of conflict and thus mental conflict provides a basis for all of the higher acts of the human mind that require careful and logical scrutiny.

Conclusion

It is to Freud's detriment that he was not more philosophically minded, and one can agree with Talvitie (2009) that it is unfortunate that Freud did not fully engage with Brentano's thesis of Intentionality when considering his formulation of mentality, conscious or otherwise. Of course, Brentano's insistence that the mental is also conscious (e.g., Brentano, 1973, p. 129) did not work in Freud's favour, but as argued here, the conceptualisation of mental acts and Intentionality is not an obstacle to postulating unconscious mentality. As demonstrated earlier, it is possible to provide an account of unconscious mental processes that is conceptually coherent. Brentano's theory does not refute the possibility of unconscious mental acts, and instead his distinction between primary and secondary objects provides a means for understanding how an Intentional mental act can be psychical and yet also unconscious: becoming conscious of a mental act requires a second mental act to reflect upon the first. This relational position further provides a means for understanding repression: repression does not push mental processes from one location to another. Instead, reflection upon the objectionable mental process is prevented. Nevertheless, psychoanalytic discourse is often confused about the nature of unconscious mentality, and the spatial metaphors and systemic positions postulating different mental systems require careful scrutiny. The primary/secondary process distinction is one such area that requires clarification through further mental acts of reflection.

Notes

1. Tamas Pataki (this volume) disputes the claim that Intentionality is the mark of the mental, claiming that moods, pains and other sensations do not have intentional objects: "… a headache, for example, is not about pain it is pain" (p. 39*n*). However, to say that a "person feels pain" is to simply say that the pain is the *object* of the mental act of feeling, or perhaps more specifically, the object of "paining" (cf. Brentano, 1874, pp. 90–91).
2. This view of cognition as a certain type of relation has a long history, tracing back to Aristotle (see Petocz, 1999), developed via medieval scholasticism (see Pasnau, 1997), and prominent in the American new realists (e.g., E. B. Holt) and the British realists (e.g., G. E. Moore), J. Laird and Samuel Alexander (see Michell, 1988). In the twentieth

century, the relational view of cognition has found prominence in the position referred to as "situational realism" (Hibberd, 2009). Further discussion of this position can be found in Anderson (1927, 1930), Boag (2005, 2008a, 2010, 2012), Mackay and Petocz (2011), Maze (1983), McMullen (1996), Medlow (2008), Michell (1988), and Petocz (1999).

3. Accordingly, when Freud writes that all "mental processes are in themselves unconscious" (1916–1917, p. 143), he is not claiming, as Solms (2003) suggests, that reality is fundamentally unknowable, even if Freud is influenced by Kantian metaphysics (see Talvitie, 2012, pp. 83–84).
4. However, since this "agent" is presumably the subject having the mental acts, and not the mental act itself, it would be misleading to describe this as a quality of mental processes.
5. This does not preclude the possibility of correcting and abandoning false beliefs unconsciously when presented with facts. Presumably this happens frequently and without reflection. Furthermore, while reflection is necessarily a second mental act that can only occur if there is first something to reflect upon, the act of reflection is not itself automatically known (which would require a further mental act) and so the concept of unconscious reflection is also comprehensible.

REFERENCES

Abbott, A. (1988). *The System of Professions: An Essay on the Division of Expert Labour*. Chicago: University of Chicago Press.

Abraham, H. C., Abraham, K., & Freud, E. L. (1965). *A Psycho-Analytic Dialogue: The Letters of Sigmund Freud and Karl Abraham, 1907–1926*. London: Hogarth Press and the Institute of Psycho-Analysis.

Adams, H., Wright, L., & Lohr, B. (1996). Is homophobia associated with homosexual arousal? *Journal of Abnormal Psychology, 105*: 440–445.

Alexander, F., & Selesnick, S. (1966). *The History of Psychiatry*. New York: Mentor.

Ammaniti, M., & Trentini, C. (2009). How new knowledge about parenting reveals the neurobiological implications of intersubjectivity: A conceptual synthesis of recent research. *Psychoanalytic Dialogues, 19*: 537–555.

Anderson, J. (1927). The knower and the known. In: J. Anderson (Ed.), *Studies in Empirical Philosophy*. Sydney: Angus & Robertson, 1962.

Anderson, J. (1930). Realism and some of its critics. In: *Studies in Empirical Philosophy*. Sydney: Angus & Robertson, 1962.

Annis, D. (1969). A note on Lehrer's proof that knowledge entails belief. *Analysis, 29*: 207–208.

Annis, D. (1977). Knowledge, belief, and rationality. *The Journal of Philosophy, 74*: 217–225.

Anscombe, G. E. M. (1957). *Intention*. Oxford: Basil Blackwell.

Arlow, J. A., & Brenner, C. (1964). *Psychoanalytic Concepts and the Structural Theory*. New York: International Universities Press.

Armstrong, D. (1969–1970). Does knowledge entail belief? *Proceedings of the Aristotelian Society, 7*: 21–36.

Armstrong, D. (1973). *Belief, Truth and Knowledge*. Cambridge: Cambridge University Press.

Ayer, A. J. (1956). *The Problem of Knowledge*. London: Penguin.

Baker, L. R. (1995). *Explaining Attitudes*. Cambridge: Cambridge University Press.

Bastuji, H., Mazza, S., Perchet, C., Frot, M., Mauguière, F., Magnin, M., & Garcia-Larrea, L. (2012). Filtering the reality: Functional dissociation of lateral and medial pain systems during sleep in humans. *Human Brain Mapping, 33*: 2638–2649.

Beardsley, M. (1958). *Aesthetics*. Indianapolis, IN: Hackett.

Beebe, B., Jaffe, J., Markese, S., Buck, K., Chen, H., Cohen, P., Bahrick, L., Andrews, H., & Feldstein, S. (2010). The origins of 12-month attachment: A microanalysis of 4-month mother–infant interaction. *Attachment and Human Development, 12*: 3–141.

Bell, C. (1914). *Art*. London: Chatto & Windus.

Bell, S. (1970). The development of the concept of object as related to infant-mother attachment. *Child Development, 41*: 291–311.

Bem, S., & Looren de Jong, H. (2006). *Theoretical Issues in Psychology: An Introduction* (2nd edn). Los Angeles: Sage.

Bengson, J., & Moffett, M. A. (2011). Two conceptions of mind and action: Knowing how and the philosophical theory of intelligence. In: J. Bengson & M. A. Moffett (Eds.), *Knowing How: Essays on Knowledge, Mind, and Action* (pp. 3–55). Oxford: Oxford University Press.

Bennett, M. R., & Hacker, P. M. S. (2003). *Philosophical Foundations of Neuroscience*. Malden: Blackwell.

Beres, D. (1962). The unconscious fantasy. *Psychoanalytic Quarterly, 31*: 309–328.

Berkeley, G. (1710/1713). *Principles of Human Knowledge/Three Dialogues*. London: Penguin, 1988.

Berlin, L., Cassidy, J., & Appleyard, K. (2008). The influence of attachment on other relationships. In: J. Cassidy & P. Shaver (Eds.), *Handbook of Attachment* (pp. 333–347). London: Guildford Press.

Bernat, J., Calhoun, K., Adams, H., & Zeichner, A. (2001). Homophobia and physical aggression toward homosexual and heterosexual individuals. *Journal of Abnormal Psychology, 110*: 179–187.

Bertenthal, B., Gredeback, G., & Boyer, T. (2012). Differential contributions of development and learning to infants' knowledge of object continuity and discontinuity. *Child Development, 84*: 413–421.

Bickle, J. (2003). *Philosophy of Neuroscience: A Ruthless Reductive Account*. Dordrecht: Kluwer.

Bion, W. R. (1967). *Second Thoughts*. London: Karnac, 1984.

Bivens, L., & Panksepp, J. (2011). *The Archaeology of the Mind*. New York: Norton.

Blass, R. B., & Carmeli, Z. (2007). The case against neuropsychoanalysis: On fallacies underlying psychoanalysis' latest scientific trend and its negative impact on psychoanalytic discourse. *International Journal of Psychoanalysis, 88*: 19–40.

Block, N. (1991). Evidence against epiphenomenalism. *Behavioral and Brain Studies, 14*: 670–672.

Boag, S. (2005). Addressing mental plurality: Justification, objections and logical requirements of strongly partitive accounts of mind. *Theory and Psychology, 15*: 747–767.

Boag, S. (2007). Realism, self-deception and the logical paradox of repression. *Theory and Psychology, 17*: 421–447.

Boag, S. (2008a). "Mind as feeling" or affective relations? A contribution to the school of Andersonian realism. *Theory and Psychology, 18*: 505–525.

Boag, S. (2008b). Making sense of subliminal perception. In: A. M. Columbus (Ed.), *Advances in Psychology Research* (pp. 117–139). New York: Nova.

Boag, S. (2010). Repression, suppression, and conscious awareness. *Psychoanalytic Psychology, 27*: 164–181.

Boag, S. (2012). *Freudian Repression, the Unconscious, and the Dynamics of Inhibition*. London: Karnac.

Boag, S., Brakel, L. A. W., & Talvitie, V. (Eds.) (2015). *Philosophy, Science and Psychoanalysis*. London: Karnac.

Bollas, C. (1987). *The Shadow of the Object*. New York: Columbia University Press.

Bornstein, M. (2014). Human infancy … and the rest of the lifespan. *Annual Review of Psychology, 65*: 121–158.

Bott Spillius, E. B., Milton, J., Garvey, P., Couve, C., & Steiner, D. (2011). *The New Dictionary of Kleinian Thought*. New York: Routledge.

Bouveresse, J. (1996). *Wittgenstein Reads Freud: The Myth of the Unconscious*. Carol Cosman (Trans.). Princeton: Princeton University Press.

Bower, T. (1977). *Development in Infancy*. San Francisco: W. H. Freeman.

Bowlby, J. (1971). *Attachment and Loss, Volume 1: Attachment*. Harmondsworth: Penguin 1971.

Bowlby, J. (1980). *Attachment and Loss, Volume 3: Loss*. London: Pimlico, 1998.

Brakel, L. A. W. (1989). Negative hallucinations, other irretrievable experiences and two functions of consciousness. *The International Journal of Psychoanalysis, 70*: 461–479.

Brakel, L. A. W. (1993). Shall drawing become part of free association? *Journal of the American Psychoanalytic Association, 41*: 359–394.

Brakel, L. A. W. (2001). Phantasies, neurotic-beliefs, and beliefs-proper. *American Journal of Psychoanalysis, 61*: 363–389.

Brakel, L. A. W. (2009). *Philosophy, Psychoanalysis, and the A-rational Mind*. Oxford: Oxford University Press.

Brakel, L. A. W. (2010). *Unconscious Knowing and Other Essays in Psycho-Philosophical Analysis*. Oxford: Oxford University Press.

Brakel, L. A. W. (2013). *The Ontology of Psychology: Questioning Foundations in the Philosophy of Mind*. London: Routledge.

Brakel, L. A. W. (2015). Two fundamental problems for philosophical psychoanalysis. In: S. Boag, L. A. W. Brakel & V. Talvitie (Ed.), *Philosophy, Science, and Psychoanalysis: A Critical Meeting* (pp. 119–143). London: Karnac.

Brentano, F. (1874). *Psychology from an Empirical Standpoint* (Translated by A. C. Rancurello, D. B. Terrell, & L. L. McAlister). London: Routledge & Kegan Paul, 1973.

Bretherton, I., & Mullholand, K. (2008). Internal working models in attachment relationships. In: J. Cassidy & P. Shaver (Eds.), *Handbook of Attachment* (pp. 102–127). London: Guildford Press.

Breuer, J., & Freud, S. (1895d). *Studies on Hysteria*. *S. E., 2*. London: Hogarth.

Buchheim, A., Viviani, R., Kessler, H., Kachele, H., Cierpka, M., Roth, G., George, C., Kernberg, O., Bruns, B., & Taubner, S. (2012). Changes in prefrontal-limbic function in major depression after 15 months of long-term psychotherapy *PLoS ONE, 7*: e33745.

Budd, M. (1995). *Values of Art*. London: Penguin.

Cairney, S. A., Durrant, S. J., Power, R., & Lewis, P. A. (2014). Complimentary roles of slow-wave sleep and rapid eye movement sleep in emotional memory consolidation. *Cerebral Cortex*, (advance access publication) doi:10.1093/cercor/bht349.

Campos, J., Barret, K., Lamb, M., Goldsmith, H., & Stenberg, C. (1983). Socioemotional development. In: P. Mussen (Ed.), *Handbook of Child Psychology* (pp. 783–915). New York: John Wiley & Sons.

Carhart-Harris, R., & Friston, K. (2010). The default-mode, ego-functions and free-energy: A neurobiological account of Freudian ideas. *Brain, 133*: 1265–1283.

Carpenter, G. (1975). Mother's face and the newborn. In: R. Lewin (Ed.), *Child Alive*. London: Maurice Temple-Smith.

Carroll, N. (1990). *The Philosophy of Horror: or Paradoxes of the Heart*. London: Routledge.

Cartwright, R. D. (2010). *The Twenty-four Hour Mind: The Role of Sleep and Dreaming in Our Emotional Lives*. Oxford: Oxford University Press.

Cassidy, J., & Shaver, P. (2008). *Handbook of Attachment*. London: Guildford Press.

Cavell, M. (1993). *The Psychoanalytic Mind*. Cambridge, MA: Harvard University Press.

Cavell, M. (2006). *Becoming a Subject*. Oxford: Clarendon Press.

Chalmers, A. (1990). *Science and its Fabrication*. Buckingham: Open University Press.

Chambers, D., & Reisberg, D. (1985). Can mental images be ambiguous? *Journal of Experimental Psychology: Human Perception and Performance, 11*: 317–328.

Chisholm, R. (1957). *Perceiving*. Ithaca and London: Cornell University Press.

Chodorow, N. (1989). *Feminism and Psychoanalytic Theory*. New Haven, CT: Yale University Press.

Chung, M. C., & Feltham, C. (2003). *Psychoanalytic Knowledge*. London: Palgrave Macmillan.

Churchland, P. M. (1988). *Matter and Consciousness, Revised Edition*. Cambridge, MA: MIT Press.

Cisek, P., & Kalaska, J. (2010). Neural mechanisms for interacting with a world full of action choices. *Annual Review of Neuroscience, 33*: 269–298.

Clark, D. A., Beck, A. T., & Alford, B. A. (1999). *Scientific Foundations of Cognitive Theory and Therapy of Depression*. New York: John Wiley & Sons.

Cooper, M. (2008). *Essential Research Findings in Counselling and Psychotherapy: The Facts are Friendly*. Los Angeles: Sage.

Coren, S. (1998). Sleep deprivation, psychosis and mental efficiency. *Psychiatric Times, 15*: 1–3.

Cox, D., & Levine, M. P. (2012). The spectacle of horror: Funny games. In: D. Cox & M. P. Levine (Eds.), *Thinking Through Film: Doing Philosophy, Watching Movies* (pp. 147–169). Malden, MA: Wiley-Blackwell. Cox, D., & Levine, M. P. (2013). Avatar: Racism, speciesism, and prejudice on Pandora. In: M. Bloodsworth-Lugo & D. Flory (Eds.), *Race, Philosophy, and Film* (pp. 117–133). London: Routledge.

Cox, D., Levine, M., Newman, S. (2009). *Politics Most Unusual*. New York: Palgrave Macmillan.

Crowell, J., Fraley, C., & Shaver, P. (2008). Measurement of individual differences in adolescent and adult attachment. In: J. Cassidy & P. Shaver (Eds.), *Handbook of Attachment* (pp. 599–634). London: Guildford Press.

Damasio, A., Damasio, H., & Tranel, D. (2012). Persistence of feelings and sentience after bilateral damage of the insula. *Cerebral Cortex, 23*: 833–846.

Damasio, A., Grabowski, T., Bechara, A., Damasio, H., Ponto, L., Parvizi, J., & Hichwa, R. (2000). Activity during the feeling of self-generated emotions. *Nature Neuroscience, 3*: 1049.

Danto, A. (1968). *Analytical Philosophy of Knowledge*. Cambridge: Cambridge University Press.

Danziger, K. (1990). *Constructing the Subject: Historical Origins of Psychological Research*. Cambridge: Cambridge University Press.

Danziger, K. (1997). *Naming the Mind: How Psychology Found its Language*. London: Sage.

Darwin, C. (1859). *On the Origin of Species by Means of Natural Selection, or the Preservation of Favoured Races in the Struggle for Life*. London: John Murray.

Darwin, C. (1903). *More Letters of Charles Darwin* (F. Darwin, Ed.). New York: D. Appleton.

Davidson, D. (1980). *Essays on Action and Events*. Oxford: Clarendon Press.

Davidson, D. (1982). Paradoxes of irrationality. In: R. Wollheim & J. Hopkins (Eds.), *Philosophical Essays on Freud* (pp. 289–305). Cambridge: Cambridge University Press.

Davies, J. (2009). *The Making of Psychotherapists: An Anthropological Analysis*. London: Karnac.

Davies, S., Higgins, K., Hopkins, R., Stecker, R., & Cooper, D. E. (Eds.) (2009). *A Companion to Aesthetics* (2nd edn). Oxford: Wiley Blackwell.

Descartes, R. (1641). Objections and replies. In: *The Philosophical Writings of Descartes, vol. II* (Translated by J. Cottingham, R. Stoohoff, & D. Murdoch) (pp. 66–398). Cambridge: Cambridge University Press, 1984.

Descartes, R. (1648). *The Philosophical Writings of Descartes, vol. III: Correspondence.* (Translated by J. Cottingham, R. Stoohoff, D. Murdoch, & A. Kenny). Cambridge: Cambridge University Press, 1991.

De Sousa, R. (1976). Rational homunculi. In: A. Rorty (Ed.), *The Identities of Persons* (pp. 217–238). Berkeley: University of California Press.

Diekelmann, S., Landolt, O., Born, J., & Wagner, U. (2008). Sleep loss produces false memories. *PLoS ONE, 3*: e3512.

Diekelmann, S., Wilhelm, I., Wagner, U., & Born, J. (2013). Sleep improves prospective remembering by facilitating spontaneous-associative retrieval processes. *PLoS ONE, 8*: e77621.

Douven, I. (2011). Abduction. In: N. Zalta (Ed.), *The Stanford Encyclopedia of Philosophy* (Spring 2011 Edition). http://plato.stanford.edu/archives/spr2011/entries/abduction/ [last accessed 20/12/2014].

Dudai, Y. (2012). The restless engram: Consolidations never end. *Annual Review of Neuroscience, 35*: 227–247.

Eagle, M. (2000). Repression: Part II. *Psychoanalytic Review, 87*: 161–187.

Eagle, M. (2011). *From Classical to Contemporary Psychoanalysis*. New York: Routledge.

Edelman, G. (1989). *The Remembered Present: A Biological Theory of Consciousness*. New York: Basic.

Edwards, J. (2011). *The Sibling Relationship: A Force for Growth and Conflict*. Plymouth, UK: Jason Aronson.

Eilperin, J. (2012). *Demon Fish: Travels through the Hidden World of Sharks*. London: Duckworth.

Ellenberger, H. F. (1970). *The Discovery of the Unconscious: The History and Evolution of Dynamic Psychiatry*. New York: Basic.

Ellison, P. (2001). *On Fertile Ground: A Natural History of Human Reproduction*. Cambridge, MA and London: Harvard University Press.

Erdelyi, M. H. (1974). A new look at the new look: Perceptual defense and vigilance. *Psychological Review, 81*: 1–25.

Erdelyi, M. H. (1985). *Psychoanalysis: Freud's Cognitive Psychology*. New York: W. H. Freeman.

Erdelyi, M. H. (2004). Subliminal perception and its cognates: Theory, indeterminancy, and time. *Consciousness & Cognition, 13*: 73–91.

Feeney, J. (2008). Adult romantic attachment. In: J. Cassidy & P. Shaver (Eds.), *Handbook of Attachment* (pp. 333–347). London: Guildford Press.

Feist, G. J. (2006). *The Psychology of Science and the Origins of the Scientific Mind*. New Haven, CT: Yale University Press.

Fisher, C. (1957). Dreams and perceptions. *Journal of the American Psychoanalytic Association, 2*: 389–445.

Fonagy, P. (1999). Memory and therapeutic action. *International Journal of Psychoanalysis, 80*: 215–233.

Fonagy, P. (2000). *Attachment Theory and Psychoanalysis*. New York: Other Press.

Fonagy, P., Gergely, G., & Target, M. (2008). Psychoanalytic constructs and attachment theory and research. In: J. Cassidy & P. Shaver (Eds.), *Handbook of Attachment* (pp. 783–810). London: Guildford Press.

Fonagy, P. & Target, M. (2000). The place of psychodynamic theory in developmental psychopathology. *Development and Psychopathology, 12*: 407–425.

Fotopoulou, A., Pfaff, D., & Conway, M. A. (2012). *From the Couch to the Lab: Trends in Psychodynamic Neuroscience*. Oxford: Oxford University Press.

Fraiberg, L. (1956). Freud's writings on art. *International Journal of Psycho-Analysis, 37*: 82–96.

Frank, J. (1976). *Dostoevsky: The Seeds of Revolt, 1821–1849*. Princeton: Princeton University Press.

Freidson, E. (1970). *Profession of Medicine: A Study of the Sociology of Applied Knowledge. With a New Afterword*. Chicago: The University of Chicago Press.

Freidson, E. (2001). *Professionalism: The Third Logic*. Cambridge: Polity.

Freud, A. (1968). *The Ego and the Mechanisms of Defence*. London: The Hogarth Press.

Freud, S. (1892–1893). A case of successful treatment by hypnotism. *S. E., 1*: 117–128. London: Hogarth.
Freud, S. (1894a). The neuro-psychoses of defence. *S. E., 3*: 41–61. London: Hogarth.
Freud, S. (1900a). *The Interpretation of Dreams. S. E., 4–5*. London: Hogarth.
Freud, S. (1901b). The psychopathology of everyday life. *S. E., 6*. London: Hogarth.
Freud, S. (1905c). *Jokes and their Relation to the Unconscious. S. E., 8*. London: Hogarth.
Freud, S. (1905d). *Three Essays on the Theory of Sexuality. S. E., 7*. London: Hogarth.
Freud, S. (1905e). Fragment of an analysis of a case of hysteria. *S. E., 7*: 1–122. London: Hogarth.
Freud, S. (1908a). Hysterical phantasies and their relation to bisexuality. *S. E., 9*: 141–154.
Freud, S. (1908d). "Civilized" sexual morality and modern nervousness. *S. E., 9*: 177–204. London: Hogarth.
Freud, S. (1908e). Creative writers and day-dreaming. *S. E., 9*: 141–154. London: Hogarth.
Freud, S. (1909a). Some general remarks on hysterical attacks. *S. E., 9*: 227–234. London: Hogarth.
Freud, S. (1909d). Notes upon a case of obsessional neurosis. *S. E., 10*: 151–249 and Addendum: Original record of the case *S. E., 10*: 253–318. London: Hogarth.
Freud, S. (1910c). *Leonardo da Vinci and a Memory of his Childhood. S. E., 11*: 59–138. London: Hogarth.
Freud, S. (1911b). Formulations on the two principles of mental functioning. *S. E., 12*: 213–226. London: Hogarth.
Freud, S. (1912f). Contributions to a discussion on masturbation. *S. E., 12*: 239–254. London: Hogarth.
Freud, S. (1912g). A note on the unconscious in psycho-analysis. *S. E., 12*: 256–266. London: Hogarth.
Freud, S. (1912–1913). *Totem and Taboo. S. E., 13*. London: Hogarth.
Freud, S. (1913j). The claims of psycho-analysis to scientific interest. *S. E., 13*: 163–190. London: Hogarth.
Freud, S. (1914b). The Moses of Michelangelo. *S. E., 13*: 209–238. London: Hogarth.
Freud, S. (1914c). On narcissism: An introduction. *S. E., 14*: 67–102. London: Hogarth.
Freud, S. (1915c). Instincts and their vicissitudes. *S. E., 14*: 109–140. London: Hogarth.
Freud, S. (1915e). The unconscious. *S. E., 14*: 159–215. London: Hogarth.
Freud, S. (1916a). On transience. *S. E., 14*: 303–308. London: Hogarth.

Freud, S. (1916–1917). *Introductory Lectures on Psycho-Analysis. S. E., 15–16*. London: Hogarth.
Freud, S. (1917d). A metapsychological supplement to the theory of dreams. *S. E., 14*: 217–235. London: Hogarth.
Freud, S. (1917e). Mourning and melancholia. *S. E., 14*: 239–258. London: Hogarth.
Freud, S. (1920g). *Beyond the Pleasure Principle. S. E., 18*: 1–64. London: Hogarth.
Freud, S. (1921b). Introduction to J. Varendonck's *The Psychology of Day-Dreams. S. E., 18*: 271–272. London: Hogarth.
Freud, S. (1921c). *Group Psychology and the Analysis of the Ego. S. E., 18*: 67–143. London: Hogarth.
Freud, S. (1922b). Some neurotic mechanisms in jealousy, paranoia and homosexuality. *S. E., 18*: 221–232. London: Hogarth.
Freud, S. (1923a). Two encyclopaedia articles. *S. E., 18*: 233–260. London: Hogarth.
Freud, S. (1923b). *The Ego and the Id. S. E., 19*: 1–66. London: Hogarth.
Freud, S. (1924b). Neurosis and psychosis. *S. E., 19*: 147–154. London: Hogarth.
Freud, S. (1924e). The loss of reality in neurosis and psychosis. *S. E., 19*: 181–188. London: Hogarth.
Freud, S. (1924f). A short account of psycho-analysis. *S. E., 19*: 189–210. London: Hogarth.
Freud, S. (1925d). *An Autobiographical Study. S. E.,* 19: 1–74. London: Hogarth.
Freud, S. (1925i). Some additional notes on dream-interpretation as a whole. *S. E., 19*: 123–138. London: Hogarth.
Freud, S. (1927c). *The Future of an Illusion. S. E., 21*. London: Hogarth.
Freud, S. (1927d). Humour. *S. E., 21*: 159–166. London: Hogarth.
Freud, S. (1928b). Dostoevsky and parricide. *S. E., 21*: 173–194. London: Hogarth.
Freud, S. (1930a). *Civilization and its Discontents. S. E., 21*: 57–146. London: Hogarth.
Freud, S. (1933a). *New Introductory Lectures on Psycho-Analysis. S. E., 22*. London: Hogarth.
Freud, S. (1939a). *Moses and Monotheism. S. E., 23*: 1–138. London: Hogarth.
Freud, S. (1940a). *An Outline of Psycho-Analysis. S. E., 23*: 139–208. London: Hogarth.
Freud, S. (1943). *A General Introduction to Psychoanalysis*. Garden City, NY: Garden City.
Freud, S. (1950a[1895]). A project for a scientific psychology. *S.E., 1*: 283–397. London: Hogarth.

Freud, S. (1950a[1887–1902]). Extracts from the Fliess papers. *S. E., 1*: 175–280.

Freud, S. (1960a). *Letters of Sigmund Freud 1873–1939*. E. L. Freud (Ed.), T. Stern & J. Stern (Trans.). London: Hogarth.

Freud, S. (1997). *Writings on Art and Literature*. W. Hamacher & D. Wellbery (Eds.). Stanford, CA: Stanford University Press.

Fry, R. (1924). *The Artist and Psychoanalysis*. London: Hogarth Press [reprinted in PSICOART n.1 2010. http://psicoart.cib.inibo.it] [last accessed 24/01/2013].

Gallese, V. (2009). Mirror neurons, embodied simulation, and the neural basis of social identification. *Psychoanalytic Dialogues, 19*: 519–536.

Gardner, S. (1993). *Irrationality and the Philosophy of Psychoanalysis*. Cambridge: Cambridge University Press.

Gaut, B. (1993). The paradox of horror. *British Journal of Aesthetics, 33*: 333–345.

Gaut, B., & Lopes, D. (Eds.) (2005). *The Routledge Companion to Aesthetics* (2nd edn). London: Routledge.

Gegestand, S. (2007). Reproductive strategies and tactics. In: R. Dunbar & L. Barrett (Eds.), *Oxford Handbook of Evolutionary Psychology* (pp. 323–332). Oxford: Oxford University Press.

Gettier, E. (1963). Is justified true belief knowledge? *Analysis, 23*: 121–123.

Gill, M. M. (1963). *Topography and Systems in Psychoanalytic Theory*. New York: International Universities Press.

Gill, M., & Holzman, P. (Eds.) (1976). *Psychology versus Metapsychology*. New York: International Universities Press.

Gillett, E. (1988). The brain and the unconscious. *Psychoanalysis and Contemporary Thought, 11*: 563–578.

Ginsborg, H. (2013). Kant's aesthetics and teleology. In: E. N. Zalta (Ed.), *The Stanford Encyclopedia of Philosophy* (Spring 2013 edn), http://plato.stanford.edu/entries/kant-aesthetics/ [last accessed 04/11/ 2013].

Glymour, C. (1983). The theory of your dreams. In: *Physics, philosophy and psychoanalysis* (pp. 57–71). Netherlands: Springer.

Godfrey-Smith, P. (2003). *Theory and Reality: An Introduction to the Philosophy of Science*. Chicago: University of Chicago Press.

Goldman, A. (1975). Innate knowledge. In: S. Stich (Ed.), *Innate Ideas* (pp. 111–120). Berkeley: University of California Press.

Goldman, A. (1976). Discrimination and perceptual knowledge. *The Journal of Philosophy, 73*: 771–791.

Goldman, A. I. (1970). *A Theory of Human Action*. New Jersey: Prentice-Hall.

Goldman, A. I. (1999). *Knowledge in a Social World*. Oxford: Clarendon Press.

Goldman, A. I. (2011). A Guide to social epistemology. In: A. Goldman & D. Whitcomb (Eds.), *Social Epistemology: Essential Readings* (pp. 11–37). Oxford: Oxford University Press.

Gombrich, E. H. (1987). Freud's aesthetics. In: R. Woodfield (Ed.), *Reflections on the History of Art: Views and Reviews* (pp. 221–239). Oxford: Phaidon.

Graham, G. (2000). *Philosophy of the Arts: An Introduction to Aesthetics* (2nd edn). London: Routledge.

Graham, G. (2010). *The Disordered Mind*. New York: Routledge.

Gray, P. B. (2013). Evolution and human sexuality. *American journal of physical anthropology, 152*(S57), 94–118.

Greenwald, A. G. (1992). New Look 3: Unconscious cognition reclaimed. *American Psychologist, 47*: 766–779.

Grosskurth, P. (1991). *The Secret Ring: Freud's Inner Circle and the Politics of Psychoanalysis*. New York: Addison Wesley.

Grünbaum, A. (1984). *The Foundations of Psychoanalysis: A Philosophical Critique*. Berkeley: University of California Press.

Grünbaum, A. (1988). Précis of *The Foundations of Psychoanalysis: A Philosophical Critique*. In: P. Clark & C. Wright (Eds.), *Mind, Psychoanalysis and Science* (pp. 3–32). Oxford: Blackwell.

Grünbaum, A. (2015). *Validation in the Clinical Theory of Psychoanalysis: A Study in the Philosophy of Psychoanalysis*. Madison, CT: International Universities Press.

Gu, X., Hof, P., Friston, K., & Fan, J. (2013). Anterior insular cortex and emotional awareness. *The Journal of Comparative Neurology, 521*: 3371–3388.

Guttenplan, S. (1994). Belief, knowledge, and the origins of content. *Dialectica, 47*: 287–305.

Haig, D. (1993). Genetic conflicts in human pregnancy. *Quarterly Review of Biology, 68*: 495–532.

Hampshire, S. (1974). Disposition and memory. In: R. Wollheim (Ed.), *Freud: A Collection of Critical Essays* (pp. 113–131). New York: Anchor.

Hart, S. (2008). *Brain, Attachment, and Personality*. London: Karnac.

Hartland-Swann, J. (1958). *An Analysis of Knowing*. New York: Unwin and Allen.

Hartmann, H. (1939). *Ego Psychology and the Problem of Adaptation*. New York: International Universities Press, 1958.

Hartmann, H. (1947). On rational and irrational action. In: *Essays in Ego Psychology*. New York: International Universities Press.

Hartmann, H. (1948). Comments on the psychoanalytic theory of instinctual drives. In: *Essays in Ego Psychology*. New York: International Universities Press.

Hartmann, H. (1959). Psychoanalysis as a scientific theory. In: S. Hook (Ed.), *Psychoanalysis, Scientific Method and Philosophy* (pp. 3–37). New York: New York University Press.

Hartmann, H. (1964). *Essays in Ego Psychology*. New York: International Universities Press.

Hartmann, H., Kris, E., & Loewenstein, R. (Eds.) (1964). *Papers on Psychoanalytic Psychology*. New York: International Universities Press.

Haslam, N., & Loughnan, S. (2014). Dehumanization and infrahumanization. *Annual Review of Psychology, 65*: 399–423.

Hassin, R., Uleman, J., & Bargh, J. (Eds.) (2005). *The New Unconscious*. Oxford: Oxford University Press.

Hawelka, E. R., & Hawelka, P. (1974). *L'homme aux rats—Journal d'une analyse* [by S. Freud, German text with French introduction, translation, notes, and commentary]. Paris: Press Universitaires de France.

Herek, G., & McLemore, K. (2013). Sexual prejudice. *Annual Review of Psychology, 64*: 309–333.

Hesse, E. (2000). The adult attachment interview. In: J. Cassidy & P. Shaver (Eds.), *Handbook of Attachment* (pp. 552–598). London: Guildford Press.

Hintikka, J. (1962). *Knowledge and Belief*. Ithaca, NY: Cornell University Press.

Hobson, A., & Friston, K. (2012). Waking and dreaming consciousness: Neurobiological and functional considerations. *Progress in Neurobiology, 98*: 82–98.

Hobson, J. A., Hong, C. C-H., & Friston, K. J. (2014). Virtual reality and consciousness inference in dreaming. *Frontiers in Psychology*, 5: 1133. doi: 10.3389/fpsyg.2014.01133

Holt, R. R. (1976). Drive or wish? A reconsideration of the psycho-analytic theory of motivation. In: M. Gill & P. Holzman (Eds.), *Psychology vs. Metapsychology: Psycho-analytic Essays in Memory of George Klein. Psychological Issues* (pp. 158–197). New York: International Universities Press.

Hook, S. (Ed.) (1959). *Psychoanalysis, Scientific Method and Philosophy*. New York: New York University Press.

Hopkins, J. (1982). Introduction: Philosophy and psychoanalysis. In: R. Wollheim & J. Hopkins (Eds.), *Philosophical Essays on Freud* (pp. vii–xiv). Cambridge: Cambridge University Press.

Hopkins, J. (1987). Synthesis in the imagination: Psychoanalysis, infantile experience, and the concept of an object. In: J. Russell (Ed.), *Philosophical Perspectives on Developmental Psychology* (pp. 140–170). Oxford: Basil Blackwell.

Hopkins, J. (1988). Epistemology and depth psychology: Critical notes on the *Foundations of Psychoanalysis*. In: P. Clark & C. Wright (Eds.), *Psychoanalysis, Mind and Science* (pp. 33–60). Oxford: Blackwell.

Hopkins, J. (1995). Reply: Irrationality, interpretation and division. In: C. Macdonald & G. Macdonald (Eds.), *Philosophy of Psychology: Debates on Psychological Explanation*, Vol I (pp. 461–484). Oxford: Blackwell.

Hopkins, J. (1996). Psychoanalytic and scientific reasoning. *British Journal of Psychotherapy, 13*: 86–105.

Hopkins, J. (1999a). Patterns of interpretation: Speech, action, and dream. In: L. Marcus (Ed.), *Cultural Documents: The Interpretation of Dreams* (pp. 123–169). Manchester: Manchester University Press.

Hopkins, J. (1999b). Freud and the Science of Mind. In: G. Howie (Ed.), *The Edinburgh Encyclopedia of Continental Philosophy* (pp. 377–389). Edinburgh: Edinburgh University press.

Hopkins, J. (2000a). Evolution, consciousness and the internality of mind. In: P. Carruthers & A. Chamberlin (Eds.), *Evolution and the Human Mind* (pp. 276–302). Cambridge: Cambridge University Press.

Hopkins, J. (2000b). Psychoanalysis, metaphor and the concept of mind. In: M. P. Levine (Ed.), *The Analytic Freud. Philosophy and Psychoanalysis* (pp. 11–35). London: Routledge.

Hopkins, J. (2003). Evolution, emotion, and conflict. In: M. Chung (Ed.), *Psychoanalytic Knowledge* (pp. 132–156). London: Palgrave Macmillan.

Hopkins, J. (2004). Conscience and conflict: Darwin, Freud, and the origins of human aggression. In: D. Evans & P. Cruse (Eds.), *Emotion, Evolution, and Rationality* (pp. 225–248). Oxford: Oxford University Press.

Hopkins, J. (2012). Psychoanalysis, representation and neuroscience: The Freudian unconscious and the Bayesian brain. In: A. Fotopoulou, D. Pfaff, & M. A. Conway (Eds.), *From the Couch to the Lab: Trends in Psychodynamic Neuroscience* (pp. 230–265). Oxford: Oxford University Press.

Hopkins, J. (2013a). Psychoanalysis, philosophical issues. In: B. Kaldis (Ed.), *Encyclopedia of Philosophy and the Social Sciences* (pp. 769–771). Los Angeles: Sage.

Hopkins, J. (2013b). Understanding and healing: Psychiatry and psychoanalysis in the era of neuroscience. In: W. Fulford (Ed.), *The Oxford Handbook of the Philosophy of Psychiatry* (pp. 1264–1291). Oxford: Oxford University Press.

Hopkins, J. (2013c). Conflict creates an unconscious id. *Neuropsychoanalysis, 15*: 45–48.

Hospers, J. (1959). *An Introduction to Philosophical Analysis*. New Jersey: Prentice-Hall.

Howe, G. (2011). *Attachment Across the Lifecourse*. New York: Palgrave Macmillan.

Howson, C., & Urbach, P. (1989). *Scientific Reasoning: The Bayesian Approach*. LaSalle, PA: Open Court.

Hrdy, S. (2000). *Mother Nature*. London: Vintage.

Hrdy, S. (2009). *Mothers and Others*. Cambridge: Harvard Press.

Inostroza, M., & Born, J. (2013). Sleep for preserving and transforming episodic memory. *Annual Review of Neuroscience, 36*: 79–102.

Jackson, F. (1982). Epiphenomenal qualia. *Philosophical Quarterly*, 32: 127–136.

Johnson, O. (1979). Ignorance and irrationality. *Philosophy Research Archives, 5*: 368–417.

Johnston, M. (1988). Self-deception and the nature of mind. In: B. P. McLaughlin & A. O. Rorty (Eds.), *Perspectives on Self-deception* (pp. 63–91). Berkeley: University of California Press.

Jones, E. (1953). *Sigmund Freud: Life and Work*, vol. 1. London: Hogarth.

Jones, E. (1957). *The Life and Works of Sigmund Freud*, Vol, 3. New York: Basic.

Jones, O. R. (1971). Knowing and guessing: By examples. *Analysis, 32*: 19–23.

Kaplan-Solms, K., Solms, M. (2000). *Clinical Studies in Neuro-Psychoanalysis*. London: Karnac.

Kenny, D. (2013). *Bringing Up Baby: The Psychoanalytic Infant Comes of Age*. London: Karnac.

Kernberg, O. F. (1966). Structural derivatives and object-relationships. *International Journal of Psychoanalysis, 47*: 236–253.

Kernberg, O. F. (1975). *Borderline Conditions and Pathological Narcissism*. New York: Jason Aronson.

Kieran, M. (2005). The value of art. In: B. Gaut & D. Lopes (Eds.), *The Routledge Companion to Aesthetics* (2nd edn) (pp. 293–305). London: Routledge.

Kieran, M. (Ed.) (2006). *Contemporary Debates in Aesthetics and the Philosophy of Art*. Oxford: Blackwell.

Kihlstrom, J. F. (1987). The cognitive unconscious. *Science, 237*: 1445–1452.

Kim, J. (1993). *Supervenience and Mind*. Cambridge: Cambridge University Press.

Kim, J. (2005). *Physicalism, or Something Near Enough*. Princeton: Princeton University Press.

Kirsch, I. (2009). *The Emperor's New Drugs: Exploding the Antidepressant Myth*. London: The Bodley Head.

Kitcher, P. (1992). *Freud's Dream: A Complete Interdisciplinary Science of Mind*. London: MIT Press.

Kitcher, P. (1993). *The Advancement of Science: Science without Legend, Objectivity without Illusions*. New York: Oxford University Press.

Klein, D. B. (1977). *The Unconscious: Invention or Discovery?* Santa Monica, CA: Goodyear.

Klein, M. (1929). Personification in the play of children. In: M. Klein, *Love, Guilt, and Reparation* (pp. 199–209). London: Hogarth, 1975.

Klein, M. (1932). *The Psychoanalysis of Children*. London: Hogarth, 1969.

Klein, M. (1946). Notes on some schizoid mechanisms. In: M. Klein, *Envy and Gratitude and Other Works 1946–1963* (pp. 1–14). London: Hogarth, 1975.

Klein, M. (1952). Some theoretical conclusions regarding the emotional life of the infant. In: *Envy and Gratitude and Other Works 1946–1963* (pp. 61–93). London: Hogarth, 1975.

Knorr Cetina, K. (1999). *Epistemic Cultures: How the Sciences Make Knowledge*. Cambridge: Harvard University Press.

Kohut, H. (1978). Creativeness, charisma, group psychology. In: P. H. Ornstein (Ed.), *The Search for the Self. Reflections on the Self-Analysis of Freud* (pp. 793–843). New York: Oxford University Press.

Kohut, H. (1982). Introspection, empathy, and the semi-circle of mental health. *International Journal of Psycho-Analysis, 63*: 395–407.

Kris, E. (1952). *Psychoanalytic Explorations in Art*. New York: Schocken.

Kuhn, T. (1957). *The Copernican Revolution*. Cambridge: Harvard University Press.

Kuhn, T. (1962). *The Structure of Scientific Revolutions*. Chicago: The University of Chicago Press.

Kumin, I. (1996). *Pre-Object Relatedness: Early Attachment and the Psychoanalytic Situation*. London: Guilford Press.

Kunst-Wilson, W., & Zajonc, R. (1980). Affective discrimination of stimuli that cannot be recognized. *Science, 207*: 557–558.

Lacewing, M. (2012). Inferring motives in psychology and psychoanalysis. *Philosophy, Psychiatry & Psychology, 19*: 197–212.

Lacewing, M. (2013). The problem of suggestion in psychoanalysis: An analysis and solution. *Philosophical Psychology, 26*: 718–743.

Lambert, M. J. (Ed.) (2004). *Bergin and Garfield's Handbook of Psychotherapy and Behavioral Change*. Fifth edition. New York: Wiley.

Latour, B., & Woolgar, S. (1979). *Laboratory Life: The Social Construction of Scientific Facts*. Beverly Hills: Sage.

Laudan, L. (1996). *Beyond Positivism and Relativism: Theory, Method, and Evidence*. Boulder, CO: Westview Press.

Lear, J. (1995). The heterogeneity of the mental. *Mind, 104*: 863–879.

Lear, J. (1998). *Open Minded*. Cambridge, MA: Harvard University Press.

Lehrer, K. (1970). Believing that one knows. *Synthese, 21*: 133–140.

Lehrer, K. (1974). *Knowledge*. Oxford: Oxford University Press.

Lemarque, P., & Olsen, S. (Eds.) (2004). *Aesthetics and the Philosophy of Art: The Analytic Tradition*. Oxford: Blackwell.

Lemmon, E. J. (1967). If I know, do I know that I know? In: A. Stroll (Ed.), *Epistemology: New Essays in the Theory of Knowledge* (pp. 54–83). New York: Harper & Row.

Levine, M. (Ed.) (2000). *The Analytic Freud*. London and New York: Routledge.

Levine, M. P. (2004). A fun night out: Horror and other pleasures of the cinema. In: S. Schneider (Ed.), *The Horror Film and Psychoanalysis: Freud's Worst Nightmares* (pp. 35–54). Cambridge: Cambridge University Press.

Levine, M. P. (2005). Arts, sex, and philosophy. In: A. Soble (Ed.), *Sex from Plato to Paglia: A Philosophical Encyclopedia* (pp. 62–74). Westport, CT: Greenwood Press.

Levine, M. P., & Pataki, T. (Eds.) (2004). *Racism in Mind.* Ithaca, NY: Cornell University Press.

Lewis, D. (1983). Mad pain and Martian pain. In: D. Lewis (Ed.), *Philosophical Papers, Volume 1* (pp. 122–132). Oxford: Oxford University Press.

Lewis, D. (1990). What experience teaches. In: W. Lycan (Ed.), *Mind and Cognition* (pp. 77–103). Oxford: Blackwell Press.

Lewis, P. A., & Durrant, S. J. (2011). Overlapping memory replay during sleep builds cognitive schemata. *Trends in Cognitive Sciences, 15*: 343–351.

Libet, B. (2004). *Mind Time.* Cambridge, MA: Harvard University Press.

Lindquist, K., Wager, T., Kober, H., Bliss-Moreau, E., & Barrett, L. (2012). The brain basis of emotion: A meta-analytic view. *Behavioral and Brain Sciences, 35*: 121–202.

Locke, J. (1690). *An Essay Concerning Human Understanding.* London: J. M. Dent & Sons, 1947.

Lordkipanidze, D., Ponce de León, M., Margvelashvili, M., Rak, Y., Rightmire, G., Vekua, A., & Zollikofer, C. (2013). A complete skull from Dmanisi, Georgia, and the evolutionary biology of early homo. *Science, 342*: 326–331.

Luborsky, L., & Barrett, M. (2006). What else materially influences what is represented and published as evidence? Theoretical allegiance. In: J. Norcross, L. Beutler, & R. Levant (Eds.), *Evidence-Based Practices in Mental Health: Debate and Dialogue on the Fundamental Questions* (pp. 257–298). Washington: American Psychological Association.

Lunbeck, E. (2012). Heinz Kohut's Americanization of Freud. In: J. Burnham (Ed.), *After Freud Left: A Century of Psychoanalysis in America* (pp. 209–231). Chicago: University of Chicago Press.

Lyons-Ruth, K., & Jacobovitz, D. (2008). Attachment disorganization: Genetic factors, parenting contexts, and development transformation from infancy to adulthood. In: J. Cassidy & P. Shaver (Eds.), *Handbook of Attachment* (pp. 666–697). London: Guildford Press.

Macdonald, K. A. (1995). *The Sociology of Professions.* London: Sage.

Macintosh, J. J. (1979–1980). Knowing and believing. *Proceedings of the Aristotelian Society, 80*: 169–185.

MacIntyre, A. (1958). *The Unconscious: A Conceptual Analysis.* London: Routledge & Kegan Paul.

Mackay, N. (1996). The place of motivation in psychoanalysis. *Modern Psychoanalysis, 21*: 3–17.

Mackay, N. (1999). Reason, cause, and rationality in psychological explanation. *Journal of Theoretical and Philosophical Psychology, 19*: 1–21.

Mackay, N., & Petocz, A. (Eds.) (2011). *Realism and Psychology*. Leiden and Boston: Brill.

Macmillan, M. (1991). *Freud Evaluated: The Completed Arc*. Amsterdam: North-Holland.

Magai, C. (2008). Attachment in middle and later life. In: J. Cassidy & P. Shaver (Eds.), *Handbook of Attachment* (pp. 532–551). London: Guildford Press.

Makari, G. (2008). *Revolution in Mind: The Creation of Psychoanalysis*. New York: HarperCollins.

Makari, G. (2012). Mitteleuropa on the Hudson: On the struggle for American psychoanalysis after the anscluss. In: J. Burnham (Ed.), *After Freud left: A Century of Psychoanalysis in America* (pp. 111–124). Chicago: University of Chicago Press.

Malcolm, J. (1980). *Psychoanalysis: The Impossible profession*. London: Pan.

Malcolm, N. (1952). Knowledge and belief. *Mind, 61*:178–189.

Malcolm, N. (1963). *Knowledge and Certainty*. Englewood Cliffs, NJ: Prentice Hall.

Maltsberger, J. T. (2008). Self break-up and the descent into suicide. In: S. Briggs, A. Lemma, & W. Crouch (Eds.), *Relating to Self-Harm and Suicide: Psychoanalytic Perspectives on Practice, Theory and Prevention* (pp. 38–44). London: Routledge.

Mannison, D. S. (1976). "Inexplicable knowledge" does not require belief. *The Philosophical Quarterly, 26*: 139–148.

Margolis, J. (1973). *Knowledge and Existence*. New York: Oxford University Press.

Marshall, G. (2000). How far down does the will go. In: M. Levine (Ed.), *The Analytic Freud* (pp. 36–48). London: Routledge.

Matusomoto, D., & Willingham, B. (2009). Spontaneous facial expressions of emotion in congenitally and non-congenitally blind individuals. *The Journal of Personality and Social Psychology, 96*: 1–10.

Maze, J. R. (1983). *The Meaning of Behaviour*. London: Allen & Unwin.

Maze, J. R., & Henry, R. M. (1996). Problems in the concept of repression and proposals for their resolution. *International Journal of Psycho-analysis, 77*: 1085–1100.

Maze, J. (2009). *Psychologies of Mind* (edited by Rachel Henry). London: Continuum.

McMullen, T. (1996). Psychology and realism. In: C. R. Latimer & J. Michell (Eds.), *At Once Scientific and Philosophic: A Festschrift for John Philip Sutcliffe* (pp. 59–66). Brisbane: Boombana.

Medlow, S. (2008). *The "Paradox" Of Mental Causation: Solutions from Anomalous Monism and Direct Realism*. Saarbrücken: VDM Verlag.

Mele, A. R. (2009). *Effective Intentions: The Power of Conscious Will*. Oxford: Oxford University Press.

Mesoudi, A. (2011). *Cultural Evolution: How Darwinian Theory Can Explain Human Culture and Synthesize the Social Sciences*. Chicago: University of Chicago Press.

Metcalfe, J., & Shimamura, A. P. (1994). *Metacognition: Knowing About Knowing*. Cambridge, MA: MIT Press.

Michell, J. (1988). Maze's direct realism and the character of cognition. *Australian Journal of Psychology, 40*: 227–249.

Mitchell, J. (2003). *Siblings*. Cambridge: Polity Press.

Mlodinow, L. (2012). *Subliminal: How Your Unconscious Mind Rules Your Behavior*. London: Penguin.

Mock, D. (2005). *More than Kin and Less than Kind*. Cambridge, MA: Harvard University Press.

Mock, D., & Parker, A. (1997). *The Evolution of Sibling Rivalry*. Oxford: Oxford University Press.

Moore, M. (1984). *Law and Psychiatry*. Cambridge: Cambridge University Press.

Münsterberg, H. (1909). *Psychotherapy*. London: Adelphi Terrace.

Nagel, E. (1959). Methodological issues in psychoanalytic theory. In: S. Hook (Ed.), *Psychoanalysis, Scientific Method and Philosophy* (pp. 38–56). New York: New York University Press.

Newberry, G. (2010). Drive theory reconsidered (again). In: N. Mackay & A. Petocz (Eds.), *Realism and Psychology* (pp. 839–871). Leiden and Boston: Brill.

Norcross, J. C., Beutler, L. E., & Levant, R. F. (Eds.) (2006). *Evidence-Based Practices in Mental Health: Debate and Dialogue on the Fundamental Questions*. Washington: American Psychological Association.

Norcross, J. C., & Lambert, M. J (2006). The therapy relationship. In: J. C. Norcross, L. E. Beutler, & R. F. Levant (Eds.). *Evidence-Based Practices in Mental Health: Debate and Dialogue on the Fundamental Questions* (pp. 208–218). Washington: American Psychological Association.

O'Brien, G., & Jureidini, J. (2002). Dispensing with the dynamic unconscious. *Philosophy, Psychology, & Psychiatry, 9*: 141–153.

Ogden, T. H. (1986). *The Matrix of the Mind*. New Jersey: Jason Aronson, 1993.

O'Shaughnessy, B. (1980). *The Will: A Dual Aspect Theory*. Cambridge: Cambridge University Press.

Panksepp, J. (1998). *Affective Neuroscience: The Foundations of Human and Animal Emotions*. Oxford: Oxford University Press.

Panksepp, J. (1999). Emotions as viewed by psychoanalysis and neuroscience: An exercise in consilience. *Neuro-psychoanalysis, 1*, 15–38.

Panksepp, J., & Biven, L. (2012). *The Archaeology of Mind: Neuroevolutionary Foundations of Human Emotion*. New York: Norton.

Paris, J. (2005). *The Fall of an Icon: Psychoanalysis and Academic Psychiatry*. Toronto: University of Toronto Press.

Pasnau, R. (1997). *Theories of Cognition in the Later Middle Ages*. Cambridge: Cambridge University Press.

Pataki, T. (1996). Intention in wish-fulfilment. *Australasian Journal of Philosophy, 74*: 20–37.

Pataki, T. (1997a). Self-deception and wish-fulfilment. *Philosophia, 25*: 297–322.

Pataki, T. (1997b). Some aspects of writing. *Quadrant, 41*: 46–52.

Pataki, T. (1998). Review of *Irrationality and the Philosophy of Psychoanalysis* (Gardner, 1993) and *The Psychoanalytic Mind: From Freud to Philosophy* (Cavell, 1993). *Australasian Journal of Philosophy, 76*: 644–647.

Pataki, T. (2000). Freudian wish-fulfilment and sub-intentional explanation. In: M. P. Levine (Ed.), *The Analytic Freud: Philosophy & Psychoanalysis* (pp. 49–84). London: Routledge.

Pataki, T. (2003). Freud, object relations, agency and the self. In: M. C. Chung & C. Feltham (Eds.), *Psychoanalytic Knowledge* (pp. 157–180). London: Palgrave.

Pataki, T. (2014a). Fairbairn and partitive conceptions of mind. In: D. Scharff & G. Clarke (Eds.), *Fairbairn and the Object Relations Tradition* (pp. 417–430). London: Karnac.

Pataki, T. (2014b). *Wishfulfilment in Philosophy and Psychoanalysis: The Tyranny of Desire*. London: Routledge.

Payne, J. D. (2011). Sleep on it! Stabilizing and transforming memories during sleep. *Nature Neuroscience, 14*: 272.

Pears, D. (1984). *Motivated Irrationality*. Oxford: Clarendon Press.

Petocz, A. (1999). *Freud, Psychoanalysis and Symbolism*. Cambridge: Cambridge University Press.

Petocz, A. (2006). Commentary on "Freudian dream theory, dream bizarreness, and the disguise-censor controversy". *Neuropsychoanalysis, 8*: 48–53.

Pockett, S., Banks, W., & Gallagher, S. (Eds.) (2006). *Does Consciousness Cause Behavior?* Cambridge, MA: MIT Press.

Popper, K. R. (1978). Darwinism as metaphysics. In: P. A. Schilp (Ed.), *The Philosophy of Karl Popper, The Library of Living Philosophers*, volume XIV (pp. 136–137). Chicago: Open Court Publishers.

Popper, K. R. (1983). *Realism and the Aim of Science*. Totowa, NJ: Rowan & Littlefield.

Pritchard, H. A. (1950). *Knowledge and Perception*. London: Oxford University Press.

Putnam, H. (1975). *Mind, Language and Reality*. Cambridge: Cambridge University Press.

Radford, C. (1966). Knowledge: By examples. *Analysis, 27*: 1–11.

Radford, C. (1970). Does unwitting knowledge entail unconscious belief? *Analysis, 30*: 103–107.

Rasch, B., & Born, J. (2013). About sleep's role in memory. *Physiological Review, 93*: 681–766.

Rechtschaffen, A., & Bergmann, B. (1995). Sleep deprivation in the rat by the disk-over-water method. *Behavioural Brain Research, 69*: 55–63.

Reddy, V., & Trevarthen, C. (2004). What we learn about babies from engaging their emotions. *Zero to Three, 24*: 9–15.

Reed, S. K., & Johnsen, J. A. (1975). Detection of parts in patterns and images. *Memory and Cognition, 3*: 569–575.

Reeder, J. (2004). *Hate and Love in Psychoanalytical Institutions: The Dilemma of a Profession*. New York: Other Press.

Reissland, N., Francis, B., Mason, J., & Lincoln, K. (2011). Do facial expressions develop before birth? *PLoS ONE, 6*: e24081.

Ribble, M. A. (1944). Infantile experience in relation to personality development. In: J. Hunt (Ed.), *Personality and the Behavior Disorders* (pp. 621–651). Oxford: Ronald Press.

Rice, J. L. (1985). *Dostoevsky and the Healing Art*. Ann Arbor, MI: Ardis.

Ring, M. (1977). Knowledge: The cessation of belief. *American Philosophical Quarterly, 14*: 51–59.

Rizzolatti, G., Semi, A., & Fabbri-Destro, M. (2014). Linking psychoanalysis with neuroscience: The concept of ego. *Neuropsychologia, 55*: 143–148.

Rizzolatti, G., & Sinigaglia, C. (2010). The functional role of the parieto-frontal mirror circuit: Interpretations and misinterpretations. *Nature Reviews Neuroscience, 11*: 264–274.

Rorty, A. (1988). The deceptive self: Liars, layers and lairs. In: B. P. McLaughlin & A. Rorty (Eds.), *Perspectives on Self-deception* (pp. 11–28). Berkeley: University of California Press.

Rosen, N. (1988). Freud on Dostoevsky's epilepsy: A reevaluation. *Dostoevsky Studies, 9*: 108–125.

Rosenfeld, H. (1987). *Impasse and Interpretation*. London: Tavistock.

Rosenthal, D. (1986). Two concepts of consciousness. *Philosophical Studies, 40*: 329–359.

Ryle, G. (1949). *The Concept of Mind*. Chicago: University of Chicago Press.

Saks, E. (2008). *The Center Cannot Hold: My Journey Through Madness*. New York: Hyperion.

Sandler, J. (1976). Dreams, unconscious fantasies and "identity of perception". *International Review of Psychoanalysis, 3*: 33–42.

Sandler, J. (1989). Unconscious wishes and human relationships. In: J. Sandler (Ed.), *Dimensions of Psychoanalysis* (pp. 65–81). London: Karnac.

Sandler, J., & Sandler, A. M. (1978). The development of object-relationships and affects. *International Journal of Psychoanalysis, 59*: 285–296.

Sayers, J. (2007). Freud. In: *Freud's Art: Psychoanalysis Retold* (pp. 9–28). New York: Routledge.

Schafer, R. (1976). *A New Language for Psychoanalysis*. New Haven, CT: Yale University Press.

Schneider, S. et al. (2011). Boys do it the right way: Sex-dependent amygdala lateralization during face processing in adolescents. *NeuroImage, 56*: 1847–1853.

Schopenhauer, A. (1844). *The World as Will and Representation, Vol. II*. New York: Dover, 1966.

Schore, A. (2003). *Affect Regulation and the Repair of the Self*. New York: W. W. Norton.

Schore, A. (2012). *The Science of the Art of Therapy*. New York: Norton.

Seabright, P. (2012). *The War of the Sexes: How Conflict and Cooperation Have Shaped Men and Women from Prehistory to the Present*. Princeton: Princeton University Press.

Searle, J. (1992). *The Rediscovery of the Mind*. Cambridge, MA: MIT Press.

Searle, J. R. (1995). Consciousness, explanatory inversion and cognitive science. In: C. Macdonald & G. Macdonald (Eds.), *Philosophy of Psychology: Debates on Psychological Explanation*, Vol I (pp. 331–355). Oxford: Blackwell.

Searle, J. R. (2002). Can computers think? In: D. J. Chalmers (Ed.), *Philosophy of Mind: Classical and Contemporary readings* (pp. 669–675). New York: Oxford University Press.

Segal, H. (1991). *Dream, Phantasy and Art*. London: Routledge.

Selinger, E., & Crease, R. P. (Eds.) (2006). *The Philosophy of Expertise*. New York: Columbia University Press.

Shedler, J. (2010). The efficacy of psychodynamic psychotherapy. *American Psychologist, 63*: 98–109.

Shevrin, H., Bond, J., Brakel, L. A. W., Hertel, R., & Williams, W. (1996). *Conscious and Unconscious Processes*. New York: Guilford Press.

Shevrin, H., Snodgrass, M., Abelson, J., Kushwaha, R., & Brakel, L. A. W. (2015). Unconscious facilitation and inhibition of phobic stimuli: N100 amplitude and latency moderate subliminal mere exposure effects. Unpublished manuscript.

Shope, R. (1967). The psychoanalytic theories of wish-fulfilment and meaning. *Inquiry, 10*: 421–438.

Shope, R. (1970). Freud on conscious and unconscious intentions. *Inquiry, 13*:149–159.

Shope, R. (1983). *The Analysis of Knowing*. Princeton: Princeton University Press.

Sims, A. (2015). Anosognosia and the very idea of a psychodynamic neuroscience, Unpublished Ph.D. Deakin University, Melbourne.

Slap, J. (1976). A note on the drawing of dream details. *Psychoanalytic Quarterly, 59*: 455–456.

Slap, J. W., & Saykin, A. J. (1984). On the nature and the organisation of the repressed. *Psychoanalytic Inquiry, 4*: 107–124.

Sluga, H. (1996). "Whose house is that?" Wittgenstein on the self. In: H. Sluga & D. G. Stern (Eds.), *The Cambridge Companion to Wittgenstein* (pp. 320–353). Cambridge: Cambridge University Press.

Smith, D. L. (2003). "Some unimaginable substratum": A contemporary introduction to Freud's philosophy of mind. In: M. C. Chung & C. Feltham (Eds.), *Psychoanalytic Knowledge* (pp. 54–75). London: Palgrave Macmillan.

Smith, R. J. (2010). Against treating introspection as perception-like. *Psyche, 16*: 79–86.

Sober, E., & Forster, M. (1997). How to tell when simpler, more unified, or less ad hoc theories will provide more accurate predictions. *British Journal of the Philosophy of Science, 45*: 1–35.

Solms, M. (2003). Do unconscious phantasies really exist? In: R. Steiner (Ed.), *Unconscious Phantasy* (pp. 89–105). London: Karnac.

Solms, M. (2013). The conscious id. *Neuropsychoanalysis, 15*: 5–19.

Solms, M., & Panksepp, J. (2012). The "id" knows more than the "ego" admits: Neuropsychoanalytic and primal consciousness perspectives on the interface between affective and cognitive neuroscience. *Brain Science, 2*: 147–175.

Solms, M., & Turnbull, O. (2002). *The Brain and the Inner World*. New York: Other Press.

Solomon, J., & George, C. (1999). *Attachment Disorganization*. New York: Guilford Press.

Solomon, J., & George, C. (2000). The measurement of attachment security in infancy and childhood. In: J. Cassidy & P. Shaver (Eds.), *Handbook of Attachment* (pp. 383–416). London: Guildford Press.

Sorabji, R. (2006). *Self: Ancient and Modern Insights about Individuality, Life and Death*. Chicago: University of Chicago Press.

Spitz, R. (1965). *The First Year of Life*. New York: International Universities Press.

Stanley, J., & Williamson, T. (2001). Knowing how. *The Journal of Philosophy, 98*: 411–444.

Stecker, R. (1997). *Artworks: Definition, Meaning and Value*. University Park, PA: Pennsylvania State University Press.

Steele, H., & Steele, M. (2008). *Clinical Applications of the Adult Attachment Interview*. New York: Guildford Press.

Stenberg, C., Campos, J., & Emde, R. (1983). The facial expression of anger in seven-month-old infants. *Child Development, 54*: 178–184.

Stepansky, P. (2009). *Psychoanalysis at the Margins*. New York: Other Press.

Sterba, R. (1940). The problem of art in Freud's writings. *The Psychoanalytic Quarterly, 9*: 256–268.

Stich, S. (1978). Autonomous psychology and the belief-desire thesis. *The Monist, 61*: 573–591.

Stoller, R. J. (1979). *Sexual Excitement*. New York: Simon and Schuster.

Strawson, G. (1994). *Mental Reality*. Cambridge, MA: MIT Press.

Stricker, G. (2006). What else materially influences what is represented and published as evidence? Dialogue: Convergence and contention. In: J. Norcross, L. Beutler, & R. Levant (Eds.), *Evidence-Based Practices in Mental Health: Debate and Dialogue on the Fundamental Questions* (pp. 285–286). Washington: American Psychological Association.

Sulloway, F. J. (1992). *Freud, Biologist of the Mind: Beyond the Psychoanalytic Legend*. Cambridge, MA: Harvard University Press.

Sunstein, C. R. (2011). Deliberating groups versus prediction markets (or Hayek's challenge to Habermas). In: A. I Goldman & D. Whitcomb (Eds.), *Social Epistemology: Essential Readings* (pp. 314–337). Oxford: Oxford University Press.

Talvitie, V. (2009). *The Freudian Unconscious and Cognitive Neuroscience: From Unconscious Fantasies to Neural Algorithms*. London: Karnac.

Talvitie, V. (2012). *The Foundations of Psychoanalytic Theories—Project for a Scientific Enough Psychoanalysis*. London: Karnac.

Talvitie, V., & Ihanus, J. (2003a). On the nature of repressed contents—A working-through of John Searle's critique. *Neuro-psychoanalysis, 5*: 133–142.

Talvitie, V., & Ihanus, J. (2003b). Response to commentaries. *Neuro-psychoanalysis, 5*: 153–158.

Talvitie, V., & Ihanus, J. (2005). Biting the bullet: The nature of unconscious fantasy. *Theory & Psychology, 15*: 659–678.

Talvitie, V., & Ihanus, J. (2006). The psychic apparatus, metapsychology and neuroscience: Toward biological (neuro)psychoanalysis. *Neuro-Psychoanalysis, 8*: 85–98.

Talvitie, V., & Ihanus, J. (2011a). On neuropsychoanalytic metaphysics. *The International Journal of Psychoanalysis, 92*: 1583–1601.

Talvitie, V., & Ihanus, J. (2011b). On the relation between neural and psychological mechanisms: Neuropsychoanalysis and the "new mechanists". *Scandinavian Psychoanalytic Review, 33*: 130–141.

Talvitie, V., Ihanus, J., & Kaitaro, T. (2013). Sigmund Freud and ways of talking about the unobservable: Romantic, positivist, Kantian, and vitalist aspects of the mental unconscious. *Bollettino di Studi Sartriani, 9*: 53–76.

Talvitie, V., & Tiitinen, H. (2006). From the repression of contents to the rules of the (narrative) self: A present-day cognitive view of the "Freudian phenomenon" of repressed contents. *Psychology and Psychotherapy: Theory, Research and Practice, 79*: 165–181.

Tauber, A. I. (2010). *Freud: The Reluctant Philosopher*. Princeton: Princeton University Press.

Thalberg, I. (1974). Freud's anatomies of the self. In: R. Wollheim & J. Hopkins (Eds.), *Philosophical Essays on Freud* (pp. 241–263). Cambridge: Cambridge University Press.

Tolstoy, L. (1896). *What is Art?* London: Oxford University Press, 1930.

Tononi, G., & Cirelli, C. (2014). Sleep and the price of plasticity: From synaptic and cellular homeostasis to memory consolidation and integration. *Neuron, 81*: 12–34.

Tremblay, R. (2002). Prevention of injury by early socialization of aggressive behavior. *Injury Prevention, 8* (Suppl IV): iv17–iv21.

Tremblay, R. E. (2008). Understanding development and prevention of chronic physical aggression: Towards experimental epigenetic studies. *Philosophical Transactions of the Royal Society B: Biological Sciences, 363*: 2613–2622.

Trevarthen, C. (2009). The intersubjective psychobiology of human meaning: Learning of culture depends on interest for co-operative practical work-and affection for the joyful art of good company. *Psychoanalytic Dialogues, 19*: 507–518.

Trivers, R. (2002). *Natural Selection and Social Theory*. Oxford: Oxford University Press.

Uleman, J. S. (2005). Introduction: Becoming aware of the new unconscious. In: R. R. Hassin, J. S. Uleman, & J. A. Bargh (Eds.), *The New Unconscious* (pp. 3–15). Oxford: Oxford University Press.

Unger, P. (1967). Experience and factual knowledge. *The Journal of Philosophy, 64*: 152–173.

van Dongen, E. V., Thielen, J. W., Takashima, A., Barth, M., & Fernández, G. (2012). Sleep supports selective retention of associative memories based on relevance for future utilization. *PLoS ONE, 7*: e43426.

van Fraassen, B. (2008). *Scientific Representation: Paradoxes of Perspective*. New York: Oxford University Press.

van IJzendoorn, M. (1995). Adult attachment representations, parental responsiveness, and infant attachment: A meta-analysis on the predictive validity of the adult attachment interview. *Psychological Bulletin, 117*: 387–403.

Vaughn, B., Bost, K., & van Ijzendoorn, M. (2008). Attachment and temperament. In: J. Cassidy & P. Shaver (Eds.), *Handbook of Attachment* (pp. 192–216). London: Guildford Press.

Velleman, J. D. (2000). *The Possibility of Practical Reason*. Oxford: Oxford University Press.

Vendler, Z. (1975). On what we know: Language, mind and knowledge. *Minnesota Studies in the Philosophy of Science, 7*: 370–390.

Wallerstein, R. S. (1995). *The Talking Cures: The Psychoanalyses and the Psychotherapies*. New Haven, CT: Yale University Press.

Wang, Y., Ramsey, R., & Hamilton, A. (2011). The control of mimicry by eye contact is mediated by medial prefrontal cortex. *The Journal of Neuroscience, 31*: 12001–12010.

Watt, D. F., & Panksepp, J. (2009). Depression: An evolutionarily conserved mechanism to terminate separation distress? A review of aminergic, peptidergic, and neural network perspectives. *Neuropsychoanalysis: An Interdisciplinary Journal for Psychoanalysis and the Neurosciences, 11*: 7–51.

Wegner, D. (2002). *The Illusion of Conscious Will*. Cambridge, MA: MIT Press.

Weintraub, R. (1987). Unconscious mental states. *Philosophical Quarterly, 37*: 423–432.

Weiss, J., & Sampson, H. (1986). *The Psychoanalytic Process*. New York: International Universities Press.

Westen, D. (1998). The scientific legacy of Sigmund Freud: Toward a psychodynamically informed psychological science. *Psychological Bulletin, 124*: 333–371.

Westen, D. (1999). The scientific status of unconscious processes: Is Freud really dead? *Journal of the American Psychoanalytic Association, 47*: 1061–1105.

Williamson, T. (2000). *Knowledge and Its Limits*. Oxford: Oxford University Press.

Wilson, T. (2002). *Strangers to Ourselves: Discovering the Adaptive Unconscious*. Cambridge: The Belknap Press of Harvard University Press.

Wimmer, H., & Perner, J. (1983). Beliefs about beliefs: Representations and constraining functions of wrong belief in young children's understanding of deception. *Cognition, 13*: 103–128.

Winnicott, D. W. (1965). *The Maturational Process and the Facilitating Environment*. London: Hogarth Press.

Wittgenstein, L. (1953). *Philosophical Investigations*. New York: Macmillan.

Wittgenstein, L. (1998). *Remarks on Culture and Value*. Oxford: Blackwell.

Wollheim, R. (1970). Freud and the understanding of art. *British Journal of Aesthetics, 10*: 211–224.

Wollheim, R. (1974). Identification and imagination. In: R. Wollheim (Ed.), *Freud: A Collection of Critical Essays* (pp. 172–195). New York: Anchor.

Wollheim, R (Ed.) (1974b). *Freud: A Collection of Critical Essays*. New York: Anchor Books.

Wollheim, R. (1979). Wish-fulfilment. In: R. Harrison (Ed.), *Rational Action: Studies in Philosophy and Social science* (pp. 47–60). Cambridge: Cambridge University Press.

Wollheim, R. (1984). *The Thread of Life*. Cambridge: Cambridge University Press.

Wollheim, R. (1991). *Freud*. London: Fontana.

Wollheim, R. (1993). *The Mind and its Depths*. Harvard: Harvard University Press.

Woozley, A. D. (1953). Knowing and not knowing. *Proceedings of the Aristotelian Society, 53*: 151–172.

Xie, L., Kang, H., Xu, Q., Chen, M., Liao, Y., Thiyagarajan, M., O'Donnell, J., Christensen, T., Nicholson, C., Iliff, J., Takano, T., Deane, R., & Nedergaard, M. (2013). Sleep drives metabolite clearance from the adult brain. *Science, 342*: 373.

Young-Bruehl, E. (1996). *The Anatomy of Prejudices*. Cambridge, MA: Harvard University Press.

Ziman, J. (2000). *Real Science: What It Is, and What It Means*. Cambridge: Cambridge University Press.

INDEX

Made in the USA
Coppell, TX
08 December 2022

88245255R00174